Austin Fisher is Senior Lecturer in the department of Media Arts and Production, University of Bedfordshire. Austin is the 'Spaghetti Westerns' editor for the Directory of World Cinema: Italy, has published articles in scholarly journals such as The Italianist and Scope and writes a blog around his research interests at www.austinfisher.me.uk.

His continuing research extends his analysis of critiques dealing with state corruption, ideology and political violence within the Spaghetti Western to incorporate an examination of the Italian police thriller (or poliziesco) genre of the 1970s. He is also investigating the discrepancies between intended political inscriptions in popular Italian cinema of the 1960s and 1970s and their patterns of reception in the English-speaking world.

*For Kirsty*

# Austin Fisher

# RADICAL FRONTIERS

## in the
## SPAGHETTI
## WESTERN

Politics, Violence and
Popular Italian Cinema

I.B. TAURIS

LONDON · NEW YORK

New paperback edition first published in 2014 by I.B.Tauris & Co. Ltd
6 Salem Road, London W2 4BU
175 Fifth Avenue, New York NY 10010
www.ibtauris.com

Distributed in the United States and Canada Exclusively by Palgrave Macmillan
175 Fifth Avenue, New York NY 10010

First published in hardback in 2011 by Tauris Academic Studies, an imprint of I.B.Tauris & Co. Ltd

ISBN: 978 1 78076 711 6

A full CIP record for this book is available from the British Library
A full CIP record is available from the Library of Congress

Library of Congress catalog card: available

Printed and bound in Great Britain by Page Bros, Norwich

MIX
Paper from
responsible sources
FSC
www.fsc.org   FSC® C023114

# Contents

APPENDICES

# List of Illustrations

# Acknowledgements

This volume began life as a PhD thesis. Consequently, my profuse thanks are due to Barry Langford for supervising the project with ceaseless support, enthusiasm and rigour over several years. I am also indebted to Christopher Frayling for his invaluable feedback and encouragement, to the ever-helpful staff at the BFI Library for their patient retrieval of countless obscure journals and to the Humanities and Arts Research Centre at Royal Holloway, University of London for funding my studies. I am most thankful to Jenna Steventon , Liza Thompson, Pat FitzGerald and all at I.B.Tauris for indulging my interests and permitting me this opportunity to disseminate them. Furthermore, my gratitude must be extended to Mark Glancy for opening my eyes to the study of film many moons ago.

Elements of Chapters Two and Four of this book have previously been published in both *The Italianist*, 30 (2) and *Scope: An Online Journal of Film and Television Studies*, 15. I would therefore like to thank their editors for providing important forums for the germination of this volume.

Every effort has been made to contact copyright holders. Any errors or omissions brought to the attention of the publishers will be made good in future editions.

Such a brief note as this is an entirely inadequate medium through which to thank my parents, John and Joyce, for thirty-three years of unconditional love, intellectual stimulation and constructive criticism. A familial rock and moral anchor (not to mention a source of proof-reading) more reliable this eternal student cannot envisage. Finally, this book is dedicated to my partner Kirsty, without whose remarkable forbearance, loving disposition, insatiable good humour and aptitude for Italian it would not have been completed.

# Introduction

The purpose of this book is twofold. Firstly, I aim to demonstrate how and why radicalised Italian film-makers identified in the Western genre an apt vehicle for communicating revolutionary political views in the national and international contexts of the late 1960s. Secondly – and more importantly – I seek to tell a story, charting the brief but intriguing lifespan of a group of films loved by fans but neglected by critics and scholars alike.

The category of film-making now known the world over as the 'Spaghetti Western' was produced on a truly industrial scale, with almost five hundred Western films emerging from the Italian studio system between 1962 and 1980.[1] In the milieu of popular Italian cinema of the era, where formulaic cycles (known locally as *filoni*[2]) would ebb and flow with the perceived whims of popular taste, this constitutes not only a vast collection of films, but a remarkable longevity. Various trends therefore emerged, flourished and expired within the Spaghetti Western format itself, from slapstick comedies to baroque tales of intrigue and horror film hybrids. It is the task of this book to chart the lifespan of one such trend: that which appropriated the Italian Western with the intention of disseminating Far Left political doctrine between the years 1966 and 1970. In this period Damiano Damiani, Sergio Sollima, Sergio Corbucci, Giulio Questi and Giulio Petroni each directed films whose locales – though lifted directly from Hollywood – barely concealed bravura, and at times militant, denunciations of advanced capitalism.

The Spaghetti Western as a whole has long been a favourite of cult film buffs, and increasingly enjoys a mainstream renaissance as audiences and critics reassess its influential place in film history (largely due to the internationally celebrated films of the now-canonised Roman director Sergio Leone). In the academic sphere, too, this once-scorned category of film-making has come to inform fields from transnational popular culture to Italian studies, through the valuable works of Dimitris Eleftheriotis,[3] Christopher Wagstaff[4] and, most notably, Christopher Frayling.[5] Yet, while this *filone*'s visibility in Film Studies departments steadily increases as it becomes admitted into the pantheon of Italian cinema, there remains a scholarly void surrounding the politically-committed variations summarised above. Academic discussion of Italy's 1960s political *auteurs* abounds (Rosi, Pontecorvo, Bellocchio to name but three), yet the complex relationship of the Italian Western to the political ferments of its era has gone almost entirely unnoticed.[6] This book is the first extended analysis of these militant trends, and therefore seeks to fill this gap.

As the plural noun in my title 'Radical Frontiers' indicates, the analysis identifies a variety of borderline exchanges which together construct this account of transcultural borrowing, political re-interpretation and generic mutation. The text is structured around an organising principle that the post-war transatlantic relationship was less one of domination by American-led modernity than one of negotiation and cultural blending: what the historian James Clifford dubs 'cultural import-export'.[7] Italian re-workings of the Western genre's ideologies naturally provide the study with its foremost case in point. The films which form my primary source material are thus interpreted as neither rejections nor imitations of Hollywood's cultural reach; more, by refocusing the Western through the lens of Italy's revolutionary 'New Left' in and around the tumultuous events of 1968, they register processes of appropriation and re-inscription which characterised significant portions of Italian culture in this era. I show how, in this new political context, the Hollywood genre's obsessive focus on the legitimacy of violence took on fresh meanings and appealed to new audiences.

My first chapter sets the cultural-political scene of post-war Italy from which these films emerged, progressing through a steady arc of contextualisation from the broad to the particular: that is, from concerns spanning Italian culture to those of a specifically cinematic nature. By opening with an emblematic case-study of Steno's satirical film *Un americano a Roma* (1954), I frame the book's subject matter within the fraught debates of the era concerning Italy's intimate encounter with US popular culture. After summarising and appraising the well-trodden arguments around transatlantic influence, I demonstrate how the increased cultural borrowing in this period frequently resulted in creative re-working. Though so-called 'Americanisation' was condemned by many on the political Left, appropriation and resistance characterised this imaginary 'America' upon which contemporary Italian mores were projected, but also contested.

Turning to the Italian film industry as a key factor in this argument, I then repudiate the era's widespread perceptions of a politically-engaged native cinema set against an anodyne, imitative genre cinema. Instead, the growth of the Roman studio system is analysed as a dynamic factor in these processes of cultural blending, from which the Italian Western emerged organically. As the chapter closes by introducing this *filone*'s political offshoot, I ask why, as Americana came to symbolise and fuel aspirant post-war notions of modernity, the Western film took on a singular resonance amongst militant constituencies.

The cultural and political coordinates surrounding the emergence of the book's key films thus detailed, my second chapter focuses on the Hollywood Western itself, assessing why this genre above all others came to be requisitioned for radical leftist ends in 1960s Italy. The previous chapter's discussion of creative appropriation is now focussed specifically on this cinematic category. Through an examination of the Western's history as both a popular format and an ideological vehicle, I arrive at the cultural 'moment' of the late 1960s, where key aspects of the genre are shown to possess compelling parallels with the concerns of Italian militants.

I argue firstly that the Western's archetypes, from their origins in the late nineteenth century, display notable concordances with dominant modes of representing the Italian South. The Wild West's status as a contested terrain for American national identity was therefore equally a mythic space with resonance within the Italian popular imagination. The genre's appropriation by radical audiences, for whom issues of banditry and redemptive violence held an additional fascination and urgency, is interpreted from within this pre-existing framework. It is in the issue of violent action and its legitimisation that I identify the foremost point of contact between the Hollywood Western's established structures and the concerns of Italian militants in the second half of the 1960s. The Spaghetti Western is frequently accused of evacuating the genre's emphasis on violence of its moral imperative. The next two chapters illustrate how ideological re-inscriptions sought to replenish it.

Chapter Three defines and analyses the first of two strands of politically-engaged Italian Westerns addressed by this book: what I dub the RSA, or 'Repressive State Apparatus', variant. The key films analysed in this chapter are *Se sei vivo, spara!/Django Kill!* (Giulio Questi, 1967), *La resa dei conti/The Big Gundown* (Sergio Sollima, 1967), *Faccia a faccia/Face to Face* (Sollima, 1967) and *Il grande Silenzio/The Great Silence* (Sergio Corbucci, 1968). The primary political function I identify in this group of films is an attempt to expose brutal mechanisms lying behind modern-day Western society. I demonstrate these films' close engagement with preoccupations characteristic of Italy's radical New Left, particularly concerning latent domestic fascism and the oppressive 'system'. The first half of the chapter is a wide-ranging analytical survey of antecedents and offshoots of this trend within the wider Spaghetti Western, revisiting famed and obscure films alike to demonstrate the gradual and organic emergence of this radicalised inclination. My appraisal considers the extent to which the trend emerged from film-makers with traumatic experiences of the Second World War and the Resistance against Nazism, positing that their films' ideological function is twofold: they seek simultaneously to evoke the horrors of the nation's past and to expose continuing threats in its present.

The chapter's focus then shifts to a close analysis of narrative and cinematography in two films which offer emblematic expressions of this trend's outlook: *La resa dei conti* and *Faccia a faccia*. I show how, with a meticulous manipulation of dramatic irony, revelation and point-of-view, Sergio Sollima attempts to position his audience to communicate his political agenda. *Faccia a faccia* in particular, through a philosophical subtext pertaining to the historical theses of Friedrich Nietzsche and Walter Benjamin, displays a level of sophistication rarely associated with the Italian Western. Ultimately, however, I argue that this film's political incoherence renders Sollima's intended messages problematic. In its ambivalence to the ethics of violence, it inadvertently reflects ideological contradictions within late 1960s protest movements, which would lead some factions towards armed struggle as the 1970s dawned.

Chapter Four defines and analyses the second trend of politically-engaged Italian Westerns, which I dub the 'insurgency' variant. The key films analysed here are *Quien sabe?/A Bullet for the General* (Damiano Damiani, 1966), *Corri, uomo, corri/Run, Man, Run* (Sergio Sollima, 1968), *Il mercenario/ The Mercenary* (Sergio Corbucci, 1968), *Tepepa* (Giulio Petroni, 1969) and *Vamos a matar, compañeros* (Corbucci, 1970; henceforth *Compañeros*). Set in the revolutionary 'Mexico' of the popular imagination, these films' endorsements of violent peasant insurrection against the Western world are as bravura as they are obvious. My analysis, however, additionally identifies how they seek to wage a cinematic campaign against the representational practices of Hollywood. I begin by surveying the allegorical motif of the border crossing as repeatedly depicted in US cinema during the Cold War. Here, the presence of white adventurers in Mexico is met with gratitude and cordiality by oppressed peasants.

I then argue that it is precisely this mode of representation which is engaged by the key films examined in the chapter, through close examination of camerawork, narrative and performance. On the surface these radicalised films reformulate the Hollywood Western into an oppositional format in remarkably explicit terms. They appropriate the commonplace depiction of aspirant Third World peasants and benevolent American interlopers, seeking quite literally to turn the film camera around and applying the Western's emphasis on regenerative violence to the postcolonial theses of Frantz Fanon. Far from rejecting the ideological functions of the Hollywood Western, however, these films in fact work with the genre's traditions, inadvertently giving the reader a glimpse into the transatlantic dynamics of popular Italian film-making of the era. Not only do their methodologies betray an ambiguous outlook on Italy's post-war encounter with US popular culture; their failure to put forward consistent ideological positions frequently tends towards banality and over-simplification (a charge most pertinently levelled at Corbucci's *Il mercenario* (1968) and *Compañeros* (1970)).

These intentions and ambiguities outlined and discussed, Chapter Five assesses the films' legacies in global popular culture, which have diverged markedly from that which their makers intended. My focus here shifts to the US film industry – where the Spaghetti Western's legacy is at its most globally visible – and the timescale of the book now widens considerably, to chart the myriad strands of influence these eccentrically radicalised films can be seen to have exerted. While the previous two chapters have shown film-makers seeking to steer the viewer towards specific political viewpoints, I now show audiences once again engaged in processes of cultural borrowing to construct their own meanings from these imports. This transatlantic relationship, however, is the reverse of that depicted in Chapter One – this time US audiences appropriating Italian popular culture – and the book's central concern turns to gauging the political and cinematic impact of the films previously assessed.

My analysis focuses, firstly, on one decisive factor in their artistic failure. These films' international releases came at a time when violence of a stylistic kind was the hot topic of debate, as Hollywood's Production Code was giving way to a new wave of brutal cinema. I assess the implications of the violence depicted in these Italian Westerns, both through analysing patterns in contemporary critical reception, and through a contrast with the stylistics being simultaneously pioneered within Hollywood's own emergent counterculture. Arthur Penn's *Bonnie and Clyde* (1967), Sam Peckinpah's *The Wild Bunch* (1969) and Don Medford's *The Hunting Party* (1971) in particular provide this segment with gory, graphic counterpoints to the surprisingly sanitised and bloodless depictions of death to be found throughout the Spaghetti Western. I argue that this stylistic divergence holds a key to understanding why, though the Hollywood Western itself became increasingly appropriated for radical ends in the 1970s, the belligerent militancy evident within the Italian films mostly failed to translate into global popular culture.

On one hand, I demonstrate that these films' postmodern re-workings of Hollywood did connect with certain disenfranchised groupings in the USA, identifying in 'blaxploitation' a strand of influence which retains the postcolonial meanings intended by the Italians. I show, however, that this 'grindhouse' association has itself contributed to a politically anodyne reception in contemporary US cinema. Appropriated and admired by Quentin Tarantino, Robert Rodriguez and Sam Raimi, these supposedly radical works have become assimilated into 'cool' pop culture and transformed into violent, but not political, films.

To conclude, Chapter Six situates these films' approaches to genre cinema within the varied cultural outlooks of the European New Left. I argue that they belong firmly within a spectrum of late 1960s political cinema and attest to the diversity of attitudes towards political dissemination amongst radical groups. Through a comparison of cinematic technique with the work of Jean-Luc Godard, I repudiate assertions that such popular political films as those addressed by this book were diametrically opposed to more experimental forms in this era. Ultimately, however, I show that their entwinement with (and reliance upon) genre convention was their undoing. Their simultaneous attempts to destroy the authority of a Hollywood format and to inscribe new authoritative structures into that same paradigm prove contradictory. As Chapter Five demonstrates, they themselves have become reformulated by disparate audiences, and emptied of their intended political imperatives. I leave these films as illuminating yet ambiguous case studies of transatlantic borrowing, which underline to the reader the key role of an audience in the negotiation of cultural meaning.

It is my intention that this volume should offer the reader a fresh, compelling and nuanced perspective on the political coordinates of European cinema and the Hollywood Western alike. Its scholarly focus incorporates discourses and arguments pertaining to *auteur* theory, trash cinema, transculturation, structuralism and postmodernism. Yet these are mere academic adornments to the book's true purpose: that of looking again at a group of stylistically eccentric and riotously entertaining films whose very flaws render them fascinating objects of study for student and film buff alike. While this is no work of enthralled hagiography (the fundamental incoherence of the films' agendas is a central concern throughout), it is born of a profound fondness for the lesser-known contributions to a filmic category so often dominated by the aegis of Sergio Leone. I hope that this enthusiasm is discernible in my writing.

I must make a couple of points for the sake of consistency, brevity and clarity. Western movies produced or co-produced by Italian studios in the 1960s and 1970s have been variously referred to as 'Spaghetti Westerns', 'Euro Westerns', *Westerns all'italiana* and even 'Macaroni Westerns'. Though Christopher Frayling quite reasonably justifies his own use of the originally pejorative 'spaghetti' moniker by identifying in it a symbolic cultural hybridity,[8] in the majority of cases I opt instead for the neutral and descriptive 'Italian Western'. I frequently add an extra prefix to categorise 'political' or 'militant' Italian Westerns, distinguishing my key group of films from the bulk of this larger *filone*. Additionally, since Chapters Three and Four analyse two distinct trends within this group, I require a further division between the 'RSA' ('Repressive State Apparatus') narrative and the 'insurgency' narrative.

Lastly, I wish to make clear my partial use of the Italian language. Throughout the book I translate films' Italian dialogue into English as faithfully as possible, only mentioning the Italian where I feel clarification of meaning is required. Likewise, I translate Italian interviews and Italian critics' analyses into English. Conversely, however, I refer to Italian films by their Italian titles. This too is primarily for clarity's sake, since most Italian Westerns have been subsequently released in cinemas, as well as on television, VHS and DVD, under numerous English language titles. To cite just one example, Giuliano Carnimeo's *Una nuvola di polvere ... un grido di morte ... arriva Sartana* (1970) was released internationally under the titles *Cloud of Dust ... Cry of Death ... Sartana is Coming, Gunman in Town* and *Light the Fuse ... Sartana is Coming*. For the sake of consistency, this policy applies equally to films whose English titles are the better known: *The Good, the Bad and the Ugly* remains *Il buono, il brutto, il cattivo*.

# PART I

# THE BACKDROP

# 1

# Imagining America:
# US Influence and American Mythology
# in Post-War Italy

Late at night, a lone figure darts between pillars and doorways to a portentous backing track. Approaching footsteps from the shadows augur a meeting in the deserted street. The 'gun' drawn in anticipation, however, is make-believe, for I describe a scene not from Hollywood film noir, but from *Un americano a Roma*: an Italian comedy directed by Steno in 1954. Nando Moriconi (Alberto Sordi) is returning home from his local cinema where, jostling for position with equally wide-eyed children, he has just seen the latest Hopalong Cassidy Western. The thrill of Wild West shoot-outs and vast desert landscapes contrasts markedly with the tenements and narrow cobbled streets of the Roman district of Trastevere; yet Nando is immersed in his private world of Hollywood mythology, and projects his fantasies onto this familiar locale. The spell is abruptly broken when a policeman approaches and the music cuts out, since Nando's 'America' is no more than a phantasm of the movie screen.

I open with this arresting and memorable vignette because it foregrounds cultural factors which would play key roles in the emergence and development of my central subject matter, and which form the basis of this chapter. Steno's film – dubbed by David Ellwood 'a milestone in the history of Italian identity'[1] – parodies and anticipates significant transformations brought about by Italy's post-war alignment with the American sphere of influence. Simultaneously, however, it depicts this flow of transatlantic borrowing as a process of negotiation and reinterpretation, instead of mere imitation.

Nando Moriconi, though infatuated with the United States as a vibrant and modern alternative to a dreary post-war Europe, is not a passive member of the cinema audience, gazing longingly at America and its mythologies. Once he leaves the picture house he attempts to re-mould the semantic structures of Americana to formulate his own identity, with comic consequences. His incomprehension of US culture, for example, is ably symbolised by his meal of bread, milk, yoghurt and mustard, which he imagines is an American dish and which proves so inedible he is forced to turn back to the familiar spaghetti and wine. With such vivid symbolism, *Un americano a Roma* captures the disorientation discernible through much of Italy's cultural output of the 1950s and 1960s, and I shall refer back to the emblematic scene on which this chapter begins at various points through the course of the book.

The films which will form the primary focus of this volume are ineluctably tied to these pre-existing processes of creative participation in the meanings of transatlantic formats. Though the notion of militant left-wing Italian Westerns may at first seem offbeat, eccentric or even downright ludicrous, this was an entirely logical, obvious and perhaps necessary conceit given the cultural-political conditions of the films' time and place. Their anti-imperialist stances and intended rejection of Occidental capitalism ostensibly place them at odds with the very concept of the 'West'. It is my contention, however, that they are in fact entwined in a dialogue with the traditions and ideologies of the Hollywood Western.

In order to analyse the complexities of this argument beyond reductive notions of imitation or rejection, it is essential that I chart both the cinematic and the wider cultural milieus which fostered these films. It is for this reason that the following two chapters assess their historical, political and cultural antecedents before I embark on the more textual and cinematic analysis at the book's core. My intention is that, through this methodology, these two chapters will allow the reader to arrive at the cultural 'moment' of the films' production and release, firstly through assessing the fraught debates surrounding 'Americanisation' in post-war Italy. I shall then refine this issue to focus on the cinema industry and then, in Chapter Two, specifically on the Western genre, to chart the myriad processes of transcultural borrowing which meet in the films of Damiani, Sollima et al.

## 'Americanisation' in Post-War Italy

By the 1950s, Gertrude Stein's 1935 declaration that 'the twentieth century has become the American century'[2] had a prescience which was all too apparent to many cultural critics in Europe. The growing hegemony of the United States had been preoccupying intellectuals for decades (William Stead, for example, published *The Americanization of the World* as early as 1902). In the post-war years, however, concerns over the degradation of traditional culture brought about by US-led modernity intensified considerably. The influx of Hollywood films, the perceived pell-mell adoption by youth culture of transatlantic fashions and the continued presence of US troops on European soil led many to express a sense that indigenous culture was being overwhelmed. Intellectuals from across the political spectrum – notably Orwell, Leavis, Marcuse and Sartre – engaged in earnest condemnations of American cultural imperialism, as US hegemony in the West became ever more apparent in the 1950s. A dystopian vision of a conformist mass culture sweeping away European traditions, foretold by Orwell renaming Britain 'Airstrip One' in *Nineteen Eighty-Four*,[3] was dubbed 'admass' by JB Priestley. Palpable in both terms is a sense of horror at the standardisation awaiting the world in the second half of 'the American century'.

Seminal theorists of early British cultural studies such as Richard Hoggart, Raymond Williams and EP Thompson were among the most vociferous of these critics. Hoggart's *The Uses of Literacy*, in studying the 'candy-floss world'[4] of mass consumerism, laments the debasement of working-class culture caused by the 'spiritual dry-rot' of homogeneous Americanisation. His despair at British youth, whose 'clothes [...] hair-styles [...] facial expressions all indicate [they] are living [...] in a myth-world compounded of a few simple elements which they take to be those of American life',[5] demonstrates Nando Moriconi's affectations to be signs of the times well beyond the borders of Italy.

These most rigorous of British critiques came chiefly from within the broad church of socialist thinking that formed the nascent New Left (Thompson, for example, was a member of the Communist Party of Great Britain until 1956, while Hoggart was a member of the Labour Party). In Italy, however, the foremost contemporaneous and analogous stance came specifically from the Italian Communist Party (PCI). This, indeed, reflected the PCI's considerably more influential status amongst national Communist parties as a mass movement, which broadly spoke for the political Left in national discourse prior to the mid 1960s.[6] The PCI's post-war ethos drew largely from the writings of the party's founder Antonio Gramsci and from the legacy of the wartime Resistance to Nazism, but was also built on a vehement opposition to American influence. In 1948, a hard-line attitude towards American culture was announced by deputy leader Pietro Secchia:

The great American trusts send us not only their riflemen, their spies, their agents, and organizers of sabotage and betrayal, but inundate our country with their books, their films, and their lowbrow ideological rubbish that should serve to weaken, disorient, and corrupt our people.[7]

'Americanisation' (that is, the emulation and adoption of habits and values associated with the USA) thus became a distinctly pejorative term in post-war Europe, implying pollution and corruption. Rob Kroes defines it as a word which 'normally serves in a discourse of rejection to point to the variety of processes through which America exerts its dismal influence on European cultures. [This view] reduces the complex processes of cultural influence [...] to the stark binary form'.[8] The issue, indeed, was not as clear-cut as Hoggart or Secchia supposed. Even within the PCI itself, the wider membership engaged in debates surrounding the political implications of US-led consumerism and mass culture for much of the 1950s. As we shall see, they did not universally accord with the leadership's hostility.

### US Influence and Italy's 'Economic Miracle'
David Forgacs suggests that 'Americanisation is, in part at least, a symptom of anxieties about one's own national identity'.[9] It follows that countries lacking a strong national culture are among the most susceptible to the superimposition of American imports, and post-war Italy was a case in point. Shortly after the War, former Prime Minister Francesco Saverio Nitti described the unified state of Italy as 'the eggshell holding the national Humpty Dumpty together, a make-believe country that never obtained the complete [...] support of all its incredulous citizens'.[10] Despite the concerted efforts of the Fascist regime to shift loyalties from the family to the state, regional identity remained the dominant pole of attraction for many, especially in the South, and a unified national culture was largely absent outside the Catholic Church and the national football team. In 1956, local dialects were the prevalent form of everyday communication for 82 per cent of the population[11] and Italy did not possess a genuinely 'national' press.[12]

Added to this, the rapid modernisation of the economy in the 1950s arrived late when compared to northern European nations such as Britain or Germany so that Italy became simultaneously an underdeveloped and an industrialised nation.[13] Stephen Gundle argues that Italy was the most receptive European country to American imports precisely because uneven economic development, combined with rapid industrialisation in the 1950s, coincided with this absence of a genuine secular culture common to all.[14] This left a considerable void in the field of mass communications media, and weakened the nation's ability to filter foreign imports. Moreover, post-war Christian Democrat (DC) governments were content to see this void filled by American models, not least because of the covert role these played in discrediting their rivals, the PCI.

American cinema in particular had been a source of fascination for Italian audiences since the 1920s, but in the immediate post-war period this intensified considerably. The Americans – an occupying force in a devastated country – monopolised the market and implemented the Motion Picture Export Association of America's 'dumping' policy, releasing a six year backlog of Hollywood films. In the first year after the Fascist embargo on Hollywood output was lifted (1946), foreign (mostly American) imports received 87 per cent of box-office receipts.[15] US films, actors and lifestyles thus became increasingly integrated into the popular Italian psyche, and this influx was purposefully tailored. Of all the Western European nations Italy, as a liminal economy with a strong left-wing sub-culture, was both a potential bridgehead and a key focus for US anxiety over encroaching communist influence. This, as well the lure of a lucrative export market, motivated the USA to play an active role in the nation's processes of modernisation since, conversely, the potentialities of renewed European prosperity as a Cold War weapon were tangible. The domestic market thus became replete with films expounding the virtues of the American lifestyle in time for the DC's 1948 election victory over the PCI.[16] In 1949, the government opted to join NATO, committing Italy to play a central role in supporting US foreign policy. The country's subsequent modernisation along American lines, in part facilitated by the European Recovery Programme (ERP), provided the USA with the propaganda victory it had sought in its efforts to create a free market economy in Western Europe.

The arrival of television in Italy in 1954 was a watershed in the fostering of consumer aspiration, fundamentally advancing the nation's linguistic unification and heralding the start, in the domestic sphere, of what would become known as the 'Economic Miracle'. The state broadcaster RAI followed a strict Catholic moral code and a DC party line, while enticing glimpses of the outside world presented Italians with a life of consumerism based broadly around the 'American Dream'. This was at its most pronounced in such programmes as the hugely popular quiz show *Lascia o raddoppia?*, and the daily half hour advertisement slot *Carosello*. Paolo Scrivano records that the first TV sets to appear were labelled 'American', thus linking post-war symbols of modernity with the transatlantic brand and its aspirational subtext.[17]

As had previously been the case elsewhere, television was at first, like cinema, a collective form of entertainment. Bars, clubs and even the PCI's *Case del popolo* ('houses of the people') purchased sets. In the five years between 1956 and 1961, however, the number of television licences in Italy increased more than sevenfold.[18] Though still far behind the UK,[19] let alone the USA, this statistic demonstrates the rate at which American models of consumption were becoming steadily more domesticated during the Economic Miracle. On the face of it these processes saw Italians become healthier, more prosperous and more cosmopolitan.[20] Car ownership helped to break down regional barriers, as the nation's post-war development broadly signalled a transition from an agrarian economy to an urbanised, mobile and industrial one with a global outlook.

The economic, political and cultural influences of the USA have therefore long been recognised as the most important factors in the transformation of post-war Italy, and the nation's rapid development of the 1950s indeed owed much to American models of modernity. Recent analysis, however, has highlighted the extent to which neither the reach nor the exact nature of this phenomenon are easily defined. In analysing the trends characteristic of Italian domestic life during the Economic Miracle, Scrivano writes:

> A multifaceted process characterized by contradictory meanings, Americanization took various forms and developed in highly differentiated ways. Indeed, it is difficult to gauge the extent to which American models were ever simply adopted: closer analysis reveals that such influences were subject to repeated misinterpretation, negotiation and even resistance.[21]

That this was a relationship of ambiguity more than one of linear displacement is illustrated by the limitations of the economic transformation fostered by the so-called 'Miracle'. To be sure, American imports had a significant impact on every stratum of Italian society but, as Scrivano concludes, 'modernization and Americanization did not necessarily coincide'.[22]

The economic realities of the era indeed depict a considerably less inexorable process. Though this intimate encounter with transatlantic culture had a profound effect on the lives of those in the South of Italy, this was more an Americanisation of consciousness and of aspiration than it was one of lifestyle. For many southerners, indeed, consumption was less a reality than a spectacle. Disparities between the industrial North-West and the rural South grew more pronounced during these years, and by the late 1950s the mass media had developed faster than had the economy. Paul Ginsborg depicts an emblematic scene of the era, as southerners could only sit and literally watch the transformations unfolding in mobility, consumerism and fashion:

> In the evenings, in the piazzas of the southern cities [...] the television of the local bar transmitted images from the North, images of a consumer world, of Vespas, portable radios, football heroes, new fashions, nylon stockings, mass-produced dresses, houses full of electrical appliances, Sunday excursions in the family FIAT.[23]

Chronic rural unemployment and the pull of northern prosperity on display so graphically saw a considerable exodus ensue, both from the countryside into the cities, and from the South into the North-West.[24] This influx of southern labour caught northern cities unawares. By the late 1960s, Turin alone had received nearly a million migrants in 15 years, and the newcomers were often deprived of basic sanitation and services. Southern cities, too, experienced considerable growth. The government provided subsidies to industrialise Naples, Bari, Catania and Palermo, but the rapidity of change led to overpopulation, with urban centres growing outwards in uncontrolled sprawls. Enduring poverty, state corruption and forced migration were the experiences many southerners had of the Economic Miracle. That Italy's economy 'Americanised' in these years is evident but, as Martin Clark argues, the ambiguity of this process is equally plain to see: 'The Northern [cities] became North American: commercial complexes surrounded by industrial estates. The Southern ones became South American: administrative centres surrounded by shanty towns.'[25] Beneath the veneer of modernisation lay persistent, and exacerbated, uneven development: a far cry from the homogeneous 'admass' feared by many European intellectuals.

By 1960, with this 'Miracle' in full swing, ambivalence towards the transformations in Italian society was becoming prominent on the cinema screen. In that year, Federico Fellini's *La dolce vita* depicted a vacuous, media-driven culture overwhelming traditional ways of life, registering the contemporary trauma beneath the affluent façade. A young Umbrian waitress with whom Marcello (Marcello Mastroianni) converses has been forced to move to the city so her father can earn money. She confesses to crying with homesickness every time she sees a car with an Umbrian registration, indicating both the breakdown of regional identity and the ubiquity, by the early 1960s, of automotive transport. Pierre Sorlin contrasts

*La dolce vita* with Luchino Visconti's *Rocco e i suoi fratelli* – released within a few months of each other in 1960 – as social documents of this dualism lurking beneath the Economic Miracle.[26] Fellini's film shows the decadence of the modern city into which Visconti simultaneously places an impoverished Sicilian family, torn apart by desperation.

The South of Italy in particular thus found itself being shoehorned into the ethos of an affluent consumer society, and socio-economic inequalities intensified as a foreign model of modernity took root. It is therefore unsurprising that metaphors of imperialism, repression and invasion were so commonly used amongst those for whom American ideologies were anathema (the PCI, for example, launched its defence of traditional Italian popular culture with a resolution entitled 'Against Imperialist and Clerical Obscurantism'[27]). Indeed, there is some credence to the argument that Italy's alignment with America in the post-war years was imposed as much as it was invited. US troops arriving on southern Italian soil in 1943 symbolised a world of prosperity in marked contrast to many of their hosts' poverty-stricken lives. Italy experienced a more conspicuous and extended presence of American troops than any other European nation during and after the War, and a culture of occupation grew as Allied forces moved northwards. GIs distributed cigarettes and food to the people, took advantage of local prostitutes, erected American road signs and established a *lingua franca* merging English and Italian. In short, as Anna Maria Torriglia puts it, 'Americans provisionally transformed Italy into their own land'.[28]

One scene from Roberto Rossellini's *Roma città aperta* (1945) anticipates the innate ambivalence towards Italy's liberators, even while the War still raged. On the one hand, America and Americans were mythologised as representatives of a distant utopia, soon to bring the bounties of modernity to a nation on its knees. On the other, their overwhelming power was a tangible and daunting reality, and in 1945 Italy's uncertain future was to be decided by foreign forces. Returning from a scene of mass looting in war-torn Rome, the neighbourhood police sergeant (Eduardo Passarelli) asks, hopefully: 'Pina, do you think Americans really exist?' Pina (Anna Magnani) looks up, as a point-of-view shot focuses on a bombed-out building. With a look of resignation on her face, she replies: 'It seems so.'

From 1948, the Marshall Plan's media campaign actively set out to construct a culture of consent, including mobile puppet shows to persuade Italian families of the virtues of American ways of life. Ginsborg describes this political intervention as 'breath-taking in its size, its ingenuity and its flagrant contempt for any principle of non-interference in the internal affairs of another country'.[29] Intense political pressure was exerted by the

American ambassador in Rome, James Dunn, and by Secretary of State George Marshall, threatening to suspend aid if the PCI won the 1948 elections. The 1953 elections saw a repeat performance, with ambassador Clare Boothe Luce issuing dire warnings of the consequences for Italy's future if the DC were to lose.

From a military and political perspective (as well as an economic one in the case of the South), it can therefore be said that Italy had been colonised by the American sphere of influence. This was also the case in much of Western Europe, where dissenting voices similarly used the language of imperial domination. Raymond Williams, for one, declared Britain to be 'at certain levels [...] culturally an American colony'.[30] Both this comment and the PCI's proclamation of resistance against 'imperialism' express a sense of unilateral coercion, and of domination and displacement of the native culture. The relevance of such a lexicon when referring to the cultural relationship between America and Europe is, however, ambiguous. Michel de Certeau also uses colonial relations as a paradigm for assessing Americanisation, but arrives at a different conclusion: 'Users make [...] innumerable and infinitesimal transformations of and within the dominant cultural economy in order to adapt it to their own interests and their own rules.'[31] Even if Italy was an American colony, the natives appropriated, subverted and adapted 'America' as much as 'America' foisted itself upon them. This notion of exchange, dubbed 'cultural import-export' by James Clifford,[32] offers a firm riposte to assertions of linear subordination such as those expressed by Hoggart and Williams in Britain, and influential PCI members in Italy.

### Transatlantic Borrowing and the Italian Communist Party

In truth, the PCI was divided in its response to the increasing influence of US popular culture in Italy, and trends of appropriation and adaptation within the party itself were testament to the inherent attractiveness of these novel imports.[33] On the one hand, Hollywood and other forms of commercial mass culture which were proliferating in this period were seen to be exerting an irredeemably corrupting influence on the working classes. Writing in the party's weekly magazine *Vie Nuove* in 1946, Lucio Lombardo Radice wrote:

> Poor quality, insignificant, and unintelligent literature is unfortunately very widespread among workers: American-style children's comics, with 'strip cartoons' and the most hideous, idiotic, and monstrous adventures, the sports press of whatever standard and shoddy, cheap

films. […] In this way their resistance is at least partially side-tracked and their capacity for struggle worn down.[34]

The PCI's leader Palmiro Togliatti remained committed to the notion that genuine 'popular culture' comprised provincial traditions, community activities and educational enlightenment (in much the same way as Hoggart viewed the British working classes' communal customs). This outlook owed much to the leadership's adherence to the memory and writings of Antonio Gramsci. Posthumously published on Togliatti's initiative between 1948 and 1951, Gramsci's *Prison Notebooks* show an awareness of the problems facing the PCI's cultural outlook, addressing the historic failure of Italian intellectuals to bridge the gap between themselves and 'the people'. Forgacs, however, writes that Gramsci's work was 'barely touched by an awareness of the new communications media [and] acted in the main as a conservative, retarding influence on the party's cultural work in the 50s and early 60s'.[35] While Italy looked to the future, the PCI followed a policy of demonising popular media of cultural expression such as television and genre cinema.[36]

In this drive for a progressive popular culture book clubs, reading groups and mass theatre societies were founded. *Case del popolo* arranged debates, meetings and film clubs, and the *festa dell'Unità* became a central event in local party efforts to promote community life and solidarity. As we have seen, the PCI was the parliamentary spearhead of a large and influential communist sub-culture. From 1948 its leadership attempted to mobilise this significant support base to champion politically-committed 'neorealist' Italian film-making over Hollywood imports. Writer and director Carlo Lizzani wrote that the aim of this movement was one of 'reawakening the critical spirit of the popular masses, directing their tastes and preferences […] in order to subtract as much as possible the masses from the noxious influence of a cinema shot through with vulgarity, banality, and gangsterism'.[37]

On the other hand, there was simultaneously a growing awareness within sections of the PCI that such a prescriptive outlook would jeopardise the party's impact upon civil society. Defending sympathetic presentations of American films in *Vie Nuove*, deputy editor Michele Pellicani argued in 1949: 'As Marxists we combat capitalist society but – as long as this is the society in which we live – we cannot ignore its laws. […] We cannot put ourselves outside reality.'[38] As Forgacs states, opposing attitudes viewing mass media as bourgeois propagators of false consciousness indoctrinating the people 'contained very little notion that "the people" might already be "within" culture, still less that they themselves produce valid forms of cultural expression'.[39] Hoggart portrayed a working class who 'take up

[Americanisms] just as they appear and use them in the manner of the child in the fairy-tale, who found toys hanging from the trees and lollipops by the roadside'.[40] So too the comments already cited from Secchia, Radice and Lizzani disregarded consumers' tendencies to negotiate with cultural imports, creating a hybrid modern identity. Though the PCI leadership's ideological revulsion for Americana largely precluded their appreciating the fact, 'Americanisation' offered vitality, novelty and escape. The party membership was no different from the rest of the populace in this respect.

Nor was such appropriation by any means restricted to the PCI's rank and file, since intellectuals within the party – notably Elio Vittorini and Cesare Pavese – also openly emulated US culture. Vittorini began his career as a translator, diffuser and advocate of American literature. During the Fascist era he was a leading propagator of the literary 'American myth' of an unreconstructed land of freedom. His translations frequently contained editorial cuts, 'improving' the source material or, as Torriglia puts it, 'appropriating America and adapting it to an Italian sociocultural code, thereby stressing his own "fictional" contribution to the shaping of the myth'.[41] In the aftermath of the War, Vittorini rode a wave of cultural renewal amongst intellectuals, condemning European culture from Ancient Greece onwards and advocating a rebuilding along American lines. In 1948, Togliatti closed down Vittorini's journal *Il politecnico* over this very issue, but the appeal of America could not be suppressed so easily.

Observing the PCI's activities in the 1950s, indeed, one can see that the communist sub-culture was widely engaged in appropriating aspects of American popular culture. Though Radice had expressed abhorrence for 'American-style comics', in 1950 the party commissioned *L'Unità* journalist Gianni Rodari to oversee the publication of a weekly children's comic book of fantasy and adventure stories. *Il pioniere* maintained a socially conscientious party line and was distributed in *Case del popolo* to children enrolled in the PCI's after-school program. Throughout the 1950s, in an attempt to cultivate an alternative popular culture to one of American derivation, the party held annual 'Miss *Vie Nuove*' beauty contests and dance evenings with transatlantic rhythms. Towards the end of that decade the leadership was forced to concede more ground to popular tastes, inviting television personalities to party festivals and utilising the format of the photo-romance magazine for electoral material. Gundle describes these as 'a striking example of how the rituals and aspirations engendered by Hollywood were absorbed by the Communist subculture'.[42]

That the PCI – the most disciplined and widespread organisation expounding anti-American messages in Italy – could not persuade much of its own membership to acquiesce on this issue gives some indication of the seductiveness of American culture in post-war Europe. Though communist critics such as Antonello Trombadori condemned De Santis's *Riso amaro* (1949) for assimilating aspects of US popular culture, the vibrant mythologies of that very culture continued to exert considerable appeal. In 1954 (appropriately enough, the year *Un americano a Roma* was released) Giuseppe Turroni interviewed a 23 year old PCI member who admitted preferring Westerns and adventure films to the neorealist cinema championed by his party, which was 'too intellectual and difficult'.[43] As is so vividly satirised in Steno's film, the 'America' with which young Europeans were becoming increasingly fascinated had little to do with the realities of contemporary life in the USA, and a lot to do with the output of Hollywood.

### The Wild West in Italian Culture

Dick Hebdige suggests that, for young working-class males, 'American popular culture – Hollywood films, advertising images, packaging, clothes and music – offers a rich iconography, a set of symbols, objects and artefacts which can be assembled and re-assembled by different groups in a literally limitless number of combinations'.[44] This second-hand, imaginary conception of US culture and society implies that, for many, the ubiquity of Hollywood imagery had distilled 'the USA' into a collection of instantly recognisable and available symbols of modernity, insubordination and emancipation.[45]

One did not have to look far to find such sentiments being expressed in Italy. Cesare Pavese, for example, described American culture in the post-war years as 'a kind of great laboratory where [...] we pursued [...] [the] task of creating a modern taste, style and world'.[46] His metaphor succinctly expresses the sense that exciting new concoctions were being formulated and blended by Europeans to create a brave new world. In the 1950s, very few European residents had actually crossed the Atlantic (neither Vittorini nor Pavese had, and the comedy behind Nando Moriconi's delusions relies on his ignorance of American life). That Americana became a touchstone for European youth culture is therefore due largely to the inherently mythic nature of that very entity: namely, 'America' itself. As Jean Baudrillard wrote on visiting the USA: 'I was here in my imagination long before I actually came here.'[47]

The Wild West was, and is, at once the most recognisable and the most escapist manifestation of this American imaginary. Famously described by André Bazin as 'the American film *par excellence*',[48] it is a Western which inspires Nando Moriconi's flight of fancy in the narrow streets of Rome.

Simultaneously a genre which exploits the excitement and the spectacle of the cinema screen, and which acts (ostensibly at least) as a synecdoche for the 'American Dream' itself, the Western functioned above all other American mythologies as a symbol of emancipation. The vast deserts and windswept plains of the mythic West depicted individual opportunity and mobility inconceivable to many in post-war Europe. Luchino Visconti's film *Bellissima* (1951) registers the lure commanded by the genre in Italy through a poverty-stricken mother (Anna Magnani) who is infatuated with the bounties on offer from the film industry. Her cry of 'guarda guarda' while watching Howard Hawks's Western *Red River* (1948) expresses more than just wide-eyed admiration for Montgomery Clift. The romance of the big screen merges with a desire for the freedom of the mythical America on show. As *Red River*'s score segues into a shot of Cinecittà studios' imposing façade, we see hordes of Italians desperate to play a part in this modernity, literally queuing to get in.[49]

It is perhaps tempting to interpret this aspirational engagement with American mythology in terms similar to those employed by David Brauer in reference to later trends of UK Pop Art: 'a relationship [...] analogous to standing outside the toy shop with one's nose pressed against the glass'.[50] As a symbolic description of the cinema screen through which Europeans gazed longingly at the excitement of a world so near and yet so far, this would be a convenient conceit. It is, however, inadequate to describe the complex interaction with these mythic structures in post-war Italy. Just as British Pop Art would in fact deploy Americana highly selectively, so Italy's relationship with American mythologies – and specifically with the Western – is more appropriately seen as a process of cultural blending. As we shall see, this was most clearly demonstrated in the 1950s and 1960s by the domestic film industry. Precedents outside the cinematic medium, however, can be traced back as far as the early twentieth century, when Giacomo Puccini appropriated the myth of the Wild West for Italian opera in *La fanciulla del West* (1910).

Puccini's opera was billed as 'a perfect fusion of the old world and the new' prior to its New York premiere, for which the Metropolitan Opera House was bedecked with both the Italian tricolour and the Stars and Stripes. It would however become the subject of cultural controversy on both sides of the Atlantic. US critics, expecting a faithful representation of American customs, were dismayed at the inauthentic and exotic treatment afforded Californian culture. A reviewer in the *Evening World* wrote:

There is nothing American about the score of *La fanciulla del West* except a suggestion of ragtime, and the suave, mellifluous Italian phrases fall strangely upon the ears from the mouths of the rough and uncouth miners in a camp of forty-niners in California.[51]

Conversely, when the production reached Rome in 1911 it was the centrepiece of the fiftieth anniversary celebrations of the Kingdom of Italy, and billed as a sign of the quality of contemporary Italian music. The musical establishment, however, expressed dismay that the country's pre-eminent composer was neglecting Italian subject matter and imitating modern fashions. In 1915 one Florentine critic wrote (in an early example of disapproval at Hollywood's influence upon Italian culture) that *La fanciulla del West* was 'a rather tedious medley of Viennese operetta with a dash of Wagner and authentic north-American film music'.[52]

Italy's relationship with the 'America' of the Western myth was, at least amongst the cultural elite, therefore one of adaptation and fusion more than linear imitation from its earliest incarnation. The setting of the 'Wild West' was a contentious repository for issues concerning national identity, on both sides of the Atlantic. Alexandra Wilson argues of the reaction afforded Puccini's production:

It tells us more about the inferiority complexes of contemporary Americans and Italians than [...] about Puccini's opera itself. The USA and Italy were both relatively new nations craving a sense of common culture, and *Fanciulla* was dragged into the project to invent two very different national identities.[53]

Recalling Forgacs's suggestion that 'Americanisation is [...] a symptom of anxieties about one's own national identity'[54] we can see that, in 1910, this was a two-way process. Italian critics were already wary of 'Americanisms' corrupting their nation's popular culture, but so too did American critics disapprove of their national foundation myth being corrupted and misinterpreted by foreign influences.

Admittedly, by the post-war era this relationship was considerably less equal, and the appropriation of the Western myth in Italy reflected the imbalance; this time in the popular culture of the news stand, with the comic strip *Tex Willer*. Italian comics, or *fumetti*,[55] had been used for propaganda purposes by the Fascist regime in such publications as *Il giornale dei balilla* and *La piccola italiana*. In 1939, foreign comics had been banned from publication. When the regime fell, and Hollywood films were released in a deluge, so too American comics – *Dick Tracy*, *The Phantom*, *Flash Gordon* and *Prince Valiant*, among others – entered the Italian market *en masse*. The comics industry experienced a boom, and locally-authored *fumetti* imitating the motifs of American culture did not take long to exploit the situation. Milanese comic book author Gian Luigi Bonelli published Western *fumetti* entitled *I tre Bill*, *Yuma Kid*, *Hondo* and *Rio Kid* in 1948. In September of that year he and illustrator Aurelio Galleppini released the first *fumetto* featuring Tex Willer. Texas Ranger, defender of the weak and righteous dispenser of frontier justice, Willer's adventures were ostensibly imitative and affectionate nods to the instantly recognisable locale of Hollywood's Wild West.

The landscape through which Tex Willer travels, however, shows this romantic evocation of a mythic America being absorbed into a more parochial representation, and adapted to the local market. The vast landscapes of the American West were by this time indelibly etched into the popular imagination on both sides of the Atlantic. John Ford's repeated and spectacular framings immortalised the distinctive buttes of Monument Valley, continuing an aesthetic tradition stretching back to the vivid descriptions of James Fenimore Cooper and the paintings of Frederic Remington and Charles Russell. Galleppini's decision to eschew this universally recognisable imagery in favour of the mountains, valleys and gorges of the Dolomites, Trentino and his native Sardinia was therefore significant. Though on one hand Tex Willer displays a fascination with the Western myth in post-war Italy, it also betrays a sense, however subconsciously, of disorientation and a desire to situate this imaginary 'America' in a familiar locale. Pertinently, Stuart Hall writes:

> When we think of or imagine cultural identity, we tend to 'see' it in a place, in a setting, as part of an imaginary landscape or 'scene'. We give it a background, we put it in a frame, in order to make sense of it.[56]

The sense of displacement by transatlantic models in the post-war era is therefore expressed through adapting and localising the Western's traditional iconography. We shall see that, even when US popular culture was seemingly imitated by Italians, it was frequently relocated culturally (and in the case of Tex Willer, physically).

The myth of the Wild West remained highly attractive throughout Europe during the 1950s, and by 1960 the second most popular European cartoon character after Tintin was the cowboy Lucky Luke. Tony Judt comments that in West Germany, 'millions […] learned about cowboys from paperback novels written by local authors who had never been to America. […] America, real or imagined, was becoming the natural setting for light entertainment of all genres'.[57] In Italy, even Carlo Lizzani, who in 1948 had roundly condemned American genre cinema, was by the 1960s making Westerns. As *La fanciulla del West* and Tex Willer suggest, however, this was by no means a one-way process of displacement, in which Italians uncritically imitated Hollywood's motifs. Italian appropriation of the Western, as with that of American popular culture more generally, was one of cultural relocation. Unsurprisingly, this point is most vividly illustrated by developments within the Italian film industry. Here, issues concerning fascination with America, 'colonisation' by America (and the various implications of this terminology) and of appropriation and adaptation of 'America' and its mythological structures converge most clearly.

### Transatlantic Appropriation in the Italian Film Industry

In 1953, William K. Everson observed with some amusement an emergent craze in European cinema: since the end of the War, Italians, Germans and even Russians had started to produce home-grown Western movies.[58] As Christopher Frayling has outlined in detail, Italians had in fact been making Westerns ever since Vincenzo Leone – father of Sergio – made *La vampira Indiana* in 1913.[59] In 1942, while the Fascist regime was still intact, local interpretations of the West, influenced by Puccini's, emerged with Carl Koch's *Una signora dell'Ovest* and Giorgio Ferroni's *Il fanciullo del West*. Everson's article refers to Italian versions of Wild Bill Hickok in what Frayling refers to as 'carbon-copies of Hollywood "B" features'.[60] The very existence of these films, as well as the ongoing popularity of the Tex Willer *fumetti*, gives us an indication of the Western myth's uninterrupted appeal in Italy.

Given the ubiquity of Hollywood imagery in Italy from the 1920s onwards, and especially the deluge of American films after 1946, such imitative phenomena were perhaps to be expected. The subsequent boom in Western production which occurred in the 1960s, however, was peculiar for its remarkable scale. Three Westerns were made in Italy in 1961, one in 1962 and five in 1963. In 1964, 32 were released, and by 1968 the annual rate had risen to 73.[61] Though many of the films of this explosion – especially some of the earliest ones – did their utmost to resemble the American product, we shall see that this exponential growth cannot adequately be explained in terms of transatlantic influence alone.

This is not to say that the Italian film industry in this period was free from pressures exerted by Hollywood; quite the opposite, but by the 1950s this relationship had become one of exchange (both financial and cultural) more than domination. We have seen that Italian society negotiated with American cultural imports with a mixture of enthusiasm, bewilderment and hostility as it recovered in the post-war years. So too the domestic film industry's rehabilitation occurred through processes of imitation and appropriation, but also resistance to Hollywood practices and formats. Indeed, cinema itself became one of the most contentious sites of the cultural and political debates surrounding the increasing influence of American culture on Italian life.

In the immediate post-war years, the direction of the film industry was high on the agenda for the major political parties. For their part, the PCI extended their drive to persuade workers that art, literature and philosophy were superior to capitalist mass culture into both a denunciation of Hollywood cinema – whose proliferation was an increasing concern – and a promotion of the socially conscientious works of the 'neorealist' trend. This campaign was predicated on the notion that such native film-making was an expression of a genuine Italian political culture, in opposition to the anaesthetising effects exerted upon the proletariat by Hollywood. In 1948, the party's cultural commission was founded in a resolution entitled 'For the preservation of Italian culture', while *L'Unità* published a collective manifesto entitled 'Defend our cinema!'[62]

Such a perspective was perhaps understandable given the intentions of the occupying Americans after the War. The Allied Military Government inaugurated the flood of Hollywood films in 1946, and set up the Film Board to address the future of the Italian cinema industry. At the Board's opening meeting its president Admiral Stone announced:

> The so-called Italian cinema industry was invented by the fascists. Therefore it must be suppressed, as must be the instruments that incorporated this invention. All of them, Cinecittà included. [...] Anyway, Italy is a farming country, what does it need a cinema industry for?[63]

The occupying forces thus aimed quite openly to monopolise the market with American films, and to dominate native industries throughout Western Europe. Rome's Cinecittà studios – the largest and most modern in Europe – had been bombed by the advancing Allies and plundered by the retreating Germans, and were used as refugee accommodation as hostilities ceased. Resourceful Italian directors such as Roberto Rossellini (who took to the ruined streets to shoot *Roma città aperta* (1945) with salvaged film stock) were understandably championed as a politically enlightened alternative to Hollywood by politicians for whom American cinema represented cultural atrophy.

As we have already seen, for its part the DC was happy to see American films flood into the country, helping to foster a consensus which viewed the United States as the touchstone for Italy's post-war recovery. The emergent trend of 'neorealist' films, full of the miseries of working-class life, on the other hand, were viewed with undisguised hostility for their subversive representations of Italian society. Giulio Andreotti, as Under-Secretary for Entertainment from 1947 to 1953, oversaw the refurbishment of Fascist laws to hand considerable control over cinema to the government. Scripts, budgets and personnel had to be vetted before a film could secure loans from the state, or even gain distribution and exhibition licences. The Church also exerted a strong influence over the exhibition sector, controlling the output of rural parish cinemas. Neorealist tales of poverty and crime were seen to be thoroughly inappropriate while, as Gundle writes, 'upbeat American comedies and Westerns were deemed eminently suitable for family audiences and were often preferred to Italian films for showing in the parish cinemas'.[64] Andreotti was unequivocal in his vision of Italian cinema's way forward: 'Less rags, more legs.'[65]

That these stark oppositions were drawn by the main political parties is symptomatic of the polarisation of Italian (and world) politics as the Cold War intensified. In truth, however, the picture was not as black-and-white as this dispute suggested. To analyse the issue (as did influential figures in both major political parties) as a dichotomy of socially progressive Italian 'art' cinema and escapist American 'genre' cinema was to make a series of erroneous presuppositions: firstly, that genre cinema was inherently a transatlantic borrowing; secondly, that popular genres were devoid of political meaning; thirdly, that the worlds of 'art' and 'popular' cinema were mutually exclusive; and fourthly, that the success of genre cinema in the 1950s and 1960s amounted to a displacement of native creativity by US models. I do not wish to dwell unduly on the party political squabble whose dualistic stances invited such readings. By addressing these issues one by one, however, the remainder of this chapter will briefly survey the history of Italian cinema to arrive at the Spaghetti Westerns of the 1960s. This genre, perhaps above all others, suggests that the post-war relationship between the Italian and American film industries was one of cultural exchange.

### i) Genre Cinema's Italian Roots

Viewing 'genre' or 'entertainment' cinema as an Americanism, as many in the PCI did, was a fundamental misreading of the history of Italian film-making. Before the Great War, Italy dominated the world market with spectacular films for a mass audience such as Giovanni Pastrone's *La caduta di Troia* (1910) and *Cabiria* (1914), Mario Caserini's *Gli ultimi giorni di Pompeii* (1913) and Enrico Guazzoni's *Quo Vadis* (1913). These 'sword and sandal' historical epics were trailblazers in the early days of cinematography. *Cabiria* in particular, employing lateral tracking shots and unprecedented special effects, was an innovative contribution to cinematic language before the advent of Hollywood's hegemony. As the reaction to *La fanciulla del West* indicates, the cultural relationship between Italy and the USA at this time was one of exchange, and Pastrone's film directly and immediately inspired DW Griffith. Viewing *Cabiria* convinced Griffith that feature-length films could be financially viable in America, and in the same year he displayed this debt to Italian cinema with his biblical epic *Judith of Bethulia* (1914).[66] *Intolerance* (1916), too, borrowed heavily from *Cabiria* in its Babylon sequence.

### ii) Italian Genre Cinema and Politics

US influence on Italian cinema increased exponentially after the Great War. Before we address the issue of political engagement in Italian genres, we must therefore take into account this shift in the transatlantic relationship from one of equality to one of subordination. That Italians had instigated popular genres did not mean that they continued to exert command over their output, and the Americans soon monopolised the 'sword and sandal' film. The decline of the Italian film industry in the 1920s, indeed, was largely due to the domination of Hollywood. In 1923 Fred Niblo came to Rome to shoot *Ben Hur* with American money then completed the project in America, sapping the Italian industry of funds. There is disagreement over the precise statistics, but there is no doubting that film production in Italy declined alarmingly from a position of strength in 1920 so that, by the decade's end, annual output was in single figures.[67] Meanwhile, 80 per cent of releases on the Italian market in the 1920s were from Hollywood.[68]

Until the mid 1930s the Fascist regime was content to indulge a growing fascination with Hollywood products, which were highly profitable and broadly thought to be a pacifying influence against subversive tendencies. This is not to say that Mussolini wholly overlooked the political potential of cinema, but newsreels and documentaries inserted as 'B' features alongside more popular films were the regime's preferred form of propaganda. Indeed, this tactic – appeasing the public taste for Americana while hoping that they would pay attention to the ideological accompaniment – was one also favoured by both Josef Göbbels and Lenin. When, in 1937, Mussolini officially opened the imposing Cinecittà[69] studio complex in Rome's Via Tuscolana, a giant banner draped across the building's façade announced 'la cinematografia è l'arma più forte' ('cinematography is the most powerful weapon'), paraphrasing a quotation attributed to Lenin.[70] During the Russian Civil War of 1918–22 the Bolsheviks had invented the *agitka*: a short propagandist film, taken around the countryside by train to spread the word to the illiterate masses. Lenin saw that Russia's huge peasant class was both passive and pliable. In such a multilingual culture where religious iconography played a significant role, the moving image was seen to be a potent instrument.

In Italy where, as late as 1951, the illiteracy rate in the largely agrarian South was 24.8 per cent,[71] Lenin's views on cinema's political power were potentially resonant. The grandeur of Cinecittà's opening ceremony, however, was testament to Mussolini's penchant for spectacle and rhetoric more than a genuine advocacy of these sentiments: a grandiloquent declaration of the regime's *volte-face* in the mid 1930s in its attitude towards the domestic film industry and the impact of Hollywood imports. In 1935, the Centro Sperimentale film school was opened and the Venice Film Festival introduced an award reserved exclusively for Italian films. Cinecittà was the centrepiece and symbol of this renewed drive for a strong national industry, free of American influence. In 1938 Hollywood films were banned from distribution.

From its inception, however, Cinecittà was intended to be a replica of Hollywood's studio system, producing mass-appeal genre films. American practices and models of modernity were therefore emulated and adapted to the native culture, even by a government which outwardly sought to nullify them.[72] Despite the bombast and ceremony of this drive for cinematic autarchy, the potential of genre cinema as a 'powerful weapon' was not appreciated much beyond the symbolic purpose of strengthening the national industry. Doubtless, this was largely due to the difficulties of persuading a public fascinated by American popular culture to sit through doctrinaire polemics, but also betrayed Mussolini's dismissive attitude towards the political possibilities of genre cinema. It is perhaps no surprise, then, that seemingly innocuous formula films of the Fascist era, such as Alessandro Blasetti's *La corona di ferro* (1941), managed to smuggle subversive content beneath the government's radar by virtue of their 'popular' tag. As we have seen, though American genres came to dominate output in the 1920s, Italy itself had a rich history of 'genre cinema'. Looking back through this history, we see a tradition that had in fact been addressing local mores or confronting political issues from its inception.

*Cabiria* itself was co-written by the ultra nationalist author Gabrielle d'Annunzio. The film's depiction of the Second Punic War between Rome and Carthage had topical ideological overtones, released as Italy conquered the North African provinces of Cyrenacia and Tripolitania. When a minor character from *Cabiria* – the slave Maciste, played by Bartolomeo Pagano – then became immensely popular in a series of films celebrating his superhuman strength, he was recruited into the government's drive to rally the Italian people in the Great War (*Maciste alpino* (1916) depicts the muscle-bound superhero single-handedly defeating the Austrian army). In the Fascist era, too, though largely overlooked by officialdom, genre cinema offered a vehicle for political theses. Angela Dalle Vacche highlights the continuity of imperialist ambitions through comparing *Cabiria* with Carmine Gallone's similarly allegorical *Scipio Africanus* (1937), released during Mussolini's Abyssinian adventure.[73] Marcia Landy records that *La corona di ferro*, in depicting a tyrant's abuse of power just after Italy had entered the Second World War on Mussolini's whim, was condemned by Josef Göbbels for its pacifist stance:

> The potential for such a [political] reading was not lost on him. […]
> The adoption of a genre mode with its penchant for fantasy does not
> preclude the film's critique of the present. By combining spectacle
> with the thematic treatment of power, the film's politics are less
> censurable.[74]

While overt criticism of the regime was often met with imprisonment, apparently harmless films like *La corona di ferro* and Ferdinando Poggioli's *Le sorelle materassi* (1944) were able to secrete their satire from Mussolini's cultural radar.

Clearly, the notion that genre cinema was intrinsically a politically vacuous art form was dubious to say the least. Nevertheless, after the War, Mussolini's view of feature films would be echoed by Giulio Andreotti, who saw cinema's function as being one of 'calming the spirits'.[75] So too did the PCI consider popular cinema to be an ideologically soporific influence. As we have seen, the politically-committed works of the 'neorealist' trend were adopted by the PCI and reviled by the DC in equal measure, viewed by both as the antithesis to Hollywood genres. In this way, the PCI's campaign in defence of native working-class culture was translated into the cinematic medium. The third issue raised by this dispute – the extent to which 'art' cinema and popular genres could be viewed as separate entities – is brought into focus by the very films championed by the Communists.

### iii) The Blurred Boundaries of Neorealism

In 1945 scriptwriter Cesare Zavattini declared that, in 20 years of Fascism, Italian studios 'have not even produced one film, I insist: not even one'.[76] This is indicative of a trend amongst critics, politicians and film-makers who wished to escape the nation's recent traumas by declaring a rupture in Italian cinema, condemning 'Fascist' films as irredeemably corrupt (and even, it seems, dismissing their very existence). A new progressive aesthetic, addressing the German occupation, the Resistance, the hunger and the unemployment of the War and its aftermath through documentary realism was seen by those within the Left as the means to start afresh. Italian cinema was to be reclaimed from the discredited regime.

Subsequent critical analyses, however, have highlighted the extent to which this 'neorealism', as it would later become known, was neither a rupture from the past nor a movement at variance with the world of 'genre' cinema. Indeed, it was never a 'movement' at all, but a heterogeneous trend of films which broadly portrayed social deprivation from a leftist political stance. Pierre Leprohon emphasises that 'the seeds of realism had [...] been germinating for many years before the fall of the regime allowed them to burst into full flower'.[77] Stylistically, if not politically, neorealism owed much to Fascist-era film-making. The state-run production house Istituto Nazionale LUCE had been perfecting documentary techniques since 1922 and, while the regime was still intact, Alessandro Blasetti, Luchino Visconti and Roberto Rossellini had experimented with non-professional actors, on-location shooting and documentary footage. All of these would later be ascribed as key features of the post-war neorealist trend.

Sorlin argues that, 'as soon as one looks for precise criteria, Neorealism vanishes',[78] since there is little consensus over what exactly the word means, or which films make up the trend's canon. If – as is commonly assumed – the foregrounding of non-professional actors is a criterion, for example, then Rossellini's *Roma, città aperta* must be excluded for its employment of comic stars Anna Magnani and Aldo Fabrizi. More importantly for the purposes of this volume, if evidence that Hollywood genres had influenced a film precludes it, then neorealism becomes a very sparse category indeed. Many of the most successful examples displayed precisely such transatlantic hybridity. Wagstaff, Bondanella and Wood list such borrowings, including *Senza pietà*'s (1948) use of gangster film motifs, the film noir elements of *Gioventù perduta* (1949), the adoption of the Western's archetypes in *In nome della legge* (1949) and *Il cammino della speranza* (1950) and the melodrama intrinsic to the plots of many 'neorealist' films such as *I ladri di biciclette* (1948) and *Riso amaro* (1949).[79] The latter film in particular drew a severe reaction from the Left both for this assimilation of genre cinema and for its indulgence in erotic titillation by employing a former Miss Italy (Silvana Mangano) in the lead role (the critic Guido Aristarco lamented that 'workers cannot be educated with the legs of Silvana'[80]). The term *neorealismo rosa* ('pink neorealism') was coined to categorise a popular[81] category of film which merged the proletarian focus of neorealism with techniques of melodrama to dilute the revolutionary agenda and increase an audience's emotional investment.

This blending of 'art' and 'genre' cinema which characterised the Italian industry's output in the 1950s and 1960s is often viewed as the 'crisis of neorealism', whereby the movement capitulated in the face of the public's desire for Hollywood products.[82] The process, however, can equally be seen in terms of continuity and evolution, when viewed from the perspective of Italian genre cinema itself. Marcia Landy, for example, identifies a continuum from popular pre-war cinema such as Blasetti's and Poggioli's films, through neorealism and into the 1950s, of social criticism in both 'art' and 'genre' cinema. Her argument refutes analyses approaching the two spheres in oppositional terms: 'The ethical and investigative spirit of neorealism was not abandoned; rather there was a greater exploration of the conditions and nature of realism in more complex and philosophical terms, often in the vein of comedy and satire.'[83]

The flowering of the *commedia all'italiana* ('comedy Italian style') from the mid 1950s owed much to the 'pink neorealist' precedent earlier in the decade. It combined, as Ellwood writes in reference to *Un americano a Roma*, 'the post-war neo-realist tradition of Rossellini and De Sica and a much older music hall and comic magazine tradition of slapstick'.[84] Comedies by Steno, Luigi Comencini, Mario Monicelli and Dino Risi thus merged 'high' and 'low' Italian culture to satirise the system presiding over the Economic Miracle and the emergent individualism of the new Italy. By the 1950s, then, Italian genre cinema had absorbed influences wholly separate from transatlantic borrowings. The rich and varied history of a national cinema interrogating and reflecting contemporary preoccupations in fact converged with the ubiquitous American formats.

Certainly, the film industry itself did not view the matter in dualistic terms of 'high' and 'low' culture. Though it is commonly thought that neorealism was a deeply unpopular category of film-making, the box-office figures suggest that it held its own in the domestic market. *Roma città aperta* for example, topped the charts for 1945–46. Out of the 53 Italian films released in 1946–47, *Il bandito* came fourth, *Vivere in pace* sixth, *Paisà* ninth and *Il sole sorge ancora* twelfth. Still, by 1949, *In nome della legge* was coming third.[85] As the volume of American imports and Italian productions both increased, neorealism's share of the home market did indeed dwindle. By the mid 1950s, however, an Italian film could make up to 40 per cent of its receipts from the export market, and it was the critically lauded, prize-winning works of neorealism which had opened the door to such profits.[86] In economic terms, a dichotomy between 'high' and 'low' culture was therefore an irrelevance, since Italian films all belonged to the same marketing strategy. This export-driven outlook saw Italy transform, in the words of Christopher Wagstaff, 'from a producer of essentially "Italian" films for an art house public to a major exporter of popular genre films for a mass audience'.[87]

It is therefore clear that the sectarian disputes which surrounded Italian cinema in the post-war years encouraged a dichotomous view at variance with the underlying realities of the industry and its production practices. Firstly, popular genre cinema of this era should not be interpreted exclusively in terms of transatlantic influence, since it fused this with a rich continuum of Italian formulae. Secondly, while US genres came to dominate output and the major Italian political parties from the 1920s onwards consistently viewed these as politically anodyne, this concealed a tradition of ideological engagement dating back to the earliest days of the Italian industry. Thirdly, the widely respected films emerging from post-war Italy were not produced in a vacuum, and frequently displayed narrative, ethical and industrial affinities with those films commonly labelled 'popular'.

These historical and cultural factors converged in the emergence of a new wave of genres (known locally as *filoni*) in the 1950s. It is to this phenomenon that I now turn, in order to analyse the final issue under consideration in this chapter: was the proliferation and success of these formulaic, internationally-oriented films a sign that Italian culture had been displaced by a globalised outlook and homogeneous 'Americanisation'? Or are these films a sign that, just as post-war Italian society's 'Americanisation' was neither universal nor a case of mere imitation, so too the film industry's experience was one of negotiation and appropriation?

### iv) Industry, Filoni, and Spaghetti Westerns

Though the DC broadly welcomed the influx of American cinema in the post-war years, the government's policies were by no means subservient to Hollywood's desires and Andreotti was fully aware of the economic advantages of a strong local industry. In 1949 screen quotas were introduced, stipulating that for 20 days each quarter every cinema had to show Italian films. Additionally, legislation was passed insisting that all future revenues in the Italian market from American films must be reinvested in Italy. The bare statistics paint a picture of remarkable recovery, which mirrored that of the economy. Cinema attendance across the Western world haemorrhaged between 1946 and 1955, yet in the same period both Italian audience figures and the number of commercially operating cinemas in the country nearly doubled.[88] In 1952 Italy became Europe's leading centre of film production, and by the 1960s the nation's output rivalled that of Hollywood itself.[89]

The Italian cinema industry in the 1950s and 1960s operated, despite Mussolini's efforts, on a very different model from the Hollywood studio system. A fragmented approach to film-making saw production, distribution and exhibition operating as separate sectors, each aiming to reach as wide an audience as possible to exploit popular trends for maximum profit. *Filoni* broadly appealed to the 'mass' audience (that is, one which traverses all social classes), via three exhibition sectors: *prima visione* ('first run' cinemas in large cities), *seconda visione* (showing the same films on their 'second run' and a selection of cheaper films) and *terza visione* (the thousands of 'third run' open-air, parish or independent cinemas, largely in rural areas). Though economic factors had brought the worlds of 'art' cinema and 'genre' cinema into the same marketing strategy, competition from American imports also helped polarise film-making into high-budget and low-budget outputs, even within individual *filoni*. An entire production sector therefore arose which was aimed exclusively at *seconda* and *terza visione* outlets. This 'popular' audience (that is, a working-class one) would therefore be consuming many films which had never been released in large cities, and which were tailored to offer formulaic entertainment to guarantee returns.[90]

The vast *terza visione* sector was not only a significant sub-culture of Italian film distribution, but also a sphere whose preferences were often at variance with mainstream culture in the 1950s. Gundle illustrates the more parochial outlook inherent to this category of film-going by analysing the extent to which the Hollywood star system was emulated in Italy. American stars had been a source of fascination and aspiration since the 1920s, and provided models of modernity to which many Italian actors aspired. Silvana Mangano, for instance, was labelled a 'Rita Hayworth of the Italian periphery' by Giuseppe De Santis,[91] anticipating Jean Baudrillard's observation that 'American is the original version of modernity. [Europeans] are the dubbed or subtitled version'.[92] Alongside such emulation, however, were those, such as the unmistakably Italian Anna Magnani, who bore little resemblance to transatlantic models. She was described as 'a star for the audiences of third-run cinemas'.[93] Gundle explains that such domestic stars 'appealed not because they were distant but because they were close to their audiences. They [...] provided symbols of continuity with the past combined with varying elements of change during a period of immense, disorienting social and economic development'.[94] Much as *Tex Willer* betrayed unease at a perceived displacement of native culture in the post-war years, so the popular audiences of the *terza visione* sector were not entirely in thrall to American models.

With this industrial context in mind, Angela Dalle Vacche differentiates *filoni* from Hollywood 'genres' as 'well-planned investments of the industry into a regulated, but also stimulating, oscillation between repetition and difference, convention and invention'.[95] The singular form *filone* literally translates as 'tradition' or 'vein', but also hints at 'filo', meaning 'thread'. Unlike a Hollywood genre, which is defined by a common theme, historical period or iconography but whose constituent parts are often diverse, *filoni* relied on rapid repetition and imitation of successful formulae: what Wagstaff dubs 'safe bets' for the industry.[96] Roman studios – most notably Cinecittà and Elios – responded to the hegemony of Hollywood by churning out as many films, and making as much money, as was possible from variations on a popular theme before it lost its mass appeal.

Between the early 1950s and the late 1960s, a succession of these cheaply-made, short-lived and often overlapping generic cycles proliferated. Comedies, spy stories, farces, peplums[97] and Westerns flooded the market in turn, often on the back of a popular American genre or film. International co-production, mostly with France, Germany and Spain, also gave *filoni* the means to compete with Hollywood in two markets at once.[98] In producing hastily-shot, low budget formulae aimed at the mass and the popular audiences, the domestic and the export markets, Roman studios were certainly emphasising the 'industry' in 'film industry'. Pier Paolo Pasolini, indeed, described Cinecittà's assembly line as 'the belching stomach of Italy'.[99]

As the *filone* phenomenon's reactive nature demonstrates, behind the resurgence of the domestic industry lay a complex relationship between Italy and the USA. Though the infrastructure was divergent from the American model, *filoni* showed that production practices in certain sectors were becoming more streamlined and efficient. Frayling demonstrates that the revolution in consumerism since the arrival of television in 1954 was palpable in such films' assembly line circumstances:

[They] resembled those of Hollywood 'B' features, or even TV series: shooting schedules which seldom over-ran a five- or six-week norm; budgets averaging below $20,000; the more solid sets used over and over again; only two or three 'takes' per shot; post-synchronised sound and dialogue tracks [...] and the same pieces of action footage frequently turning up in 'disguised' form.[100]

While mainstream analysis of the American Western tends to overlook Republic's 'B' features of the 1930s, Peter Stanfield has demonstrated how their interplay of Western iconography and Depression-era maladies kept the genre afloat by addressing the immediate concerns of lower-class audiences in rapidly-produced series following familiar heroes.[101] The quick production turnover of the *filoni* similarly offered a potential responsiveness to topical themes which prestige productions could not match. As the *terza visione* sector's emphasis on comforting familiarity suggests, these Italian films represent an equivalent underbelly, pulling in audiences with regular instalments of popular heroes' adventures.

Frayling's comparison with television is also pertinent. Christopher Wagstaff insists that, when analysing such formulaic cinema, the assumptions of traditional film theory alone – that the individual film, as the object of the viewer's attention, is the unit worthy of study – are not sufficient. He advocates practices more commonly associated with television studies concerning the social function of cinema-going, as a model offering a more faithful deconstruction of the *terza visione* sector's ongoing dialogue with provincial audiences.[102] Elsewhere, Wagstaff points out that television viewers did not identify individual hour-long 'Kojak' episodes by their titles, but knew them as weekly appointments with the iconic hero.[103] International *filone* distribution followed this pattern, so that individual films were tailored to suit the demands of different export markets. For example, Giacomo Gentilomo's Peplum *Maciste e la regina di Samar* (1964) was marketed in America as *Hercules Against the Moon Men*. Maciste and Hercules were interchangeable heroes – both taciturn, muscular and clad in loin-cloths – but Hercules was the more popular in America, and therefore the 'safest bet' for the Italian exporters.

Investment, as well as distribution, showed that the influence of America was still strong. Though the 1949 legislation locked earnings from foreign films released in Italy into local film production, this did not discourage Hollywood exploitation of the market. Instead, it forced American distributors to seek loopholes. A gamut of Italo-American co-productions over the ensuing 15 years saw Italy's position in world cinema boom, while offering considerable profits to Hollywood through 'exporting' the films back to America. Roman studios thus attracted large numbers of American actors and directors taking advantage of cheap, technically-skilled native crews and a ready-made industry infrastructure in a phenomenon dubbed 'Hollywood on the Tiber'. Del Buono and Tornabuoni argue that the Americans enjoyed 'the ease of living in a colony as if they were the bosses, and with greater freedom than in the controlled, moralist and McCarthyist Hollywood of the era'.[104]

Once again, we find the language of imperialism employed to describe the cultural relationship between Italy and America. So too, Michel de Certeau's extension of this colonial conceit, whereby locals engage with and appropriate the dominant culture's mythic structures, again applies. The above argument underlines the fact that conditions back in California were not entirely favourable for American film-making at the time. The *Paramount* decision of 1948 had broken up the major studios' monopolisation of production and marketing. Declining cinema attendance was jeopardising domestic profits, while output was falling. US producers therefore needed to sell their films in Europe, whose markets were growing just as those in America declined. From 1950 onwards American films acquired 50 per cent of their earnings abroad, and Italy's rapidly growing industry was a high priority.[105] In other words, the Americans needed the Italians as much as the Italians needed them. US influence in the film industry, as in society, remained the most significant catalyst for change, but the relationship was not one of domination. Areas in which the industry appeared to imitate transatlantic habits in fact displayed, time and again, processes of cultural blending. The *filoni* of the 1950s and 1960s are the single most illustrative example of this.

As the major US studios scaled down their output, the fusion of cultures in 'Hollywood on the Tiber' scored significant box-office successes with such 'runaway' productions as Mervyn LeRoy's *Quo Vadis* (1951), Robert Wise's *Helen of Troy* (1955) and William Wyler's *Ben Hur* (1959). Budding Italian film-makers learnt their trade on these films' sets alongside giants of the US industry (Sergio Leone, for example, worked on all three of the above ancient epics). The Italian peplum, with its irreverent, humorous take on Hollywood's earnest grandeur, was therefore the archetypal *filone*, fusing the iconography of the 'sword and sandal' spectacles of early Italian cinema with contemporary Cinecittà/Hollywood epics, whose skilled local second unit crews it borrowed. The craze began with Pietro Francisci's melting-pot of disparate Greek and Roman myths, *Le fatiche di Ercole* (1957). Both this and its sequel, *Ercole e la regina di Lidia* (1958), proved highly popular both domestically (especially in the *terza visione* sector) and abroad.[106] Success spawned imitation, and the peplum remained an extremely lucrative formula into the early 1960s. Eccentric hybrids sent interchangeable muscle-bound heroes such as Ercole/Hercules, Samson, Ursus and (directly from *Cabiria*) Maciste into Norse sagas, pre-Revolutionary France and eighteenth-century Scotland, displaying the versatility (not to mention the humour) of this *filone*.

The peplum ran out of steam when a series of financial disasters for Cinecittà peaked with Robert Aldrich's *Sodom and Gomorrah* (1961) going wildly over budget and becoming beset by recriminations between the American director and his Italian crew (including second unit director and up-and-coming peplum-maker Sergio Leone). The film's Italian producer Goffredo Lombardo recalled of the Americans: 'They treated us with a certain disdain, as if we were underdogs, from a lower caste. When Italian film culture started to show signs of life, they did all they could to kill it stone dead.'[107] 'Hollywood on the Tiber' imploded, and as American financiers pulled out, Cinecittà faced mass unemployment and an uncertain future.

Though, in the 1960s, Italy had almost equal attendance figures to the combined markets of France, Germany and Britain,[108] cinema began steadily to lose its monopoly on popular leisure to television from the beginning of the decade. At first, the number of operating cinemas dropped back only slightly,[109] but annual attendance was decreasing at a more marked rate, while television was becoming ever more popular.[110] Erosion of big city audiences in particular alarmed the industry, and a new *filone* was required to alleviate the crisis. The early 1960s therefore saw thrillers, Gothic horrors, swashbuckling adventures and Viking sagas, among countless other action-packed formulae and hybrids, attempt to capture the imagination of the mass audience.

The Roman studios' future was heralded by the success in Italy of two European Westerns co-produced by Rialto Film of Hamburg and Jadran Film of Zagreb: *Der Schatz im Silbersee* (1962) and *Winnetou I* (1963). Adapted from the German novels of Karl May, directed by the Austrian Harald Reinl, shot in Yugoslavia and starring the American ex-Tarzan Lex Barker, these films displayed the profitable potential of an international 'Wild West'. The production of American Westerns was in decline, but the genre had retained its appeal in the European market.[111] As the Hollywood product dried up, Cinecittà saw a lucrative niche. Europeans had in fact been making Western films in the deserts of southern Spain since 1959, when Raoul Walsh directed *The Sheriff of Fractured Jaw* with British money. Spanish production companies had also constructed Wild West town sets in Madrid and Almería for their own versions. That the Western could provide a new *filone* was therefore a logical conclusion for Italian distributors. The cheap, ready-made desert sets would be used alongside Cinecittà's new Western town stage in Rome. Through co-production with West Germany and Spain, Cinecittà had thus identified its next formula.

The short life-spans of the various *filoni*, and their emergence from the same studios, meant both that hybrid genres arose (notably the 'horror peplum', typified by Mario Bava's *Ercole al centro della terra* (1961)) and that a relatively circumscribed set of directors made a living across this spectrum. Antonio Margheriti, for example, directed peplums, horrors, spy thrillers, adventure films and Westerns. As the gothic horror influences in the Westerns of Giulio Questi (*Se sei vivo, spara!*), Sergio Garrone (*Django il bastardo*) and Margheriti himself (*Joko, invoca Dio… e muori!*) testify, these films were just as amenable to generic hybridisation as were other *filoni*. Sharing an irreverent take on popular Hollywood genre convention, as well as the same crews and international co-financiers, the transition from one *filone* to another was fluid. Seasoned Cinecittà directors such as Sergio Corbucci, Duccio Tessari, Sergio Sollima and Sergio Leone therefore left the peplum behind to embark on the next cycle.

Peculiar to the Westerns, however, was a mixture of such genre-hopping artists with politically-committed directors and screenwriters who did not become involved in any other *filone*. The PCI leadership's dogmatic reaction against 'entertainment' films blinded them to the fact that, as already discussed, the divide between 'high' and 'low' Italian cinema was narrowing in the 1950s and 1960s. The northern intelligentsia and the Roman assembly line were increasingly merging. Carlo Lizzani's *volte-face* was an extreme example, but not an isolated one. Militant film critic and neorealist pioneer (writing the screenplays for *Germania anno zero* (1948) and *Riso amaro* (1949)), Lizzani directed two Westerns in the 1960s, bringing Pier Paolo Pasolini on board to star in his Mexican peasant parable *Requiescant* (1967). Lizzani and Pasolini were just two of many figures from the world of 'art' cinema who saw no contradiction in making Westerns. Other notables included Bernardo Bertolucci (original story for Leone's *C'era una volta il West* (1968)) and Ennio Flaiano (screenplay for Tessari's *Vivi o, preferibilmente, morti* (1969)).

By 1966, a radicalised sub-*filone* variously offering critiques of latent fascism, engaging with contemporaneous protest movements and expounding bravura anti-imperialist doctrine had arisen from within the Italian Western. This ostensibly most 'American' of all the *filoni* was identified as fertile space for such appropriation and dissemination by intellectuals and dissident PCI members. Of these, six men played key roles in the central films under consideration in this book.

Sergio Sollima enrolled at the Centro Sperimentale di Cinematografia in 1940, and cut his cinematic teeth working with Chiarini, De Santis, Antonioni and Visconti. He later became an assistant journalist for the periodical *Cinema* alongside the future figurehead of the PCI's militant left, Pietro Ingrao. His post-war career fused his political beliefs with screenwriting and directing in an eclectic mix of genres. Sergio Corbucci also trained as a journalist, before entering the film industry by directing *Salvate mia figlia* in 1951. By the 1960s he was one of Cinecittà's most prolific directors of *filoni*, but was at pains to stress the sincerity of his films' politics: 'In my Westerns there was always something of a political element; there were always racial or revolutionary backdrops.'[112]

None of Giulio Petroni, Damiano Damiani, Giulio Questi or Franco Solinas, however, were previously connected with, or involved in, the production of *filoni*, yet they too were attracted to the Italian Western as a means of political communication. Petroni left Italy for Ceylon after the War, returning in 1951 to make political documentaries. Damiani, a graduate of the Brera Academy of Fine Arts in Milan, illustrated *fumetti* before becoming involved in cinema through art direction and neorealist scriptwriting. Questi wrote for political journals, including Elio Vittorini's ill-fated project *Il politecnico*. Solinas worked as a novelist and militant journalist for *L'Unità* before being introduced to the film industry by Gillo Pontecorvo, and embarking on a career writing political screenplays such as *Kapò* (1959), *Salvatore Giuliano* (1962) and *La battaglia di Algeri* (1966).

In Chapter Three, we will see that the political roots of Petroni, Questi, Sollima and Solinas lay in their involvement in clandestine anti-Fascist groups during the wartime Resistance: a factor which is infused throughout their Westerns. The legacy of these experiences is manifest in Solinas's and Sollima's Western collaboration, *La resa dei conti* (1967), and to an even greater extent in Sollima's solo effort, *Faccia a faccia* (1967). The latter film is a unique contribution to this sub-*filone* for its eschewal of action sequences, its denial of generic expectations and its philosophical engagements with fascistic ideologies. Wider trends within the Italian Western also informed these films' political content. Many such movies set in the American West, for example, register contemporary countercultural outlooks on capitalist society, culminating in Corbucci's *Il grande Silenzio* (1968). As Chapter Four will demonstrate, those crossing the Mexican border, meanwhile, consistently utilise the Mexican Revolution to comment upon US foreign policy. The four Westerns attributed to the pen of Franco Solinas in particular signal a consistent advocacy of insurrection from a Third Worldist perspective through tales of agrarian political awakenings and violent rejection of the capitalist West (*Quien sabe?* (Damiani, 1966), *La resa dei conti* (Sollima, 1967), *Il mercenario* (Corbucci, 1968) and *Tepepa* (Petroni, 1969)). The same is true of Westerns directly influenced by Solinas's work, such as *Corri, uomo, corri* (Sollima, 1968) and *Compañeros* (Corbucci, 1970).

Petroni (born 1920), Sollima (1921), Damiani (1922), Questi (1924), Corbucci (1926) and Solinas (1927) all matured in a period when US influence was a decisive factor in shaping a modern consciousness. A sense of cultural bewilderment redolent of that displayed so memorably by Nando Moriconi in *Un americano a Roma* is palpable through Sollima's recollection of his childhood in Tivoli, near Rome:

> My heroes were Tom Mix and Hopalong Cassidy! I remember the Westerns of William Hart. [...] I was five or six years old, and I suffered my first shock when someone told me that I was not an American, that the prairies and the Indians were out of my reach.[113]

Damiani similarly recalls that as a boy in Pasiano, near Udine, he would go to the cinema twice a day. At the age of 14, having just watched Frank Capra's *It Happened One Night* (1934), he decided to become a film director: 'That film really impressed me. That did it.'[114]

Despite the wide-eyed admiration intimated by these responses to US popular culture, we should not forget Nando Moriconi's creative requisitioning of Hollywood's output, which is mirrored by the films at the heart of this volume. They give a clear indication that transatlantic influence in Italian cinema was just as much a process of negotiation and blending as it was in society. Economically, the industry was once again reacting to American trends, but these films were by no means merely receptacles of Hollywood iconography. By appropriating a popular American genre and adapting it both to the native market and to contemporary politics, they register the interplay of reference points evident throughout the nation's culture in the post-war years.

When the Western became the latest *filone* phenomenon, an opportunity presented itself to these film-makers to reach a mass audience and address the immediate concerns of Italy's revolutionary Left. The question of why this genre above all others should have offered such a pressing format for these radical polemics is the subject of my next chapter. I now turn to the Hollywood Western itself, to assess how this appropriation invited such a reading. The key functions ascribed to this narrative model display notable affinities both with issues surrounding Italian national identity and with themes and disputes at the heart of the country's militant discourse in the 1960s.

# 2

# A Marxist's Gotta Do What a Marxist's Gotta Do:
# National Identity and Political Violence on the Italian Frontier

Upon hearing that their mother has been killed by an agent of the St Louis Midland Railroad, Jesse and Frank James are impassive. After exchanging a brief look with his younger brother, Frank (Henry Fonda) calmly exclaims: 'Well, let's go.' Jesse (Tyrone Power), equally composed, rejects his fiancée's plea for him not to follow. 'I've got to', he declares, before purposefully riding into Liberty, Missouri and gunning down the man responsible in broad daylight. So begins the legendary outlaw's criminal career in Henry King's 1939 film *Jesse James*.

*Jesse James* was released in the same year that John Steinbeck's *The Grapes of Wrath* was published. It was scripted by Nunnally Johnson, who also converted Steinbeck's novel into a screenplay for John Ford. King's tale of a hard-working farming community torn apart by ruthless big business therefore owes more to the political and economic context of Depression-era America, the Dust Bowl and the New Deal than to that of nineteenth-century Missourian banditry. Described by Jon Tuska as 'a pastoral fantasy',[1] the film pays little heed to historical verisimilitude.[2] Indeed, the romantic myth of the James-Younger gang had superseded reality in the popular imagination ever since 1872, when John Newman Edwards reported their deeds in the *Kansas City Times* under the headline 'The Chivalry of Crime'.[3] Dime novelists had long since entrenched the notorious outlaw Jesse James as a latter-day Robin Hood, and the concordances between this myth and the plight of agrarian labourers in the 1930s made invoking the legend once more a profitable step.

It is significant that in addressing contemporary mores, King's film does not alter the generic conventions of the Western. Indeed, *Jesse James* synthesises themes which had been central to the genre's dynamics since its inception, and which invite such reinterpretation at times of traumatic social upheaval. The railroad's strong-arm tactics force innocent farmers to leave their land, as the inexorable advance of industrialisation runs roughshod over rural values. The James brothers' banditry is depicted as a noble rebellion in defence of an agrarian community. The locals' suspicion of outside interference, alongside their admiration for the gang, displays the ambivalence towards centralised government and the onset of modernity found throughout the Western genre. Most significantly, in that brief, understated exchange between the James brothers is distilled a moral code so self-evident and so ubiquitous to the Western that is does not warrant articulation: since institutional law cannot be trusted, such an outrage must be avenged with violence, and no feminine pleas for pacifism can deter the Western hero from this masculine duty. Throughout the genre's development, ritualised violence ('Count three and duck', Jesse advises the bartender before avenging his mother), in self-defence or as a regenerative force for the greater good, is accepted and implicitly advocated.[4]

In this chapter I examine the Hollywood Western, from its earliest traditions up to the 1960s, to explain why this genre became an available and appropriate conduit for revolutionary doctrine in Italy. I invoke *Jesse James* because the Western themes distilled in this film, and summarised above, possessed affinities with dominant modes of representation in the Italian peninsula. Here, especially in the South, discourses concerning pastoral nostalgia, agrarian fantasies of resistance and ambivalence towards central government had more immediate and local significance than being confined to the parameters of the 'Wild West'. So too, as the political oppositions of the late 1960s became ever more fractious, issues surrounding romanticised banditry, the use of violence and its legitimacy became the focus of earnest and heated debate amongst Italian protest movements. By the end of this chapter I hope that the appropriation of the Western by radical left-wing Italian film-makers will make more sense than it might otherwise have done since, far from rejecting Hollywood's mythic structures, they requisitioned and adapted these aspects of Americana to the pressing concerns of contemporary militant discourse.

### Out West, Down South: Representing the Italian Frontier

In 1966 Franco Solinas co-wrote a story set in his native Sardinia, in which a police officer pursues an elderly peasant accused of molesting a child. The climax reveals the peasant to be innocent, framed by corrupt local officials to cover up their own misdeeds. Awoken to the true nature of the system he has served, the policeman still sees no alternative but to shoot the innocent man in cold blood and protect himself. Sergio Sollima saw in this tale of agrarian oppression the outline for his first Western, and enlisted the help of Sergio Donati to transpose the plot to the Texas/Mexico border for their screenplay *La resa dei conti* (literally, 'The Settling of Accounts', 1967).

Concessions, it is true, were made to the demands of the market. By reversing the protagonists' ages, for example, they facilitated the highly profitable casting of Lee Van Cleef (fresh from Leone's *Il buono, il brutto, il cattivo*) as the pursuer, and by altering the ending allowed the innocent Mexican peasant to enact righteous revenge on the corrupt system. Otherwise, the transposition from southern Italian parable to Western is remarkably fluid, involving little formal subversion of either the original story or the parent genre. As is the case in *Jesse James*, the villain of *La resa dei conti* is a railway magnate whose ruthless profiteering disregards the plight of rural folk, one of whom is driven outside the law by resisting his plans for expansion. As will be made clear in Chapter Three, Sollima's film differs markedly from Hollywood models in its political trajectory. Nevertheless, Sollima and Donati were clearly alert to representational concordances between the Italian South (or, colloquially, the *Mezzogiorno*[5]) and the Wild West, as well as the political (and financial) potential of such a conceit.

Of course, the industrial context within which Sollima was working was not that of the Hollywood Western, but that of the Italian Western: by 1967 a firmly established and flourishing *filone* which constituted a considerable fusion of native and transatlantic influences. Given the explicit nature of the above example, however, remarkably few critics of these films have identified representational parallels between the American West and the Italian South. Frayling was the first to raise such a thematic concordance:

> Perhaps the hostility to codified law (and to the encroachments of central government) which is often enshrined in Hollywood Westerns [...] *and* which was to become central to the Spaghetti Westerns, finds a parallel [...] in the equivalent hostilities of Southern Italian society.[6]

Marcia Landy offers a hypothesis emphasising that Italy's intimate ties to American culture begin with nineteenth-century emigration, which arose largely in the South as a result of stark inequalities after the *Risorgimento* (the union of the Italian states):

Therefore, it is not at all unusual or surprising that the Italian westerns have assimilated and appropriated Americanism to their own ends. In the Italian films, there is a congenial union between the themes and styles attributed to the North American western, involving the American continent, both north and south of the border, and portrayals of Italian life – in representations of the Mezzogiorno in particular.[7]

This notion – that the Italian Western is a hybrid, absorbing and reflecting both American and Italian traditions of representation – is self-evident, and *La resa dei conti*'s cultural fusion affirms such a reading (though, curiously, Landy only mentions Sergio Leone in her argument).

Of more interest, for the purposes of this chapter, is the question raised by Frayling: to what extent did the themes of the American Western, which Cinecittà had inherited and reformulated, possess pre-existing parallels with the preoccupations of Italian society? In other words, was Sollima's film merely another example of the Italian Western's fusion of American and native influences? Or had the director in fact identified in the Hollywood model a set of themes whose concerns made their adoption for issues concerning Italian national identity appropriate and obvious?

Frayling goes on to extrapolate from Jean-Luc Godard's film *Vent d'Est* (1970) a critique of Cinecittà's likely marketing strategy with the Italian Western: by making films which echoed traditional southern concerns, cinemas were attracting southern audiences who would reinforce their crudest self-image, while northerners would turn up to confirm their prejudices about southerners.[8] Certainly, to make such a reading would be to posit a more dichotomous north/south divide than actually existed in the 1960s: a period during which many southerners had been forced north to find work. Contemporary social realities, however, are not necessarily the most relevant basis upon which to build such cultural concordances.

Gabriella Gribaudi argues that the South of Italy 'can only be understood if we analyse the processes through which [its] image has been created. [...] The South is much more than a geographical area. It is a metaphor which refers to an imaginary and mythical entity'.[9] Focusing on northern stereotypes of the South, as much as on the society of the South itself, is therefore a necessary and informative approach if we are to examine this concordance with the Western in any depth.[10]

### Representing the South and the West

This imaginary 'South' emerges from a long tradition, in both scholarly and popular literature, of locating the region as the polar opposite both of northern Italian and of northern European aspirations of bourgeois modernity. Accordingly, it possesses numerous parallels with representations undertaken by eastern Americans looking west in the late nineteenth and early twentieth centuries. Compare, for example, the following excerpts: firstly, from French anthropologist Ernest Renan writing home from Salerno in 1850:

> I am unable to tell you the strange feeling I had in thus finding myself in full barbarousness. What! I am hardly six or seven days from Paris, and I am at the end of civilization! At the center, one believes that the circumference extends to infinity; what a surprise when one runs into the edge.[11]

Secondly, the narrator's first impressions of Medicine Bow, Wyoming, in Owen Wister's 1902 novel *The Virginian*, commonly read as a (if not the) founding text of the cinematic Western:

> The East-bound [train] departed slowly into that distance whence I had come. I stared after it as it went its way to the far shores of civilisation. It grew small in the unending gulf of space, until all sign of its presence was gone save a faint skein of smoke against the evening sky. [...] A sort of ship had left me marooned in a foreign ocean.[12]

Both narrators, in expressing bewilderment at their surroundings, use the alien locale as a contrast to define their own more civilised worlds. Their ideological agendas, however, are divergent. Renan's Eurocentric perspective is characteristic of northern European and northern Italian stereotypes of the South from the mid eighteenth century up until the *Risorgimento*. John Dickie and Nelson Moe both demonstrate the extent to which the South became increasingly represented as an 'Africa' or an 'Orient' as northern momentum gathered behind this nation-building project.[13] Widely perceived as a backward, degenerate obstacle to ambitions of Italian unity, the Kingdom of Naples was represented and conceptualised by the North at a cultural remove. Dickie writes that the imagined national space was defined 'by the exclusion of the alien or the unpatriotic, by the projection of Others'.[14] While northern Italian states such as Lombardy and Piedmont fell into line with prevailing European conceptions of civilisation, the *Mezzogiorno* was therefore increasingly marginalised, as commonplace representations of degeneracy display. The economist Nassau William Senior wrote of Naples in 1851: 'You never are free from the sight, or indeed, from the contact, of loathsome degradation. I never saw so hateful a people; they look as wicked as they are squalid and unhealthy.'[15]

The passage from *The Virginian*, on the other hand, has a somewhat different ideological purpose. Firstly, the narrator is just that: a fictional first-person storyteller, whose eastern prejudices are dismantled the more he encounters the West. Far from decrying the degenerate nature of a savage land, Wister's novel synthesises themes established by dime novels and historical romances towards the end of the nineteenth century to assert a morally regenerative force for eastern sensibilities. Above all else, *The Virginian* reflects *fin de siècle* anxieties over a decline in traditional American values brought about by industrialisation.

In looking west for the nation's moral and social elixir, Wister's agenda was akin both to his friend Theodore Roosevelt's 'rough rider' political spin, and to Frederick Jackson Turner's 'Frontier Thesis' of 1893. Roosevelt's perspective similarly arose from an upper-class eastern consciousness, eager to stem a perceived moral decay in American life by emulating the values of an already mythologised recent past. Turner saw the frontier as the defining element in the construction of American national identity: a vast safety valve for social tensions, offering boundless opportunities for rebirth and enterprise. Though his was a progressive outlook, in contrast to Wister's and Roosevelt's aristocratic perspectives, he too expressed anxiety for the future of the nation after the frontier was officially declared closed in 1890. This ambivalence towards the modern era is most vividly expressed in *The Virginian*'s narrator's realisation that the seemingly squalid West could be a force for regeneration: 'Yet serene above their [Western towns'] foulness swam a pure and quiet light, such as the East never sees; they might be bathing in the air of creation's first morning.'[16]

This contrast between the two passages' representations, however, in no way negates the fact that the pre-history of the cinematic Western and the origins of twentieth-century stereotypes of the Italian South arise from equivalent cultural and political processes. This notion becomes clearer when we observe how representations of the *Mezzogiorno* evolved after Italian unification in 1860, when the region's plight had increasingly profound implications for national identity in the peninsula.

Italy, as a part of Europe's own 'south', had itself been stereotyped as backward, squalid and corrupt, yet picturesque and quaint since the seventeenth-century northward shift in geopolitical and economic power on the continent. For much of the eighteenth and nineteenth centuries the chief global dividing line between civilisation and savagery was unequivocally drawn by Europeans, not between east and west, but between north and south. Attributes situated firmly to the south such as laziness, servility and illiteracy were thus set against the freedom and industriousness of northern peoples in works such as Montesquieu's *The Spirit of the Laws* (1748).

The *Risorgimento* itself was driven by a steady migration of political influence in the Italian peninsula to the North. Piedmont and Lombardy in particular aligned themselves with the liberal bourgeois world beyond the Alps, and distanced their societies from frequent accusations of barbarism levelled at the Kingdom of Naples. The South thus inherited the stereotypes previously applied to the entire Italian peninsula, from which northern states had been trying to escape for over a century. By the mid 1870s, however, the erstwhile Kingdom of Naples was the subject of earnest debate amongst intellectuals highlighting the abject living conditions of southern peasants at a time when the northern bourgeoisie was booming.[17]

Such socio-political discourse (which came to be known as *meridionalismo*; its proponents the *meridionalisti*) offered damning criticism of the *Risorgimento*'s failures. It played a major role in framing the South as what Dickie terms 'the testing-ground of Italy's modernity, the measure of its claims to civility, and the focus of national solidarity'.[18] With unification the *Mezzogiorno*'s symbolic power moved closer to the role played by the West in Wister's, Turner's and Roosevelt's representations: that of a window into Italy's past, a mirror for national identity and an arena for discourse around the failings of the modern state. Culturally, the South was situated at the extremity of 'Italian-ness': Italy, only more so.

While such parallels attest to a notable degree of equivalence, this is not to say that the Italian South and the American West possessed identical symbolic roles in the development of their respective national imaginaries. As the contrasting tones of Renan and Wister indicate, the West became imbued with valorised notions of nationalism and 'authenticity': a regenerative formulation of US exceptionalism which the Italian South – as a conquered and derided 'Other' – was denied.[19]

Yet even in this productive ambivalence afforded the West – the savage wilderness whose danger and allure offer the effete easterner the chance for virile renewal – there are parallels to be found in the representational models commonly ascribed to the South. Here, conflicting perceptions of a savage wilderness and a bounteous idyll are reflected in the commonplace epithet applied to Naples which arose in the seventeenth century: 'a paradise inhabited by devils'. In underlining perceived contrasts between the natural beauty and the human degradation of the South, this also echoes the ambivalent position of Native Americans in the European imagination: half noble savage, half devil on Earth. Drawing such parallels between the *Mezzogiorno* and the Americas, indeed, is far from a new enterprise. In 1575 the Spanish missionary Michele Navarro reported back to his father superior after working in Calabria and Sicily:

> Just as some of our brethren go to the Indies, in this India they could labour so as to render a service to God that is not inferior to that rendered by those who go down there. [...] I am certain [...] that whoever does well in these Indies of ours, here, will be fit for those across the ocean as well.[20]

The New World and the South of Italy – both under Spanish rule at the time – were seen to be analogously savage, superstitious and lawless. The geographically closer of the two was identified as a training ground for the grave task of civilising the other.

Concurrently, however, the New World was also conceived as a virgin paradise and a primitive escape from civilisation. The first British colony in Virginia in 1585 was depicted as an untouched Eden in the paintings of John White, and as settlement pushed further inland the still wild West inherited these attributes. In the early nineteenth century, long before Wister conceived the West as a utopian social model, James Fenimore Cooper popularised the commonplace of a romantic wilderness. Simultaneously, however, he permeated the landscape with an impending sense that its days were numbered, as civilisation must inevitably overrun it. Such an elegiac tone would remain dominant throughout the Western myth's development, forever representing the West as the disappearing remnants of a dying age. Cooper's evocation of the Vanishing American myth (notably in *The Last of the Mohicans*) is a precursor to Wister's polemical preface lamenting that the modern world has overtaken the romantic era of the cowboy:

> A transition has followed the horseman of the plains; a shapeless state, a condition of men and manners as unlovely as is that moment in the year when winter is gone and spring not come, and the face of Nature is ugly.[21]

Similarly, alongside the social critiques of the *meridionalisti*, illustrated periodicals full of exotic images of the picturesque and seductive South – a place of vitality and escape for the burgeoning middle classes – became enormously popular in the North of Italy. Such pastime journals as the *Cosmorama pittorico* had been engaging the growing fascination with exotic parts of the world, including the South, since 1835. In the 1870s, a

Milanese publishing boom coincided with increasing northern urbanisation, and magazines fostering a vision of the South as a virgin land gained in popularity. The pages of one such publication – the *Illustrazione Italiana* – commonly represented the South in illustrations with cacti and bare-footed peasants from a bygone classical age. In 1890 its correspondent Rafaello Barbiera depicted Sicily as an elemental Arcadia:

> Amongst the prickly pears, a boy who seems like an ancient bronze statue appears. His hair is black and curly, the tint of his face is olive. […] Here it is not only in the flaming sky that Africa abides; there is even more if it in the race of the Conca d'Oro [region of Sicily].[22]

The South's role as the last remnant of poetic backwardness and tangible antiquity persisted into the mid twentieth century. In Alberto Moravia's novel *Contempt* (1954), for example, the narrator visits Capri to get inspiration for a screenplay of *The Odyssey*: 'Homer had wished to represent a sea just like this, beneath a similar sky, along a similar coast, with characters that resembled this landscape and had about them its ancient simplicity.'[23]

The perspectives of Wister, Turner and Roosevelt, of the *meridionalisti*, and of the *Illustrazione Italiana*, are all reflections of late nineteenth-century anxieties over national identity during a transition to bourgeois modernity. All of them inherit earlier perceptions of the least technologically advanced region of their own land, and all of them project fears and aspirations of nationhood onto this region. Given that these two traditions of representation – the one of the South, the other of the West – arise from equivalent and coinciding perspectives, it is not surprising that they share numerous iconographic and thematic motifs. Moe writes that the South became 'a region of extraordinary symbolic force in Italian culture'[24]: a force whose potency was certainly not diminished in the mid twentieth century when stark inequalities were laid bare by the Economic Miracle. Such themes which, by the 1960s, had been subsumed internationally by the Hollywood Western would therefore equally possess a more parochial significance in Italy.

The notion, ascribed to Godard by Frayling, that northern audiences might indulge their stereotypes of southerners by viewing Italian Westerns suggests that this genre perpetuated the fascination with the exotic displayed in the *Illustrazione Italiana*. This viewpoint, however, overlooks the important symbolic role played by the South in framing Italian national identity, which accords with the function of the Wild West in US culture. Given that this mythic 'South' remained a key focus for such discourse, and that by the

1960s Americana was a highly visible presence throughout Italy, one notion becomes clear: that US popular culture's most analogous and applicable format to 'southern' themes – namely, the Western – was an apt vehicle for such ongoing debates, both in the North and in the South. Sergio Sollima for one, in transposing a Sardinian parable to the Wild West to explore issues surrounding peasant politics, appears to have accorded with this hypothesis.

It remains, however, to consider the southern audiences themselves. It would be easy to fall into the trap of engaging in similar processes of stereotyping to those already outlined when trying to ascertain the nature of these audiences and their expectations. Given the political, social and economic conditions of southern Italy both after the *Risorgimento* and in the post-war years, however, preoccupations central to the Western can be seen to possess relevance beyond mere representations of this region. The genre's key themes equally pertained to the concrete concerns of many in the southern states themselves.

### The Western Genre and Southern Italy

In his memoir *Cristo si è fermato a Eboli* (1945) Carlo Levi relates his exile to Basilicata during the Fascist regime, and describes the peasants' opinion of the Italian state thus:

> The State, whatever form it might take, meant 'the fellows in Rome'. 'Everyone knows', they said, 'that the fellows in Rome don't want us to live like human beings. There are hailstorms, landslides, droughts, malaria, and […] the State. These are inescapable evils; such as there always have been and there always will be'.[25]

Levi was himself a northerner, and wrote from the perspective of an outsider in an alien locale. Nevertheless, his account emphasises the important fact that the history of the South's peasantry had been for the most part not only one of poverty (which, as we have seen, was a quaint and picturesque stereotype to many in the North), but one of disenfranchisement. Such an attitude as is cited here is indicative of widespread feelings of hostility towards central government evident in the populace of southern states throughout the eighteenth, nineteenth and twentieth centuries. Paul Ginsborg cites Levi's account to illustrate how the peasantry in particular 'developed a philosophy which mixed fatalism, solidarity and distrust'.[26]

This distrust of authority emerged from decades of economic neglect and of governmental perceptions – largely fostered by the very stereotypes discussed above – that the South was immobile and incapable of looking after itself. In 1806 southern peasants had been promised a share of the common land, only to see barons and landowners usurp their claims. In 1860 national unification brought no agrarian reform, instead heralding the foisting of Piedmontese models of modernity upon the former Kingdom of Naples. Shortly after Garibaldi had conquered the South, the united Italy's first Prime Minister, the Count of Cavour, was advised by Diomede Pantaleoni that 'with our force, our greater courage, with our superior intelligence and superior morality, with our experience and character, we can hope to govern and master them [southerners]'.[27]

Throughout the late nineteenth and early twentieth centuries, *latifondi* (large estates) accounted for the majority of rural employment in the South.[28] The landless labourers here enjoyed no stability, little pay, and were often compelled to work barren soil for absentee landlords. In the post-war era the situation for many southerners was little better. Infant mortality rates in 1950s Palermo were at 'Third World' levels[29] and in 1954, 85 per cent of Italy's poorest families lived south of Rome, with per capita income in Calabria coming to 52 per cent of the national average.[30]

Peasant agitations, firstly in 1944–47, then again in 1949 heralded occupations of Calabrian *latifondi*, in part organised by local PCI sections, with demands for extensive agrarian reform. Change, when it came, was dictated from above, and betrayed continuing adherence to age-old stereotypes of a dependent and backward region on the part of the DC. In 1950 the government announced extensive reforms, expropriating over 700 thousand hectares of landed estates for redistribution amongst the peasantry. Meanwhile, the *Cassa per il Mezzogiorno* – a state fund for the rehabilitation of the South – was building an ambitious programme of industrialisation by the late 1950s. The redistributed land, however, was mostly of poor quality,[31] and modernisation projects left the agricultural interior to its fate while state-of-the-art steelworks and refineries were set up on the coast. These 'cathedrals in the desert' were mostly subsidiaries of northern companies taking advantage of the state subsidies in the South, and did little to benefit local labourers. The *Cassa per il Mezzogiorno* became little more than a channel of state funds into Christian Democratic interests.

Stereotypes of the South as a vanishing idyll notwithstanding, the rapid modernisation of the post-war years heralded a tangible loss of older traditions. Time-honoured ways of life were disappearing, with ancient communities being abandoned by those fit enough to find work. We have already observed the extent of migration away from the South during the Economic Miracle, and Martin Clark records that 'in the land reform areas of Metaponto and southern Calabria [...] men moved *down* from the hills to settle on the plains for the first time in 1,500 years'.[32]

Francesco Saverio Nitti's acerbic dismissal, cited in Chapter One, of the unified Italy as a 'national Humpty Dumpty [...] a make-believe country that never obtained the [...] support of all its incredulous citizens' was made in specific reference to the disenfranchisement of southerners in the Italian state.[33] In 1960 Luchino Visconti described his recently released film *Rocco e i suoi fratelli*, which depicted poverty-stricken southerners forced to emigrate northwards to find work, as 'a contemporary drama, because the inability of these two Italian regions to communicate continues in a disquieting way. [...] We have our racism too'.[34]

Visconti's comment highlights the fact that, in the post-war years, the South found itself being shoehorned into the ethos of an affluent consumer society. The minority of urban southerners who spoke standard Italian found work a lot easier to come by in the North than those rural immigrants who spoke only regional dialects. In a very real sense, such people were foreigners in their own country. Though the increased factory militancy of the late 1960s occurred mostly in the North, this mass migration of southerners to cities such as Turin in the first half of the decade had created a volatile unskilled and semi-skilled labour force in northern factories. The parliamentary Left was seen to be failing to address their grievances, while hostilities towards the state were exacerbated and required an outlet. As we shall see, the formation of armed insurgent cells in the 1970s offered just such a means of militant expression. One of the foremost such groups emerging in these years was the Turinese *Prima linea*, 32 per cent of whose membership was of southern origin.[35]

These socio-economic factors considered, a cinematic genre which frequently questions the wisdom of central government's laws, which depicts the traumatic onset of modern civilisation while lamenting the loss of a more simple age, which asserts the dignity of rural communities in the face of hardship and which conjures up avenging heroes to defend those communities against threats from outside would stand a good chance of becoming popular. It is indeed reasonable to suggest both that Westerns were successful amongst southern Italian audiences, and that producers took their desires and expectations into account, especially in the *terza visione* sector.[36] Wagstaff states that 'adventure formulas did well in provincial and *terza visione* cinemas, especially in the south',[37] and Frayling argues both that the majority of Italian Westerns were 'pitched at the "Roxy, Calabria"' and that producers were 'opportunistic about relating their films to the known audience expectations of the Southern Italians'.[38] As Stephen Gundle suggests, *terza visione* audiences often had considerably more parochial tastes than the mainstream, internationally-oriented, urban demographics of the *prima visione* sector. Such (chiefly) rural communities were apt to seek symbols of continuity and familiarity in such a period of immense social upheaval as the 1960s.[39] The success of Westerns in the *terza visione* sector indicates that the thematic parallels outlined in this chapter were not lost on these audiences.[40]

That Levi's 'fellows in Rome' could be represented by fellows in Washington is largely due to the Western genre's thematic traditions: traditions with relevance to rural audiences whose experiences of the Economic Miracle were a world away from the affluence of the North, yet whose awareness of American popular culture had grown exponentially during the 1950s. The ever-changing ideological uses to which Westerns have been put since Wister apotheosised the cowboy in 1902 render the genre elusive, and generalisations about it precarious. Nevertheless, throughout the myth's development has been enshrined a sense that legislation handed down from central government is often at variance with the realities of remote communities.

One of the most recognisable motifs of the Western is that of the townsfolk or – more often – a skilful individual being forced to take the law into their own hands in order that justice is served. The pen-pushers back East (or up North) rarely understand how life works out West. *The Virginian*'s narrative centres on a particularly brutal example of this ethos in action, when Steve is lynched for cattle rustling. Wister, through the character of Judge Henry, explains the necessity of this action to the outraged easterner Molly Wood:

> The courts, or rather the juries, into whose hands we have put the law, are not dealing with the law. They are withered hands, or rather they are imitation hands made for show, with little life in them, no grip. They cannot hold a cattle-thief. [...] [Lynching is] the fundamental assertion of self-governing men.[41]

The sentiment, if not the morality, of this passage remained a feature common throughout the cinematic Western until the 1960s, in films whose ideological stances were otherwise at variance with one another. Though with *Stagecoach* (1939) John Ford helped to transform and rejuvenate the prestige Western, the final scene retains this sense that official law is inadequate, and must be subjugated to the moral code of the West. When the Ringo Kid (John Wayne) avenges his brother by killing the Plummers in the centre of Lordsburg, Sheriff Curley turns a blind eye and lets him escape into the night, recognising the necessity of such an act.

In the same year as *Stagecoach*, *Jesse James* depicted federal law as a tool of corrupt big business, which is resisted by brave freedom fighters. In *High Noon* (1952) – a film otherwise notable for its inversions of Western codes of honour – it is made clear that Will Kane is only faced with his dilemma because 'the politicians up north' interfered by saving the malevolent outlaw Miller from hanging in the first place. By the 1960s, when the genre's traditional morality was under increasing scrutiny, John Ford preserved this fundamental generic premise in *The Man Who Shot Liberty Valance* (1962). James Stewart's tenderfoot lawyer Ransom Stoddard is forced to reassess his faith in institutional law when faced with the violence of life in the West, underlining once again that the ethos of a distant government is insufficient.

In his book *Sixguns and Society*, Will Wright distils the Western down to four plot variants.[42] He has been oft criticised both for his generalisations and for his criterion of only including films which made over 4 million dollars in rental.[43] It is certainly true that box-office receipts alone are an unscientific criterion, especially in such a fragmented film industry as Italy's (where tickets in *terza visione* theatres were considerably cheaper than those in the *prima visione* sector). For the purposes of studying Italian perceptions of this foreign genre, however, such a criterion serves a purpose. As I have stated in the previous chapter, from 1950 onwards Hollywood films acquired 50 per cent of their earnings abroad, and Italy was a vital market for American distributors.[44] Post-war prestige Westerns (such as *Red River*, gazed at so longingly by Anna Magnani in *Bellissima*) were the most widely distributed examples of the genre, and would thus play a considerable role in shaping perceptions of the Western abroad. Of these, George Stevens's *Shane* – described by Wright as 'the classic of the classic Westerns'[45] – synthesises themes with relevance to the lives of rural Italian communities in the clearest terms.

*Shane* was released in Italian cinemas in September 1953, under the title *Il cavaliere della valle solitaria* ('The Horseman of the Solitary Valley'): a label which instantly stresses both the remote, rural setting and the imminent arrival into that locale of a saviour figure. Wright identifies the most important factor in a Western to be the relationship between the hero and society, and the function of each plot type to be the communication of oppositions which help an audience make sense of the world around them. *Shane*'s Italian release came at a time when the *Cassa per il Mezzogiorno* was promising much but failing to deliver on key demands concerning the working conditions of landless labourers. The film narrates, in overtly mythic terms, the historic struggle between lowly homesteaders and powerful cattle ranchers on the Wyoming plains. It barely requires comment that a lethal yet benevolent gunman appearing from nowhere onto a struggling farmer's plot of land and offering his services (with both farm tools and firearms) free of charge might constitute a rural labourer's ultimate fantasy. Though Wright fails to appreciate the cultural origins of the Italian Western, the parallels outlined here suggest that the genre's dramatisation of social oppositions would resonate in this foreign context.

If Westerns indeed appealed to southerners for their nostalgic engagement with the past, and if the genre is to be read as an appropriate model for the defence of rural ways of life against heavy-handed legislation, there is however an irony in this application. In valorising the 'American Way', many Westerns fuse this elegiac tone with a fundamental assertion of the virtues of US-led modernity (as early as John Ford's *The Iron Horse* (1924), the genre acted as a champion for technological advancement). There is therefore a contradiction in grafting *Shane*'s mythic structures onto the preoccupations of rural southern Italian communities, since the labourers whom the film's plot valorises are themselves harbingers of progress, whose occupation of the land signals the death of the open range, the cattle drive and the 'Old West'. Stevens's film is in fact one of the most vivid reversals of Owen Wister's political outlook in the entire Hollywood genre. Its Wyoming-set narrative exactly echoes *The Virginian*'s engagement with the Johnson County War of 1892. Its sympathies, however, lie on the side of the very sodbusters whom Wister sees as thieves and rustlers, whose representatives have taken over governmental posts and led the nation to ruin.

There is no doubt that *The Virginian* had a decisive influence in the early development of the cinematic Western. The taciturn cowboy winning the affections of an eastern lady despite her objections to his violent lifestyle; the greenhorn outsider gaining a Western education; the climactic walk-down shoot-out in the main street; and the strict adherence to a code of honour transcending institutional law: all of these prefigure key tenets of the myth which reappear in the films of William S. Hart and the novels of Zane Grey. To claim, as does John G. Cawelti, however, that 'Owen Wister initiated the modern Western'[46] is to exaggerate the importance of *The Virginian*. Wister's polemical mourning at the death of the world of the cowboy is unambiguously conservative, lamenting the emasculating effects of modern civilisation. Patrick McGee emphasises the fact that, after 1939, the genre took a wholly divergent route from this supposed 'founding text'. 'By the fifties Western movies and many of the fictions they were based on had so transformed the "code of the West"', he writes, 'that Wister's novel read like a violation of its own rule'.[47] Joe Starrett's heroic oration to the threatened group of farmers in *Shane* distils a sense that though its onset is traumatic, the settlement of the West is inherently a force for good:

> Who is Rufe Riker or anyone else to run us away from our own homes? He only wants to grow his beef, and what we want to grow up is families, to grow 'em good and grow 'em up strong the way they was meant to be grown.

I am suggesting neither that *terza visione* audiences necessarily questioned or cared about the finer points of frontier ideology, nor that they engaged in analyses of a given film's source material. One thing seems evident, however: Westerns which retained the recognisable iconography and many of the central oppositions at the heart of the Hollywood genre, but which jettisoned this focus on the necessity of progress, were by the 1960s more suitable to act as surrogate fantasy narratives for southern Italians. Frayling identifies the Spaghetti Western's appeal in the South by applying Edward C. Banfield's theories of 'amoral familism' (whereby southern loyalty to family transcends civic responsibility) to the societies represented in the Italian *filone*.[48] Banfield's hypothesis identifies much the same attitude amongst southerners as does Carlo Levi: those in power are by definition corrupt, so one must look after one's own interests and assume that everybody else will do likewise.

The Hollywood Western itself had by this time departed ever further from its roots. What Wright terms the 'transitional' plot (in such films as *Broken Arrow* (1950), *High Noon* (1952) and *Johnny Guitar* (1954)) places society as the hero's enemy, to be saved despite itself. The 'professional' plot, which is identifiable as far back as *Vera Cruz* (1954), dispenses altogether with the hero's duty to that society. By the 1960s the Western hero had become a more alienated, nihilistic and individualistic figure than had been the case previously. Similarly, if common features can be identified across the vast spectrum of Italian Westerns, one must surely be that the majority drain the myth of any pioneering doctrine whatsoever, and in so doing remove the ambiguity (some might say subtlety) inherent to the Hollywood genre. Domenico Paolella, who directed two Cinecittà Westerns in 1967 and 1968, stated unequivocally that his films were aimed at those who felt alienated 'by the dominance of modern technology'.[49] In the Italian version of the myth the hostility towards authority, the frontier towns and the lethal gunmen remain; the Manifest Destiny of a nation does not.

One has only to contrast the crowded streets and boisterous saloons in *Stagecoach*, *My Darling Clementine*, *Winchester '73* and *The Man Who Shot Liberty*

*Valance* with the 'society' which greets us at the opening of Sergio Leone's Western debut to appreciate the evacuation of 'progress' from the Italian *filone*. San Miguel – *Per un pugno di dollari*'s deserted, whitewashed Andalucían ghost-town – is populated mostly by scurrying widows. This must have resonated to a southern Italian audience at a time when urbanisation and the exodus to the North left southern villages, in the words of Martin Clark, 'inhabited only by the women, the children, the old, and the dead – for burial plots back home remained popular even with long-term emigrants, and in some places grave-digging was the only flourishing local industry'.[50] Piriperro, San Miguel's coffin-maker, is the only thriving businessman in Leone's village, and Silvanito tells Joe that 'we spend our time here between funerals and burials'.

Just eight months after Leone's film had defined a new formula for success his script-writer, Duccio Tessari, released his own profitable take on it. The narrative of *Una pistola per Ringo* (1965) is closer to the traditions of the Hollywood genre than is that of *Per un pugno di dollari*. It retains many of the Western's central oppositions and adheres to Wright's 'classical' plot, of which *Shane* is the archetype. When a ranch is seized by bandits, the sheriff of the nearby town is faced with the realisation that institutional law is insufficient against such brutality. The civilised community thus finds itself in need of assistance from a deadly gunfighter whose lifestyle places him outside that society's accepted morality. After confronting and killing the bandits, the hero rides off into the mountains.

This eponymous hero lives by a strict moral code, constantly repeating that everything is 'a matter of principle'. His code, however, is born not of concern for society's common good, but purely of self-preservation. While both Shane and Ethan Edwards (in *The Searchers* (1956)) depart as representatives of the old ways of life, to allow a new society to grow up without them, Ringo leaves with the payment promised him in return for his services. Even Leone's ruthless hero displays sentiment in donating his money to a needy family, but Ringo is 'amoral familism' personified. He sees shooting people in the back as common sense ('If you're out to kill somebody, it's stupid to take unnecessary chances'), while his role-model is his father, who switched sides in the Civil War when the South started losing. Tessari's nihilistic Wild West, though retaining the narrative traditions handed down from Hollywood, robs these of their received ideological purpose. Ringo's sardonic dismissal of the Civil War in particular takes one of the most potent symbols of the USA's traumatic transition towards modernity and dispenses with its significance. In much the same way, Leone literally consumes the conflict's political complexities in a cloud of dust in *Il buono, il brutto, il cattivo* (1966).

It is notable, however, that in a *filone* whose interpretations of Hollywood's hallowed turf are so unrepentantly irreverent, the Civil War is actually one of the few symbols frequently to be treated with seriousness. Leone's and Tessari's wry grins notwithstanding, numerous Italian Westerns – for example, *Un dollaro bucato* (Ferroni, 1965), *Un fiume di dollari* (Lizzani, 1966), *I crudeli* (Corbucci, 1967) and *Faccia a faccia* (Solima, 1967) – follow a narrative tradition stretching back to Thomas Dixon and Thomas Nelson Page of depicting Confederates who are faced with the death of their way of life, bewildered by the rapidity of change. This 'Lost Cause' motif is faithfully reconstructed in *I crudeli*, which tells the story of southern renegades refusing to let the war end and fighting on as outlaws against the victorious Union. Though Henry King's *Jesse James* makes very little mention of it, the James brothers' criminal careers in fact began in precisely this manner: a fact explored in more depth in both Gordon Douglas's *The Great Missouri Raid* (1951) and Nicholas Ray's *The True Story of Jesse James* (1957).

It is no coincidence that in this particular feature of the Hollywood Western can be found its most apt symbolic parallels with both the history and the folklore of the South of Italy, since it is in this theme that the genre possesses its clearest elegiac evocations of a bygone age. The 1860s were years of bloodshed in the name of national unification in both the USA and Italy. In both countries, the industrialised North emerged victorious over the semi-feudal South, whose archaic social structures were problematic to the prevailing liberal ethos of the era. In both, too, southern renegades continued to resist the imposition of northern values after hostilities had formally ceased. The Italian army's war against rural brigands in the South lasted throughout the decade and claimed more lives than the other battles of unification combined.[51]

The stereotypes of a degenerate and backward South discussed earlier in this chapter were exacerbated by this conflict, as the concept of 'brigandage' became synonymous with the *Mezzogiorno* in the minds of Europe's middle and upper classes. Alexandre Dumas wrote in 1861 that 'Southern Italy produces wheat on the plains, oil in the valleys, brigands in the mountains',[52] while the Italian army came to see itself fighting on a frontier of mysterious savagery. The politician Gaetano Negri commented: 'Everyone says [brigandage] exists, but no one knows where it is; and I am beginning to believe that their existence is the product of the over-active imagination of the local population.'[53] In bestowing on outlaws an arcane co-existence with the land these texts apotheosise them, cultivating a myth omnipresent in oral narrative, popular folklore, and bourgeois novels and plays alike.

Eric Hobsbawm defines the 'social bandit' not only as a historical reality, but as an apparition in the minds of peasant communities: a virtuous paladin fighting against the injustices that blight rural life. Defining the South of Italy as 'the classic region of Western bandit myth',[54] and the 1860s brigand war as the prime example of a major uprising led by social bandits, Hobsbawm lists features of this archetypal hero. Many of these features accord with those of the Western hero already discussed. Resistance to the encroachment of outside authority, attainment of masculine hero status amongst rural communities and the use of justified violence in defence of these communities, for example, are all common to both. The folkloric social bandit is typically driven to outlawry by oppression from outside, and is not deemed 'criminal' by the local population.

Henry King's *Jesse James* posits exactly this myth in framing the James brothers as heroes, and the brigands of the *Mezzogiorno* were often outlawed in just such a manner. In 1863 the Italian 'Pica Law' stipulated that any group of three or more people caught in the countryside with offensive weapons (including farm tools) could be arrested for the new crime of 'brigandage' and executed. In the increased harassment of southern villages that ensued, many peasants fled to the hills, instantly defining themselves as bandits in the eyes of this law. The social bandit thus relies on a wall of silence (*omertà*) amongst the rural population for survival, and here again *Jesse James* adheres to the archetype's criteria, which accord with key features of the Western outlaw.

To explain the persistent fascination with 'social bandit' figures such as Ned Kelly, Jesse James and Bonnie and Clyde in Australia and the USA, Hobsbawm writes:

> The bandit myth is also comprehensible in highly urbanized countries which still possess a few empty spaces of 'outback' or 'west' to remind them of a sometimes imaginary heroic past, and to provide a concrete *locus* for nostalgia, a symbol of ancient and lost virtue, a spiritual Indian territory from which […] man can imagine himself 'lighting out' when the constraints of civilization become too much for him.[55]

As we have seen, the *Mezzogiorno*'s representational role in the eyes of the North remained precisely this into the twentieth century, and social bandit mythologies had lost none of their local significance in the South by the 1960s. Indeed, while in America banditry was by this time a reminder of the past, in Italy it remained a contemporary phenomenon. In the mountains of the Sardinian interior bandits continued to evade the law into the 1960s, while mythic traditions of virtuous outlaws in Calabria and Sicily retained their local currency in figures such as Giuseppe Musolino at the turn of the century and Salvatore Giuliano after the Second World War.

By the time the Italian Western *filone* was flourishing in the mid 1960s, a local cycle of films concerning the position of banditry in the modern nation had already emerged. *Banditi a Orgosolo* (Vittorio De Seta, 1961) uses neorealist stylistics to depict a Sardinian shepherd wrongly accused of a crime and driven by circumstance into outlawry. In the same year, Francesco Rosi directed *Salvatore Giuliano* in a similarly neorealist tenor. By presenting conflicting flashbacks, while never allowing the audience to encounter Giuliano himself, Rosi dissects in minute detail the processes through which the historical Sicilian outlaw came to be apotheosised as a social bandit in the eyes of his home town of Montelepre. When the Italian army are sent in to capture Giuliano they encounter the *omertà* which both protects the outlaw and builds his mystique. One soldier hisses: 'Damn it! I survived a war, only to get killed by savages in this godforsaken wasteland', echoing both the history of southern bandit wars and perceptions of the South widespread in the nation since 1860.

The emergence of these films in post-war Italy is explained by Angelo Restivo in terms of the South's dislocation from the affluence of the Economic Miracle, and of its continuing role in the 1960s as an arena for discourse concerning the nation's role in the modern world:

> We can see [...] how interesting the bandit figure will appear to a society in the throes of the social dislocations connected with modernity. [...] Thus, for the North, Sardinia [and continuing banditry] was at the same time a problem and a site for its own anxieties about modernization.[56]

The close affinity between such films and the Italian Western should therefore come as no surprise. Indeed it is more than likely that the 'Western' format itself was not the chief frame of reference within which Italian audiences – and in particular southern Italian audiences – comprehended the 'Western' *filone*. The original Sardinian story on which *La resa dei conti* was based bears a remarkably close resemblance to *Banditi a Orgosolo*, and was co-written by Franco Solinas, who also wrote *Salvatore Giuliano*. Frayling speculates whether Carlo Lizzani was drawn to the Western *filone* because he had previously made films dealing with bandits (his feature film debut, *Achtung banditi!* (1951), tells a tale of partisan guerrillas fighting the Nazis near Genoa).[57] This would resolve the apparent contradiction between his early dismissal of American genres and his engagement with Western bandit narratives in the mid 1960s.

Figure 1    George Barnes takes aim in Edwin S. Porter's *The Great Train Robbery* (1903)

When Sollima, Solinas and others chose to engage the Italian Western *filone* with militant politics, they were therefore simultaneously investing in traditions of Italian social interaction and utilising transatlantic themes which possessed pre-existing affinities with these traditions. I am not claiming their films to be direct attempts to incite revolution in the South. There is no evidence that this was their aim, and this would be a simplistic interpretation in light of the complex nature of the South/North dichotomy in this era. By the late 1960s, however, themes of banditry and violent resistance to central government possessed an increasing appeal in the North as well.

### Terrorist Parables Way Out West

'A non-violent western', writes Philip French, 'is as odd, as unthinkable, as a vegetarian steakhouse'.[58] From the bar-room brawl to the lynch mob, the bank robbery to the showdown, the burnt-out homestead to the cavalry charge, this genre has always been characterised by memorable and spectacular imagery of wounding, trauma and death. The earliest iconic sequence in the cinematic Western – a still from which adorns many critiques of Edwin S. Porter's *The Great Train Robbery* (1903), including this one – is a close-up of an outlaw shooting his six-gun directly at the camera. The shot serves little narrative purpose, existing exclusively to emphasise the visceral excitement of cinema and the suitability of dime novel action for the medium. Violence is the Western's single most consistent and defining preoccupation. The means by which it is dispensed act variously as catalysts for regeneration, moral touchstones and rites of passage.

When Robert Warshow helped to initiate scholarly criticism of the genre in 1954, he identified its appeal as lying in its 'serious orientation to the problem of violence such as can be found almost nowhere else in [American] culture'.[59] In contrast to the amoral brutality of the gangster film, Warshow maintains that the Western performs a dual function. It seeks to solve the modern world's obfuscation of issues surrounding the ethics of violence, and provide an outlet for the modern audience's desire for violent action while all the time expounding values of honour and self-discipline. The Western hero, though inhabiting a morally ambiguous position as a killer, only resorts to violence when all other avenues are exhausted: in other words, when he's 'gotta do what he's gotta do':

> The gun tells us that he lives in a world of violence, and even that he 'believes in violence'. But the drama is one of self-restraint: the moment of violence must come in its own time and according to its special laws, or else it is valueless.[60]

In 1954 this version of the Western's ethical standpoint, handed down from Owen Wister, William S. Hart and Zane Grey, remained broadly true. Though Warshow expressed distaste for the recently-released films *High Noon* and *Shane*, both adhere to this archetype whereby latent violence is contained until the explosive finale. In this respect, the otherwise oppositional *Shane* and *The Virginian* share a common trait. In each, violence is perpetrated for the common good and is not undertaken lightly.

As we have seen, this is an issue which runs through the Western from its inception. Wister's Judge Henry debates the ethics of lynching with Molly Wood; King's Jesse James tells his fiancée 'I've got to' when implored not to avenge his mother; the Ringo Kid's act of triple homicide in *Stagecoach* is deemed legitimate by a higher moral code than institutional law; and Ethan Edwards confronts his own lust for vengeance when pursuing Chief Scar in *The Searchers*. While the pre-1960s Western frequently debates the legitimacy of such acts, however, it is notable that, exceptions such as *The Ox-Bow Incident* (1943) and *Johnny Guitar* (1954) notwithstanding, very rarely does the genre conclude that violence is something to be condemned. Where institutional law fails, the hero is duty-bound to take the law into his own hands, and use aggression of equal or greater force than that of his enemy. It is informative to note that all of the above examples of 'justified' violence are committed against the wishes of a woman who stands for love, forgiveness and compassion. Jane Tompkins eschews Frederick Jackson Turner's conventional 'frontier' explanation of the Western's success (whereby the genre acts as an escape valve for social tensions during rapid modernisation). Instead, she identifies in the literary West of Wister and Grey a debunking of the femininity, Christian charity and pacifism which proliferated in evangelical popular fiction in the mid nineteenth century. For Tompkins, the genre exists as a justification for lethal force to re-assert masculine identity in a world increasingly dominated by emasculating modern ethics:

> Time after time, the Western hero commits murder, usually multiple murders, in the name of making his town/ranch/mining claim safe for women and children. But the discourse of love and peace which women articulate is never listened to [...] for it belongs to the Christian worldview the Western is at pains to eradicate.[61]

Both Warshow and Lee Clark Mitchell[62] also discuss the decisive role played by violence in the Western. They, too, argue that the genre's central preoccupation is that of defining and constructing masculinity (or 'making the man') through violent trauma. Jenni Calder also highlights a common link between violence and virility in Western fiction, citing the phallic symbolism of the powerful sidearm in Jack Schaefer's 1953 novel on which *Shane* was based: 'Belt and holster and gun. [...] These were not things he was wearing or carrying. They were part of him, part of the man, of the full sum of that integrate force that was Shane.'[63] 'The Western would fail in its appeal', writes Calder, 'if it were not continually suggesting a creative force. [...] The frontier must not only be tamed but be populated. The man must not only be skilful with his weapons he must be virile'.[64] Masculine Western violence, then, works for the same regenerative ends as do the hard-working farmers to whom Joe Starrett proclaims: 'What we want to grow up is families, to grow 'em good and grow 'em up strong.'

Jim Kitses has criticised Tompkins's notion that women are marginalised in the Western for overlooking the films of John Ford, which often subsume motifs of melodrama and position women at the genre's centre (quite an oversight, given Ford's dominance of the genre after 1939).[65] It is indeed true that Ford's films complicate Tompkins's argument, but the fact remains that in each of *Stagecoach*, *My Darling Clementine*, *Fort Apache*, *She Wore a Yellow Ribbon*, *The Searchers* and *The Man Who Shot Liberty Valance*, women operate as domesticated, peaceful counterpoints to men who understand the necessity of violence in the West. These female figures have direct precedents in the literature of Owen Wister and Zane Grey (with Molly Wood, and Jane Withersteen from *Riders of the Purple Sage* respectively). Though Ford does place women at the moral centre of his films' plots, the civilised future which they represent must still, as in the majority of Westerns, be secured by men killing other men. Masculine violence is therefore frequently located as a cleansing, regenerative entity while pacifism, though morally pure, is shown to be naive and feminine. Similarly, when Marian objects to Shane's violent ways, he insists that 'a gun is a tool [...] no better, no worse than any other tool – an axe, a shovel, or anything'. Like the axe and the shovel, the Westerner's six-gun is a progressive force, playing a necessary role in the formation of a brighter future.

Of course, as both Warshow and Mitchell are at pains to emphasise, in the pre-1960s Hollywood Western this advocacy of violence usually has strict limits. If killing can be a force for good, it is only permitted within the codes of honour inherent throughout the genre. We have already observed Warshow's identification of violence as a grave duty, a regulated code and a last resort. Mitchell similarly argues that restraint, composure and temperance are the essential features of the Western's construction of masculinity. That a genre in which violent acts were so pervasive was, until the 1960s, largely regarded as morally safe by Hollywood's Production Code Administration (PCA) is largely due to this mitigating context.

On the rare occasion that the Western did transgress PCA taboos, it was not the presence of violence that drew censure, so much as the motivations behind it. When *The Deadwood Coach* (1922) incurred the wrath of Chicago censors for its glorification of violent acts, for example, the court condemned the film for its focus on 'gun-play, or the shooting of human beings [which] does not pertain to the necessities of war, nor to the preservation of law and order'.[66] It follows that violence which preserved law and order was permissible, allowing the Western's code of honourable restraint to excuse the genre from reprimand. Tompkins, however, highlights the extent to which this restraint itself impels the viewer to desire the moment of violence all the more. If the audience is to feel satisfied with the outcome, the admirable self-control displayed by Shane and Ransom Stoddard, despite insults and jeers from Ryker and Liberty Valance respectively, must ultimately be broken by the hero turning to violence: 'He wants to, and we want him to, too. At this juncture, the point where provocation has gone too far, retaliatory violence becomes not simply justifiable but imperative.'[67]

While audiences' desire for explosive action may be provoked by such a build-up of tension, it remains the case that Shane and Ransom Stoddard (as well as *High Noon*'s Will Kane) all vacillate over the use of violence and see it as a last resort, before ultimately realising its necessity. Increasingly, during the 1960s, however, the Western retained its violent content but dispensed with both the restraint and the moral imperative which had hitherto served as validation. What Richard Schickel dubbed the 'dirty Western',[68] in reference to such films as *The Wild Bunch* (1969) and *The Hunting Party* (1971), heralded a fundamental shift in the genre's dynamics. Violence ceased to be a last resort and became a means of survival in an unforgiving world. The genre's position as a paragon of self-restraint and moral fortitude was increasingly ambiguous.

Pauline Kael was unequivocal in identifying the chief catalyst for these transformations:

> It was the spaghetti Westerns [...] that first eliminated the morality-play dimension and turned the Western into pure violent reverie. [...] What made these [...] popular was that they stripped the Western form of its cultural burden of morality. They discarded its civility along with its hypocrisy. In a sense, they liberated the form: what the Western hero stood for was left out, and what he embodied (strength and gun power) was retained. *Abroad, that was probably what he had represented all along* [emphasis mine].[69]

There are two flaws in this argument. Firstly, the extent to which the Italian genre can take the credit for the removal of violence's moral justification in the Hollywood Western is neither as linear nor as straightforward as Kael suggests.[70] A considerably broader shift in the genre's narrative and ideological trajectory was evident long before Cinecittà's conveyor belt reached the USA. In a cycle of earlier Westerns such as *The Naked Spur* (1953), *Man of the West* (1958) and *One-Eyed Jacks* (1961) violence was presented as degrading and unlikely to provide a force for redemption or regeneration. The increase in brutality which characterised Westerns of the late 1960s should not be divorced from this precedent.

Secondly, building on Warshow's seminal hypothesis of 1954, Mitchell argues that the Western's perennial concern with testing the legitimacy of violence, far from being rendered meaningless, took on added significance in 1960s America. He sees in the genre's amplified brutality towards the end of the decade a return 'to a set of traditional preoccupations corresponding to larger social and political uncertainties during the 1960s about the legitimate uses of violence'.[71] As television relayed the repression of civil rights activists, urban riots, assassinations and the carnage of Vietnam into American homes, violence indeed rose to the top of political and moral agendas. Films which confronted the genre's traditional celebration of violent spectacle directly, through increased brutality or parody, Mitchell holds, found a new relevance in the mores of 1960s America.

Most interesting in Mitchell's hypothesis, for my purposes, is the source material from which he extrapolates this argument concerning American society: Sam Peckinpah's *The Wild Bunch* and Sergio Leone's *Per un pugno di dollari*. Leone's film was released in America in February 1967, as political tensions over Vietnam were taking on a greater intensity, and around the corner lay the campus occupations and increasing political violence of the late 1960s. Given the internationally-facing nature of Leone's output, it should perhaps come as no surprise to find his films being discussed in such a context (and Will Wright uses *Il buono, il brutto, il cattivo* in a similar fashion). Mitchell's emphasis, indeed, is quite properly on the reasons for the appeal of such films' violence to an American public.

What he largely disregards, however, is the Italian context from which Leone's film emerged. When he does address this, the argument becomes strained: 'Leone adopts (as one might have imagined from an Italian leftist) a fiercely liberal position.'[72] There are two suspect claims here, neither of which should be taken at face value. Firstly, though he had grown up in a left-wing household and described himself as 'a disillusioned socialist',[73] Leone was not, beyond offering the occasional platitude in interviews,[74] a politically-committed 'leftist' director. He was in fact scathing in his contempt for 'so-called "political" or "intelligent" Westerns',[75] accusing such political readings to be 'typical of the European mentality; our false intellectualising'.[76] Furthermore, Mitchell's statement presupposes that Italian leftists would be inclined to adopt a liberal position concerning the issue of violence in society.[77] This, as will become clear, is far from the truth.

If, as Mitchell argues, the Western genre found a new relevance amongst 1960s American audiences for its engagement with the role of violence in society, it follows that a similar process of identification might occur in countries whose awareness of American culture had grown exponentially but whose political traditions were divergent. Contemporaneous and equivalent social tensions in Italy to those in America increasingly elevated issues surrounding violence in the public eye as the 1960s progressed. Here too, after students had revolted in 1968 an increasingly confrontational 'New

Left' began to debate armed insurrection against the state. Here too, outrage would eventually spill over into violence, culminating in the formation of clandestine terrorist cells.[78] In both countries, the preoccupations of the Western genre simultaneously became co-opted into this larger discourse by film-makers with radical sympathies. While countercultural Westerns in America, such as *Little Big Man* and *Soldier Blue* (both 1970), expressed such political leanings through pacifism, reconciliation and remorse, however, the political tenor of equivalent Italian appropriations was altogether more extreme.

The PCI's failure to connect culturally with the generation of the Economic Miracle meant that when, in the late 1960s, sections of that very generation expressed disillusionment with the values fostered therein, the party was seen as a part of the establishment against which they were rebelling. The Italian student movement, though initially a reaction against the nation's ill-equipped education system, arose from an increasing disdain for individualism, the nuclear family and consumerism. Equally, however, this anger was aimed at the traditional forces of the 'Old Left', who had singularly failed to fulfil their remit of achieving a proletarian hegemony.

When students in Trento, Milan and Turin occupied campus buildings in the autumn of 1967, they cannot have foreseen the violent extremes to which sections of the extra-parliamentary Italian Left would go in the ensuing decade. The rhetoric of the student movement, however, employed various violent idioms borrowed from an international amalgam of revolutionary thought. Acolytes of Lenin, Mao, Guevara, Fanon, Marcuse, Debray and Trotsky jostled for position in defining the movement's aims and, along with the legacies of Resistance and anti-fascism, provided a forum for debate on the implications of insurrection and revolution. In February 1968, campus demonstrations in Rome sparked rioting and running battles with police. By the summer, inspired by similar events across the advanced industrial world, students were joining picket lines alongside striking workers in a wave of spontaneous militancy in northern Italy. Favoured slogans among the Turin student demonstrations of June 1968 included 'only violence helps where violence reigns'.[79]

The relationship between these relatively innocuous and widespread Italian student demonstrations of 1967–68 to the small-scale but deadly violence of the 1970s has been the subject of much debate and disagreement. Rossana Rossanda described the 1970s insurgent groups as the 'unwanted children' of 1968,[80] while Joseph La Palombara draws a direct relationship of cause and effect from the student movement to the outbreak of terrorism.[81] Renato Curcio and Margherita Cagol – founder members of the Red Brigades (also known as the BR [*Brigate rosse*]) – indeed both studied at Trento University and became involved in campus occupations before turning to violence.

On the other hand, only 11 per cent of the membership of revolutionary cells which emerged in the early 1970s came from universities, and only a third of the 814 activists subsequently convicted of terrorist acts were veterans of the student movement.[82] Both Sidney Tarrow and Donatella Della Porta emphasise that, despite the confrontational rhetoric, the student movement's demonstrations were no more prone to descend into physical conflict than were any other protests at the time.[83] Tarrow argues that the turn to violence was neither a direct graduation from campus occupation to armed insurrection nor a rupture from the student movement. Instead, he identifies it as the progeny of clashing ideologies within Italy's extra-parliamentary Left:

> Violence developed not in a linear fashion out of the movements in the universities in 1967–8 but as part of a competitive process of tactical innovation within the social-movement sector that led some groups into the party of armed struggle but forced others to reject it and to join the institutional system.[84]

Tarrow's hypothesis underlines the extent to which insurrectionary violence was at once the most divisive and the most pressing issue within the Italian New Left of the late 1960s and early 1970s. Virtually all of the disparate revolutionary groups which eventually emerged from the ferment of the student movement either became riven by disputes over the legitimacy of armed resistance, or were founded as the direct result of such splits. Born of the union between student protesters and striking factory workers, such extra-parliamentary groups emerging in 1968–69 as *Potere operaio* and *Lotta continua* worked to coordinate protest around a 'workerist' philosophy, continuing Marxist-Leninist objectives abandoned by mainstream left-wing institutions (the PCI and the trade unions). This adoption of a revolutionary vanguard ethos, however, coincided with a narrowing of political options for these groups. The 'Hot Autumn' of 1969 saw labour agitation become more widespread than at any time since the War, yet the trade unions directed this, re-asserting their institutional dominance over the working-class movement.[85] The PCI, meanwhile, were steering themselves ever further down the path of reformism and parliamentary democracy, winning over a larger electorate than ever before but alienating extreme Marxist factions.

As the option of productive legitimate action became perceived as more remote, left-wing violence, which during the student movement had mostly broken out in self-defence against police or neo-fascists, became more premeditated. Small extremist wings of the revolutionary organisations competed for kudos with increasingly aggressive tactics, while larger factions steered towards electoral legitimacy. By 1973 both *Potere operaio* and *Lotta continua* had split irrevocably over arguments concerning the use of violence, while 'autonomist' factions had formed clandestine terrorist cells such as *Rosso, Prima linea, Senza tregua* and the BR. If direct links can be drawn from the mass mobilisations of the late 1960s to the armed insurgencies of the early 1970s, they lie in this very relationship. Activists in the earlier movement were engaged in fraught debates concerning the legitimacy of tactics which would later be taken up by the Red Brigades and similar minority organisations.

The trend of radical Italian Westerns under consideration in this volume spanned this very period in the nation's history, when the extra-parliamentary Left's activism was at its most widespread, dynamic and fractious. In December 1966, as international tensions over US foreign policy were becoming increasingly volatile, *Quien sabe?* was released in Italy. *Se sei, vivo, spara!* followed in January 1967 and *La resa dei conti* in March 1967. *Faccia a faccia* emerged in November 1967, as the campus occupations were growing in size and political significance. In late 1968 and early 1969, as the 'workerist' groups were forming and international headlines were increasingly filled with stories of political violence, *Corri, uomo, corri, Il grande Silenzio, Il mercenario* and *Tepepa* were in Italian cinemas. By the time *Compañeros* came out in December 1970, Milan's Piazza Fontana had been bombed by neo-fascists, unarmed American students had been killed by police at Kent and Jackson States and the BR had formed a couple of months previously.

This sub-*filone* therefore traversed the period during which debates over the legitimacy of violence were preoccupying Italian protest movements, and lasted into the early 1970s when tensions were starting to spill over into terrorism. Mitchell's description of the Western as 'a genre devoted to testing the legitimacy of violence'[86] highlights its potential resonance to such radical audiences whose contemporary preoccupations it dramatises. When Jean-Pierre Gorin looked back at the era of protest, indeed, he identified it as a time when 'every Marxist on the block wanted to make a Western'.[87]

Furthermore, while the Hollywood Western had traditionally imbued its violent content with the solemn task of fostering US national identity, the irreverent tenor of the Italian version dispensed with any such imperative. Once again, Duccio Tessari's *Una pistola per Ringo* (1965) – in fact one of the least extreme cases of the Italian Western's impertinence – offers a clear illustration of this departure from the Hollywood model. As before, this is well demonstrated through a comparison with George Stevens's *Shane* (1953). Each film's eponymous hero is an exemplar of his genre: Shane is a paragon of self-restraint, Ringo a sardonic killing-machine.

The first time Shane resorts to lethal force is in the final reel of the film, and comes only when all other avenues to a resolution have been exhausted. When he rides purposefully to face his enemy, the entire narrative has pointed to this inevitable climax: an accumulation of tension and latent violence expressed through little Joey Starrett's frustrated cry of 'Ah, Shane!' when the hero refuses to promise a violent resolution. Even in the final scene, the hero offers Ryker the chance to do a deal, underlining violence's status as a last resort. When the desire for explosive catharsis is at last sated, however, the same child looks on, awe-struck. This denouement is preceded and framed by a grave dialogue between Shane and Ryker concerning the death of the Old West, which this final act of violence will hasten:

> Shane: 'You've lived too long. Your kind of days are over.'
> Ryker: 'My days? What about yours, gunfighter?'
> Shane: 'The difference is I know it.'

Contrast this to Ringo's first violent act, which comes just three minutes into *Una pistola per Ringo*, and interrupts his game of hop-scotch. Here, as with *Shane*, the presence of fascinated children represents the audience's admiration for the hero, but Tessari's wise-cracking gunfighter consciously performs for them, comically deflecting the gravity of his violence: 'The first of these gentlemen that steps forward gets a new lead bullet between his eyes. [...] It's a new game I invented. I figured it might amuse the kids.' Within a few seconds, he has killed four men, and his plea of 'self-defence' is merely another recurring mantra in his light-hearted patter. The event is quickly forgotten and the hero pardoned when his skills are required to help the sheriff. Emptied of ideological overtones, in Tessari's West killing is no longer a last resort or a regenerative force, but merely a stylish, casual and frequent game. Moreover violence in *Shane*, when it does occur, is altogether more shocking and visceral. When Stonewall is shot by Wilson, the force of the bullet lifts him off his feet into the mud. Ringo's victims, on the other hand, expire with no signs of pain or distress, but simply slump to the ground in what Stephen Prince terms the 'clutch-and-fall' technique.[88]

That there is no 'serious orientation to the problem of violence' in *Una pistola per Ringo* is due to the fact that violence has ceased to be a 'problem' at all. Pauline Kael's remark that 'abroad, [strength and gun power] was probably what [the Western hero] had represented all along'[89] emphasises the extent to which the traditional significance of Western violence – the winning of the West, Manifest Destiny, inexorable progress – would have been subordinated to familiar iconographies amongst Italian audiences. The Italian Western takes aspects of the Hollywood genre with appeal to local tastes – banditry, stylish gunfighters, disrespect for authority and explosive violence – and enlarges them, whilst dispensing with their ideological accompaniments.

If the wider Italian *filone* was indeed guilty of draining the Hollywood Western's pervasive violence of meaning, however, this is not a charge that can be levelled at such directors as Damiano Damiani or Sergio Sollima. Though they inherited this Italian version of the myth, which had emptied the genre of its moral weight, they sought to replenish the form with radicalised doctrine, addressing contemporary issues in direct and uncompromising terms. In the following two chapters I shall therefore set out how these film-makers both identified in the Italian Western format a forum for debating contemporary political issues, and amplified aspects of the Hollywood genre which chimed with the outlooks and motivations of emergent protest groups. I examine the cinematic and narrative means by which they re-negotiated the pre-existing structures of the Western to put forward their polemics.

The 'bandit' archetype in particular was by no means simply a focus for a southern Italian self-image. Both the student movement and the later insurgent groups, for example, identified with historic and contemporaneous examples of this phenomenon. International events in particular were bringing an ever more significant influence to bear on the European Left. Escalating American involvement in Vietnam and Latin America, as well as anti-colonial uprisings across the developing world, fuelled sympathies for oppressed peoples outside the political borders of Europe. By building a mystique around themselves as virile social bandits fighting against oppressive state mechanisms, the BR and other armed groups would subsequently claim to be adapting contemporary examples of guerrilla insurgency, such as the Viet Cong and the Uruguayan Tupamaros, to an Italian context.

In Chapter Four I demonstrate how such outlooks were foreshadowed within the Italian Western *filone*. The genre's 'serious orientation to the problem of violence' is most noticeably restored in the work of Franco Solinas. In his screenplays, the traditional emphasis on regenerative and redemptive violence finds a parallel preoccupation in Frantz Fanon's seminal postcolonial treatise, *The Wretched of the Earth* (1961). Such an anti-imperialist outlook informs a significant sub-group of these films, which re-moulded the Western into a narrative format both offering legitimising motivations for armed struggle, and romanticising banditry as a means by which such causes could be victorious. This trend also further engages with the dominant modes of representation analysed in this chapter, with *Quien sabe?* and *Tepepa* in particular offering an alternative reading of the Western's relevance to southern Italian stereotypes.

Firstly, however, I turn to a group of films which addressed the more domestic concerns of the Italian New Left, such as latent fascism and the perception of an oppressive governmental 'system'. By articulating contemporaneous critiques of advanced capitalism emanating from the student movement and inspired by theorists such as Herbert Marcuse, these films seek to expose the violent underbelly of their ostensibly democratic society. Their narratives evolved organically from within the Italian Western's industrial conventions, but also reflect what would later become key motivations for insurgent violence.

The 1943–45 Resistance against Nazism was appropriated within the extra-parliamentary Left as an example of 'necessary' armed struggle by rural bandits in a noble cause. The ongoing blood feud between fascists and communists in Italy presented both sides with legitimating historical reference points for the escalation of violent tactics as the 1970s dawned. This confrontation is prefigured most clearly in the films of Sergio Sollima, emerging through a discourse concerning the ethics of the Resistance, fascism and political conflict. His work, though presenting arguably the most politically sophisticated examples of the Western *filone*'s engagement with the counterculture, also registers the incoherence of that constituency's ideologies.

# PART II

# THE FILMS

# 3

# Go West, Comrade!
## Defining the Absolute Enemy

One violent man is an outlaw; a hundred violent men are a gang; a hundred thousand, an army. This is the point: beyond the confines of individual violence, which is criminal, one can reach the violence of the masses, which is history!

The Wild West is perhaps an incongruous locale in which to find a diabolical Fascist gleefully torturing a bound captive. Sergio Sollima, however, saw it as an apt vehicle for such allegory in his film *Faccia a faccia* (1967). Professor Brad Fletcher proceeds to execute his wretched victim after opining the above epigraph, and the film's director – a former partisan – explained the scene thus: 'I knew a lad of 18 who was tortured in [the Nazi prison at] Via Tasso because he knew our names and didn't hand them over, and he died in the *Fosse Ardeatine* [massacre].'[1]

Through depicting the transformation of this liberal-minded New England academic into a violent megalomaniac, Sollima sought to present an extended critique of the seductive and dangerous nature of Fascist brutality, which he had experienced first-hand both before and during his years in the Resistance.[2] Upon travelling to the Wild West, Professor Fletcher realises that beneath the surface of progress, tolerance and propriety, human society is driven by violent, coercive urges, through which its rulers perpetuate their power. Far from fighting his epiphany, Fletcher grasps the opportunity to assert his own authority over a primitive community. He applies his newly-discovered understanding of the usefulness of violence to force its inhabitants into hard labour and the stockpiling of weaponry. The intended allegory for the Fascist era of Italian history is at its most apparent when, taking on the aspect of a rabble-rousing demagogue, Fletcher expounds his vision of power to recruit a private militia: 'I'm calling for men who are fighters, who are ready for anything, but above all else, who will obey!'

*Faccia a faccia* is, by some distance, the most loquacious and intellectually sophisticated of all Spaghetti Westerns. At first glance, its uniquely direct engagement with issues surrounding political violence and Fascist ideology set it apart from the *filone* production line. By dramatising contemporary neuroses surrounding the workings of the modern state, however, Sollima's film emblematises a surprisingly large trend within the Italian Western, which repeatedly satirises the failure of bourgeois liberalism to live up to its pretensions of freedom and tolerance. Many of these films merely treat this topic with the sardonic humour for which this *filone* is famous. The most acerbic – such as *Faccia a faccia* – however, draw direct parallels between modern society and latent fascism, thus documenting outlooks which characterised protest movements emerging during the Italian student demonstrations of 1967–68. This chapter charts the development, and analyses the contemporary political engagement, of this trend.

That the spectre of Fascism and the Second World War remained a significant cultural factor in 1960s Italy is self-evident. In 1970, for example, half of all Italians were old enough to remember the Resistance years (1943–45).[3] Furthermore, though Mussolini's regime had been defeated in the Italian peninsula in 1943, its ideologies were by no means simply phantoms from the past. As the 1960s drew to a close, such movements loomed large on the political landscape, bolstered by an electorally significant presence in parliament, a resurgent clandestine underbelly and support from fascist power bases in Greece, Spain and Portugal. Gangs known as *picchiatori* ('dive bombers') had terrorised *L'Unità* and PCI offices in the post-war era, and as left-wing protest gathered momentum in the late 1960s so right-wing mobs saw an opportunity to revitalise their historic confrontation with communism.

Though the student movement was largely peaceful, those factions for whom terrorism would later become a justifiable option were largely inducted into political confrontation through this ongoing blood-feud with fascism. The seeds of the armed struggles which erupted in the early 1970s were planted as early as April 1966, when neo-fascists killed a protesting Rome University student named Paolo Rossi. As the 1960s wore on, right-wing extra-parliamentary groups such as *Ordine nuovo*, *Fronte nazionale* and *Avanguardia nazionale* stepped up militant activities in confrontation with their counterparts on the Left, and both *Lotta continua* and *Potere operaio* formed armed wings – known as *servizi d'ordine* – in direct response to this threat.

Moreover, inspired by Herbert Marcuse's book *One Dimensional Man* (1964), the international student movement did not limit its definition of 'fascism' to street gangs, blackshirts and neo-Nazis. The notion of Western capitalism as a repressive system hiding behind a façade of democracy and tolerance, against which resistance was justified, was widespread amongst the New Left in Italy, West Germany and the USA. In Germany and Italy in particular, protesters and insurgents alike conceptualised the ostensibly liberal governments of the 1960s and 1970s as an 'absolute enemy' and an extension of fascist authoritarianism.

Abortive *coups d'état* – firstly by General De Lorenzo in 1964, then by Prince Valerio Borghese in 1970 – heightened a widespread fear that Far Right mobilisation posed a real threat to Italian democracy. Amongst radical leftist groups such incidents as the 'Battle of Valle Giulia' in February 1968, which ensued after police baton charges broke up a university occupation in Rome, served to entrench further a conception of the state as a mechanism of repression and a covert continuation of fascism. Most significantly of all, the bombing of Milan's Piazza Fontana in December 1969, along with the cover-up by the secret service over neo-fascist culpability, had a profound effect on attitudes towards the state, both within and without the Far Left.

In some radical circles, these incidents merely confirmed the long-held belief that fascism, right-wing terror and state power were one and the same, and such outlooks would later play a key role in the emergence of militant violence in the 1970s. Co-founder of the Red Brigades Renato Curcio, for example, conceived the organisation's insurgent activities as a direct continuation of the partisan cause,[4] and his was one of many such factions for whom the struggle represented an extension of the wartime Resistance (as the nomenclature of such groups as *Nuova resistenza* and *Gruppi di azione partigiana* attests). In March 1973 an announcement from *Potere operaio* defined the enemy as 'not only the fascism of [parliamentary neo-fascist leader] Almirante's blackshirts but the fascism of Andreotti and the Christian Democrat white shirts'.[5]

While *Faccia a faccia*'s allegorical narrative outwardly connects with the politics of the 1940s, then, its preoccupations with violence in society and the ruthlessness of the fascist mentality equally accord with the embryonic stages of such countercultural viewpoints. Sollima's film was released in Italy in November 1967, when student demonstrations were erupting in Trento and Milan, and tensions between Left and Right were starting to intensify. Through transposing and reinterpreting his own recollections of the Fascist era, the director was simultaneously engaging in a contemporary discourse, using the very frames of reference which would soon become dominant in debates surrounding the efficacy and legitimacy of political violence.

In the same year as both *Faccia a faccia* and *La resa dei conti* (which similarly dealt with Sollima's wartime experiences), other Resistance veterans – Giulio Questi and Giulio Petroni – also released Westerns which depicted a symbiotic relationship between violence and power in bourgeois society. Over the ensuing four years, this theme was to inspire a recurring strand in the Spaghetti Western *filone*. With varying levels of seriousness and political commitment, these films condemn Western society (in both senses: the Wild West and bourgeois liberalism) as a syndicate of cruelty, corruption and coercion. This brand of radicalism was modish, populist and frequently reductive but, as we shall see, it also reflected the ideological confusions of contemporary protest movements in their attitudes to political violence. The muddled political message of *Faccia a faccia* in particular, in its failure to put forward a cogent viewpoint, registers contradictions characteristic of Italian (and international) countercultures which were flowering at the time of its release.

### The Spaghetti Western's 'RSA' Narrative

Towards the end of Sergio Corbucci's *Il grande Silenzio* (1968) a bound captive pleads: 'No! Have pity! We don't want to die!' Tigrero (Klaus Kinski) is unmoved, and at his signal the innocent men and women, lined up in Snow Hill's saloon, are summarily executed. As the firing squad departs, the camera zooms in on the dead bodies lying in pools of blood, with Tigrero's parting comment hanging in the air: 'All according to the law.'

Throughout *Il grande Silenzio*, 'the law' is shown to be not only a thin veneer of respectability, but a tool by which the most vicious and depraved psychopaths get rich. Those driven to outlawry by its mechanisms are reduced to mere commodities, of value only for the prices on their heads, and Tigrero and his fellow bounty hunters are the logical corollary of such a system: businessmen meticulously adhering to the letter of the law. The film's penultimate shot – our last glimpse of Tigrero, reflected in the saloon window (Figure 2) – symbolises this central premise that behind the shell of bourgeois propriety a violent and exploitative base is clearly discernible. As the camera pulls away his image becomes superimposed upon the limp bodies of his victims on the other side of the glass, suspended like slabs of meat in a butcher's shop. The surface of legality which covers the brutal realities beneath is, in this film at least, transparent.

As previously discussed, Will Wright pays little heed to Italian Westerns, merely naming Sergio Leone's *Il buono, il brutto, il cattivo* (1966) as an

Figure 2    Tigrero's adherence to the law cannot conceal his bloody toll in
*Il grande Silenzio* (1968)

example of his 'professional plot'.[6] Frayling counters that such assimilation
is insufficient in explaining the complexities at work in this *filone*, since
Spaghetti Westerns do not fall neatly into Hollywood plot categories.[7] The
three protagonists in Leone's film do not, for example, form a 'group' (as
Wright's definition of a 'professional plot' requires) but are actively trying to
kill or thwart each other.

Frayling therefore proposes a chronological subset of plot variants
common to the Italian Western or, more appropriately, trends within the
*filone* which spawned imitations: the 'foundation' narrative of 1964–67,
whereby a lone hero rides into a town divided by two factions or clans as
with *Per un pugno di dollari* (1964); the 'transitional plot' of 1966–68, where
a historical backdrop is placed into the 'foundation' narrative to widen the
scope of the characters' actions such as in *Django* and *Il buono, il brutto, il
cattivo* (both 1966); and the 'Zapata-spaghetti plot' of 1967–71, which places
a gringo and a Mexican in an uneasy partnership revolving around the
Mexican Revolution. Bert Fridlund, too, takes Wright's model as a starting
point for deeper examination of the *filone*'s structural patterns, categorising
a host of variants and sub-variants including the 'infiltrator', the 'unstable
partnership', the 'avenger' and the 'social bandit' plots.[8] While such
structuralist exercises risk over-simplification and occasionally necessitate
tenuous constructions,[9] they serve a clear purpose. By demarcating recurrent

structures they illustrate the extent to which the *filone* system relied on rapid repetition of successful formulae.

To this end, and with the caveat that all such groupings are to some extent amorphous and symbiotic, I feel the addition of another variant is required. Though *Il grande Silenzio* is the most nihilistic, pessimistic and uncompromising example, it is by no means a lone voice in its denunciation of a state ruled by coercion and corruption. This trend, which lasted roughly from 1967 to 1971, I shall dub the 'RSA' or 'Repressive State Apparatus' plot. I have tentatively borrowed this terminology from Louis Althusser's essay 'Ideology and Ideological State Apparatuses' (1970).[10] I do not seek needlessly to aggrandise these films with such a lofty association, but the label succinctly emphasises the trend's consistent determination to unmask an outwardly civilised society whose covert mechanisms are predicated on violent tyranny. The 'RSA' moniker also distinguishes these films from the Italian Western's more overtly militant 'insurgency' trend, which I shall examine in Chapter Four. While this RSA narrative seeks merely to identify and expose state-sanctioned oppression, the 'insurgency' plot goes further, proffering confrontational and violent solutions.

Of course, hostility towards governmental and commercial institutions is a feature common to many Hollywood Westerns too (as shown by such figures as the crooked banker in *Stagecoach* and the railway magnate in *Jesse James*). The RSA trend, however, possesses a striking feature which requires that it is set apart from the categories listed by Frayling and Fridlund. Its films consistently appropriate symbols of law and order, civilisation and propriety common to the Hollywood Western and reverse their significance so that they come to denote violence and dishonesty. Heroes are trapped in labyrinthine webs of vice; the 'law' is both a tool of oppression for those in power and a commodity on sale to the highest bidder; and those who profess to stand for justice, tolerance and civilised virtue are shown to be thoroughly, irredeemably corrupt.

To list but a few such films, Giulio Questi's *Se sei vivo, spara!* (1967) and Gianfranco Parolini's *Ehi amico ... c'è Sabata, hai chiuso!* (1969), both present Western societies whose most respected citizens are psychotic megalomaniacs: a motif which reappears time and again in a variety of guises. Sollima's *La resa dei conti* (1967), Giuliano Carnimeo's *Sono Sartana, il vostro becchino* (1969) and Tonino Valerii's *Il prezzo del potere* (1969) all depict innocent men framed to cover up crimes committed by a violent and powerful bourgeois syndicate. Valerii's *I giorni dell'ira* (1967) and Corbucci's *Il grande Silenzio* (1968) present vicious criminals in positions of authority and power. Furthermore, both Giulio Petroni's *Da uomo a uomo* (1967) and

Parolini's *È tornato Sabata ... hai chiuso un altra volta* (1971) depict traditional Western boom-towns outwardly embracing progress, while beneath the veneer of respectability the economic growth is merely a career-ladder for crooks.

While utilising the motifs of the parent genre, this goes beyond the ambivalence towards the onset of modernity discernible in many Hollywood Westerns. This point is best illustrated by examining more closely the uses to which one of the genre's most potent symbols of 'law and order' is put. In the opening scene of Carnimeo's *Una nuvola di polvere ... un grido di morte ... arriva Sartana* (1970) a judge's daughter is dragged screaming from her home by a man wearing, as a close-up shot emphasises, a tin star pinned to his waistcoat. As the judge is similarly manhandled, another deputy informs him: 'I advise you to obey us.' Pointing to his badge, he adds: 'Meaning the law.' Soon afterwards, the judge lies dead and the sheriff tortures a prisoner with acid to find the location of hidden gold, hissing: 'You know I'm the law, and I can do anything I want.' His private army of deputies then proceeds to terrorise the town, arbitrarily condemning innocent people to death with liberally-placed 'Wanted' posters.

Both *Sono Sartana, il vostro becchino* (1969) and *Il prezzo del potere* (1969) similarly depict gangs of star-wearing deputies carrying out the diabolical orders of respected members of the community. The corrupt 'sheriff' in the former sums up the ubiquitous deception lying behind symbols of law and order by wryly admitting: 'The star is just for show.' In the RSA narrative, the tin star – shorthand for virtue and justice in Hollywood's visual syntax – frequently becomes a legitimating cover for murderers and a signifier for brutality, coercion and greed.

Worn with pride by sheriffs such as Henry Fonda's Wyatt Earp in *My Darling Clementine* (1946) and John Wayne's John T. Chance in *Rio Bravo* (1959), the tin star is a synecdoche for those charged with the duty of upholding the law. Moreover, as a potent social symbol, it represents the aspirations (or pretensions) of a community towards order, stability and peace. Rejecting or questioning this symbol therefore implies society's failure to live up to these aspirations, and when former communist Carl Foreman was subpoenaed by the House Un-American Activities Committee, the tin star was his chosen means of symbolic retribution. The iconic final scene of his screenplay *High Noon* subverts the badge and simultaneously condemns the spinelessness of contemporary Hollywood, as Will Kane tosses his star away in disgust at the cowardly society he had hitherto defended. So powerful a gesture was this that *Rio Bravo*'s defence of the small-town sheriff was made as a direct riposte, John Wayne angrily branding Foreman's script 'the most un-American thing I've ever seen in my whole life'.[11]

In a similar vein to *High Noon*, Anthony Mann's *The Tin Star* (1957) narrates the disillusionment of Henry Fonda's ex-sheriff turned bounty hunter. Deserted by society in his time of need, he brands anyone expecting the badge to earn them respect 'a fool'. The film's denouement, however, upholds the sanctity of the law, as Anthony Perkins's now worldly-wise sheriff defends justice in spite of, not for, the townsfolk. Despite questioning the transcendence of law and order, both *The Tin Star* and *High Noon* confirm the symbolic potency of the sheriff's badge. Subverting its role by tossing it away in disgust, indeed, merely fortifies its instantly recognisable power.[12]

*Il grande Silenzio* quotes *High Noon* directly during the hero's childhood flashback, when the tin star is again discarded, though in a considerably more acerbic framing. A man wearing the badge approaches the family home with his partners, one of whom is the cruel and manipulative Pollicut. This sheriff seemingly placates Silenzio's father by pleading: 'You'd better give yourself up and stop this or some bounty hunter will kill you. [...] Give yourself up and get a fair trial. [...] A good lawyer will prove your innocence.' He then shoots the family, slits the infant Silenzio's throat to silence the witness and tosses away the star. It is never explained whether he is a real sheriff or not, but this is an irrelevance. Like every other traditional symbol of justice in this film, the badge is corrupted. This tin star is not tossed aside by any Will Kane to assert righteous disgust. Again, it is merely subterfuge for a killer.

*Il grande Silenzio* is the 'RSA' film *par excellence*. An uncompromisingly bleak assault on notions of justice and authority, this more than any other contribution depicts the law as an overwhelmingly repressive force. The plot revolves around the desolate, blizzard-bitten settlement of Snow Hill, and the morality of Corbucci's world is as barren as the landscape. Silenzio (Jean-Louis Trintignant), a mute gunslinger, rides into town to exact vengeance on Pollicut (Luigi Pistilli), who has risen to become Justice of the Peace. The world in which Silenzio finds himself is inescapably unjust, and whilst its morality is polarised, it is also inverted. The film depicts an insane and utterly malevolent West, in which the 'law' is an active agent of evil. In *Il grande Silenzio*, the murderous realities beneath the façade of law and order are plain to see. Much as Tigrero's departure is punctuated by the imagery of a window revealing barbarous depths beneath surface legality, so Pollicut sits in the warmth for much of the film, looking out through his window at the cruel world he has created. By denying work to his enemies he forces them to steal and flee, so that he can put prices on their heads, guaranteeing a swift execution at the hands of Tigrero. Klaus Kinski's villain, meanwhile, is the most diabolical representative of the law in the entire 'RSA' trend.

Conversely, and rarely for an Italian Western, the hero is an unambiguously virtuous figure, fighting not just to avenge his family, but to defend the innocent and the weak. Pauline imagines him as an avenging fury ('They call him Silenzio, because wherever he goes, the silence of death follows') who represents the only beacon of hope in this bleak moral landscape. That he is fighting against, not for, the law therefore serves to underline the society's confused morality. Nearly every moral judgement in the film is either misplaced or inverted: Tigrero calls the innocent outlaws 'enemies of God, of humanity, of morality, of order. It's a patriotic duty to exterminate them'; his henchman Charley eats with a bestial repulsiveness befitting the satirical bite of Sergei Eisenstein, emptying his nose and ripping flesh from bone, yet it is he who hunts the outlaws like they are animals; and when the avenging angel Silenzio kills Charley, a lawman says: 'For all I know, [Silenzio] is the devil.'

Our first encounter with Tigrero comes as he masquerades as a lawyer, claiming to have come to represent one of the outlaws, and advising him that 'you're wise to put your trust in the law, son', before executing him. The shock value of this betrayal is not so much that a social role associated with justice and the law is used for evil, but that this is shown to be a thoroughly appropriate application as the film progresses. Tigrero is indeed on the side of the law, and is earning an honest wage according to the prevailing moral code. As he says to the wailing mother of this victim, 'è nostro pane' (translated idiomatically, 'it's our bread and butter'). Though a monstrous embodiment of evil, he is the natural product of such a world, and in justifying his work he again speaks like a hard-working American trying to make ends meet: 'He's only worth $500, but every little helps. […] Well, a man has to provide for his old age.'

The only scene in the film not set in Snow Hill and the surrounding mountains gives us a glimpse of the wider political world from which such corruption has arisen. The state governor grants amnesty to the outlaws, not because it is the right thing to do, but because the credulous electorate will approve: 'I'm only interested in the voters, who believe in the law.' The appearance of civilised propriety in this democratic society is a sham, and it is made clear that real power comes from the barrel of a gun when Sheriff Burnett (Frank Wolff) comments jovially that the governor is the fastest draw in the state. In the RSA narrative, lawmen are either a part of the syndicate of violence which covertly controls society, or else they exist in a state of false consciousness, oblivious to the fact that they are mere pawns in an oppressive system. Burnett falls into the latter category, naively believing that the law is a transcendent code which defends the weak and punishes the guilty (this despite the clear evidence to the contrary with which he is faced time and again). When he eventually falls foul of Tigrero's scheming, the villain unmasks the true nature of society's mechanisms before killing him, hissing: 'You end up buried in the ice and I stay alive to defend the only real law: the survival of the fittest.'

*Il grande Silenzio* thus crystallises this trend's themes of legal malice and institutional corruption in stark and explicit terms, and the film exerted a visible influence on the RSA narrative's subsequent development. This is most notable in *Sono Sartana, il vostro becchino* (1969). Carnimeo's film again brings Klaus Kinski and Frank Wolff together, and *Il grande Silenzio* is quoted directly when Kinski's psychotic bounty hunter stops a stagecoach to load the bodies of outlaws onto the roof. Additionally, Burnett's ironic failure to comprehend the fact that the law which he strives to uphold is itself cruel and violent ('We're going to abolish crime. The United States of America must be governed by justice, not by violence. [...] The day you're hanged, I'll be the one applauding') is repeated almost verbatim when a sheriff informs Sartana: 'We're doing you a favour. Now no bounty killer will get you. You'll just be hanged.'

The parallels between these two films go beyond simply borrowing scenes, however, since Sartana operates in an equally bleak moral universe as does Silenzio, albeit one depicted in a considerably more light-hearted manner. Sartana, framed by a banker for a crime he did not commit, is pursued by bounty hunters who hide behind every corner to collect the reward for his death. In both films, outlaws are commoditised by the prices on their heads. Tigrero meticulously keeps the bodies and Wanted posters of his victims for identification, ticking off names in his notebook 'all according to the law'. His colleagues come from miles around to cash in on the outlaw hunt as if involved in a gold rush. The bank which Sartana is alleged to have robbed, meanwhile, boasts 'Our bounty killers are the best' as its tillers count Wanted posters like banknotes and outlaws' bodies are 'deposited' in exchange for rewards. The latter film's ubiquitous gambling imagery (the town itself is called 'Poker Falls') acts as a metaphor for a society in which the law is itself a giant gamble, in which the dice are loaded, the roulette wheels fixed and the cards stacked in favour of 'respectable' men such as the sheriff and the bank manager. Beneath the comic-book façade, *Sono Sartana, il vostro becchino* remains a sinister film with assassins hiding in every shadow, working for a conspiracy run by society's guardians and using the law as cover.

It is true that many of the films cited here (especially those of Carnimeo and Parolini) use this moral universe as a backdrop for eccentric action and physical comedy, and should not be mistaken for committed Marxist expositions. Nevertheless, narratives which unambiguously assert that the forces of law and order in an outwardly liberal society amount to an authoritarian conspiracy must, in the volatile political arena of the late 1960s, be appraised in their full historical context. This trend of Westerns spans the very period during which the international student movement and some of its attendant extra-parliamentary groupings emerged, flourished, and descended into armed insurgency.

Moreover, the world-view expounded in these RSA narratives possesses conspicuous parallels with contemporaneous critiques of Western capitalism taking place amongst the generation of malcontents occupying campuses and joining picket lines across the advanced industrial world. In Italy, the Frankfurt School's trenchant critiques of commercial mass culture served as a basis for much of the student movement's ideology, locating fascism as a cognitive structure of power and violence ever-present in contemporary Western society. In particular, Herbert Marcuse's notions of 'democratic unfreedom' and 'repressive desublimation' condemned advanced capitalism as an oppressive totality whose stranglehold on public consciousness conceals a violent perpetuation of power.[13] In his 1965 essay, 'Repressive Tolerance', Marcuse writes:

> Even in the advanced centers of civilization, violence actually prevails: it is practiced by the police, in the prisons and mental institutions, in the fight against racial minorities; it is carried, by the defenders of metropolitan freedom, into the backward countries.[14]

The oppressive bourgeois syndicate covertly controlling society, the pretence of liberal propriety concealing the crimes of those in power from an oblivious populace, and the brutal law-enforcers carrying out their whims: these are all features ubiquitous to this cycle of films which broadly characterised the belief-systems of the international New Left. Equally, such an outlook would serve as the single most powerful justification for violence amongst extra-parliamentary leftist groups in the late 1960s and early 1970s. Italian militants internalised the state as an 'absolute enemy' and an extension of fascist totalitarianism. Simultaneously in West Germany, shortly before his shooting at the hands of a right-wing fanatic in 1968, New Left activist Rudi Dutschke announced: 'Our oft-praised free and democratic system [...] is itself a gigantic act of violence [which] manifests itself only reluctantly and in exceptional situations with batons and guns.'[15] In both countries, the perceived failure of pro-American administrations in the post-war era both to eradicate the spectre of fascism and to live up to progressive expectations was a key factor in the eventual turn to militancy.

These parallels most certainly help to locate the RSA narrative in the political climate of the late 1960s. They do not, however, go very far towards explaining the reasons for the emergence of this plot variant, beyond implying the self-evident notion that Cinecittà and Elios studios were opportunistic in plugging into aspects of the contemporary zeitgeist. As Wagstaff and Dalle Vacche make clear, *filoni* and sub-*filoni* were well-planned investments in successful formulae, producing imitation and repetition as often and as profitably as possible.[16] Carnimeo's quotation of *Il grande Silenzio* suggests that the RSA narrative was no exception. It too evolved organically from pre-existing strands within both the Hollywood genre and the Italian *filone*, responding to successful paradigms by fusing convention and invention. As stated previously, defining structural categories is an imprecise science. What is notable about this variant, however, is that some of its most characteristic and influential contributions have their political roots firmly located in critiques of Fascist violence, openly addressing their makers' memories of the War and the Resistance.

Even before Sergio Leone's *Per un pugno di dollari* ensured the Western *filone* a prolific future in September 1964, two Italo-Spanish co-productions directed by Joaquín Romero Marchent – *I tre implacabili* and *I tre spietati* (both 1963) – had placed villains in respected social roles. Giorgio Ferroni's *Un dollaro bucato* (1965) further anticipates the arrival of the RSA narrative by depicting a sheriff and a banker forming a conspiracy to frame the hero's innocent brother. Corbucci's *Johnny Oro* (1966) similarly displays early signs of this pattern with a clear nod to *High Noon*, as a cowardly citizenry desert their sheriff in his time of need, forcing him to re-evaluate his rigid faith in the law. The same director's *Un dollaro a testa* (1966) also shows thematic influences, as a respected doctor colludes with the sadistic villain.

Fridlund's 'big boss' category, in which a hero is pitted against a socially powerful villain, is closely related, but he subsumes this as a sub-category of his 'infiltrator' plot.[17] Though the RSA narrative, it is true, possesses numerous points of similarity with both this and Frayling's 'foundation' model,[18] these both take *Per un pugno di dollari* as their founding text. The depictions of society expounded in this alternative category in fact mark a significant departure from this influential archetype. Leone's border town San Miguel, for example, has no real 'society' to speak of. Silvanito's saloon is deserted, the only thriving industry is a coffin maker's and the only 'citizens' we see are widows hurrying indoors. The Rojos and the Baxters are self-interested clans with no concerns for the greater good of the town (if 'town' we can even call it), and when Joe is finally offered the chance to become involved in a political structure beyond these horizons he declines, departing before the troops arrive: 'You mean the Mexican government on one side, the American government on the other, and me in the middle? No, too risky.'

Conversely, the RSA plot depicts a vibrant and advanced social structure which traps the hero in a conspiratorial web, with no such option to escape his political surroundings. Alex Cox identifies in this recurring feature of the Western *filone* an influence from Jacobean tragedy (many such plays were set in the court life of Renaissance Italy, with its attendant legends of murder, revenge and intrigue).[19] The notion that Italian Westerns reflect the sins of the Borgias and the Medici is testament to a frequent engagement with the politics of power, and in this respect Cox defines the RSA narrative.

The extent to which such trends within the *filone* began to take divergent paths from those of Leone in the late 1960s is best illustrated by a comparison between its most influential director (Leone) and one of its most prolific (Corbucci). Corbucci's early Westerns, such as *Massacro al Grande Canyon* (released before *Per un pugno di dollari* in May 1964), *Minnesota Clay* (1964) and *Johnny Oro* (1966), were relatively traditional films, owing more to Hollywood models than to any recognisably 'Italian' West. As the 1960s progressed, however, his work became steadily more eccentric, iconoclastic, and eventually militant. *Django* (1966) presents a nightmarish Pop Art West, pitting its hero against Klansmen, while *Un dollaro a testa* (1966) depicts a parochial, suspicious and racist community barely worth saving from the vicious villain. By the later years of the decade, Corbucci was directing films about political fanaticism (*I crudeli* (1967)) and the violent underbelly of society (*Il grande Silenzio* (1968)), then militant parables about the Mexican Revolution (*Il mercenario* (1968) and *Compañeros* (1970)).

Conversely, Leone's first Western is a prime example of Dalle Vacche's definition of a *filone* as 'a regulated, but also stimulating, oscillation between repetition and difference, convention and invention'.[20] As the 'B' feature to Mario Caiano's *Le pistole non discutono*, it used the same crew, costumes, extras and sets as the higher-budget 'A' feature. The latest item from the Cinecittà production line, Leone's film became the archetype for the future development of the *filone*. Though begotten by the Cinecittà system, however, Leone's appropriation of the myth incrementally became more indebted to the Hollywood model as his reputation (and his budgets) grew. His Western towns are at first deserted (*Per un pugno di dollari*), then boisterous (*Per qualche dollaro in più*), and finally pioneering (*C'era una volta il West*).

This is not to say that Leone's work does not anticipate the emergence of the later RSA category. Indeed, *Per un pugno di dollari* itself dismantles the progressive symbolism of the tin star. A corrupt gun-runner fumbles in his pocket for the badge to threaten Joe (Clint Eastwood) with punishment for his crimes, and the hero's response undermines the empty symbol with the muzzle of a Colt 45. *Per qualche dollaro in più* offers an even closer precedent, when a corrupt sheriff is shown to be in cahoots with a wanted man. Monco (Eastwood) confiscates his badge, chiding: 'Tell me, isn't the sheriff supposed to be courageous, loyal and above all honest? I think you people need a new sheriff.' Neither case presents a society so irredeemably corrupt as those we see in the RSA narrative, whereby the tin star is an active force for evil. The former example drains the badge of all meaning, while the latter is an extraneous introductory footnote to the narrative. Both, however, prefigure the irreverent extremes to which the *filone* would go in the second half of the decade.

Much as Leone's films appropriate, adopt and subvert features common to the Hollywood Western by the 1960s, so too the RSA model has clear antecedents in American cinema. While Leone draws chiefly upon mainstream trends within the genre, however, the same cannot be said for this divergent plot category. The arrival of the lone hero in *Per un pugno di dollari* has obvious, and acknowledged, roots in *Shane* (1953),[21] and Ramon Rojo's ritualistic adherence to his Winchester rifle echoes Anthony Mann's *Winchester '73* (1950). Among other films, Edward Dmytryk's *Warlock* (1959) and John Ford's *The Man Who Shot Liberty Valance* (1962) offer precedents to Leone's debunking of the traditional emphasis on regenerative violence (he described the latter as 'at long last, a work of disenchantment'[22]). While Frayling's criticisms of Wright hold true, it remains the case that both *Per qualche dollaro in più* and *Il buono, il brutto, il cattivo* adapt and develop features common to the 'professional plot' which arose in the 1950s. Mann's *The Naked Spur* (1953), for example, lays bare the ethics of mercenary violence, while Robert Aldrich's *Vera Cruz* (1954) and Howard Hawks's *Rio Bravo* (1959) narrate uneasy partnerships between professional, world-weary gunfighters. Contemporaneously with Leone's films, Richard Brooks's *The Professionals* (1966) and Hawks's *El Dorado* (1966) continued Hollywood's exploration of these themes. Leone's bounty hunter films similarly narrate mercenaries leaving society behind to collect a reward and, while subverting their inherited structures, clearly engage with these mainstream trends.

The source material from which the RSA narrative inherits its attitude towards society, however, serves further to illustrate its departure from Leone's otherwise highly influential archetypes. Alongside the obvious debts to Wright's 'professional' plot, Frayling's 'foundation' plot and Fridlund's 'infiltrator' plot owed by the often mercenary activities of this variant's central characters, there is a clear line of influence from the Hollywood strand dubbed the 'transitional' plot by Wright. Here society itself, not just factions within it, acts as the film's 'villain'. Wright lists only Delmer Daves's *Broken Arrow* (1950), Fred Zinnemann's *High Noon* (1952) and Nicholas Ray's *Johnny Guitar* (1954) in this category, underlining its nature as a minority strand within the genre. As already discussed in the case of *High Noon*, these depictions of a hero's battle against a malevolent community comment as much on their directors' and writers' political attitudes to contemporary America as they do on the mythic West. Such themes were not, however, restricted to addressing the paranoia of the 1950s.

A clear precedent to this 'transitional' plot can be found in 1943, when William Wellman adapted Walter Van Tilburg Clark's book *The Ox-Bow Incident*. Here, a Western town's pretensions towards civilisation are shown to be hollow and the genre's traditional advocacy of vigilantism (inherited largely from Owen Wister) is exposed as a sinister capitulation to mob rule. The majority of the lynch mob insist that their victims' punishments cannot be deferred to the courts since institutional law is fallible. Having carried out the sentence they discover that they have killed three innocent people. Clark explained the motivations behind his book by linking the credulousness and brutality of the mob to the spread of Nazism:

> [It] was written in 1937 and '38 when the world was getting increasingly worried about Hitler and the Nazis. [...] I had the parallel in mind all right, but what I was most afraid of was not the German Nazis [...] *but that ever-present element in any society which can always be led to act the same way.* [Emphasis mine][23]

*The Ox-Bow Incident* provides the closest parallel within the Hollywood genre to the RSA narrative, not only for its presentation of a weak-minded society easily led by malevolent demagogues, but for this intentional social commentary on a fascistic mentality in an ostensibly civilised society. In *Se sei vivo, spara!* (1967), Giulio Questi similarly decided to use the Western genre as the canvas upon which to project his memories of Fascist violence during his time in the Resistance. He explains: 'I put the avarice, the violence on the side of the establishment. [...] Violence is a Western tradition. I just used [it] to exorcise what I had known during the war.'[24] He, too, presents a brutal, lynch-happy town which listens too easily to the shallow affectations of propriety voiced by its most respected citizens.

There remains in *The Ox-Bow Incident*, however, a clear sense that, though sections of society may choose to disregard it, there is a transcendent law which reflects the inherent tolerance and humanity driving Western civilisation, and which is worth defending. The virtuous sheriff, who arrives too late to stop the lynching, is outraged and promises real justice for those responsible. The posthumous reading of a victim's last will and testament, voiced in a subdued tone by that paragon of American wholesomeness Henry Fonda, declares:

> Law's a lot more than words you put in a book, or judges, or lawyers or sheriffs you hire to carry it out. It's everything people ever have found out about justice and what's right and wrong. It's the very conscience of humanity.

The lynch mob is suitably chastened as Clark's cautionary tale draws to a close, suggesting that society will learn the errors of its ways.

*Se sei vivo, spara!* allows no such sentiment. Here, 'law' and 'justice' are indeed mere words, existing solely in the mouths of avaricious hypocrites as justification for their actions. When Questi's townsfolk are similarly whipped up by respected citizens into lynching a group of strangers, it is purely so that those citizens can lay their hands on the victims' gold. Tembler's justification for the lynching ('They're a bunch of killers, murdering outlaws, and we did what we felt had to be done. [...] We just brought them to justice') is instantly undercut by the gruesome spectacle of a survivor's chest being torn open by townsfolk desperate to lay their hands on the golden bullets with which he has been shot. When the vultures turn on each other to possess the outlaws' gold, Tembler's fiancée distils the RSA narrative by prophesying her own demise: 'I don't stand a chance against Hagerman. He's a highly respected citizen. He'll have me killed and make it seem legal.'

The parochial frontier town, the casual vigilantism, the violent spectacle and the hypocrisy of respected citizens are all present in Hollywood Westerns, but each is exaggerated by Questi to a stylised extreme. As Oaks's gang rides into the town[25] we are presented with a settlement more in keeping with a Mario Bava horror film than a Western, as the hardened outlaws flinch at child abuse, domestic violence and a man retching into the gutter. The hangings are depicted in gruesome detail, as tongues protrude and the mutilated bodies are hoisted aloft to rot in the sunlight. 'Law', meanwhile, is nowhere to be seen except as a justification for greed. The film was banned after just one week in Italian cinemas in January 1967 for its excessive brutality, and it certainly constitutes an eccentric take on the violence of the Fascist era.[26] Most notable about Questi's decision to utilise the Western *filone* to filter these wartime traumas, however, is that he was not alone. *Se sei vivo, spara!*, *La resa dei conti*, *Faccia a faccia* and *Da uomo a uomo* (all released in 1967) are among the most uncompromising and influential examples of the RSA narrative in their exposition of a society governed by violence, corruption and deceit. Each depicts psychopathic undercurrents rising to the surface from beneath a façade of respectability and each was directed by a veteran of the Resistance.

Sergio Sollima locates *La resa dei conti*'s thematic oppositions in the polarised political milieu of the 1940s. Ex-sheriff Jonathan Corbett is faced with the realisation that the peasant he has chased throughout the film is innocent, framed by a corrupt railway magnate. Sollima identified in this moral dilemma a parallel with his own stark choice when the Nazis descended on Rome and partisans fled to the hills: 'It was the story of men faced with a crossroads, men who must choose; it was this that became a political fact. [...] Behind it was always my experience of 8 September,[27] the problem of choice.'[28] Sollima, like Corbett, had to choose between risking everything by fighting for his beliefs, or keeping his head down to survive. The 22 year old film student joined the Resistance rather than assent to the Nazi occupation of his city: a choice he recalls as being between 'one thing, which would surely lead to my being killed like a dog, and another which would see me survive, but as a coward'.[29]

Carlo Lizzani, who had previously directed films about the partisans, released *Un fiume di dollari* in August 1966. *Se sei vivo, spara!* emerged in January 1967. *La resa dei conti* was released in March 1967.[30] Giulio Petroni, another Resistance veteran and director of political documentaries such as *L'arte della Resistenza* during the 1950s, released *Da uomo a uomo* in August 1967. *Faccia a faccia* – as we shall see, the most politically sophisticated incarnation – came out in November 1967.

That the RSA narrative, which proliferated in the years following the release of these films, owed much to these directors' visions of the Western genre is shown on a superficial level by tracing the lineage of one of the trend's most characteristic plot devices. In Lizzani's *Un fiume di dollari* a recently-released criminal tracks down his deceitful former associate, who has become an upstanding member of society in his absence. This device has clear precedents in Hollywood. It recalls both *Man of the West* (1958), in which Link Jones (Gary Cooper) is reacquainted with his violent ways when he meets his former partners in crime, and *One-Eyed Jacks* (1961), which depicts a criminal hunting down his treacherous ex-partner who has since risen to a position of respectability. The formula is repeated almost unchanged in Petroni's *Da uomo a uomo* (1967) and Valerii's *I giorni dell'ira* (1967), both of which cast Lee Van Cleef as a vengeance-seeking outlaw hunting down his former associates. In turn, Petroni's film displays direct precedents to *Il grande Silenzio*. Both films feature a flashback (again displaying the influence of Hollywood: in this case Raoul Walsh's *Pursued* (1947)) in which an infant hero witnesses a gang butchering his family, then grows up to hunt the perpetrators down. In both too, Luigi Pistilli portrays a member of the gang who has since risen to become an influential citizen. In *Da uomo a uomo*, Walcott (Pistilli) has become a respected banker in the boom-town of Lyndon City, but uses his newly-found prestige to steal from the government and frame his erstwhile colleague Ryan (Van Cleef). The credulous populace believe Walcott's every word, and demand that Ryan hangs. Pistilli's portrayal of Pollicut in *Il grande Silenzio* is thus a formulaic echo, and the latest in a long line of Italian Western villains who have become powerful members of their community despite their homicidal backgrounds.

On a more substantial, and politically significant, level, *Il grande Silenzio*'s affinity with these films comes not only through its narrative opposition of a hero's struggle against a corrupt legal system, but in its allegorical resonance. Though set in the Utah Rockies, the film's exterior scenes were shot in the Veneto in northern Italy, presenting a 'West' in a recognisably Italian locale akin to that of Bonelli and Galleppini with their Tex Willer *fumetti*, and inviting parallels with local history. The outlaws whom Tigrero hunts like animals are outside the law, not because they have broken society's rules, but because society itself has turned morality upside down, rendering those who resist wanted men. As we have seen in the previous chapter, the brutal application of the Pica Law during the 1860s brigand wars rendered southern Italian rural labourers 'outlaws' in a similarly arbitrary fashion. Ignacio Ramonet sees a parallel between the film's bleak exposition of starving bandits and the peasant revolts in Italy at the turn of the century.[31]

Furthermore, it is entirely plausible to suggest that in a tale of desperate bandits who have fled to the mountains set against powerful and insane psychopaths who subjugate the citizens of the nearby town there is a clear echo of the partisan movement. Though he had not himself fought in the Resistance, Corbucci, born in 1926, was of the same generation as Petroni (1920), Sollima (1921), Questi (1924) and Solinas (1927), who had. He was a Roman, and a self-confessed militant leftist. The savagery of the final mass execution in particular evokes such atrocities as the massacre at the *Fosse Ardeatine* in Rome in 1944. This event subsequently became a symbol for Italy's wartime traumas and a focus for national remembrance. The film's epilogue suggests a conscious parallel: 'An inscription was legible for years in Snow Hill, the area of the massacre: "Man may walk over this place for a thousand years, but will never wipe out the blood of those who fell".'

Clearly, Questi, Petroni, Sollima and Lizzani did not 'invent' the RSA plot. The passage from one narrative category to another was fluid, and the recurrence of a particular motif reliant more on the whims of the market than on any programmatic political campaign. The extent to which individual films were responsible for repetition of these themes is also hard to quantify. *La resa dei conti*, *Faccia a faccia* and *Da uomo a uomo*, for example, were highly successful at the box-office; *Se sei vivo, spara!* and *Un fiume di dollari* less so.[32] What is clear, however, is that amongst the earliest and most characteristic examples of this sub-*filone* were films which arose directly from first-hand experience of Fascist totalitarianism. Equally clear is that a younger generation of film-makers subsequently identified a lucrative and politically relevant formula (Carnimeo was born in 1932; Valerii in 1934). The RSA narrative was simultaneously a model indebted to recollections of Fascist violence, and an apt receptacle for outlooks pertaining to the contemporary New Left concerning corruption and power in the modern state. This notion is starkly illustrated by Valerii's *Il prezzo del potere* ('The Price of Power', 1969).

As we are told in Carnimeo's *Una nuvola di polvere ... un grido di morte ... arriva Sartana* (1970), in the RSA narrative 'the lawmen are snipers. [...] Those fellows do what they want, with the excuse of the law'. Valerii takes this notion to an extreme and in the process draws overt parallels with contemporary America, since even the most cursory summary of *Il prezzo del potere*'s plot betrays its intended meaning. A progressive president, despised by the racist locals, visits Dallas and tours the city in an open topped carriage, in which he is assassinated by deputies working for a powerful conspiracy. Even down to the pink dress worn by the president's wife, the allegory for the assassination of John F. Kennedy is explicit. As the president's carriage turns a corner to approach us and he grasps his throat as he is shot, the camera is placed to replicate (rather clumsily, it must be said) Abraham Zapruder's infamous film of the assassination, while Valerii offers his own theory concerning the culpability for the crime. The guilty deputies are perched on an overpass ahead of the president's 'motorcade', while the man who is wrongly arrested is found in a high window behind.

Oswald was a patsy; the CIA did it; there was more than one gunman: hardly sophisticated or, indeed, original. That the weak Texan vice-president, sworn in hurriedly after the assassination, is a puppet for the plotters is somewhat more provocative less than a year after Lyndon Johnson left office, but the film's specific engagement with conspiracy theories surrounding the JFK killing are less important than its relationship to the larger sub-*filone*. *Il prezzo del potere* is worthy of comment because it adheres closely to the RSA narrative's established patterns. In this film, Dallas is an outwardly respectable Western town where hatred and malevolence fester under the surface, tin star-wearing hoodlums carry out the orders of a grand conspiracy of respected citizens and an innocent man is framed to cover up their diabolical deeds. That these recurrent motifs are utilised to assert quite openly that modern America is predicated on violence, corruption and the abuse of power is a clear indication that the RSA narrative was amenable to more than mere memories of totalitarian brutality. *Il prezzo del potere* displays the format equally pertaining to assertions of that brutality's continued presence beneath the surface of Western liberalism.

## Sergio Sollima's Incoherent Texts

Of all the 'RSA' plots here considered, the oeuvre of Sergio Sollima offers the most illuminating insights into countercultural mores of the era. This is particularly evident in the complex interplay of wartime recollection and contemporary radicalism which is inscribed throughout *Faccia a faccia*. On the one hand Sollima's didactic manipulation of the cinematic medium in both this film and *La resa dei conti* seeks to steer an audience into acceptance of his modish outlook on bourgeois liberalism, state power and latent fascism. On the other hand, beneath the film-maker's unified authorial intent lie contradictions, silences and ideological gaps – what Pierre Macherey would call a 'certain absence'[33] – which inadvertently reflect the confusions characterising emergent protest groups in and around the Italian student movement.

### *Sollima's Point-of-View*

*Faccia a faccia*'s narrative[34] revolves around the gradual realisation by Professor Brad Fletcher of his own innate power. We see his abduction by the notorious bandit Beauregard ('Beau') Bennett, his joining of Bennett's gang and his ultimate epiphany as he takes command of the outlaw community and applies his own theories of authoritarian leadership.

Returning to the sequence on which this chapter began it is evident that, though Sollima's film is a unique Italian Western in many ways, it shares much thematically with the 'RSA' plot category. As Brad tortures an agent from the Pinkerton law enforcement agency, he reveals the extent of his transformation from the passive, tolerant professor who leaves Boston at the start of the film to the virile, violent Western bandit we see before us. 'What is surprising', he declares, 'is that a man like me can remain all those years watching life as a spectator before he discovered the force that was in him'. Brad's epiphany, indeed, is recounted through an opposition of passive spectating and active participation. His position vis-à-vis the 'on-stage' action and the omnipresent audience is liminal; his intellectual deconstruction of society's machinations frequently bestowing upon him a privileged perspective of analytical detachment from the mythic West which surrounds him.

Nowhere is this opposition more clearly constructed than in the episode at Purgatory City where, having been kidnapped then released by Bennett, Brad awaits the eastbound train back to civilisation and is provided with some violent 'cabaret'. Purgatory City is an archetypal 'RSA narrative' frontier settlement. Beneath the surface of propriety its social leaders conspire to manipulate their inferiors, while corrupt law-enforcers carry out their bidding. As their minions move into position to shoot it out on the main street, the powerful citizens Taylor and Williams take their seats to watch the show, their lofty position resembling a theatre's upper circle.

'You have a beautiful view from here' remarks Taylor. 'Ah, we're ready at last'[35] replies Williams, as the action begins. Repeatedly, during the gunfight that ensues, the camera leaves the action to show lengthy reaction shots of these two men, engrossed in the performance below. More than mere spectators, however, those who covertly control society are positioned as puppet-masters, and are hidden from view, their manipulation of the action visible only to the audience through dramatic irony. Across the street, Brad Fletcher enjoys an equally aloof perspective, and is treated to a running commentary courtesy of the hotel landlady. '"I want you all out of town within the hour, and if you're not, I'll come and get you one by one"', she recites. 'Those were his very words. What a man!' Her words serve a dual purpose. As a third person narrator, she aids the film's diegesis through her exposition of Beau Bennett's ultimatum to the corrupt sheriff. Additionally, that Sollima's omniscient narrator is in the room with Brad as he spectates serves further to emphasise his privileged position of negotiation between the audience and the action.

Brad then descends to street-level and intervenes in the narrative unfolding before his eyes. Watched from on-high by Williams and Taylor, he concludes the performance by entering stage right and saving Beau's life with his inaugural act of lethal force. Though Fletcher decides to join the action, however, his consciousness remains on a level with the corrupt businessmen on their balcony, with the landlady/narrator on hers, and with the audience. When the gang later arrive at their mountain refuge, Brad's role is once again to spectate. As the bandits kiss their womenfolk, dance and sing, he gazes covetously at Maria yet remains passive, declining the offer to dance with her and analytically observing: 'I have never seen people so real, free, alive and happy as these.' His subsequent epiphany of innate power, too, is framed by spectatorship: as he stands on a knoll above a river, looking down on two naked bathers, one of the women chides: 'What are you looking at?' Once again, he descends from his aloof position to intervene in the narrative, raping Maria on the river bank, before victoriously brawling with her virile lover. The West through which Brad travels is a transparent and malleable construction, and he identifies a blank canvas upon which to build a masculine 'bandit' persona.

That the film incrementally bestows upon Brad the same understanding of society's coercive mechanisms that the audience (by seeing Taylor and Williams on their balcony) has been party to all along, allows him eventually to manipulate the narrative itself. The Willow Creek bank heist is meticulously planned, and as Brad explains his strategy to the gang his voice is superimposed over footage of its execution. Now it is he who serves Sollima's diegetic needs. Moreover, while the Purgatory City landlady's narration related events already in the past, his words are in the future tense, and as each component of the plan leaves his mouth it transpires before our eyes. Brad's virile epiphany has taken him out of passive spectatorship, through active participation, into omniscience. The West, meanwhile, has surpassed mere performance to become fantasy fulfilment.

While Sabata, Silenzio and Sartana unambiguously fight evil yet powerful foes, both *Faccia a faccia* and *La resa dei conti* depict an 'Everyman' at first blind to the violent underbelly of society, naively believing in the wholesomeness of bourgeois values. Only in the course of the narratives do Brad Fletcher and Jonathan Corbett awaken from this false consciousness to realise that beneath the surface, the principles they had hitherto held dear are hollow. In both films, Sollima carefully recounts the awakening through manipulating the camera's point-of-view, guiding his central character towards epiphany through dramatic irony, negotiation with genre convention and revelation. In both, too, the director seeks to steer his audience into identification with, then rejection of, the Everyman figure.

At the outset of *La resa dei conti*, Jonathan Corbett's moral universe is constructed on the notion that the law is a transcendent code of honour, protecting the innocent and punishing the guilty: a reductive outlook symbolised in the opening two scenes. After Corbett has killed three outlaws, Sheriff Jellico takes the last three Wanted posters down, exclaiming: 'I never thought I'd see that wall empty. Yes sir, any good man can live in our state. All the bad ones will meet the great Jonathan Corbett.' Lee Van Cleef (Corbett) is ostensibly resuming where he left off in Leone's films.[36] The deadly, taciturn persona so popular with international audiences is now centre-stage, with no Clint Eastwood to overshadow him. Accordingly, the first half hour of the film narrates his pursuit of the Mexican peasant Cuchillo Sanchez entirely from Corbett's perspective.

When we see Cuchillo for the first time, we are therefore given no reason to suspect that he is innocent of the accusation of rape and murder. An old man with a mutilated face warns Corbett: 'Be careful señor. He's quick with a knife, as you can see.' When Cuchillo is shown cavorting in a river, he is framed as a menace to the unsuspecting Mormon girl undressing nearby. As he lures the vulnerable child into the water and approaches her with a playfully hunched posture, he shouts: 'You be the Mormon girl and I'll be the wolf. […] What pretty feet you have!' The ominous background music enhances his role as a child-molester, making his exuberance seem psychotic, his playfulness perverted. Such didactic cinematography guides the audience into identification with Corbett's outlook, but the narrative instantly renders reliance on surface appearance problematic. Corbett assumes that the 13 year old girl is the middle-aged Mormon's daughter, when it transpires that she is his wife.

Cuchillo, though entering the narrative framed as a child-killer, becomes incrementally more sympathetic as the film progresses, and as the narrative switches to his point-of-view. Tomas Milian based his exuberant performance on Toshiro Mifune's role in Akira Kurosawa's *Seven Samurai* (1954) – a mixture of clown and ice-cold duellist – but the character also fuses archetypes from literature and folklore. He is a close relation of Puck, or Robin Goodfellow. This elusive trickster of Western European tradition leads travellers astray in oral narratives, fairy tales and in Shakespeare, Jonson, Goethe and Kipling. Cuchillo also closely resembles the figure of Arlecchino/Harlequin from the *commedia dell'arte*, instantly recognisable to many Italian audiences. An illiterate peasant displaced from his native Bergamo to seek fortune in Venice, Arlecchino is a restless, nomadic acrobat and clown. These folkloric figures share not only the guile, chutzpah and wit which we see in the character of Cuchillo, but also a privileged position of aloofness over their narratives. Before *La resa dei conti* is halfway through, the audience is accordingly sharing his point-of-view. When he fools Corbett into thinking he has been bitten by a deadly snake, for example, we can see, courtesy of the camera's position behind Cuchillo, that the 'bite' came from no more than a cactus thorn carefully gripped between the trickster's toes. In this morality play, Arlecchino dictates the terms of Everyman's/ Corbett's education, remaining tantalisingly and inexplicably one step ahead and leading him through labyrinthine paths ever nearer to the truth.

As the climax approaches, the story is being told entirely from Cuchillo's perspective, showing him to be virtuous and heroic, and his adversaries demonic. We see him dreaming of escaping hardship while lying in bed with his wife, and intervening to stop Don Serano's thugs from assaulting her. The railway magnate Brockston, who had seemed so jovial at the beginning when the story was from Corbett's point-of-view, hisses with malevolent relish befitting a burlesque villain: 'There's still one type of animal that I haven't hunted. [...] The hunting of man.' Corbett, meanwhile, becomes completely marginalised from the narrative after Cuchillo expounds some home truths to him in the Mexican jailhouse: 'You must have proof huh? No, not you. They told you I was guilty and right away you start running after me. [...] You didn't even ask if it was true or not.'

In the 17 minute[37] period between this revelation and the start of the final hunting scene, Corbett is almost entirely mute and inactive, observing the scheming of his wealthy hosts. Like Brad Fletcher, therefore, his epiphany is preceded and framed by spectatorship. Unlike Brad, however, he has become entirely extraneous to the diegesis and his point-of-view irrelevant. When the audience hears conclusively for the first time that Cuchillo is innocent, Corbett is out of earshot.

The concluding 20 minutes of *La resa dei conti* are narrated through a persistent exploitation of the camera's point-of-view, purposefully guiding both Corbett and the audience towards the explosive denouement. The camera follows Cuchillo's flight as he is chased into cane fields by Brockston's hunting party, and the audience hears the approaching hounds at the same time as he does. Once again, dramatic irony allows us to appreciate Cuchillo's guile as he remains in a privileged position over the other characters. When he hides in the long grass, the audience is privy to his location thanks to a close-up shot, which then pulls away to show the group on horseback hovering above the crops, failing to locate their quarry. When a hunter then comes close to Cuchillo, we see the horseman from below (that is, from Cuchillo's point-of-view). Corbett, meanwhile, has not only lost his role as the audience's narrative conduit; he is no longer even framed as an important character. He has become just one of the faceless hunters who appear as a group in the distance as Cuchillo selects another hiding place, of which the audience alone is permitted cognizance when the camera pans over him, crouched under a boulder.

Only when Corbett decides to rebel against the corrupt system he has hitherto served is he permitted to rejoin the narrative, and take possession once again of the camera's point-of-view. When at last he speaks it is to separate Shep (the real perpetrator of the original crime) from the rest of the party, and to send him down a path where he knows Cuchillo lies in wait. As the camera pans across to follow Shep's route, revealing Cuchillo creeping up behind him, the shot construction appears to continue the narrative's adherence to the peasant's privileged perspective. As becomes apparent when Corbett appears in the bottom-left foreground, however, we have been viewing Cuchillo through his eyes, and the film's point-of-view has switched once again. Accordingly, when Corbett finally announces his decision to fight his employers and join the peasant, we are privy to his conversion as the camera follows his gun's aim from Cuchillo to Shep (Figures 3 and 4).

Figures 3–4 Corbett takes control of the camera once more in *La resa dei conti* (1967)

Through such painstaking manipulation of his audiences' perspectives and assumptions, Sollima seeks in *La resa dei conti* to allegorise his wartime politicisation and to deliver a cogent ideological statement. On a narrative level, these cinematic techniques are successful in steering an audience's sympathies from one character to another. The coherence of the film's political exposition is however compromised by inconsistencies in its approach to genre convention and audience expectation.

For most of its narrative the film relies on a series of reversals, challenging the audience's preconceptions and defying surface appearances. As the chase commences, for example, Corbett and Cuchillo are framed in familiar Italian Western roles of 'cool' Anglo bounty hunter and vicious Mexican bandit, but these applications are both shown to be false. Cuchillo, it transpires, is not a bandit but a poverty-stricken peasant, while Corbett is no bounty hunter, but a vigilante. Since he is no longer a sheriff, his blind faith in the law does not have the mitigating context of professional duty, as does Sheriff Burnett's in *Il grande Silenzio*, and he does not even share Tigrero's financial excuse for his violence. He does not collect rewards, as is expected of Van Cleef's previous persona from *Per qualche dollaro in più*, but is simply conducting a personal campaign ('In my country even a private citizen who believes in justice can help out the law'). His 'hero' status is further complicated by his fledgling political career which is set to succeed, not due to virtue or progressiveness, but because of his reputation as a deadly law-enforcer and sponsorship from a corrupt magnate. As such, he is a more morally bankrupt politician than is the governor in *Il grande Silenzio*, and his motives are decidedly dubious.

Howard Hughes highlights the film's debt to Henry King's *The Bravados* (1958).[38] Here, Van Cleef himself plays a man on the run from Gregory Peck's avenger who, in his obsession with retribution, loses his humanity. Corbett's mania in pursuing his prey clouds his judgement so that, though he professes to be upholding righteousness, 'law' and 'justice' are mere words, used to excuse his frequent acts of violence. As Keith Hall writes, until the film is very far advanced, 'we haven't seen Cuchillo kill anybody while Corbett has already rivalled *Rambo* for a body count'.[39] Corbett's assumption that the law in any way corresponds to a transcendent moral code is undercut by every person he meets on the way questioning his supposedly virtuous motives. The Willow Creek sheriff advises him to give up on Cuchillo, and a widow whose advances he shuns says: 'You saved him for only one reason: so you could kill him yourself.' A Good Samaritan who saves him in the desert cannot comprehend the mania that keeps him going, and Captain Segura tells him: 'I don't get you.' A monk counsels him, prophetically: 'That pistol's been hanging from your belt a long while I see. In time its weight always changes a man.' By the time he draws near to his goal, he is repeating his desperate plea of 'don't you understand?' to people who, clearly, do not.

As would become a common feature of the RSA narrative, in *La resa dei conti* institutional law is no more than a cover for coercion, and the tin star quite openly denotes assimilation into the violent syndicate which exists beneath its surface. Corbett's misplaced faith in the 'system' allows him to be duped into collaboration with Brockston. To confirm his integration further he is deputised by the drunken, apathetic sheriff, who says: 'The star becomes your life: a life with the law.' Brockston counters Corbett's reluctance to accept the badge by advising: 'Wear it. A star can come in handy.' The villain then nods agreement to Corbett's wry inquiry: 'And shine brightly on your plans?' The tin star here is a tool for the rich and powerful, and a symbol of Corbett's false consciousness. When he then loses it, it is thanks to Cuchillo and denotes his first step towards epiphany, which is facilitated by the peasant. On noticing its absence, the Willow Creek sheriff speculates that Corbett must have thrown it away, so little is it respected in the Italian West. It turns up, appropriately, attached to the stocking of a whore. Sollima's appropriation of the Western as a vehicle for his polemic, and of an ex-sheriff turned vigilante as the personification of his own wartime dilemma, thus presents him with ample opportunity to subvert generic expectations and challenge audience preconceptions.

All the more curious, then, that the conclusion of *La resa dei conti* reverts to stock situations, genre clichés and crowd-pleasing resolutions. As noted in Chapter Two, the film's final scene is a reversal of Franco Solinas's original screenplay, in which the Corbett figure kills the peasant despite having been awoken to the corruption of the system he serves. When Cuchillo is finally cornered by Corbett he says, bitterly: 'I always thought you were an honest man Americano, and now I see how blind I was. You will kill me to cover up the truth.' Here, Solinas's shocking ending is still possible, but it is instantly discarded when Corbett's gun turns on Shep.

In a film which until this point has carefully dismantled audience expectation, what transpires is an incongruous departure, and the remainder of the narrative a capitulation to genre convention. Cuchillo and Corbett step forward in turn to partake in drawn-out and rapidly cross-cut showdowns. Along with the presence of Van Cleef and idiosyncratic Ennio Morricone scores, these serve only to place the film in a 'Sergio Leone derivative' sub-category. The corrupt businessman gets his comeuppance, and the relationship between Corbett and Cuchillo becomes the uneasy gringo/ Mexican friendship by this time recurrent in Italian Westerns. As the two heroes ride away in the final shot, Corbett's future is not addressed. Will he still run for Senate? Have the implications of his experiences had any meaningful impact upon his morality? Devoid of such contextualisation we are left with a thoroughly traditional Western ending, whereby big business and institutional law are untrustworthy and the individual gunfighter must do what he's gotta do.

Alex Cox argues that a recurrent weakness in Italian Westerns is that, unlike the Jacobeans (in whose plays Cox identifies the primary source material for these films), their directors seem not to appreciate the necessity of the hero's death.[40] Certainly, Sollima's happy ending has none of the iconoclastic power with which *Il grande Silenzio*'s brutal conclusion leaves its audience in a state of moral outrage. Indeed, it undermines the ideological premise upon which the whole narrative has been so painstakingly built: that the coercive 'system' irresistibly seduces those who profess to stand for law and order. Prior to the hunting scene, the grandee Don Serano dismisses Brockston's notion that Cuchillo is, as a Mexican, in any way similar to himself, saying: 'Oh no, this man's a poor peon.' The hypothesis that class loyalties cross international boundaries serves to reinforce the message that society is covertly controlled by a consortium of corrupt bourgeois megalomaniacs. This line of political thinking, however, is never pursued further, and is compromised by the abrupt ending.

As the film draws to a close, this supposedly malevolent landowner seems suddenly to see the error of his ways, calling off his personal militia and stating meekly: 'There has been enough bloodshed.' According to co-writer Sergio Donati, the reversal of the final scene was the suggestion of Sergio Leone.[41] Sollima did not acknowledge this,[42] but the veracity of the claim is irrelevant. Clearly, both the pressures of the market and the hand of the *filone*'s most successful *auteur* are influential in this ending, whether directly or not.

### Inadvertent Subtexts

As we have seen, Sollima professed a personal and allegorical significance to *La resa dei conti*'s ending, which ties it thematically to *Faccia a faccia*. That Corbett redeems himself by taking up arms in resistance against the oppressive machine while Brad Fletcher is seduced by power is supposed to depict the stark choice with which the director was faced in 1943. The dual message which arises from the two films, however – that on the one hand the fascist mentality which festers under the surface of respectable society can only be resisted adequately with violence (*La resa dei conti*), yet on the other fascism is a pernicious force because it uses violence for its own ends (*Faccia a faccia*) – betrays the ambiguity of Sollima's position. It is, indeed, in this uncertain approach to violence that the political tumults of the era speak most intriguingly through these two films, as the reference points and ideological confusions of incipient countercultures simmer beneath their contradictions. Catanzaro suggests that the ideological difficulties facing the extreme Left in the late 1960s arose in part from this very ambiguity concerning the legitimacy of armed resistance:

> Part of the tradition of the left-wing is its problematic or traumatic relationship with violence. This is in strong contrast to the extreme right-wing, which conceives of society as being governed by violence; it does not propose to change this state of affairs but rather to take it to the extreme. [...] We can in fact argue that the real problem of the historical experiences of the revolutionary left in the twentieth century has been its relationship to violence.[43]

As the announcement from *Potere operaio*, cited at the start of this chapter, attests, the Far Right was certainly not alone in internalising modern society as a mechanism of coercion. Catanzaro's argument, however, draws attention to the difficulties facing Sollima's agenda, since this very objection to state-sanctioned violence was paradoxically to become one of the primary justifications for insurgent violence in the early 1970s. The international New Left's conception of a covert continuum of fascist authoritarianism was perhaps best articulated by Gudrun Ensslin, the future founder of West German insurgent group the RAF (*Röte Armee Fraktion*). She declared in 1967: 'This fascist state means to kill us all. [...] Violence is the only way to answer violence.'[44]

Sollima's corresponding ambivalence towards both the legitimacy and the appeal of political violence is expressed inadvertently through the complexities of *Faccia a faccia*'s exposition. This sets out to condemn and expose fascism for its brutality, but ultimately neither endorses nor opposes the seductive nature of armed struggle. If *La resa dei conti*'s engagement with audience expectation is inconsistent, *Faccia a faccia*'s is considerably more sophisticated, yet in its complexity jeopardises the coherence of Sollima's intended message. Robin Wood sees in certain 1970s Hollywood films such as *Taxi Driver* (1976) – whose authorial vision is neither identical with, nor clearly distinguishable from, that of its central character – an incoherence arising from ideological confusions in society. Wood argues that, emerging amidst such major eruptions in American culture as Vietnam and Watergate, along with increasingly vociferous protest movements, these films fail to deliver a consistent message: 'Ultimately, they are films that do not know what they want to say.'[45]

*Faccia a faccia* is just such an 'incoherent text', reflecting the flux in left-wing thought during the 1960s. The very issue of audience identification, which the film so carefully manipulates through the character of Brad Fletcher, itself problematises the message. While on the one hand he is framed as an omniscient narrator, a negotiator between the audience and the action, and a mouthpiece for Sollima's polemics, on the other he is a brutal fascist, rapist and murderer. Doubtless, his ethical choices are intended to be the target of the film's critique, but his transformation is exhilarating as well as repulsive, his violence masculinising as well as vicious.

This incoherence is best charted through an analysis of Sollima's philosophical subtext, which provides a good illustration of the film's fundamental ambivalence towards the central character. Though this subtext is testament to Sollima's appreciation of fascism's ancestry, it leaves an audience in limbo by nominating Brad Fletcher as its chief narrative conduit. Brad learns early on that the universe of *Faccia a faccia* is largely inhabited by the strong, who carve out their own destinies, and by the weak, who are trampled underfoot. Paco, a young Mexican boy ostracised from his community, is gunned down during the Willow Creek bank heist, and Brad reads out a letter accompanying life savings from an elderly couple to their son which the gang have just stolen, revealing the pitiful consequences of their crime: 'Your Ma and I are pretty old. Old people don't need very much. All we care about is you.' This unforgiving world is a common feature in the Westerns of Leone, and increasingly in those of Hollywood by the mid 1960s. *Faccia a faccia*, however, is set apart not only by its intended depiction of fascistic ruthlessness, but by its application to this formula of fascism's philosophical antecedents.

*Cahiers du cinéma* dubbed Brad 'a Nietzschean of the Sierra',[46] and the central character's epiphany is indeed narrated through a remarkably direct parallel with Friedrich Nietzsche's ideas. Firstly, Brad realises that all so-called morality is driven purely by the will to power: a notion first demonstrated to him when Beau Bennett punches him, then asks: 'What would you do if you were stronger than I am?' Brad's revelation that 'there's only one kind of right in the world, the kind you make for yourself if you're big enough and strong enough' is likewise in accord with Nietzsche's efforts in *The Genealogy of Morals* (1887) to expose late nineteenth-century ethics of justice, equality and compassion as expressions of 'slave morality'.

The film's employment of Nietzsche is not, however, so simplistic as to present such theses only in the context of the philosopher's oft-distorted status as a forebear of fascism. Though Brad indeed comes to see himself as a Nietzschean superman and descends into sadistic megalomania, Sollima's authorial voice equally pertains to this philosophical reference point by expounding, through Brad, a deconstruction of the ideology of history. In the 1960s Nietzsche, alongside Marx and Freud, was widely studied as a practitioner of what Paul Ricoeur called the 'hermeneutics of suspicion', uncovering latent meanings through suspicious readings of surface appearances.[47] Nietzsche's repudiation of late nineteenth-century ascetic morality was more than just a rejection of the values of equality and compassion. He argues that these values, though masquerading as transcendent and absolute, are the result of the violent struggle between the ruthless 'aristocratic morality' and the reactive 'slave morality'.

*Faccia a faccia*'s 'philosophy of violence' (cited as the epigraph to this chapter) emerges from an analogous historical outlook on the part of the authorial voice. Brad's early pitiful pleading ('I'm too weak!') and compassion ('All members of a civilised society have fundamental human rights') are replaced by his realisation, not only that humanity is fundamentally driven by 'the lust to acquire power', but that morality and history are ideological constructs, presented as natural by the winners of past conflict. Therefore, 'beyond the confines of individual violence, which is criminal, one can reach the violence of the masses, which is history!'.

Nietzsche's historical theses brought a significant influence to bear on the work of the Frankfurt School, most notably in the writings of Walter Benjamin. Indeed, the film's extensive philosophising on the ideological construction of history is most compellingly read through the theoretical prism of Benjamin's 'Theses on the Philosophy of History' (1940), which owe much to Nietzsche's concepts of culture and history as the ideologically-laden spoils of past strife. Firstly Benjamin, like Sollima, argues that liberal values and social democracy are built on the ruins of violent conflict, and that fascism ('the "state of emergency" in which we live') is 'not the exception but the rule'.[48] The affinities between such hypotheses and both Marcuse's visions of Western capitalism and the countercultural movements of the late 1960s herald Benjamin's posthumous elevation in the annals of Western Marxism and his cult status amongst the New Left. Secondly, in his concepts concerning the revolutionary energy of recollection and the Messianic power of past epochs, Benjamin's theses illuminate Sollima's attempts to expose and combat this latent fascism. Sollima's appropriation of the Western as the lens through which his memories are interpreted, indeed, connects with pre-existing affinities between such theses and the genre's founding myth.

Owen Wister's elegiac tenor in *The Virginian* is, as discussed in the previous chapter, realised through an ideological agenda decrying the perceived moral decay accompanying industrialisation in the early twentieth century. In the individual, masculine values distilled in 'this brief epoch' of the cowboy, Wister argues, lies the vital elixir with which the modern nation can cure its degeneracy.[49] The Western myth, and the valedictory strain of its cinematic manifestation in particular, was from its inception predicated on the concerns and neuroses of contemporary society. As Jack Nachbar writes, 'the subject matter of Westerns has usually been the historical West after 1850, but the real emotional and ideological subject matter has invariably been the issues of the era in which the films were released'.[50] The mythic West was ever an epoch of malleable signifiers charged with not only a moral, but a contemporary imperative. Wister's 'brief epoch' is perceived as a period whose moral clarity has the power to illuminate contemporary society, but which is fast disappearing: an analogous notion to that which Benjamin labels *Jetztzeiten*, or 'now time':

> Every image of the past that is not recognized by the present as one of its own concerns threatens to disappear irretrievably. […] To articulate the past historically does not mean to recognize it 'the way it really was'. […] It means to seize hold of a memory as it flashes up in a moment of danger.[51]

*Jetztzeiten* is 'a past charged with the time of the now which [is] blasted out of the continuum of history'.[52] Departing from Enlightenment views of linear historical progress, this notion hones in on focal points in history which are laden with transcendent 'now time', to redeem the past for the present. Benjamin cites ancient Rome as a fertile space for such transcendence. Wister's agenda claims just such a status for the epoch of the Wild West.

Additionally, many post-war Westerns, and especially those of the 1960s, were marked by what Barry Langford terms a 'growing self-consciousness about [their] role in fabricating the national self-image'.[53] Constantly poised between yesteryear and modernity, many such films – most notably *The Man Who Shot Liberty Valance* (1962) – dwell upon the processes through which history is selectively constructed, underlining the genre's awareness of its own status as narrative. When John Ford's newspaper man opts to 'print the legend' instead of the less heroic fact he joins the ranks of dime novelists for whom the West is always already myth, even as they live through what can only hesitantly be termed the 'reality'.

'History', then, is only that which is recorded, and Sollima displays an appreciation of this legacy when, in *La resa dei conti*, Brockston advises Corbett: 'There's light and shadow in the life of every man, but history preserves the light and cancels the shadow.' As its emphasis on self-conscious spectatorship and performance indicates, *Faccia a faccia* enters and exploits this pre-existing discourse by framing the Wild West as a fertile arena for the construction both of legendary status and contemporary allegory. In displaying a consciousness of the individual's place in history, as well as the pliable nature of that history, Brockston's advice to Corbett is a precursor to the self-awareness which pervades the narrative of this later film.

*Faccia a faccia* takes this emphasis on mythic status, recollection and one's place in history to an obsessive extreme, where being remembered is the sole aim in life for the film's characters. When Pinkerton agent Siringo betrays a train hold-up by returning a stolen locket with a tip-off hidden inside, he allays suspicion by saying: 'If folks get to talking about how gently we treat the ladies, they won't talk about what we've robbed. That's how legends are born.' The ageing outlaw Rusty Rogers is quite consciously a relic of the 'Old West'. With a name straight out of a Hollywood 'B' feature, and a desperate desire to be 'Wanted', Rusty's dream is fulfilled by Brad's white lie: 'You're a legend. [...] I thought you'd been invented as a symbol of the Wild West, a figment of the public imagination.' This fabrication serves both to fulfil the old outlaw's fantasy and to accentuate the extent to which the characters in this film are constantly aware both of the mythic nature of the West which surrounds them, and of the imminent disappearance of their world.

As illustrated in Chapter Two, the 'Lost Cause' motif provided the Western genre with its clearest evocations of a bygone age, and Wister's agenda synthesised the mythic traditions of the Wild West and the Deep South as synonymously heroic, pre-industrial and fast disappearing cultures. It is appropriate, then, that *Faccia a faccia*'s most vivid valedictory sentiment should come from the southern gentleman Max de Winton:

> All of us [...] are ghosts of the past. Buffalo hunters where there are no longer any buffalo, cowboys where there are no cows, prospectors where there's no gold. The dregs of the old romantic frontier, who are unable to accept the coming of the telegraph, the railroads, or reality for that matter.

It must be said that setting this 'end of the road' lament during the Civil War is historically eccentric on Sollima's part. De Winton, however – a Confederate renegade recalling such figures as Jesse James – is the film's clearest representative of a culture soon to be consigned to the dustbin of history.

Sollima is not content, however, merely to echo the elegiac tradition of Wister, for he seeks to exploit the genre's innate capacity for contemporary commentary quite openly to critique fascism. Benjamin's intention in the

1930s was to act as a vanguard in the battle with Nazism for control over the historical past as it would live on in memory. At a time when neo-fascist violence was erupting anew in the 1960s, the intended message behind *Faccia a faccia* appears to correspond. By transposing the Fascist period into this mythic setting, and highlighting the Wild West's nature as a narrative construct, Sollima paradoxically emphasises that period's persisting relevance to contemporary Italian politics, at this 'moment of danger' in the 1960s. His agenda is similarly to 'brush history against the grain',[54] and to redeem this past epoch to illuminate the present in the ongoing conflict with fascism.

If this philosophical subtext seems convoluted, it is with good reason. Though, as we have seen, Sollima seeks to guide his audience into accordance with an authorial voice, the source of this voice, as well as the precise message arising therefrom, is muddled. Of all the characters in *Faccia a faccia* for whom the selective nature of history and the malleability of the mythic West become apparent, it is Brad Fletcher who most often articulates Sollima's intended insights. Herein lies the problematic nature of the film's expositional technique. Since Brad is the audience's primary point of contact with this agenda, his status remains that of omniscient Everyman, even after he has transformed into a diabolical fascist.

This uninterrupted identification with the central character is due to the fact that each stage of his epiphany is used to further the agenda of this supposed authorial voice, which is at variance with the ideological trajectory of the character himself. The film's very first scene, for example, uses Professor Fletcher's departing lecture to his class to initiate a dialectic surrounding the individual's capacity to make a mark on history:

> Though all men must die in time, other men will make history live, and each man can choose his own part in history. [...] If a small bit of knowledge can help you in the future, then I am truly privileged, for my part in history will not have been useless.

Brad's subsequent realisation that the West offers him opportunities to carve out a virile 'outlaw' persona begins in Purgatory City, when his narrative aloofness bestows upon him his position of negotiation between the audience and the action. The landlady/narrator insinuates that beneath the civilised surface of this society lies a violent core, observing blithely: 'We're friendly people here in Purgatory City. We prefer someone who smiles at us, especially if he's carrying a gun.' Once Brad has saved Beau's life and departs for the railway station he sees the veracity of her words, as the wide-eyed townsfolk inflate his deed into the actions of a legendary Western hero: 'Will you sign my notebook Professor Fletcher?'; 'Do you always shoot them in the front? You got a price on your head too?' Brad's realisation of his own power is then punctuated by a shoot-out, a bank heist, the violent seduction of Maria and a victorious brawl, as he consciously and wilfully constructs a fantasy masculine existence.

Ultimately, then, is it not Brad Fletcher instead of Sergio Sollima who blasts open what Benjamin labels 'the continuum of history',[55] by identifying its ideological construction and its status as narrative? Any efforts to separate his epiphany from the intended political meaning can surely only complicate further what is already an ambiguous message.

Sollima, it would appear, does indeed wish to wrest this narrative control from Brad, by repeatedly denying the audience the 'Western' spectacles and action sequences they have been led to expect amidst all the talk of legendary banditry, mythic status and the construction of history. Time and again, the film wilfully eschews a common feature of Italian formula cinema, which Christopher Wagstaff describes as the 'pay-off'. He elucidates:

> The viewer was being offered either one or a combination of three pay-offs: laughter, thrill, titillation. [...] Italian formula cinema simply juggled with items to produce the required recipe that would stimulate the appropriate number and kind of these 'physiological' responses.[56]

Sollima's refusal to grant such moments persists throughout the film. Brad rapes Maria, but the potential titillation of viewing the act itself is denied. Instead, an abrupt (in fact, clumsy) cut takes us straight to Beau's gang holding up a train. Here, we again 'miss' the action, joining them after it has taken place, and hearing that there were no killings involved (this after Beau had warned that there would be a 'bullet in the belly for those who resist'). When Beau later challenges Brad to a duel, an Ennio Morricone-composed crescendo punctuates camerawork rhythmically splicing close-ups and deep-focus shots, pointing to a seemingly inevitable explosion of gun-smoke (all of Sergio Leone's Westerns to this point had climaxed thus). Brad's gun, however, is unloaded, the duel a mere ruse to test his ruthlessness. Later on, Beau escapes from Silvertown jail, but we only hear about it the next morning. Though the climax of the film involves a brutal massacre, Sollima shows us only the aftermath, of burnt-out shacks and dead bodies. Finally, the audience is denied the spectacle of Beau and Brad single-handedly taking on a fifty-strong vigilante army, since Siringo intervenes, clearing the stage for the denouement between the three men. By having Beau kill Brad in the final scene, Sollima attempts to confirm his rejection of the character, registering Brad's failure to make a mark on history. We have missed much of the action so cannot 'remember' his virility, and his demise is an un-heroic slump out of shot.

Though Sollima seems at pains to refuse generic spectacle, however, the West ultimately retains its regenerative function in this film. This occurs because, though Brad becomes a monster, his transformation is presented as a revitalising and masculinising process, by which he turns into a charismatic and virile bandit. Maggie Günsberg sees in the parodic displays of masculine prowess throughout the Italian Western a masquerade of phallic power betraying castration anxiety.[57] As already discussed, *Faccia a faccia*'s exposition of virile awakening occurs through metaphors of performance and artifice. Furthermore, the very moment of Brad's transgression in the main street of Purgatory City itself unmasks the masculine imperative behind Sollima's agenda through a visual allusion to *High Noon* (1952). As a lawman sneaks up behind Beau, an out-of-frame gunshot sends the deputy hurtling through the saloon window. We then cut to a view from inside the building to see the airborne casualty continuing his progress through the glass, revealing Brad standing resolutely, gun pointing towards the camera. Clearly discernible here is a quotation of the moment in *High Noon* when Amy Kane (Grace Kelly) intervenes to save her husband Will (Gary Cooper) in the final shoot-out. Here, the camera faces one of Frank Miller's henchmen as he reloads. After a gunshot is heard, he falls dead, to reveal Amy standing in the window behind, gun in hand.

Both Brad Fletcher and Amy Kane are preparing to board a train and leave the town for good when they decide to intervene in its violent narrative being played out on a deserted main street. Pertinently, this is the moment in *High Noon* at which Amy's feminine pacifism is conclusively eschewed, exposed as naive in the face of a ruthless foe. By replicating Fred Zinnemann's shot construction, Sollima further emphasises the effeteness of Brad's initially humanitarian persona, tying it by association to the femininity and weakness of Amy Kane's ideological position. In *High Noon* a cut switches to Amy's point-of-view, as she gazes at the dead body, emphasising the gravity of her decision to kill. In *Faccia a faccia* the camera ignores the body once it has broken the window to dwell upon the gun-toting figure of Brad, demanding that we focus on his virile awakening.

The near ubiquitous rejection of femininity in the Italian Western (occurring on a far greater scale than that identified by Jane Tompkins in the American genre) here finds its common outlet. Günsberg writes of this *filone* that 'femininity generally appears in much reduced form merely to establish masculinity as heterosexual'.[58] Certainly, in *Faccia a faccia* women act purely as agents of Brad's awakening. His early protestations of humanity and compassion coincide with evidence of repressed desire, as he objects to the passionate love-making of his vivacious hostess then gazes at a photograph of Miss Wilkins (whom he has left behind in Boston without revealing the feelings he clearly harbours for her). The hotel landlady narrates the intrigue of Purgatory City in Brad's presence, allowing him his first glimpse into the hidden depths beneath society's surface propriety. Finally, his epiphany of power liberates his sexual and violent urges simultaneously, as he shoots a gun alone in the wilderness then rapes Maria.

This fetishistic conflation of firearms and phallic power is a feature common to the Western myth. We have already seen in the previous chapter the progressive function with which the side-arm is frequently endowed, absorbed as an adjunct of the masculine body. Jenni Calder cites as an example Van Cort's Western novel *Journey of the Gun* (1966), in which the young hero, Clay Rand, loses his virginity and kills a man within a few pages.[59] When Brad first holds a pistol, he similarly confirms the weapon's phallic potency: 'There's no doubt that holding it gives one a curious sense of power. It seems so natural, as though it had become part of me.' By the end of the film, Sollima's shot composition leaves an audience in little doubt as to the power with which he has been bestowed by his encounter with firearms. As Brad prepares to execute Siringo, who kneels helplessly before him, a deep-focus shot reveals the pistol which has fallen in the sand protruding from the ground in the near foreground. The shot's perspective enlarges the weapon to a gargantuan size, the giant handle pointing towards Brad the virile superman.

On one hand, this conflation of mechanised power and masculine virility is testament to an appreciation on Sollima's part of the psychopathology of fascism. In Brad's phallic revelation can be read echoes of Filippo Tommaso Marinetti's hymn to progress in his 'Manifesto of Futurism' of 1909, which planted the roots of the Italian Fascist movement. Moreover, Klaus Theweleit illustrates the extent to which the forebears of Nazism harboured intense and violent hatred of women.[60] Many members of the Freikorps, who fought against revolutionary workers in Weimar Germany and would subsequently form the vanguard of Nazi power, expressed disgust, fear and hatred towards femininity in their memoirs.

On the other hand, however, *Faccia a faccia*'s ambiguity and ultimate failure to put forward a clear agenda is further illustrated by a pernicious misogyny which the narrative singularly fails to reject. Giulio Questi's hint of a homosexual rape at the hands of cackling black-shirted *muchachos* in *Se sei vivo, spara!* offers a somewhat more condemnatory slant on fascist sexual deviance than does Brad's act. Maria, it transpires, thoroughly appreciates being raped and becomes his passive, voluptuous moll immediately afterwards. Women in general, indeed, are entirely desirous of such treatment at the hands of virile men in Sollima's world, as Annie reveals when chiding Beau for ignoring her. Looking sideways at Maria and Brad, she shouts: 'You're not the only man in the world. [...] I found out today that certain men, when they want a girl, take her whether she likes it or not.'

All of which leaves an audience with more questions than answers. Are we to condemn Brad for his ruthlessness and his authoritarianism, or admire, even aspire to, his virile awakening and his lucid identification of violence's usefulness? Certainly, while on the one hand Sollima seeks to condemn a brutal fascistic mentality, on the other he leaves us in no doubt as to the charismatic nature of the fascist Mr Hyde as opposed to the pathetic liberal Dr Jekyll. Far from a radical revision of the Western, Brad's violent epiphany is an exhilarating, yet entirely traditional, emancipation from the shackles of civilised morality: a vicarious fantasy of masculine power played out in front of the Italian Western's largely male audience.[61] As a condemnation of the seductive, empowering nature of violence, *Faccia a faccia* is a failure.

Sollima's film, however, is worthy of attention precisely because it inadvertently expresses the incoherence and volatility of the countercultural milieu from which it arose. This ambiguous attitude towards virile violence is characteristic both of many of the films analysed in this chapter and of the ideological confusions amongst contemporary New Left factions. *Il grande Silenzio*, too, fails conclusively to reject violence. Corbucci's film ends on the execution of the angelic hero and the brutal massacre of innocent outlaws, but this only transpires because Tigrero is less honourable than Silenzio and has a sniper disable his adversary before dispatching him. Herbert Marcuse, while framing the capitalist state as a violent mechanism of repression, was cautious in his language around the use of violence, yet his thesis on the 'natural right of resistance' was cited by West German insurgent Andreas Baader to justify murder at his trial.[62] In the moral outrage provoked by Corbucci's ending can similarly be read a message that in order to fight such evil one must be equally ruthless.

*Faccia a faccia* was released one month after the Trento University occupation hit the headlines and explosive disgust at the antiquated bureaucracy of the education system was impacting on every aspect of social and political life. It accordingly displays a populist political tendency in depicting a sanctimonious history professor turning into an insane fascist and finally being shot dead. When the long-haired drop-out Beau Bennett decides to kill him, he says: 'It was what I had to do.' Ultimately, then, while

*Faccia a faccia* displays undoubted prescience in critiquing the fascist mentality just as right-wing extra-parliamentary gangs were undergoing a resurgence, this is mixed with a considerable myopia in ascribing virile fascination with violence purely to the extreme Right. Leftist extra-parliamentary groups emerging in the 1970s would also exploit the allure of firearms and the empowering revitalisation of violence to appeal to young activists. Catanzaro records the following interview with a member of one such group – *Prima linea* – whose accord with Brad Fletcher's outlook is striking:

> Arms have a fascination of their own, it is a fascination that makes you feel in some way more … more virile … this sensation of feeling stronger, more manly, … I found myself … showing them to women to try to impress them.[63]

*Faccia a faccia*'s unspoken subtext – that violence is indeed an attractive and masculinising process – registers an equivalent ambivalence and portends this valorisation of armed struggle which lay around the corner. Though Sollima professes to present us with a condemnation of violence, what emerges through his production is a tacit admiration for those who have the courage to use it.

In the next chapter I shall analyse films – in some cases made by the same directors and writers as the works discussed in this – whose attitude towards violence possesses none of the ambiguity manifest in *Faccia a faccia*. Through engagement with contemporary theorists of Third World revolution such as Franz Fanon and Régis Debray, they instead openly and programmatically endorse armed insurrection, using Mexico as their surrogate for contemporary anti-colonial uprisings across the globe.

# 4

# Violent Mexico: 'Crossing the Border' into Armed Insurgency

Though the narrative of Sergio Corbucci's *Compañeros* (1970) places us amidst the turmoil of the 1910–20 Mexican Revolution, both the film's political subtext and its authorial voice arise from the aftermath of 1968. Amidst the remains of a shelled church, an impromptu student debating chamber unmasks this contemporaneity. 'Words are of no use to us any more', shouts a student revolutionary, armed to the teeth. 'The time has come to respond to violence with violence. To respond any other way is cowardice.'

'The strength of our ideals is that we have no fear of death, and have no need of rifles to triumph', retorts the pacifist revolutionary Professor Xantos, lecturing his radicalised students. 'If the ideals you are struggling for are just, you can win without violence.' As the previous two chapters have made clear, similar debates surrounding both the efficacy and the justification of armed resistance played a significant role in the fractious discourse characterising the Italian (and international) New Left in the late 1960s and early 1970s. For all its comic-book exuberance and slapstick humour, Corbucci's film openly articulates and symbolises these oppositions in the short sequence cited above.

*Compañeros* was the culmination of a trend which began with Damiano Damiani's *¿El Chuncho, quién sabe?* (1966, hitherto and henceforth abbreviated to *Quién sabe?*), then continued with Sergio Sollima's *Corri, uomo, corri* (1968), Corbucci's own *Il mercenario* (1968) and Giulio Petroni's *Tepepa* (1969). This chapter outlines the myriad influences which converge in this trend, and analyses the film-makers' attempts at political communication.

Each of these films seeks to articulate radical debates surrounding political violence, and each engages with related and pressing issues of anti-imperialism through its setting in revolutionary Mexico.[1] The decision to employ this mythic locale for Cold War allegory cannot be separated from the 'Mexico' of Hollywood's imagination, which had been co-opted into just such a framework throughout the post-war era. Such films as *Vera Cruz* (1954), *The Magnificent Seven* (1960) and *The Alamo* (1960) offered rationalisations for the USA's emergence as a superpower, a bastion of freedom and a 'global sheriff' as the Cold War intensified. It is precisely this narrative model of US cinema which is appropriated and re-moulded by this chapter's key films.

I label the Italian trend the 'insurgency' plot. Firstly, this appellation underlines these films' consistent advocacy of violent resistance to US imperialism. Secondly, it directly opposes their political agendas to that of the Hollywood paradigm mentioned above, which Richard Slotkin dubs the 'counterinsurgency' plot.[2] The ideologically-laden border crossings undertaken by Hollywood's Western heroes in the Cold War years are precisely the target when, in each of this chapter's central films, the Mexican hero comes to realise that such intervention in native affairs is a pernicious intrusion which must be violently repelled.

Though the high visibility of Hollywood formats is a key factor in explaining the emergence of the 'insurgency' sub-*filone*, these films are also the progeny of radical trends closer to home. The sequence from *Compañeros* cited above is an explicit moment of contemporary discourse, fusing as it does scenarios and ideological viewpoints pertaining directly to the experiences of Italy's extra-parliamentary Left. Ernest Mandel envisioned the international student movement as a 'new, young revolutionary vanguard' on whom the hopes of Trotskyism could be pinned.[3] Herbert Marcuse similarly identified in the student rebels a revolutionary force, free from absorption into the capitalist system. Notions emerging from 1968 such as the 'red bases in the colleges' sought to adapt Régis Debray's *foco* theory to the university campus, forming compact cells of activists to bring about the conditions for revolution. Corbucci's guerrilla unit of student insurgents fighting both North American imperialists and Mexican counter-revolutionaries is a crude and obvious enactment of these contemporary countercultural vogues.

Furthermore, *Compañeros* actively proffers a resolution to the debates it dramatises, for no sooner has Professor Xantos's plea left his lips than his pacifism is exposed as naive. The students, defiantly gripping their firearms, respond as one that his forgiveness is futile and that, faced with a violent

enemy, lethal force is the only adequate response: 'The others have rifles
[…] and when they have killed us all our principles and our ideals will be
dead too.' Xantos himself is eventually forced to admit that the argument
is lost. Turning towards the camera and mounting an out-of-shot 'podium',
he partially exits the narrative, addressing his students and the viewer
simultaneously to admit that his philosophy is outmoded. 'I have become
too old, and you are too young, all of you', he states. 'It could very well be
that this way of thinking is more in keeping with the times that we live in
than mine.' The low-angle shot serves further to emphasise the gravity of
these words, while supplying a visual clue that this is a public address. At both
the Trento and Turin campus occupations, students emulated the Chinese
Cultural Revolution to interrupt lectures and force professors to confront
the ideologies of the movement.[4] While Xantos is not exactly denounced, he
is similarly impelled to question his own beliefs, and ultimately to 'confess'
his ideological failings. 'The times' to which he refers are quite evidently
closer to home than the narrative's ostensible setting.

Equally apparent in this speech is a symbol for the generational divisions
which largely defined the New Left's contemporary activism. The 'old' in
'Old Left' was conspicuous on both sides of the Atlantic, as radicalised
youths increasingly saw fit to reject established structures of authority and
political expression in favour of militant insubordination. When the PCI-
supporting father of Red Brigades activist Roberto Ognibene recalled his
son's turn to violence, he echoed Xantos's admission: 'He was young and I
was not. […] He wanted action. […] He had an enormous eagerness […]
to act, to see things done.'[5] The ferments of the era, indeed, were driven by,
and provoked, generational conflict as much as they reflected class-based or
racial tensions in Western society.

Outside left-wing subcultures, this generation gap took on an even
more unsettling mantle to political establishments throughout the advanced
industrial world, as student movements and related ferments increasingly
adopted the idioms of the communist foe. In Italy, the students came to
be known as the *Cinesi* for their emulation of Mao, and Tom Engelhardt
summarises the culture shock in Middle America of youths proclaiming pro-
NLF ideologies during the Vietnam War: 'As in some 1950s science fiction
fantasy, the enemy now looked exactly like your child!'[6] The 'revisionist'
American Western *Soldier Blue* (Ralph Nelson, 1970) caricatures this unease
when Colonel Iverson laments the disrespect towards authority shown by
Crista: 'When I see young people today behaving like that, I just can't help
wondering what this god damn country's coming to!'

The unmistakably contemporary nature of Iverson's comment resembles that of Xantos's with good reason. *Soldier Blue* and *Compañeros* – released in the same year – both represent contemporary generational conflict by adapting the established codes of the Western. Both Nelson and Corbucci see fit to make this parallel manifest through such direct address. The two films also arise from equivalent ideological positions of revulsion at US imperialism, but here the parallels cease.

Iverson's moralistic utterance serves merely to emphasise his hypocrisy on the eve of committing an act of genocide. *Soldier Blue*'s graphic depiction of the Sand Creek massacre of 1864 deliberately evokes the carnage of the My Lai atrocity, news of which had entered the public domain at the end of 1969, scandalising America.[7] Ronald Haeberle's recently-published photographs of the massacre in Vietnam are recreated way out West, expressing the oft-repeated countercultural claim that the US government was the latest in a long line of murderers and criminals to preside over the nation. Marcuse's 'Repressive Tolerance', alongside David Wise's and Thomas B. Ross's notions of a coercive and violent 'invisible government',[8] took on a singular relevance to the student movement in the context of Vietnam. In particular, Marcuse's accusation that 'even in the advanced centers of civilization, violence actually prevails […] carried, by the defenders of metropolitan freedom, into the backward countries' offered an oft-cited paradigm for protest and insubordination.[9]

The ideological journey from this revulsion to the taking up of arms against what is perceived to be a repressive 'system' is, as we have seen in Chapter Three, fraught with ambiguity. Nelson's polemic, like that of the contemporaneous *Little Big Man* (Arthur Penn, 1970), is one of pacifism, disgust and anger at the violence perpetrated in the name of white America. Though the incendiary rhetoric of the Weathermen had recently lent the US counterculture a more confrontational appearance,[10] neither Nelson nor Penn offer a programmatic statement that such imperialist violence should be met with insurgent violence. Here, Corbucci departs radically from Hollywood's revisionism. It is indeed precisely these contemporary philosophies of pacifism which *Compañeros*, by asserting the futility of Professor Xantos's ideals, seeks openly to expose as naive. Appropriating the symbolic 'Mexico' of Hollywood mythology gives Corbucci free rein to engage with the cult of Third World revolution: one of a precious few reference points uniting the disparate factions of the New Left in the late 1960s. While echoing Fanon, Debray, Mao and Guevara, Corbucci's armed students also indirectly quote Gudrun Ensslin's declaration that 'this fascist state means to kill us all. […] Violence is the only way to answer violence'.[11]

Amongst the Italian New Left, the surrogate 'American' imaginary permeating popular culture in the post-war years took on an altogether darker appearance than the seductive ticket to modernity explored in Chapter One. Napalm, nuclear war and 'pig Amerika' were more likely reference points than were Coca Cola or Cadillac. As Ginsborg records: 'For Italian youth of this period the "real" America became another: the anti-war protests on the campuses, the Californian communes and counter-culture, the Black Power movement.'[12]

In Italy, as in Hollywood, the Western genre became appropriated as a countercultural tool offering acerbic critiques of US foreign policy. Insurgent violence in Italy, when it broke out in the 1970s, would be of an altogether more extreme nature than that of the American Weathermen. Analogously (and perhaps portentously) so too Italy's anti-imperialist Westerns endorsed ideologies of a considerably more brutal temperament than did their US counterparts. Their ideological trajectory offered neither reconciliation nor pacifism. The 'insurgency' variant is therefore a melting-pot of political and cinematic references, incongruously fusing the tropes of Italian political cinema with those of the American Western. It is the task of this chapter to chart a route through this transcultural tangle. I begin with Hollywood.

## Out West Down South Part II: Borderline Disputes

*Quien Sabe?* is not a Western. [...] The Western belongs to Protestant North American culture. If one leaves this culture, one is not making a Western anymore. South of the Rio Grande it is not the West, it is Mexico. [...] To say that a film which is set in Mexico is a Western shows that you have understood nothing. [...] [*Quien Sabe?* is] a film about the Mexican Revolution, set in the Mexican Revolution, and therefore it is clearly a political film and nothing else.[13]

(Damiano Damiani)

Horace Greely's advice to 'go West, young man' not only offered the settler, the prospector and the entrepreneur the aspirational promise of playing a part in the Manifest Destiny of the United States of America; it also gave, if such were required, clear directions. The inexorable quality of westward expansion, as the 'vanishing American' made way for the technologically superior white man, would become the touchstone of American exceptionalism in print, theatre and, of course, celluloid. The frontier – the social safety valve of Frederick Jackson Turner's thesis – draws the gaze eternally to one horizon: the West.

As Cold War tensions became ever more fraught in the post-war era, however, a significant trend within the Western genre increasingly shifted its symbolic focus to the south: a re-orientation anticipated in the last of John Ford's 'Cavalry Trilogy', *Rio Grande* (1950). As Lt Colonel Kirby Yorke returns to base from an unsuccessful pursuit of renegade Apaches, he informs his commander that his quarry 'reached the Rio Grande and crossed into Mexico. Pursuant to orders I halted on our side of the river. The men didn't like it very much'. The seemingly boundless American frontier has come to an abrupt halt, and reaching the periphery of the nation has thrust Yorke's command reluctantly into the arena of international politics.

Made as relations with the Soviet Union were souring, as that same enemy attained nuclear capability, as China 'fell' to communism and as North Korean forces launched raids on their southern neighbours, *Rio Grande* posits a dualistic world-view. The Apache once more assumes his role of devil on Earth, attacking wagon trains and abducting children. 'The blood-crazed insurgents of [*Rio Grande*]', writes Michael Coyne, 'were scantily disguised frontier equivalents of the communist threat'.[14] The title of the film draws our gaze to the border for good reason, for the threat to American freedom can no longer be fought exclusively within the nation's boundaries. When Yorke's men make an audacious, and illegal, foray into Mexican territory to rescue the abductees, there are no repercussions. It is simply seen to be the right thing to do. This scenario presages the direction in which the Western genre would find itself moving with increasing regularity as the Cold War intensified. The act of crossing this national boundary line in particular gained an ever more contemporary imperative, but the moral certitude of the covert operation would simultaneously become ever more ambiguous.

Doubtless, Damiano Damiani's attempt to distance his film *Quien sabe?* from the generic boundaries of the Western was largely driven by a desire to avoid the intellectual stigma associated with the Cinecittà/Elios production line – by 1966 churning out Westerns at a rate of over 50 a year – and to align the film alongside the revered oeuvre of its co-screenwriter Franco Solinas. Certainly, as I shall demonstrate, *Quien sabe?* displays notable hallmarks of this politicised inheritance. Equally evident in Damiani's argument, however, is a statement of intent that the film is an outright rejection of the cognitive formulations peddled by the Hollywood myth machine. Here, he comes unstuck.

In seeking to eschew the Western genre he posits a series of tenuous assumptions and reductive, binary oppositions. The border between the United States and Mexico provides both a symbol and a paradigm, through which he seeks to delineate concrete oppositions between mutually exclusive entities: the North and the South; Protestantism and Catholicism; the USA and Mexico; and the Western and the 'political film'. All are presented as dichotomies between clearly-defined categories, glaring at each other from opposing sides of a boundary line. In practice these polarities, whether national, cinematic or political, were neither as discernible nor as antagonistic as Damiani supposes. His film – an amorphous blend of leftist polemic and Western – is a case in point.

That Damiani felt the need so vociferously to deny his film's categorisation within the Western's framework is inescapably related to the shift in the symbolic functioning of the Hollywood genre in the post-war era. From amongst his misapprehensions emerges a clear sense that the Mexican border, as a political and national boundary line, possesses a fundamentally different function to the largely mythic role of America's internal frontier. Frederick Jackson Turner himself depicted the frontier, as the defining feature of his nation's development, to be constantly mobile and ambiguous: an overtly mythic function famously summarised by Jim Kitses's 'shifting antimonies' paradigm.[15] Here, wilderness and civilisation, individual and community, nature and culture, and the West and the East form binary, yet flexible, oppositions within and between which the folkloric mechanisms of the frontier negotiate US national identity. As Lt. Colonel Yorke discovers, and as the heroes of *Vera Cruz* (1954), *The Magnificent Seven* (1960) and *Major Dundee* (1965) come to realise, the Mexican border presents an alternative boundary line. The crossing of it holds an altogether different set of implications for both the protagonists and the allegorical pertinence of the Western genre. The 'Mexico' of Hollywood's collective imagination was always already both a projection of North American values, and a reflection of US self-perception on the world stage.

This premise is emblematised in an early sequence from Robert Aldrich's *Vera Cruz* (1954). A pan shot follows Ben Trane (Gary Cooper) as he rides into a town, ties his horse up outside a bar and with a genial 'howdy' walks inside. Hollywood's 'A'-list cowboy star is imperturbably going about his usual business but the iconography the camera registers is curiously alien. Instead of a saloon there is a cantina; instead of boardwalks and wooden façades, the buildings flanking this main street are made of ancient stone; instead of the industrious hustle of a boom-town there are peasants in sombreros leaning against walls and Latina women carrying food atop their heads.

Both outside and inside the cantina, however, there are North American gunslingers, scowling at Trane's repeated attempts at politeness. When, a few choice words later, Donnegan (Ernest Borgnine) is sent flying courtesy of Trane's fist, the camera tracks his progress from inside the cantina, to the door, and out onto the dusty street where a row of peasants stands watching the show. The rough-and-tumble bar-room brawl, the gang of menacing outlaws and the virtuoso gunplay with which Joe Erin (Burt Lancaster) enters and defuses the situation are all spectacles 'out West, down South'. As Erin approaches the camera, a low-angle shot emphasises his looming presence. When he then observes with amusement Borgnine's ample physique hurtling exaggeratedly outside and slumping unconscious, the camera's position inside the cantina allows the audience to share his view, and his broad grin. The Mexicans themselves, meanwhile, are a backdrop gazing in wonder at the antics of American supermen yet excluded from the cantina itself.

The gaze of the peasants at this Western action 'on tour' in Mexico is, however, not all it seems, for *Vera Cruz* equally demands that the Westerner gazes south towards the exotic, turbulent and alien culture lying over the Rio Grande. Early representations of Mexico in American cinema, such as *Barbarous Mexico* (1913) and *Patria!* (1915), had reflected governmental unease at the presence of an indigenous revolution on the USA's doorstep. These depicted Mexicans as barbarians who threatened the very fabric of American civilisation. The myths of Mexico and its various periods of revolutionary turmoil, indeed, were sources of both tangible danger and voyeuristic fascination for many in the United States even while the actuality was still being played out. Hall and Coerver record that, during the 1910–1920 Revolution, gathering in El Paso to view the fighting on the other side of the Rio Grande at Ciudad Juárez 'was a major spectator sport for Americans'. The occasional stray bullet even found its way into enraptured spectators.[16]

The *campesino* warlord Pancho Villa, many of whose battles occurred next to the US border, exploited the spectacle of the Revolution to enhance his own public image. He not only gave interviews to American journalists such as John Reed, but invited American film crews along to record his campaigns. Films of Villa's battles at Chihuahua, Ciudad Juárez and Torreon, such as *The Life of General Villa* (Cabanne, 1914) and *Life of Villa* (Cabanne/Walsh, 1912), were shown commercially in the United States by the Mutual Film Corporation. These arose amidst claims that he had agreed to attack only in daylight hours to enable filming, and to re-enact manoeuvres which had not been shot adequately the first time around.[17] Whatever the truth of these rumours, Villa's approach to warfare was impeccably media-conscious, and his mystique carefully cultivated.[18] He accordingly became assimilated into Hollywood's mythic structures, joining Jesse James and Billy the Kid in the pantheon of social bandits ripe for revision in subsequent incarnations such as *Viva Villa!* (1934), *Let's Go With Pancho Villa* (1936), *Pancho Villa Returns* (1950) and *Villa Rides* (1968).

Carlos Monsiváis writes: 'The Hollywood attraction for Villa [...] would perhaps be explained in terms of the self-complacent hypnosis that the "primitive" provokes in the "civilized"; in terms of the fascination that, from the metropolis, Tarzan or King Kong awaken.'[19] Clearly discernible in this fascination with a neighbour perceived to be backward, degenerate and exotic is another parallel with northern Italian conceptions, outlined in Chapter Two, of the *Mezzogiorno*. This alternative reading of the Western's pertinence to Italian social relations focuses on the perception of an ancient civilisation, a feudal society and a backward, superstitious and 'southern' people. In the danger, allure and culture-shock inherent to Hollywood conceptions of Mexico such as those in *Vera Cruz* and *The Magnificent Seven*, is an equivalent gaze at the ethnic 'Other' to that which Nelson Moe terms the 'delectation of cultural difference' experienced by northern travellers to the Italian South.[20] This 'gaze' manifest in Milanese illustrated periodicals was essentially aimed at a reflection of the national self for northern Italians, much as Wister, Roosevelt and Turner by looking to the West saw their own national character looking back at them. The fascination with the Mexican exotic in Hollywood's representations is also a gaze at oneself. This looking-glass, however, reflects back over the Rio Grande a vision of US identity on the world stage: the manner in which the USA is perceived (or would like to be perceived) by other, less advanced, cultures. The peasants in *Vera Cruz* who stand gazing in awe at North American heroes are Mexicans as imagined and idealised by Hollywood. They inhabit a mythic Mexico fascinated by the United States of America, and aspiring to be like white Americans. As we shall see, it is precisely this reflected gaze at the aspirant subaltern which the Italian 'insurgency' plot seeks to appropriate and reverse.

The fantasy 'Mexican' construct presented in *Vera Cruz* inherits a formulation of the USA's neighbour which had been fostered outside the Western genre itself in the preceding decades. The vision it perpetuates of Mexicans as aspirant Americans dated back cinematically at least to the 1930s, when Hollywood's appropriations of the country's revolutionary ferment began to depict Mexico as a nation emulating North American ideals. Jack Conway's *Viva Villa!* (1934), for example, draws upon both Edgcumb Pinchon's literary source material and John Reed's book *Insurgent Mexico*, but disregards both authors' socialist beliefs. Ben Hecht's screenplay instead establishes Villa as a primitive bandit with 'revolutionary' ideas of land-reclamation described by Richard Slotkin as 'not really very far left of the tenets of movie-populism and New Deal reform'.[21]

The figure of the exotic Mexican revolutionary became an ambassador for Roosevelt's liberalism once more in William Dieterle's *Juarez* (1939). Here, despite the ostensible absence of North American characters, one looms over the narrative to such an extent as to dominate the eponymous hero's motivations. Every time Benito Juárez expounds his egalitarian visions of a Mexico liberated from feudal tyranny, peering over his shoulder is a portrait of Abraham Lincoln. The US president writes to commend the rebel leader for defending 'the democratic principle', and the terms of the Monroe Doctrine are the driving force behind every political decision in the film. Though depicting internal Mexican affairs, *Juarez* was made with the intention of furthering Roosevelt's 'good neighbor' policy on the eve of war. Above all else, the film affirms the role of the USA as the paragon of freedom and the scourge of hierarchical oppression through the eyes of a Mexican revolutionary.

With Elia Kazan's *Viva Zapata!* (1952), this paradigm appropriating a turbulent, revolutionary Mexico emulating the freedom of the USA enters the political arena of the Cold War. Through an action-adventure format it also augurs this contemporary conceit's incorporation into the structures of the Western genre two years later with *Vera Cruz*. 'Up there they protect political refugees'; 'Up there they're a democracy'; 'Up there the government governs but with the consent of the people.' While *Viva Zapata!* ostensibly draws the viewer's gaze towards Mexico, towards its turmoil and its peasants' struggle for freedom against Porfirio Díaz, the aspirant gaze of Pablo and Aguirre is resolutely to the north in this early scene.

In *Vera Cruz* this imaginary Mexico welcomes white American adventurers stepping out from the familiar scenarios of the Western into alien territory and intervening in its revolutionary turmoil. 'Crossing the border', in the context of Korea and Vietnam, became a highly politicised act, replete with signifiers of interventionism, containment and imperialism. In Mexico, more than in any other recurring locale in the Western genre, the USA's promise of assistance, famously articulated by JFK in 1961, to 'those peoples in the huts and villages across the globe struggling to break the bonds of mass misery' is acted out on the big screen. Both Richard Slotkin and Stanley Corkin highlight the overtly allegorical nature of films influenced by *Vera Cruz*, such as *Bandido* (1956), *The Last of the Fast Guns* (1958), *The Wonderful Country* (1959) and especially *The Magnificent Seven* (1960).[22] Each portrays North Americans entering Mexican territory to offer technical and military assistance to backward yet freedom-loving peasants wishing to throw off the yoke of tyranny.

Labelling this trend the 'counterinsurgency scenario', Slotkin draws explicit parallels between Cold War-era Westerns and US governmental policy. Dwight D. Eisenhower himself, for example, evoked the Mexican Revolution as a precedent for contemporary Third World ferments, where the Cold War was being fought by proxy in response to nationalist uprisings.[23] Slotkin thus identifies in *Vera Cruz* a direct parallel with Eisenhower's contemporaneous decision to intervene in South-East Asia, and in Burt Lancaster's amoral mercenary Joe Erin a parallel of the very dilemma expressed in the 1954 Doolittle Report: 'Just how dirty, how like the enemy an American hero can become and still remain an American hero.'[24] As the chivalric ex-Confederate Ben Trane inquires: 'What gets into Americans down here?'

Certainly, as Slotkin's thesis holds, Ben Trane's incredulity reflects the problematic nature of responding to an elusive guerrilla enemy, openly articulating the contemporary dilemmas facing US military command in far-flung corners of the globe. The focus of his question above all highlights the extent to which *Vera Cruz*, though set in Mexico, is a story of US citizens acting out their own narrative from which the natives are largely marginalised. As the meek Mexican barman in the cantina is shoved aside, the conversation between Erin and Trane concerns the American Civil War, and the locals' rebellion against Maximilian is referred to as 'the civil war they've got down here'. Mexican concerns are thus subordinated to familiar frames of reference, while heterogeneous white adventurers graft archetypal Western scenarios onto the alien surroundings. The locals, meanwhile, gather in hordes, seduce with Latin charm or parade in conspicuously feudal military uniforms. The massed hordes of Juaristas who triumph with Trane's and Erin's aid at the climax are a Cold War fantasy of compliant and grateful peasants in a Third World country gladly accepting US assistance in effecting an indigenous revolution.

In the post-war era, more than in any other period of the Western's development, the ethics of violent confrontation were debated time and again in overtly contemporaneous terms pertaining to the USA's changing role in international politics. As the dominant popular means by which US national identity had been negotiated, fostered and articulated, this genre came increasingly to be co-opted into the task of redefining that very identity on the world stage. Though the frontier remained the Western's dominant cultural and political entity, the border with Mexico therefore came to play an increasingly central role in conceptualising the moral and pragmatic parameters of US foreign policy within the genre. Corkin compares John Wayne's *The Alamo* with John Sturges's *The Magnificent Seven* (both 1960) to show how the Western's traditional discourse on expansionism, nationalism and the ethics of violence offered an outlet for disparate political perspectives on contemporary crises.[25] With the intensification of nationalistic ideologies, perspectives both liberal (*The Magnificent Seven*) and conservative (*The Alamo*) saw fit to intervene in benighted regions of the globe, and crossing the border became the genre's favoured symbol for such contemporary allegory. 'The historically resonant images found in Hollywood films', writes Corkin, 'provided a map for a great many Americans that helped them navigate the stresses and contradictions of Cold War life'.[26]

By expressing misgivings over the conduct of Americans abroad, however, Ben Trane's comment also possesses an inadvertent prescience, auguring the crises to come in US identity on the world stage. This moral and political shift from the confidence of the early 1950s to the predicament brought about by 'Zippo squads' and My Lai is well illustrated by analysing the self-righteousness at the heart of *Viva Zapata!* (1952). When the counter-revolutionary leader Venustiano Carranza and his generals discuss the difficulties of defeating Zapata's guerrillas, the new president offers a brutal solution:

General: 'How can you fight an enemy you can't see?'
Carranza: 'You're looking for an army to fight. There is no army. Every man, woman and child in the state of Morelos is Zapata's army. There's only one thing to do. Wipe them all out. All of them.'
General: 'Excuse me sir, we can't find anybody to wipe out. We go there, the corn is growing, there's a fire in the hearth and no-one. We burn the house, we destroy the corn. We go back, there are new shelters and the corn is growing again.'

In 1952, before the Korean War had ended in a frustrating stalemate, such a portrayal of evil was unambiguously one against which the USA felt it could assert its own moral righteousness. *Viva Zapata!* is a significant departure from its original screenplay by Edgcumb Pinchon and Mexican socialist Gildardo Magana. Re-written by John Steinbeck, the film endorses a conception of 'freedom' in keeping with a US polity ('a man sitting safely in front of his home in the evening'). Released at the height of the 'Red Scare', this didactic allegory seeks quite openly to condemn Stalinist oppression.

While the intended message in this scene is that totalitarian regimes can try as they might to eradicate freedom but will always fail, in the following decade the USA itself would become portrayed as the perpetrator of such 'extreme prejudice' against an invisible enemy. With the hindsight of the Tet Offensive, My Lai, Napalm and Agent Orange, these words offer a chilling premonition of both the problems faced, and the solutions attempted, by US military command in the 1960s. The disbelief that the enemy survives extreme measures, the inability to locate that enemy, the shooting of women and children, the burning of villages, the destruction of crops: all of these describe the 'quagmire' of Vietnam. Tom Engelhardt writes that, during the course of the Vietnam War, the USA steadily surrendered the narrative of inexorable triumph which had informed the nation's progress since the landing of the Pilgrim Fathers. It found itself framed in the role hitherto reserved for the non-white 'savage':

> It would no longer be the enemy who left the log cabin, the fort, the town in smoldering ruins. Fire was now in the wrong hands. [...] The Vietnamese, a people subjected to a trial by fire, were visibly being transformed into victims and the Americans into savage aggressors.[27]

As young Americans marched under NLF flags and yelled confrontational slogans such as 'LBJ, LBJ, how many kids did you kill today?', the imagery of atrocity and the language of righteousness passed over to the enemy.

As the war in Vietnam progressed, this steady dismantling of the moral certitude of US imperialism was increasingly reflected in the Western genre itself. Engelhardt's central thesis – the end of the USA's 'victory culture' – argues that established models of triumphalism largely arising from the Western myth ceased to function in the new international context. The years 1945–75 thus saw 'the slow-motion collapse of a heroic war ethos', even while governmental and military decisions continued to rely on a ubiquitous narrative of triumph: 'circling the wagons', pushing back the boundaries of non-white savagery and overwhelming the enemy with technological superiority.[28]

The Western's traditional validation of violence in the name of white America had in fact been subverted for ideological ends at variance with US foreign policy from the early 1950s onwards. Increasingly, as with such films as *Broken Arrow* (1950), *The Gunfighter* (1950) and *Warlock* (1959), the Hollywood genre began to express doubt over the legitimacy of violence, as the Cold War progressed and myths of Manifest Destiny began to unravel. In the 1960s, the genre's ongoing symbolic engagement with the Mexican border in particular came under increasing scrutiny. *The Magnificent Seven* (1960), for example, is ostensibly an affirmatively interventionist parable.

Even this film, however, expresses seeds of doubt over the extent to which American warriors' participation in foreign conflicts would be welcomed by the natives, when the Seven are betrayed by the village they have come to save.

By mid-decade, the 'counterinsurgency Western' was openly questioning its own mythologies. This is most conspicuous in Sam Peckinpah's *Major Dundee* (1965) which, as a direct counterpoint to *Rio Grande*, illustrates this steady erosion of US self-righteousness. The illegal pursuit of renegade Indians over the Mexican border and the rescue of abducted children recreate John Ford's 1950 scenario to the letter, but assumptions of legitimacy and success which in the earlier film are taken for granted now become problematic. Far from the clinical strike effected by Yorke's command, Dundee and his men become inadvertently embroiled in Mexico's revolutionary turmoil. The French lancers who are brushed aside without a second thought in *Rio Grande* catch up with the American adventurers at the climax of *Major Dundee*, inflicting huge losses and forcing the survivors to flee back to Texas.

This catastrophic reversal is indicative of the sea-change in American culture, outlined by Engelhardt, which would gather pace in the late 1960s. The evacuation, in *Major Dundee*, of unambiguous righteousness motivating US adventurers abroad anticipates the cynical 'band of rogues' schema of *The Dirty Dozen* (1967) and *Kelly's Heroes* (1970). The realisation that America's moral high-ground is being steadily surrendered, meanwhile, contributes to a nihilistic ideological trajectory within the Western genre itself which would culminate in *Soldier Blue* and *Little Big Man* (both 1970).

Escalation in Vietnam thus brought about a leeching away of self-confidence and moral certitude from Hollywood's mythic structures. Simultaneously, however, opposition to that very conflict manifested itself in increasingly confrontational tones. As we shall see, in Italy another 'victory culture' was bleeding into ascendant militant circles. It is no coincidence that the emergence of bravura expressions of revolt emanating from Cinecittà coincided with this crisis in the Hollywood Western. Though diametrically opposed to the ideological assumptions of the 'counterinsurgency' narrative, the 'insurgency' sub-*filone* inherits the American variant's framework and exploits its crises. In 1966 – the very year *Quien sabe?* was released – Richard Brooks's *The Professionals* unmasks the increasing self-doubt of this Hollywood scenario. When these US adventurers in revolutionary Mexico observe the conflict first-hand, Ehrengard (Robert Ryan) asks: 'What are Americans doing in a Mexican revolution anyway?' Dolworth (Burt Lancaster[29]) replies: 'Maybe there's only one revolution, since the beginning.

The good guys against the bad guys. The question is: who are the good guys?' The remainder of this chapter will examine how radical Italian film-makers offered uncompromising answers to both of these questions.

## Straddling the Divide: The Political Inheritance

The role of a cinematic filter mediating and polemicising the antagonisms of the Cold War was therefore a burden with which the Western had long been laden by the time *Quien sabe?* opened in Italy on 2 December 1966. This film's representations of revolutionary Mexico and of a 'gringo' crossing the border, as symbols for Third World insurgency and US interventionism respectively, were merely the latest in a continuum of films employing these very conceits. In cinema at least, the concept of a 'revolutionary Mexico' had never referred exclusively to the historical events of the 1867 overthrow of Maximilian or of the 1910 uprising against Díaz. In the latter case in particular, from the moment the actuality erupted it was an ideologically-charged entity (which had been appropriated and elaborated upon by Hollywood). As I shall demonstrate, Damiani's film and its descendants seek to confront Hollywood's language of representation, reversing the objectifying gaze at the primitive subaltern. In short, they are entwined at every turn in a dialogue with the American Western.

Briefly to return to Damiani's proclamation that *Quien Sabe?* is a 'political film' rather than a Western, however, his comment highlights the fact that the film's origins simultaneously lie in a divergent cinematic tradition from that of Hollywood: one whose sense of moral purpose, ideological certitude and political determination were becoming fortified, not dismantled, by Vietnam. When Italy's foremost Marxist screenwriter Franco Solinas was asked to adapt a story by Salvatore Laurani, set during the Mexican Revolution, his brief was not to write a Western. The resulting screenplay (*Quien sabe?*) above all addressed themes central to Solinas's contemporary oeuvre. The irreconcilable dichotomy between Western civilisation and the underdeveloped Third World, the arrogance of the West's interventions in native affairs, the necessity of violent resistance against this intervention: all are explored, and to varying degrees affirmed, not only in *Quien sabe?*, but in each of Gillo Pontecorvo's *La battaglia di Algeri* (1966) and *Queimada!* (1969).

In *The Wretched of the Earth*, Frantz Fanon insists: 'Violence is a cleansing force. It frees the native from his inferiority complex and from his despair and inaction; it makes him fearless and restores his self-respect.'[30] Solinas's work in and around the 1960s engages in a meticulous (almost obsessive) dialogue with the central tenets of this seminal postcolonial treatise. In a style he and Pontecorvo dubbed 'the dictatorship of truth',[31] Solinas sought through his screenplays to analyse clashing forces at violent moments in history: the Holocaust (*Kapò*, 1959), Algerian independence (*La battaglia di Algeri*, 1966), colonial revolt in the Portuguese Antilles (*Queimada!*, 1969) and the Uruguayan Tupamaros struggle (*State of Siege*, 1973). The Mexican Revolution provided just such an historical crossroad, replete with signifiers pertaining to Western imperialism and US intervention in the Third World. The extent to which *Quien sabe?* is a constituent, and indeed central, part of this oeuvre is most conspicuous in its structural parallels with Solinas's later screenplay, *Queimada!*. De Fornari reads Damiani's film as a 'blueprint' for this subsequent, more prestigious project.[32] Indeed, it foreshadows *Queimada!*'s plot structure to the letter.

As the British *agent provocateur* Sir William Walker (Marlon Brando) prepares to board a ship bound for home, he is stabbed to death by a black porter. *Queimada!*'s final scene echoes its first, in which the Westerner entered the Third World country at this very spot and the natives who flocked around this conspicuous outsider affirmed a paternalistic imperial fantasy. The *déjà vu* which we share with Walker in the final scene, however, is distorted. As he walks towards his ship the crowds ignore him, only one street vendor attempting to attract his business. A close-up tracking shot then registers his nostalgic smile as he hears, from out-of-shot, the words 'your bags, Señor?'. The knife-wielding porter's ruse repeats the very words with which Jose Dolores, in the opening scene, affirmed the black man's subservience by offering his services to the British interloper. With Jose now dead, having been trained as a revolutionary then hunted down by Walker, the white man's counterinsurgency mission is complete. The surrogate 'Jose' who now approaches him in this nightmarish re-enactment of the opening displays none of the cordiality with which Walker was first greeted. The crowd of natives now looks on impassively as the Westerner bleeds to death on the quayside. This native gaze registers none of the aspirant admiration of the peasants in *Vera Cruz*. The nightmare, indeed, is that of the white man rendered extraneous.

The symmetry of this plot structure, as well as the liminality of the murder's location, repeat those found three years previously in *Quien sabe?*. Here, the imperialist is a US citizen, Bill Tate; the underdeveloped country in whose internal affairs he interferes, Mexico; and the site both of his arrival in the country and of his final comeuppance, Ciudad Juárez on the US/ Mexican border. Both Tate and Walker befriend then exploit a local bandit for their own mercenary ends, and both are killed at the brink of their return to Western civilisation. Walker lies bleeding next to a Royal Navy vessel – a symbol for British imperial power – which will presumably carry his body home. Chuncho, the Mexican bandit, shoots Tate as he boards a train home, itself a symbol of the technological and economic power of his home country. His instruction to Tate's limp body to 'go back to the United States' as the train pulls away sends a bloodied message back over the border that Western intervention will no longer be tolerated.

The dualistic constructions articulated by Damiani concerning the Western world and its neighbours thus accord with those expressed throughout the oeuvre of Solinas, which in turn adhere to the dichotomous world view put forward by Frantz Fanon.[33] 'The native's work is to imagine all possible methods for destroying the settler', writes Fanon. 'To the theory of the "absolute evil of the native" the theory of the "absolute evil of the settler" replies.'[34] The uncompromising rejection of the West by the native – the touchstone of Fanon's thesis – is symbolised by the demise of both Walker and Tate. Equally, both Jose Dolores and Chuncho discover the emancipating force of violent resistance by murdering a representative of the oppressor (in Jose's case a Portuguese soldier; in Chuncho's, Tate).

*Quien sabe?* was to be the progenitor of what I have dubbed the 'insurgency' variant: a group of films whose ideological premises similarly sought to affirm Fanonist tenets through the allegorical appropriation of revolutionary Mexico. All of them display the imprint of Solinas, whether directly or not. As we have seen *La resa dei conti*, released three months after *Quien sabe?* in March 1967, was adapted from a Solinas screenplay concerning the peasantry of Sardinia. The poverty-stricken Mexican Cuchillo's oppression at the hands of ruthless Western capitalists asserts an equivalent dualism to Solinas's contemporaneous screenplays. Sergio Sollima would re-use the character, without the writer's permission, in *Corri, uomo, corri* (1968). Giulio Petroni's *Tepepa* (1969), again replicating the Western-interloper-in-Mexico schema, was co-authored by Solinas and Ivan Della Mea.[35] Gillo Pontecorvo himself subsequently asked Solinas to write a film for him set in the Mexican Revolution. The resulting screenplay, *Il mercenario*, told the story of a North American criminal entering Mexico, who is hired by peasant revolutionaries to train them in techniques of modern warfare. After befriending their leader he is sentenced to death for his presumptuous exploitation of his position in the group, but the bandit leader cannot bring himself to kill his friend, setting him free. When the group is later captured and the roles reversed, the Western mercenary, now on the payroll of the army, has no hesitation in shooting the bandit. As we shall see the eventual film, directed by Sergio Corbucci (1968), was steered down a considerably more light-hearted path, and led to a sequel which replicated the original film's structure, tenor and politics: *Compañeros* (1970).

All but one of these films narrate the political awakening of a Mexican peon.[36] All of them depict an outsider or group of outsiders (either European or North American) crossing the border from the United States to interfere in Mexican affairs. All show the Mexican and an outsider forming an uneasy friendship. Finally all insist, to varying degrees, that in the face of Western imperialism armed resistance is the only answer. From a structural, thematic and political perspective, therefore, they are all the progeny of Italy's foremost radical screenwriter, and owe much to his Fanonist oeuvre.

On the other hand however the manner, outlined above, in which these films repeat, imitate and develop the plot of a founding text (that of *Quien sabe?*) is familiar from the *filone* system of popular Italian cinema. From an industrial perspective – that is, viewing this output as a commodity in a market – the group of films with which this chapter chiefly deals is indistinguishable from a sub-*filone*, relying on repeated exploitation of a successful formula.[37] Frayling's 'correction' of Will Wright's plot categories defines this very formula as the 'Zapata-Spaghetti' plot.[38] Fridlund labels these same films as a 'social bandit' narrative.[39] Both writers subordinate this group of films to the larger *filone*. In recognising the symbiotic nature of such categories, both also draw influences from other Italian Western plots on this schema, most notably identifying the arrival of the 'gringo' as one of many variations of the stranger's entrance in Frayling's 'foundation' narrative. The evolution of Solinas's Mexican scenario cannot be separated from the conveyor belts of Cinecittà and Elios studios.

There is, moreover, a considerably smaller gulf between Solinas's Fanonist polemics and not only the Italian Western, but that of Hollywood, than Damiani will allow. A focus on turbulent points in history illuminating contemporary oppositions and an emphasis on cleansing, regenerative violence form the cornerstones of Solinas's oeuvre. These, as we have seen, are also features fundamental to the Western myth from its inception. Indeed, not only must *Quien sabe?*, as a self-conscious critique and ideological subversion, be assessed in the context of the Western myth; it paradoxically returns to the genre its earnest endorsement of 'legitimate' violence. What Warshow termed its 'serious orientation' to the issues therein, so conspicuously stripped from the wider Italian Western and so rapidly becoming soured in contemporary Hollywood, is restored. An ennobling necessity in the building of a brighter future, the Western's traditional validation of killing finds an incongruous bedfellow in the postcolonial treatises of Frantz Fanon.

In the closing moments of *Quien sabe?*, the moral imperative to use lethal force for the greater good is restored, when Chuncho decides to kill

Tate. The outlaw's political awakening certainly affirms Solinas's agenda. His attempt to articulate this imperative, however, also echoes *Jesse James*'s insistence that violence is necessary ('I've got to'), attesting to the fluidity of the transposition: 'I must hurry up and kill you. [...] I must. [...] I must.' Once the physical, ideological and ethical borderline has been crossed a Fanonist, it would appear, has got to do what a Fanonist has got to do.

### Crossing the Border: The 'Insurgency' Plot

In the course of this book, we have observed numerous instances of spectatorship; some creative, others passive. Both Nando Moriconi's gaze at the silver screen and Brad Fletcher's participation in the narrative unfolding before him, for example, offer apt symbols for the processes of transcultural negotiation which surrounded their films. On the other hand, the evocative scenario cited by Ginsborg, of southerners viewing northern Italian prosperity on their television sets, depicts a more submissive and aspirant form of spectatorship.[40] Similarly, *Vera Cruz* represents the gaze of the Mexican peasant reflected back at the technologically superior Westerner. When Damiani, Petroni and Sollima contributed to the 'insurgency' variant of the Spaghetti Western, it was this last mode of representation which they set out to undermine. By manipulating the medium to give possession of the narrative to the Mexican peasant, they posit a radically oppositional notion: that the subaltern's gaze at his affluent neighbour does not express admiration, but violent and deep-seated animosity. To communicate this political message their films employ a variety of didactic techniques, which I shall detail in the following pages.

### *Dramatic Irony*

The attentive gaze of the Mexican, directed at the gringo adventurer on foreign soil, reappears near the climax of *Quien sabe?*. As Chuncho waits at Ciudad Juárez train station, he turns to face the camera, and the carefree bandit's stare becomes fixated. A point-of-view shot reveals the subject of his attention to be Bill Tate. At this moment Chuncho is dressed in Westernised finery, standing at the very periphery of the USA and preparing to leave his country behind for a life of decadent luxury. He appears every inch the compliant Mexican emulating his North American superior. The formal construction of the film, however, has by this point worked at every turn to steer Chuncho towards his final political awakening. This penultimate scene displays the film-makers' purposeful employment of signifying processes both aural and visual in its clearest terms.

As Tate pushes in at the front of a queue of peasants, we hear the conspicuously affluent Westerner ordering them to 'get out of my way'. 'But I was here first', protests a Mexican. 'Now I'm here', retorts Tate. As a reaction shot returns to Chuncho, the camera zooms in on his frowning visage, still staring in the direction of this spectacle (Figure 5), and an ominous musical refrain indicates that he, too, has heard and seen this impertinent act. The soundtrack then registers one of the locals asking 'who does this gringo think he is?'. 'It's always like this', complains another. The camera has left *Vera Cruz*'s cantina to share the native's gaze, and at this climactic point in the film's construction foregrounds the arrogance and presumptuousness of the Westerner in Mexico. Nowhere in this gaze does the US fantasy of a compliant peasantry reside. It signals neither the passive spectatorship of *Vera Cruz* nor the aspirant fascination with the USA of *Juarez* or *Viva Zapata!*. The narrative has changed hands. The North American is now the object of our gaze and, framed as the enemy, his impending demise is imperative.

For much of the film up until this point the framing of the shots, the timing of the cuts and the positioning of the film camera bestows upon the audience alone clues pertaining to Tate's real purpose in Mexico, while hiding those same pieces of information from Chuncho himself through dramatic irony. The 12 minute long[41] denouement steadily reverses this pattern, revealing the truth to the Mexican hero piece-by-piece. In this climactic scene, he takes possession of the camera's viewpoint himself, at last attaining a consciousness of the events which surround him equal to that of both the viewer, and Bill Tate.

Figure 5    The Mexican's gaze is no longer deferential as *Quien sabe?* (1966) draws to a close. Image by kind permission of Surf Film/Argent Films Ltd.

When Tate presumptuously pushes into the front of a ticket queue in the opening scene, foreshadowing his identical act in the last, we literally see at the very start what it takes Chuncho the entire course of the narrative to see for himself: that this American's presence in Mexico is both arrogant and disdainful of local culture. 'Do you like Mexico?', a peon boy asks at the start. 'No, not very much', replies the gringo. As his train then heads into the Mexican interior, his disgust at the breast-feeding native mother who sits next to him is made obvious as he wipes his shoulder with a handkerchief.

Two zoom shots – one of Tate watching a Mexican firing squad at the beginning; the other, studied above, of Chuncho watching Tate at the end – indicate the contrasting perspectives employed in *Quien sabe?*. The gaze of the North American and that of the Mexican are aimed at one another and act as book-ends for the film's political exposition. The opening scene, indeed, is juxtaposed with the last, since they take place at the same railway station but are shot from opposing perspectives. *Quien sabe?* opens with a fast-moving montage, as four revolutionaries are marched up against a wall and executed, one of their number defiantly shouting insurgent slogans as he is shot. The crowd gathering to watch largely comprises peon women and children, but no sooner have the firing squad pulled their triggers than the camera zooms in on Tate's face, watching the grisly spectacle with an impassive detachment.

The rapid editing and the cacophony of sound emanating from the peasants in this opening sequence evoke a frenetic perceptual ambience in keeping with the exuberance, exoticism and danger of a cinematic 'Mexican Revolution' lifted directly from Hollywood. Tate's position as a detached observer therefore mirrors our own, and invites the viewer to accept him as the primary point of contact with the on-screen action. The cutting and the soundtrack combine actively to encourage this reading. Immediately after Tate's reaction shot we cut back to the firing squad with what now appears, by virtue of its positioning in the sequence, to be a point-of-view shot from his perspective. A voice-over then affirms the impression of an exotically turbulent culture: 'Scenes of this kind were commonplace, as the various factions tried to dominate the others and bring order out of chaos.'

By the time the camera tracks Tate's progress across the railway line as he boards his train, the viewer is therefore predisposed to view Mexico through recourse to the familiar tropes of the Western genre. Tate is dressed in conspicuously urban clothes against an alien cultural milieu of sombreros, peasant overalls and *Rurales*. The first sign of Chuncho's gang, meanwhile, assimilates them into this 'Mexican Revolution' backdrop, when shots ring out from the hills surrounding the munitions train. *Rurales* drop dead but, with no sign of any snipers, the guerrillas are disembodied, ethereal and at one with the landscape, framing Mexico as a recognisably dangerous and alien environment for the Westerner.

The ensuing exposition reveals to the audience a series of clues which, while not fully explaining the nature of Tate's counterinsurgency mission, clearly indicate that he has a hidden agenda. In each case, Chuncho is blind to the information, either absent from the scene, out-of-shot or with his back turned. Firstly, as the train pulls away to escape the ambush, the camera follows Tate as he climbs onto the engine car, kills the driver, stops the train, and handcuffs himself to fool the gang into thinking that he is a prisoner. Later, once he has joined the bandits, Tate operates a machine gun to kill soldiers pursuing a messenger from the revolutionary General Elias. When Chuncho takes his rifle to finish the fight in single combat, we view his heroic act from Tate's point-of-view behind the machine gun, as the bandit runs away from us. As soon as Chuncho has exited the frame and is otherwise engaged, Tate blithely turns the machine gun on the messenger. He then searches the messenger's body to find money brought to pay for armaments and surreptitiously hurls the coins over a cliff. The dramatic irony of Chuncho's meticulous, and vain, search for the money in the background of a deep-focus shot places us cognitively, and literally, closer to Tate, as he nonchalantly reloads the gun in the foreground.

The first time the film offers Chuncho a chance to share a clue with us is when, searching Tate's valise for quinine, he finds a single golden bullet. Momentarily, as he examines it, a close-up hints at the Mexican's curiosity but the tense background music which briefly accompanies this shot gives a further clue to the audience alone, and the bullet is put back in the bag. Chuncho's curiosity later resurfaces, when he asks why the bullet is there. His back, however, is turned when Tate's expression shows brief alarm, which is registered in centre-frame close-up by the camera. By the time Chuncho has turned around, the gringo has regained his composure and deflects suspicion by explaining: 'It brings me good luck.' Finally, when the pair at last arrive at Elias's mountain encampment, Tate's agenda becomes clear to us before it does to Chuncho. As the American loads the golden bullet into his rifle and takes aim, the camera is once again placed behind him, looking down on the camp and his target – the back of General Elias's head – from his perspective.

From the moment Tate fires his rifle, however, the viewer's privileged position of aloofness over Chuncho begins to diminish. Firstly, though we see the gringo taking aim, a reverse shot emphasising his target to be Elias, and a final shot showing Tate pulling the trigger, we do not see the general

being hit by the bullet. Instead, the sound of the gunshot announces a cut
back to Chuncho and his brother Santo. We therefore hear the gunfire at the
same time as they do, and when another shot occurs immediately afterwards,
we do not see who has fired it. Our hero once again has his back turned,
this time to his brother, but turns around in time to see what we cannot. As
Santo's grasping hand enters at the left of the frame, it is revealed to us that
the second gunshot was not, as we expected, Santo shooting Chuncho. It
was instead aimed at Santo himself.

As the first instance of the hero possessing a privileged epistemological
position over the audience, albeit for a split second, this timing is significant.
From this moment onwards Chuncho's understanding of events begins
incrementally to attain a level on a par with the viewer. When the golden
bullet is paraded to the gathered crowd, it is revealed in close-up from the
right hand side of the frame, less than a minute after Santo's dying hand
had entered from the left. Now, Chuncho's back is not turned. A close-up
reaction shot shows that Tate's betrayal is immediately apparent to him as he
looks up to the mountain top, where Tate had been hiding, in disbelief. He
also hears that 'Señor Elias is dead' at the same time as we do. Meanwhile,
revelations which Chuncho sees directly are occurring for us only as they
enter the camera's field-of-view, denying the audience prior knowledge of
their presence.

As Tate arrives back at Ciudad Juárez, the camera lingers to reveal
Chuncho sleeping on a bench, merging seamlessly with beggars. When the
Mexican draws a pistol and follows the gringo into the building, it is now
Tate who has his back turned to events. Chuncho's revelatory gaze in the
train station is also directed at the American's back, offering an apt symbol
for the fact that it is now Tate, rather than Chuncho, who is ignorant of
what is occurring around him. The bandit, on the other hand, is increasingly
thirsty for knowledge as the climax approaches. As the two men talk in
Tate's hotel room, he asks question after question, enlightening him ever
further: 'It is a trick maybe?'; 'Why did you murder Elias?'; 'My brother, why
did you kill him?' In the very final moments of the film, Tate explains his
initial ruse of travelling on munitions trains and masquerading as a prisoner
to get close to Elias, and Chuncho at last knows everything we do. It is only
at this point, at the very moment when the last piece of information has
been ascertained from Tate and the Mexican's eyes are fully opened, that he
announces: 'You've been a very good friend to me haven't you? […] It's a
shame I have to kill you.'

### Performance Style

Such didacticism infuses the 'insurgency' variant, and goes beyond cinematic technique, for the manner in which these films are performed also seeks to guide the viewer into acceptance of the trend's political imperative. To illustrate this point, I shall briefly compare two of the most memorable portrayals in the films under consideration in this chapter: Tomas Milian as Cuchillo in *Corri, uomo, corri* and Gian Maria Volonté as Chuncho in *Quien sabe?*. The former elicits sympathy for the peasant figure by placing himself alongside the audience; the latter further demands that we question the representational norms of the Hollywood Western. Both performances, by toying with both the medium and the cognitive position of the viewer, are testament to an emphasis on their films' own status as text and artifice. They frequently interrupt the narrative to deny an audience passive acceptance of character or plot.

After Tomas Milian's Italian debut in Mauro Bolognini's *La notte brava* (1959), the early to mid 1960s saw the Cuban actor work for giants of 'art' cinema – Bolognini again (*Il bell'Antonio* (1960) and *Madamigella di Maupin* (1966)), Visconti (*Boccaccio '70* (1962)), Pasolini (*Ro.Go.Pa.G.* (1963)) – as well as appearing in Carol Reed's epic, *The Agony and the Ecstasy* (1965). Whilst working on such critically acclaimed projects, he was introduced to the world of popular Italian cinema, with which his career would become chiefly identified, in Sergio Corbucci's wartime comedy *Il giorno più corto* (1963). Milian's debut in the Western *filone* came in Eugenio Martín's *El precio de un hombre* (1966): an Italo-Spanish co-production in which he played an amoral, psychologically tormented Mexican outlaw on the run. His starring role in Giulio Questi's *Se sei vivo, spara!* (1967) positioned him as an understated observer of the horrors unfolding amongst the corrupt townsfolk, while in *Quattro dell'apocalisse* (1975), Milian portrayed the deranged sadist Chaco. Here, dressed as Charles Manson out West, drugging, raping and terrorising a group of drop-outs, the actor's Method training comes to the fore in a brooding, intense and sinister performance.

Milian was nothing if not versatile, for the exaggeratedly loud role of Cuchillo required him to portray the polar opposite of such characterisation. We have already seen that this character occupies a position of negotiation between the audience and the on-screen action, occasionally observing the narrative from our level. Of course, *La resa dei conti* (as well as *Faccia a faccia*) revolves around the awakening, not of a Mexican, but of a Westerner, whose political and moral choices define Sollima's agenda. The trickster figure of Cuchillo, while occupying a privileged position, is in essence a plot device, and facilitator for the conversion of the Everyman.

When Sollima reprised this character in *Corri, uomo, corri* (1968), however, he not only placed the peasant at the centre of the plot; he elevated the character's detachment from the narrative to a parodic extreme. When Penny and Dolores wrestle on the ground, for example, Cuchillo's role as a mediator between the audience and the action (be it as Robin Goodfellow or Arlecchino) is paraded openly. As the two women grapple in the dirt, refusing to listen to his pleas that they stop, he accepts defeat and takes a seat to watch the show. Resignedly, the character points a hand towards the spectacle and looks to one side in amused detachment, clearly confiding in an imaginary fellow spectator (Figure 6). Except, of course, the fellow spectator is not imaginary. Milian later speculated that his peasant roles were popular because 'the Third World figure could in some sense have also been an Italian sub proletarian'.[42] Cuchillo is now not only on a cognitive level with the audience; he is among them, and consciously so.

As *Corri, uomo, corri* opens, Cuchillo is the same poverty-stricken, opportunistic vagabond we left at the end of *La resa dei conti*, entering an empty house to scavenge tortillas. When he arrives in the village the film's theme tune peters out, only to be taken up immediately by Cuchillo himself, humming and whistling surreptitiously as he lurks behind the door. Continually, throughout the course of the film, the character disrupts the audience's illusion of viewing an inviolable narrative through such extra-diegetic performance. His repeated singing of the theme tune in particular effects a peculiar displacement. This exuberant, uplifting Latin music is played during the credit sequence: a segment of the film for the audience's eyes only. It also reappears in the background of emotionally-charged scenes, such as when Cuchillo frees the revolutionary poet Ramirez from

Figure 6    Cuchillo takes a break to join the audience in *Corri, uomo, corri* (1968). By kind permission of Blue Underground Inc.

prison. In general, such a score's traditional function is to aid the absorption of the audience into acceptance of the fictional world presented on-screen. That Cuchillo is aware of this music's presence breaks the 'fourth wall' to an extent beyond that of Sollima's previous films. His energetic performance, moreover, is that of a court jester. His exaggerated facial tics (what Frayling dubs 'toothsome charisma'[43]), his loud exclamations, and his guileful clowning are elevated above even his previous incarnation in *La resa dei conti*.

In a slightly different vein, the schizophrenic performance of Gian Maria Volonté in *Quien sabe?*, by communicating Chuncho's conversion from mercenary bandit to committed revolutionary, continues the didacticism we have already seen at work in the film's camerawork. Volonté – one of Italy's foremost militant actors – insisted on the importance of Brechtian alienation in cinema, theatre and television to comment on and expose the mechanisms of modern industrial society.[44] While remaining a member of the PCI during the 1960s, Volonté was on the radical left of the party, and lent his support to the increasingly militant ARCI (Italian Recreational and Cultural Association). His theatre productions gained international publicity (*The Times* recording in 1965 that a group of actors led by Volonté evaded a police cordon in Rome after authorities suspended their production of Rolf Hochhuth's *The Representative* over its accusations of Pope Pius XII's complicity with Nazism[45]). In later years Volonté took to performing on the streets of Rome to provoke such reaction from the authorities. Through militant cinema he aimed to unite workers throughout Italy by filming in occupied factories (*La tenda in piazza* (1970)) and by offering counter-information to official versions of contemporary events. *12 Dicembre* (1972) was made in response to the Piazza Fontana bombing in Milan in December 1969, refuting mainstream media analysis blaming left-wing revolutionaries.

Volonté dismissed his work for Sergio Leone as a mere rung on his career ladder, and expressed doubt over the efficacy of Westerns for disseminating his political views. He maintained, however, that *Quien sabe?*, as a pertinent allegory for CIA intervention in Latin America, remained an exception.[46] Certainly, his performance as Chuncho is a more complex and intertextual one than those of Ramon Rojo in *Per un pugno di dollari* or Indio in *Per qualche dollaro in più*. Eager to steer his career down a more politically-committed path, Volonté turned down Leone's offer of playing Tuco in *Il buono, il brutto, il cattivo* to take the role.

When Chuncho first appears over the lip of a hill, beating a drum and yelling at the top of his voice, he is presented as every bit the alcoholic, virile and stupid Mexican bandit of Hollywood stereotypes, from *Broncho Billy and the Greaser* (1914) to *In Old Arizona* (1929) and *Viva Villa!* (1934).

Adorned in sombrero and gun-belts and laughing manically, he is concerned only with making money out of the Revolution, but lacks the intelligence to be able to add up his earnings. After a successful assault on a governmental fortress he is mostly concerned with getting drunk, and when he hears of San Miguel's liberation his primary motivation in rushing to help is that there will be women there. This comic-opera *bandido* persona is, however, one side of a dialectic, expressed through Volonté's performance style. In jarring contrast, his various moments of political revelation are marked by a subdued, contemplative calm.

This bipolar performance goes beyond naturalistic representation of emotion, motivation or characterisation. The pendulum swing occurs in correlation to which pole – bandit or revolutionary – is in the ascendancy at a given moment. In the penultimate scene, for example, immediately prior to Chuncho's revelatory gaze at Tate in the train station, the mercenary is set to leave the Revolution behind to enjoy his blood money. He turns around to admire a well-dressed woman, and with a smirk quips: 'Hey baby.' Behind his back we can see Tate walking to the front of the queue, ready to repeat the presumptuous intrusion to which we were party at the film's opening. Once again, Chuncho's back is turned to the truth and his demeanour is jovial, but as he turns around to face Tate, meeting the reverse camera angle in close-up, his final revelation is signalled by his features suddenly dropping. Far from the grinning mercenary of a few seconds previously, this gaze at the Western interloper anticipates the stillness, determination and menace of the black porters who stare into the camera in the closing moments of *Queimada!*[47]

The primary target of this portrayal is genre convention itself. Volonté's performance is resolutely intertextual, in turn adhering to, then eschewing, conventional depictions of Mexican bandits inherited from US cinema. Given the actor's Brechtian background, it seems fitting that his performance works to alienate the audience from accepted patterns, exposing the stereotyped norms of Hollywood's 'Mexico'.

### Racial Masks, Dual Identities

Nowhere is the 'insurgency' variant's engagement with the representational practices of Hollywood more evident than in Giulio Petroni's *Tepepa* (1968), in which direct quotations of Elia Kazan's *Viva Zapata!* (1952) place the audience at a remove from the on-screen action. While Tepepa is ostensibly a fictional character, Tomas Milian's eponymous hero continually quotes Emiliano Zapata's radical demand for peasant emancipation: 'Tierra y libertad' ('land and freedom'). Moreover, the details of Tepepa's life explicitly locate him as a representation of Zapata: a peasant from the Morelos region who fights for Francisco Madero to overthrow Porfirio Díaz, before becoming disillusioned and declaring war on the new government.

When Tepepa asserts his dissatisfaction with land reforms he is revealed from amongst his fellow peons, who part to show him standing defiantly, facing the governmental representatives and the camera. This exact shot construction occurs in *Viva Zapata!*, when the hero refuses to accept Díaz's promises. Both Marlon Brando's Zapata and Milian's Tepepa subsequently confront Madero to argue with his demand that the guerrillas disarm now that the Revolution is won. The latter quotes the former almost verbatim:

> Zapata: 'Who will enforce the laws once we have them?'
> Madero: 'The regular army. The police.'
> Zapata: 'They're the ones we just fought and beat!'

> Tepepa: 'I took this rifle from the army, to fight against the army, and now I have to give it back to the army. Who won: the revolution or the army?'

Kazan's film closes with Zapata's followers refusing to believe that the hero is dead and looking up to the mountains. A panoramic shot then shows the hero's white horse standing on an outcrop, symbolising his posthumous apotheosis. *Tepepa*, similarly closing on the hero's death, superimposes his laughing face over his band of guerrillas and cuts to a silhouetted *bandido* on horseback in the mountains.

Milian himself identified in the relationship between the two films a critique of Hollywood's ethnic representation:

> You know, Latin Americans are always dirty little spics, and I'm still a spic, but I have made of the spic a hero. [...] Zapata, Mexican, is played by Marlon Brando, American. He's not a spic, he's Marlon Brando interpreting a spic.[48]

As a Cuban, Milian implies, he is in a position to subvert Hollywood's portrayals which frequently homogenised ethnic groupings and cast white actors in those non-white roles which demanded complexity or hero-status. As is demonstrated vividly in *Vera Cruz* and *The Alamo*, Mexicans often formed a picturesque but homogeneous backdrop for a drama in which complex white characters, both fallible and heroic, enacted their own story. Tom Engelhardt summarises the roles commonly given to the non-white ethnic 'Other' in Hollywood's traditional generic structures: 'The invisible, the evil, the dependent, and the expendable.'[49] He observes the following of cases where the 'native' is on the side of the Americans:

> A grateful nonwhite face would be there to reflect back to the audience American (or Western) generosity and humanity. [...] Such movies added up to a vast minstrel show in which the Other was represented by a limited set of red-, black-, brown-, or yellow-face masks created by, and if important enough, worn by whites.[50]

In *Vera Cruz*, *The Alamo*, *The Magnificent Seven* and *The Professionals*, the Westerners entering Mexico retain both the cinematic point-of-view and the heterogeneous complexity required to retain the audience's sympathy and interest. As we have seen, their gaze at the backward culture south of the border is a gaze at their own country's perception of itself on the world stage.

Common to the 'insurgency' plot is a reversal of this pattern, turning the analytical gaze back onto the gringo and refusing to affirm the pro-American perceptions of the native frequently propagated by Hollywood. In *Quien sabe?*, for example, Tate's sense of alienation steadily increases, so that it is he who becomes an objectified 'Other'. Throughout the film, Chuncho refers to him as 'Niño' ('little boy'), turning the common schema of infantile natives and paternalistic gringos on its head. Additionally, while Chuncho's characterisation is, as we have seen, complex, the American is a cold-hearted gringo stereotype (a role, it must be said, which is aided by Lou Castel's somewhat wooden performance). Tate's role as an ethnic outsider also means that he comes face to face with hostile attitudes towards his nationality. A Mexican officer laughs derisively at him, shouting: 'American! Not too much heart, but plenty of dollars', while Raimundo is reluctant to trust him because 'the United States hosts the rival forces. [...] His country helps the enemy'.

*Corri, uomo, corri*, too, enacts conspicuous ethnic reversals. While many of the set-pieces, as we shall see, self-consciously echo those of its prequel (*La resa dei conti*), the structure is inverted. The earlier film begins in Texas, and narrates the gradual political awakening of a North American as he enters Mexico. The sequel opens in Mexico, where the ex-sheriff Nathaniel Cassidy is already a conspicuous outsider and the narrative is from Cuchillo's perspective from the start. Our peasant hero then heads for Texas, and the first sign that he has reached the border is when a polite request for help is met with 'I ain't your amigo, dirty Mexican. Get outta here'. In this film it is

Texas, not Mexico, which is represented both as a threatening, alien 'Other' and as a refuge for outlaws on the run.

In *Tepepa*, an early scene shows the white man being both caricatured by the film-maker and homogenised by the hero. When Tepepa calls Dr. Henry Price 'Americano' and refers to drinking coffee, the outsider replies, pompously: 'I am English, and I drink tea.' Unconvinced, Tepepa muses: 'Americano, inglese, tutti biondi!' (translated idiomatically, 'you all look the same'). Likewise, the fat, avaricious North American capitalist Mr. Rosenblum in *Compañeros* is testament to a very different Mexican perception of the USA from that hopefully expounded in *Vera Cruz*.

As befits this reactive, wilfully subversive sub-category, these ethnic reversals ostensibly offer acerbic critiques of Hollywood's representational practices. In focusing on the ethnic 'authenticity' of his portrayal, however, Milian overlooks two key factors: firstly, the extent to which issues of miscegenation, hybridity and the donning of ethnic masks are central to the very milieu from which this militant sub-category emerges (the Italian Western *filone* itself); and secondly, the fact that the 'insurgency' variant is inextricably tied to these genre conventions, as well as those of Hollywood. Maggie Günsberg's study of 'masquerade' in the Italian Western highlights the constantly unstable nature, not only of masculine prowess, but of ethnic representations evident throughout this multi-national *filone*. The blond-haired Sergei Kowalski of *Il mercenario*, for example, is referred to as 'Americano', yet is Polish, and played by an Italian. The Mexican bandit Chuncho, too, is played by an Italian, while both Tuco in *Il buono, il brutto, il cattivo* and Juan in *Giù la testa* – again, Mexican characters – are played by North Americans.[51]

Moreover, a clear precedent to the disorienting ethnic reversals found in *Quien sabe?* and *Tepepa* is discernible within the wider genre in Duccio Tessari's *Il ritorno di Ringo* (1965). Here, an American soldier returns from the Civil War to find his home town taken over and oppressed by a group of Mexicans. The cowed sheriff refuses to stand up to the bandits, who have annexed this little bit of the USA as Mexican territory, protesting: 'I'm not a Mexican. I'm an American: an inferior race.' Outside the saloon hangs a sign displaying the words: 'No entry for dogs, gringos and beggars.'

As we have seen, the Italian Western emerged from processes of transatlantic borrowing evident across post-war Italian culture. They re-formulate the symbols of US popular culture in a similar process to that dubbed by James Clifford 'cultural import-export'.[52] The transcultural nature of this *filone* leads Dimitris Eleftheriotis to the following conclusion:

[It is] a phenomenon closely linked to the process of globalization. This not only follows accounts of Hollywood as global cinema but also highlights the accelerated mobility of cultural products around the world and their increasing detachment from national contexts.[53]

Perched on a borderline between two cultures, the Italian Western *filone* itself is therefore ably symbolised by the political border between the USA and Mexico. The near ubiquity of precisely this setting leads Günsberg to identify 'a metaphor for other types of border crossing between the various social categories defining identity'.[54] The frequently porous nature of the border in the Italian Western, indeed, reflects an equally unstable ethnic identity among many of its central characters. The blonde-haired, pale-skinned hero of *Il ritorno di Ringo*, for example, 'blacks up' to infiltrate the Mexican gang. *Per un pugno di dollari* is set entirely on the Mexican side of the border, yet both the locale and the protagonists are hybridised. The deserted town of San Miguel is in thrall to two families: the Rojos (Mexican) and the Baxters (American). When the action moves to the border itself, the regiment of 'Yankees' turns out to be Mexicans in disguise. The hero, though dressed in a poncho and riding a mule, is an American.

Moreover, Eleftheriotis's observation underlines the extent to which this 'globalised' Western locale is no longer replete with US-specific signifiers. While border crossings are frequent in the Italian West, rarely does the act of crossing itself have serious implications for the characters. This is in marked contrast to the ideologically-laden crossings to be found in post-war Hollywood, particularly those in the 'counterinsurgency scenario'. The (half Mexican) eponymous hero of Corbucci's *Johnny Oro* (1966), for example, crosses the boundary line at will, his sole aim in life being to collect bounties from either side of the divide. Leone's *Per qualche dollaro in più* (1965) presents an increasingly surreal spatiality which precludes a clear geographical comprehension. The action begins in Tucumcari, New Mexico, and switches to Indio's jail break on the Mexican side of the border. The three main protagonists then meet at El Paso, on the border itself, but from this point onwards the specificity diminishes. The denouement occurs in a town called 'Agua Caliente', which Indio says is east of El Paso. This would place it in Texas, yet it would appear that this whitewashed, alien settlement familiar to Indio and his *bandidos* is in Mexico. The only real Mexican Agua Caliente is near Guadalajara, 800 miles south of El Paso. This ambiguity speaks volumes. Leone's picaresque tale renders the political border of little consequence, and crossing it so common that the narrative ceases to register the act.

This is not to say that border crossings go universally unnoticed in the *filone*; far from it. In addition to *Il ritorno di Ringo* and amongst many other examples, *Una pistola per Ringo* (1965), *Sette pistole per i MacGregor* (1966) and *Django* (1966) narrate groups of Mexican bandits causing trouble on US soil. *Texas, addio* (1966), *Da uomo a uomo* (1967) and *Indio Black, sai che di dico: sei un gran figlio di…* (1970) all depict North American gunfighters crossing into a conspicuously feudal Mexico. Furthermore, as is vividly displayed in the character of *Django*'s General Hugo, the *filone* as a whole does very little to eschew retrograde stereotypes of cackling, dirty and stupid Mexican *bandidos*.

*Texas, addio* is the closest this *filone* comes to replicating the political dynamics of Hollywood's forays south of the border. Here, a Mexican revolutionary pleads with the heroes to help the cause because 'you two are Americans. You're both free. You went through this already. You understand'. Far from engaging with the specific political contexts of the Cold War, however, this film typifies what Eleftheriotis terms 'a system of objects detached from their cultural and historical specificity […] an exotic background and location for the travelling outsiders of the spaghetti'.[55] *Texas, addio*, indeed, merely serves to underline the inherently hybridised nature of the Italian Western. Its blatant pastiche of both *Vera Cruz* and *The Magnificent Seven* operates solely on a textual level. It apes the popular Hollywood paradigm yet, emptied of the specific cultural imperative of formulating US national identity, contains none of the political or allegorical engagement of the 'counterinsurgency' Western.

We have seen that the wider Italian Western *filone* retained the Hollywood genre's proclivity towards violent spectacle while draining it of its moral imperative. So too, the Mexican border, emptied of the specific ideologies of US expansionism, becomes in the Roman 'West' merely a conveniently Latin setting for the hordes of Spanish extras. As is also the case with the treatment of violence, however, the same cannot be said of the 'insurgency' variant. Here both the specific political and allegorical contexts of the Cold War and the symbolic significance of the border are restored. Crossing, indeed approaching, this boundary line once again becomes an act with serious consequences for a protagonist's identity. In the opening scenes of *Quien sabe?* (and therefore of the 'insurgency' variant itself) Chuncho, though yet to undergo his awakening, signals the impending replenishment of this signifier, when he and Tate first meet. Pretending to be a captive, Tate lies that he is being taken to 'the frontier', but the bandit corrects him: 'The border?' Though the gringo cannot see the difference between the USA's own mythic boundary and this political and international one, the Mexican sees the border as the point at which two cultures meet. By the end of the film Chuncho comes to realise the dichotomous and incompatible nature of those opposing entities.

Slotkin identifies a recurrent motif in post-war Hollywood which depicts Mexico as a dangerous yet alluring mythic space, confronting the Westerner with a primitive alternative to the corruption of industrial civilisation in such films as *The Treasure of Sierra Madre* (1948).[56] The influence of this conceit on the Italian 'West' can be seen most vividly in *La resa dei conti*. Here, Sollima presents Mexico as an arena in which Corbett's political awakening is facilitated, and the closer the chase gets to the border the more his moral code collapses. A monk warns him: 'When you cross over that line, you'll be as bad as [Cuchillo] is. It becomes a personal matter, and you know it.' Mexico is Corbett's Purgatory, which opens his eyes to the machine which had deceived him. Though the film begins by narrating the chase from the ethnocentric perspective of the Westerner, this is progressively dismantled as the narrative draws nearer to Mexico. When Corbett crosses the border, he is an alienated outsider, amongst a bewildering array of sombreros, whitewashed walls, Catholic pageantry and Day of the Dead trinkets. In this film, however, despite Cuchillo's interventions, Mexico remains an exotic, alien territory offering both moral regeneration and the delectation of difference to the Westerner. The dramatic irony, the point-of-view and the intended political message are returned to Corbett at the climax.

The figure of the lone 'outsider' is both common to the American Western and ubiquitous to the Italian version. The detachment of the hero from the community defines Wright's 'classical' and 'vengeance' plots and *Shane*, as we have seen, exerted a significant influence on the development of what Frayling terms the 'foundation' narrative. Alienated gringos arriving in a predominantly Mexican milieu pervade the *filone* to such an extent that the conspicuousness of Bill Tate, Jonathan Corbett, Dr. Henry Price and Nathaniel Cassidy is mostly inherited from the industrial context of Cinecittà and Elios.

It is however in the cultural miscegenation and ethnic instability inherent to the *filone* that the 'insurgency' variant most purposefully utilises its generic inheritance for political purposes. Itself a by-product of contact zones between two cultural poles, the Italian Western makes, in de Certeau's phrase, 'innumerable and infinitesimal transformations of and within the dominant cultural economy'.[57] By restoring the dichotomous nature of the border, as a dividing line between opposing cultural forces, this militant sub-*filone* seeks to apply its inherited hybridity to the postcolonial theories of Frantz Fanon. The bipolar performance of Volonté in particular symbolises the psychological 'dual identity' imposed upon the native in colonial society which, Fanon writes, 'forces the people it dominates to ask themselves the question constantly: "In reality, who am I?"'.[58]

In both *Quien sabe?* and *Tepepa*, a Mexican finds himself alienated as he approaches the border. Both Chuncho and Paquito are taken to a Ciudad Juárez hotel by the gringo, from where they are to be 'Westernised' in the USA. Both find themselves dressed in Western clothes[59] at the periphery of their nation, and both are given money and infantilised by their companion (less surprisingly in Paquito's case, since he is a child, but more so in Chuncho's, since it has been he paternalistically calling Tate 'Niño' throughout the film). When both then tear off their new clothes in favour of peon overalls and flee to join the Revolution, they head back into the Mexican interior, rejecting the pull of the West. As Fanon writes: 'Going back to your own people means to become a dirty wog, to go native as much as you can, to become unrecognizable, and to cut off those wings that before you had allowed to grow.'[60]

### Third Worldist Politics

This adherence to the tenets of Fanonism of course brings us back to the political agenda of Franco Solinas, and situates the 'insurgency' narrative firmly in the political context of the 1960s. The American Western had, as we have seen, frequently been co-opted into the task of explaining the need for conflict in a Cold War context. Mexico had offered an efficient surrogate therein for Third World communities to set against the military might of the USA. In Italy, film-makers and actors with an ideological revulsion for US imperialism saw the subversion of this very paradigm as a suitable framework within which to assert the legitimacy of armed resistance to the American war machine. As Damiani was at pains to emphasise, these films send both the events and the audience's sympathy south of the border. The 'insurgency' variant, however, also crosses a political and ethical boundary.

While the RSA narrative, and *Faccia a faccia* in particular, seeks to expose inherent violence and latent fascism within Western society, the films stop short of openly advocating a violent response. In *Quien sabe?* and the movement which it inspired, however, not only is the objectifying gaze of America at its exuberant neighbour turned on its head; the paradigm of the 'counterinsurgency' Western itself is appropriated to expound contemporary political perspectives in radical and violent opposition to American imperialism.

The aggressive cult of 'Third Worldism' became increasingly *de rigueur* amongst the ascendant European New Left towards the end of the

1960s. This vogue for viewing world politics from the perspective of the 'Wretched of the Earth' gave rise to a radical opposition to the perceived oppressive 'system' and offered a model for action by valorising guerrilla resistance movements across the globe. Jeremy Varon writes that, by the end of the 1960s, isolated and facing overwhelming state power, many New Left activists felt the need to secure 'a body of theory or a set of narrative resources – a model or paradigm for change – ensuring that revolution was indeed possible'.[61] In the implausible successes of guerrilla cells against the US military in South-East Asia appeared an answer. Theoretical models drawn from the writings of Mao, Fanon and Debray, amongst others, thus provided militant extra-parliamentary movements with notional platforms upon which to launch domestic insurgency. After October 1967, Che Guevara's death provided a martyr around whom to valorise the cause and call for 'two, three, many Vietnams'.

Arguing that the industrial proletariat had become integrated into capitalism and had ceased to be the class of world revolution, Herbert Marcuse saw 'outcast' groupings as the solution: in the West itself, urban blacks, students, the unemployed; across the world, the disparate guerrilla movements fighting US military might. Furthermore theories such as Debray's stressed that the guerrilla cell, or *foco*, need not wait for the preconditions for revolution, but instead could hasten the crisis in capitalism through propagandist actions. This invited militants in Europe and the USA to go ahead with insurrectionary activities, despite their living in advanced Western nations. This was a far cry from PCI leader Palmiro Togliatti's *Via italiana al socialismo* ('Italian road to socialism') policy of wooing the middle classes in a broad alliance. Many young activists on the left of the party were attracted to the more aggressive response to American imperialism.

Gérard Chaliand writes that European New Left youth created an amalgam of reference points to define its historical influences: '[It] absorbed pell-mell into its imagination fragments of the Spanish Civil War, the October Revolution, the resistance to Nazism, the Mexican Revolution, the Long March and Che Guevara.'[62] The historical position of Mexico in this list took on a contemporary political significance all of its own on 2 October 1968. Nine weeks of student strikes in Mexico City culminated with the Tlatelolco Massacre as the world's eyes were turning towards the city for the Summer Olympics. Mexico's position as both a representative of Latin American insurgency and the site of incendiary political movements was therefore particularly highly charged amongst the European Far Left. This political milieu was one with which Solinas, Sollima, Corbucci, Petroni and Damaini were demonstrably sympathetic. Allied to the established iconography of the Italian Western, the very concept of 'Third Worldism', indeed, provided a pre-existing mythology within which their films could advocate armed resistance. The development of Tomas Milian's Cuchillo persona clearly illustrates this notion.

As Cuchillo stands facing his Western tormentor, cross-cut shots flash before our eyes for two whole minutes while Ennio Morricone's majestic score builds to a climax. The Almerían setting, the cinematographic style and the prolonged showdown place us firmly in the generic conventions of the Italian Western, but the weaponry on display is curiously ill-matched. The fetishism for firearms displayed by Colonel Mortimer in *Per qualche dollaro in più* was merely the start of a love affair within this *filone* with an increasingly ingenious machinery of death. Johnny Oro's golden pistol, Django's coffin-cum-machine gun, Sabata's customised Derringer, Sartana's deadly church organ: this litany of exuberantly lethal technology barely scratches the surface of this fascination evident throughout the Roman West. It is, therefore, a curious sight to behold that Cuchillo faces his enemy's six-gun with nothing more than a throwing-knife. The film's intended symbolism is hardly subtle, but Sergio Sollima saw fit to offer guidance all the same: 'It could be the story of an American Green Beret against a member of the Viet Cong.'[63] The technological superiority of the North American interloper in the Third World counts for little when faced with native ingenuity. So ends *La resa dei conti*, and so perishes the villainous Shep, Cuchillo's knife protruding from his forehead.

In studying the numerous 'Django' films which proliferated in the aftermath of Corbucci's runaway success of 1966, Frayling applies Umberto Eco's theory concerning the comic-book hero Superman to the development (or lack of it) of this icon of the Italian West. By breaking down the sense that time has passed between episodes, writes Eco, and by denying the character permanent relationships or changes in outlook, a new story is started 'from zero' each week. In order to maintain a readership's interest, the comic-book writer bestows this 'inconsumable hero' with 'recognisable personality traits, idiosyncrasies, or "tics", which "permit us to find an old friend in the character portrayed"'.[64]

When Cuchillo resurfaces in *Corri, uomo, corri*, he adheres to this formula. Milian's extrovert clowning, the white peon garments and the unerring ability to find himself in the wrong place at the wrong time all signify the return of the charming rogue we last saw in *La resa dei conti*. He also appears to have overlooked the fact that, in the first film, he had a wife, since he is now engaged to Dolores. The passage of time, indeed, appears to be of little consequence. In *La resa dei conti*, we are informed that Cuchillo 'stood with Juárez', and the sequel tells us that the French assassins worked in turn for Maximilian, Juárez, and now Díaz. Benito Juárez died in 1872, so both films must logically be set at an early stage of the *Porfiriato* (1877–80, 1884–1911). The frequent references to 'the revolution' in *Corri uomo corri* therefore cannot point to the conflict which is most commonly associated with the phrase – that of 1910–20 – or indeed to the earlier uprising against Maximilian, but to a generic 'Mexican revolution'. On one hand, this continues Sollima's tendency to treat chronological concerns with carefree abandon (most noticeable in *Faccia a faccia*'s anachronistic lament for the passing of the 'Old West' while the Civil War still rages). On the other, however, this temporal dislocation, along with the removal of permanent relationships and the insertion of repetitious tics, affirms a reading of Cuchillo as one of Eco's 'inconsumable' heroes.

Foremost among these tics is the character's predilection for throwing knives, and in this respect, too, our 'old friend' does not disappoint. Indeed, the ritual established in the first film is not only repeated, but self-consciously analysed, in the second, openly drawing attention to its symbolic mechanisms while exposing its narrative illogicality. Firstly, when Cuchillo is arrested, the prison guard conducts a search and finds, preposterously, a total of six knives hidden amongst his scant peon garb. This comedic scene confirms to the audience that Cuchillo has retained his crowd-pleasing idiosyncrasy, and promises a repeat of his heroics.

When the inevitable gun-versus-knife duel arises, however, he finds the ritual itself scrutinised to a degree not seen in the previous film. Just prior to the duel, the characters engage in a debate over the imbalance brought about by Cuchillo's chosen method of fighting. 'We must stick to the rules', states his opponent, the French counterinsurgency agent Jean-Paul, as he allows the peon to choose his weapon. Naturally, Cuchillo chooses the knife, but finds his adversary moving too far away. 'This isn't the right distance for a knife fight', he complains. 'It's you who chose the knife', quips Jean-Paul. 'I chose the gun.' Only the intervention of Cassidy allows Cuchillo to get in range, and the process is comically and laboriously exaggerated as the peon and his friend take time out to debate the precise distance Jean-Paul should be moved for a fair fight to ensue. Eco's theorem remains a pertinent reference point here, but the unmasking of this 'tic' denies mere acceptance of its inevitability. Furthermore, though Cuchillo was not to reappear by name, the next outing for Milian's peon persona displays a narrative development precluding any further application of the 'inconsumable hero' model.

As we have seen, the 'insurgency' variant is marked by films which seek to expound, through manipulation of point-of-view, performance style and engagement with Fanonist tenets, an agenda in direct opposition to US imperialism. It is in the self-referential evolution of the Cuchillo persona where we find the most vivid example of such ideological exposition. As Dr. Henry Price drives his motorcar into the Mexican countryside, the man sitting next to him is immediately familiar. Tomas Milian's carefree clown, dressed in peon whites, whistles along to the film's theme tune while grinning at his narrow escape from trouble with the law. All the visual and aural signifiers point to the fact that this is our 'old friend' Cuchillo continuing his adventures under the assumed name 'Tepepa'. When governmental troops appear behind the vehicle, however, the character does something which Cuchillo, throughout the course of his two previous films, refuses to do even once: he fires a gun. No longer is this the 'inconsumable hero', for he has learned, as Superman cannot, a valuable lesson. Still, the repetition of Cuchillo is emphasised. As the motorcar explodes and falls from a cliff, Price, the army and the onlooking peons assume Tepepa is dead. A zoom shot reveals to the audience alone his hiding place amongst the cacti. This exactly replicates the dramatic irony of the shot construction in *La resa dei conti*, when Cuchillo is chased through the cane fields and his position is revealed time and again to the camera but not his pursuers.

When next we see Tepepa, however, he has transformed from Cuchillo to Zapata. Dressed in black, carrying a rifle and adorned with cartridge-belts and sombrero, the revolutionary general who breaks into the jail to free political prisoners is a considerably more ruthless breed of Third World hero. Moreover, while Cuchillo merely enjoyed positions of aloofness over the action, sharing the camera's point-of-view and exiting the narrative to 'join' the audience, Tepepa attains control over the exposition itself through epistolary flashbacks. He literally writes history and in the process self-consciously interrogates, and rejects, Cuchillo's insistence on knife-fighting. When he recalls the army slaughtering his fellow peasants, he comments bitterly: 'All those peons are dead, because the machete is one thing; the rifle is another.' Cuchillo's propensity for symbolic revenge on corrupt Westerners is renounced, his fighting only with knives shown to be absurd in the face of such force. Milian's peon persona now sees that he must wield firearms, and his specific focus on dates and historical events of the 1910–20 Mexican Revolution reverses the temporal dislocation experienced by Cuchillo. As this now-ruthless revolutionary marches Colonel Cascorro to his execution, however, he once again begins whistling the film's theme tune. The loveable rogue is still with us; he has simply learned the error of his ways. 'Cuchillo' has progressed from knife to gun, from peon to revolutionary, and from Arlecchino to narrator.

Overlaid directly onto this awakening of 'Cuchillo' are contemporaneous arguments preoccupying the various factions of the New Left pertaining to uneven development, armed insurrection and responses to state violence and the oppressive 'system'. The symbolism of armed resistance in the Third World in particular provided legitimating structures for violence amongst those factions for whom terrorism would subsequently become a viable option. Certainly, the centrality of Third Worldism should not be overstated, and the international New Left should not be homogenised. Della Porta, for example, emphasises that anti-imperialism, while a key catalyst amongst West German activists, played second fiddle to anti-fascism and factory disputes in legitimating violence amongst the Italian extra-parliamentary Left.[65] Additionally, and as I have already demonstrated, one should not simply draw a straight line of cause and effect from the rhetoric of the student movement to the violence of the Red Brigades.

Nevertheless, identification with anti-imperialist movements in Asia and Latin America was a significant pole of attraction across the student movement in the late 1960s. Judt records that '"Maoism" – or at any rate, an uncritical fascination with the Chinese Cultural Revolution then in full swing – was more extensive in Italy than anywhere else in Europe'.[66] Moreover, when extremist wings of the protest movement did turn to armed resistance, such reference points informed the tactical and ideological premises upon which clandestine insurgent groupings were built. The Red Brigades in particular sought to emulate the Uruguayan Tupamaros and the Viet Cong in their terrorist campaigns.

The years in the immediate aftermath of 1968 were the most influential for the political education of Italian militants. The national congress of the Italian student movement in September 1968 was, in the words of Luigi Bobbio, 'the last moment in which the debate was open and the common participation in the student movement was a shared assumption'.[67] As New Left groups became increasingly centralised, exclusive and isolated, what Tarrow dubs the 'spiral of competitive tactical innovation'[68] began to take root amongst radical factions. As we have seen, the state response to the revolutionary movements arising in the following years fostered the notion that armed struggle was necessary 'self defence' against a new form of fascism. The Red Brigades formed amidst precisely this ethos that the firepower of the enemy must be matched if revolution is to be achieved.

*Tepepa* was released in Italy in January 1969, at the very time that such debates were becoming ever more fraught. Only a month previously police had fired on a labourer demonstration in Avola, Sicily. The 'workerist' movement was in its infancy as student demonstrators joined factory picket lines, and in the ensuing 12 months working-class militancy would steadily increase. The transformation of Cuchillo – the 'poor peon', petty thief and vagabond – into a brutal Third World pragmatist is a reflection of such debates. The development of Milian's peasant persona in *Tepepa* equally develops the patterns of dramatic irony and extra-diegetic performance evident in *Quien sabe?*, *La resa dei conti* and *Corri, uomo, corri* into overtly contemporaneous political commentary. To find, in *Compañeros*, Milian's peon hero adorned once more in cartridge-belts, this time at the head of a student battalion and sporting a 'rebel chic' beret, seems merely to confirm the persona's integration into this discourse. As this film's student debate concludes, the camera zooms in on his guns, earlier discarded at the request of Professor Xantos but soon to be taken up once more. The debates over the legitimacy of violent confrontation which pervade the film are symbolically resolved.

### Conclusion: Stylistic Flaws

Far from leading this sub-*filone* further down the path of committed Third Worldist militancy, however, Sergio Corbucci's eccentric interpretations of the 'insurgency' variant in fact lay bare the trend's inherent weaknesses. This is most apparent in *Il mercenario*. In the very first scene Paco, the film's 'revolutionary peon' figure, emerges into an arena dressed as a clown. The majority of the narrative is framed by this circus act, to which we return towards the denouement. The plot's fictive qualities are emphasised by the positioning of the outsider (in this case a Pole – Sergei Kowalski – an ethnic characterisation in itself confusing any anti-'Western' political message) as both spectator and narrator. Amongst the audience in the arena, as a zoom shot reveals, sits Kowalski, watching the show with amused detachment and narrating: 'So Paco Roman is a clown. Well, better a live clown than a dead hero. [...] When our story began, Paco was only a peon, but one with a difference.' The majority of the narrative is recounted thus, through Kowalski's flashback.[69]

Kowalski remains the detached observer, rising above (and at times controlling) the narrative throughout the film. When he organises a bank heist, for example, he ticks off the various stages of the plan, in full view of the camera, as they happen. This bestows upon the Pole a narrative control akin to that of Brad Fletcher when he similarly narrates a bank robbery for our benefit. As we have seen, *Il mercenario* was based on a Franco Solinas story in which a North American joins, and is then rejected by, the Mexican hero. Thematically and structurally similar to both *Quien sabe?* and *La resa dei conti*, this initial bestowal of the cinematic point-of-view on the outsider figure is consistent with these related narratives.

At the point where Paco is about to reject the interloper, as the original screenplay demands, however, he is forced to turn to him once more for help as the army attacks. As we return to the circus ring, Kowalski still sits observing Paco's elaborate tomfoolery. The gaze of the audience, through our laconic Polish conduit, remains resolutely directed at the exotic Mexican. Shorn of any meaningful shift in the audience's perspective, *Il mercenario* fails to expound any political message whatsoever. While Damiani and Sollima incrementally shift the perspective away from the Westerner towards the peon, Corbucci instead places Columba – Paco's lover – in a position of narrative control towards the end, as she organises Paco's and Kowalski's daring escape. Far from making any serious attempt to elicit our sympathy for the peon, however, her actions simply precipitate yet more violent comic action. In both *Il mercenario* and *Compañeros*, the killing of Jack Palance's gringo counterinsurgent and the conversion of the Mexican from bandit to revolutionary become mere *filone* echoes from *Quien sabe?*. In both, too, when Franco Nero picks up a machine gun and mows down hordes of Mexican soldiers, the stylistic fetishism for deadly machinery simply echoes *Django*. The orgiastic violence once more loses the regenerative political qualities in part recovered by the Fanonist agenda of Damiani's trail-blazer.

This is by no means to say that *Il mercenario* is alone amongst the 'insurgency' variant for its failure to marry an intended political agenda to a consistent manipulation of the cinematic medium. Indeed, it merely amplifies similar flaws evident in films whose exposition is otherwise more sophisticated. We have already seen an identical reversal of another bleak Solinas script into a crowd-pleasing, yet politically anodyne, ending with *La resa dei conti*. Additionally, the otherwise meticulous pendulum swing of Volonté's studied portrayal of the bandit/revolutionary dichotomy in *Quien sabe?* is jeopardised in the film's very final moments, when this supposedly committed Fanonist runs away whooping and jumping for joy. More fundamentally flawed is the flashback structure of *Tepepa*, which simultaneously seeks to elicit sympathy with the hero's political stance while it alienates the audience from his actions.

A significant portion of *Tepepa*'s narrative is expounded through subjective flashbacks, each framed by the camera according to the current narrator's version of events. When Cascorro recalls the massacre of Tepepa's companions, he claims to have given the order to his troops not to fire, and Tepepa's charge towards his car is shown to be irrational and deranged. Henry Price's elusive version of events reveals piece-by-piece his accusation that Tepepa had raped his fiancée and driven her to suicide. When Tepepa dictates at length his letter to Francisco Madero, the camera portrays the past events of the Revolution faithfully according to his account, and from his perspective. We see him standing up to a landowner, framed centre-screen in medium close-up, clearly denoting a heroic presence. When we then see once more his fellow peons being massacred by the army, this time from his perspective, their powerlessness is emphasised as they stand, machetes in hand, facing the machine gun.

Once these subjective narrative devices have ceased, however, the camera retains the heroic framing of Tepepa in the 'present'. When he finds his village burned out by governmental troops, for example, both the camera and the hero miss the event itself, and we share both his hiding place and his point-of-view as the soldiers ride away. When he sees the carnage wrought by those soldiers, he is once again framed in frontal close-up. As he then makes a speech denouncing Madero and declaring war on the government, the camera pans around him to settle at a low-angle shot, again obviously positioning Tepepa as a hero.

This didactic framing means that when Price's accusations are vociferously denied by the hero both we and the Englishman are led to doubt Tepepa's guilt, only for Cascorro's recital of independent testimonies to prove it beyond all doubt. This renders Tepepa's hero status problematic, but he retains the heroic framing in the present despite the revelation that he is a rapist. As his guerrilla band ambushes Cascorro's convoy, for example, Tepepa, atop a white horse, leads his cavalry over the lip of a hill into single combat against a numerically superior foe. That our sympathy for him is brought into question jeopardises the intended political message that the final killing of Price is justified because 'that gringo didn't like Mexico'.

It is possible that Petroni intends here to affirm Fanon's doctrine that 'when the native is tortured, when his wife is killed or raped, he complains to no one. [...] For the native, life can only spring up again out of the rotting corpse of the settler'.[70] By massacring landowners and violating their families, Tepepa may be fighting fire with fire. *Quien sabe?* openly advocates this position when Adelita asks why, when she was raped as a child by aristocrats, Don Felipe's wife should be spared, but *Tepepa* completely ignores the issue of the hero's culpability for the crime. Its political implications are not addressed and, despite this act, he is afforded a posthumous apotheosis as the embodiment of the Revolution (this obfuscation of the issue of rape is equally a reflection of the *filone*'s general atmosphere of misogyny, already discussed in the case of *Faccia a faccia*).

Ginsborg writes that the emergent groupings of the Italian New Left in the late 1960s 'accepted a dangerously casual attitude towards violence, adopting contemporary South American and Asian struggles as their models, with little reflection on their applicability or likely consequences in the Italian situation'.[71] This blasé outlook is aptly symbolised by Petroni pushing on with his pro-insurgency polemic in *Tepepa*, while sweeping the wider ethical and political implications of this stance under the carpet. Leone's *Giù la testa* (1971) offered a direct rebuke to the high pretensions and the irresponsible advocacy of revolutionary theory in political Italian Westerns. It is significant that it singles out *Tepepa* in particular for direct quotation and parody: with Sean's motorised entrance into revolutionary Mexico; when Juan tries to rob a bank but ends up freeing political prisoners; and when the Westerner rescues the Mexican from a firing squad by driving past on a motor vehicle.

Even while he offers assistance to Juan, *Giù la testa*'s revolutionary intellectual Dr. Villega's book forms a physical barrier between him and the peasant. Meanwhile Sean, the idealist insurgent, discards his Bakunin tome after a lecture in agrarian *realpolitik* from Juan:

> The people who read the books go to the people who can't read the books, the poor people, and say we have to have a change, so the poor people make the change. Then the people who read the books they all sit around the big polished tables and talk and talk. [...] But what has happened to the poor people? They're dead!

As the painstaking efforts of Damiani and Sollima suggest, a film's advocacy of violent political acts is more likely to succeed in a narrative sense if sympathy for the perpetrator is first elicited from the audience. They subvert the generic conventions of Hollywood, reverse the objectifying gaze, manipulate the cinematic point-of-view and exit the diegesis to address the viewer directly. They thus make concerted efforts to frame the enemy – in this case, the West – as a foe against whom violent resistance is imperative. Without this framework, the violence which ensues is liable to be conflated with that which is commonly labelled 'gratuitous'. 'When I started using dynamite, I believed many things', says *Giù la testa*'s Sean Mallory. 'Finally, I believe only in dynamite.'

Jack Woddis criticises Frantz Fanon's *The Wretched of the Earth* for creating a mystique around violence at the expense of genuine political engagement.[72] This same accusation can ultimately be levelled at the 'insurgency' variant. By transposing complex political stances advocating armed insurrection into a popular medium, they invite a viewer to interpret nothing other than advocacy of violence for violence's sake. With this in mind, the next chapter explores the reception political Italian Westerns received on their international releases, and appraises what, if anything, their political legacy might be.

# PART III

# THE LEGACY

# 5

# Revolutionising Violence:
# Radical Translation and Postmodern
# Residues in US Cinema

The opening sequence of Sam Peckinpah's *The Wild Bunch* (1969) is remarkable not only for its uncompromising brutality, but for its acerbic critique of bourgeois society. Spatial and temporal relationships are manipulated by the film-makers to construct a stage upon which corporate America is interrogated and condemned.

While San Rafael's tree-lined avenues, park benches and smartly-dressed gentlefolk denote the gentrification of the Old West and the onset of bourgeois modernity, the town is depicted as an assembly of artifice. The courteous soldiers helping an elderly lady across the street are in fact ruthless outlaws in disguise (the eponymous 'Bunch'), while behind the town's incipient decorum lurks a brutal corporate machine, symbolised by the legally-sanctioned posse under the employ of the railroad hiding feverishly on the rooftops waiting for impending carnage. That the respectable citizens of this burgeoning middle-class society live in ignorance of the forces conspiring beneath the surface is patent in the stark imagery of the Temperance Union parade, blissfully anaesthetised to the hidden dangers and marching headlong towards violent death. Their hymn 'Shall We Gather at the River' – long a staple ingredient of the wholesome, regenerative West of John Ford – here constitutes a sanctimonious and deluded faith in civilised values.

Descriptive framings alternating between the parade, the Bunch's covert robbery of the depot and the bounty hunters hiding on the roof permit the viewer cognizance of the full scenario. As the violent spectacle approaches, however, interspersed are point-of-view shots alternating between low-

and high-angle, allowing us to share the perspective of the Bunch and the posse respectively. On a purely narrative level, this shot construction builds tension as the parade and the gunfight draw ever nearer. Symbolically, however, it is significant both that Tector Gorch and Angel – members of the Bunch – are the only people at ground level perceptive enough to espy the imminent threat, and that we share their viewpoint of rifles barely visible above the parapets. The Bunch, we are later told, 'share very few sentiments with [their] government' and are under no illusions as to the coercive mechanisms hiding behind bourgeois propriety. Consequently, they are permitted a glimpse of the threat that awaits them, while the oblivious townsfolk march blindly to their doom.

In this chapter I assess the legacies of the political Italian films analysed in the book so far, examining the extent to which their intended radicalisation of the Western survived the journey back across the Atlantic upon their international releases. My focus now shifts to the American film industry because the globalised dissemination of US popular culture has dictated that this is the filter through which political appropriations of this *filone*, as 'Westerns', were received and are still read. I chart a broader timescale than in the previous two chapters and for this reason my analysis is more selective, with key films chosen for their representative nature over a 40 year period in American cinema.

While the US counterculture increasingly appropriated the mainstream Hollywood Western for political purposes after 1969, the overtly militant tenor to be found in the Italian *filone* failed to gain a foothold. In the following pages I identify various issues surrounding cinematic violence in this era as important factors in this failure. These include: the Spaghetti Western's stylistic conventions of depicting violent acts, which diverged markedly from the practices of Hollywood's countercultural community; the dramatic increase in cinematic violence across the board which embroiled this book's key films in debates specifically surrounding this cultural shift; and the resultant consumption of Spaghetti Westerns alongside other violent genres proliferating in the late 1960s and early 1970s such as 'blaxploitation', 'splatter' horrors and martial arts films. It is concerning these issues in particular that *The Wild Bunch* provides both an illuminating context and a useful starting point for assessing the legacy of Italy's political Westerns.

Peckinpah's film is frequently discussed as evidence for the transformations visited upon the American Western by the commercial successes of the Italian version, whether through imitation or reaction. On its release, William Hall described it as 'a blatant, sensational attempt to recapture the market won by [...] *A Fistful of Dollars* and *The Good, the Bad and the Ugly*.[1] With the more measured benefit of hindsight, Jim Kitses argues that it is impossible to discuss Peckinpah and Sergio Leone independently of each other, since between them they deconstructed and reinvented the genre.[2] The primary basis of such a conflation is the increased level of death and destruction evident in the work of these two highly influential directors. They are frequently discussed as joint pioneers in the proliferation of ultra-violence on American screens in the late 1960s.

While, as we shall see, Peckinpah's stylistic depictions of violence in fact differed markedly from those arising in Italy, my intention is not to refute these claims. *The Wild Bunch*'s producer Phil Feldman, indeed, specifically urged his director to look at Leone's films before deciding how far he could push the envelope of cinematic brutality.[3] Instead, I seek to highlight the extent to which the 'meanings' ascribed to the key films discussed in this book would rely more on the industrial, political and social contexts into which they were released than on their (in any case frequently incoherent) intended expositions. As we have seen, these 'political' Italian Westerns were in part designed as discourses concerning the ideological legitimacy of violent acts. In the event, though violence has certainly defined their cinematic legacy to the present day, the attendant messages have not survived the translation.

*The Wild Bunch*'s San Rafael massacre displays some degree of political equivalence with the outlooks of Damiani, Sollima et al. Through such amplified depictions of violence, Peckinpah professed to be shaking Americans out of passively accepting officially-sanctioned killing both in the cinema and, as Vietnam entered its bloodiest phase, on newscasts.[4] His modish affinity with the youth counterculture's critiques of industrial society is discernible in this opening scene, which displays certain parallels with *Faccia a faccia*'s Purgatory City episode. As in Sollima's scene, so too in Peckinpah's powerful men occupy elevated vantage points while manipulating a massacre occurring in the street below. Moreover, in both films the audience's privileged insight into these brutal mechanisms is shared with characters that the narrative will soon render our primary conduits. Peckinpah's deployment of the cinematic medium is certainly more sophisticated than Sollima's, with rapid cross-cutting of slow-motion and real-time stylistically heightening the impact of violence in what Stephen Prince terms 'an artistic transformation of space, time, and perception'.[5] His use of symbolic spatial relationships, however, echoes that of the earlier film.

The concordances between the ideological standpoint of *The Wild Bunch* and that of the Italian plot variants I have identified in this book can also be seen in terms of characterisation and allegory. The railroad boss Mr. Harrigan's venomous excuse that 'we represent the law' as the dead bodies of innocents shot by his men are mourned in the street, for example, places us in a similar political labyrinth to those experienced by Sabata, Sartana and, most of all, Silenzio (the animalistic bounty hunters in particular recall Corbucci's film). Furthermore, by proceeding to send his outlaws south of the Mexican border Peckinpah sought quite openly to undermine the Western genre's recent proclivity towards justifying US interference in far-flung corners of the globe. If the opening massacre at San Rafael offers a parallel with the 'RSA' plot, then the closing carnage at Agua Verde debunks myths of benign intervention fostered by *The Magnificent Seven* and *The Alamo* in a manner akin to the 'insurgency' narrative.

*The Wild Bunch* was shot during the spring and summer of 1968. This was the time of the Paris uprising and the international student movement, the Tet Offensive, the assassinations of Martin Luther King and Bobby Kennedy, and the turbulent Democratic Convention in Chicago: an era ripe, one might think, for countercultural messages to be received and understood. Crucially, however, this was also the year in which Hollywood's Production Code finally collapsed, ushering in a new wave of filmic ultra-violence. Consequently, though Peckinpah claimed to be expounding a radical thesis, the critical response instead focused on *The Wild Bunch*'s palpable contribution to depictions of brutality in American cinema.

The ambiguities of Peckinpah's technique – 'at once compelling and repelling', in the words of John Goff[6] – have provoked divisive debate ever since the film's release, frequently interpreted in a cinematic context at a remove from the director's avowed political message. In pushing the boundaries of acceptable screen brutality, Peckinpah set out both to condemn the violence on which, he proposed, modern America was predicated, and to implicate the audience in their desire for violent action by heightening its aesthetic qualities. Little wonder, in the industrial context summarised above, that this attempt to unmask traditional screen violence was often seen to be a glorification of the very thing it sought to undermine. So we find, on *The Wild Bunch*'s international release, William Hall's review concluding that 'on this showing Hollywood has finally succumbed completely to the current era of screen violence'.[7] For every Vincent Canby ('When I came out of it, I didn't feel like shooting, knifing or otherwise maiming any of Broadway's often hostile pedestrians'[8]) or Michael Sragow ('The technique objectifies our vision of violence rather than enflame our lust for it'[9]) there was a Nina Hibbin ('One of the most gratuitously blood-loving Westerns ever to have hit the screen [...] a conscious exercise in the glorification of the kill'[10]).

The opinions of the critical establishment, of course, are not necessarily a reliable gauge of public opinion, and I shall return to this issue with specific focus on the Italian Westerns in due course. Whether we choose to take Peckinpah's claims of radicalism at face value or not, however, one thing is clear: films of this era whose professed function in depicting death and destruction was to evaluate the ethics of political violence had their work cut out if they wished to be taken seriously. Consequently, we shall see that the radicalised Westerns emanating from Rome in this period have been from their international releases subsumed into an entirely divergent cinematic discourse from that which was intended. The industrial context of late 1960s Hollywood rendered their political content invisible.

There is, however, something of a contradiction in this argument. If these industrial factors alone precluded a violent film from serious political discussion, why is it that *The Wild Bunch* has since been afforded extensive academic attention for its radical imperative, while the Italian Western has not? Given the ideological concordances between Peckinpah's and the Italians' uses of the Western genre it is notable that, while the amoral (and largely apolitical) universe of Sergio Leone is often located alongside *The Wild Bunch*, the films of Damiani and Sollima are consistently omitted from discussions concerning Peckinpah's film. Indeed, their very existence is largely overlooked when discussing this director's work in its generic context, even in cases where his radicalism is fully acknowledged. Christopher Sharrett, for example, writes: 'In *The Wild Bunch*, capitalism's veneer of democracy is transparent and irrelevant, and Peckinpah insists on this rapacity and murderousness as the true nature of this society. *Before other revisionists of the Western, Peckinpah accomplishes this basic unmasking* [emphasis mine].'[11] This alludes to the spate of countercultural Hollywood Westerns which followed in the wake of *The Wild Bunch* – for example, Robert Altman's *McCabe and Mrs Miller* (1971), Peckinpah's own *Pat Garrett and Billy the Kid* (1973), Arthur Penn's *The Missouri Breaks* (1976) and Michael Cimino's *Heaven's Gate* (1980) – which similarly depicted corporate America as a brutal machine. Absent from this timeline, however, is the fact that *La resa dei conti* was released in the USA in August 1968 and *Quien sabe?* followed in April 1969: both before *The Wild Bunch*.[12]

This omission partly reflects the phenomenal achievements of Sergio Leone in the international marketplace, which eclipsed all other contributions to the Western *filone* in both commercial success and popular stylistic currency (especially revealing is that Sharrett includes *C'era una volta il West* (1968) as a precedent to Peckinpah's vision of society). Such avenues of investigation, however, are also overlooked due to 'internal' factors pertaining to cinematic style which, allied to the 'external' industrial aspects already discussed, have served to obscure Italian Westerns' political content. It is the purpose of this chapter to identify and delineate these various nuances, and explain the evacuation of these films' polemics.

### Caught in the Crossfire

When *La resa dei conti* and *Quien sabe?* were released in the USA, the populist Italian radicalism so painstakingly inscribed into their narratives had to compete in an unfamiliar industrial and political context. We shall see that in this alien milieu their political intentions were almost completely unrecognisable. To a variety of audience constituencies, their frames of reference and their cinematic language did not signify any political imperative whatsoever. In each case, this can be attributed to the Italian Western's conventions of depicting violence, to which these radical films adhered. Firstly, I shall demonstrate that stylistic choices rendered Sollima's and Damiani's political messages largely invisible within the terms of the US counterculture itself. Secondly, the very presence of abundant killing obscured their narrative content amidst the contemporaneous furore over on-screen violence *per se*.

With the emergence of 'New Hollywood' around 1967, the cognitive frameworks of American countercultures increasingly became overlaid onto mainstream film-making. The tone of insubordination in Arthur Penn's *Bonnie and Clyde* (1967) and Dennis Hopper's *Easy Rider* (1969), for example, is accompanied by despairing representations of the annihilation of free-spirited youth by the repressive 'system'. This outraged sense that American democracy was mere window-dressing for coercive power-mongers is characteristic of Hollywood's countercultural film-making of this era. As we have seen with *The Wild Bunch*, *Little Big Man* and *Soldier Blue*, such nihilism had equally infused the Western by the decade's end, with the genre's 'serious orientation' to violence becoming assimilated into revelatory exposés of state brutality and military genocide. This ideological outlook, indeed, was at its most apparent in the attendant revolution in the cinematic depiction of bloodshed, which sought to lay this principle bare by foregrounding the brutality of violent death. Peckinpah and Penn in particular amplified the effect of physical trauma by introducing into mainstream cinematic language such techniques as blood-squibs, head-shots and slow-motion bodily convulsions. The prolonged, agonising and graphic demise of Buck

Barrow (Gene Hackman) at the hands of the state in *Bonnie and Clyde* typifies this aesthetic representation and attendant ideological outlook.

The countercultural Westerns simultaneously arriving on American shores from Italy arose from a different outlook, and practiced different methods of representing death and destruction. We have seen in Chapter Four that *Quien sabe?* in particular registers a considerably more belligerent form of radicalism than that prevalent in contemporary America. Indeed, the very frames of reference from which these films' intended meanings arose were not the same as those inhabited by many radical communities within the USA. Briefly to reprise my recourse to Louis Althusser's terminology from Chapter Three, the outraged and revelatory identification of repression in the depictions of Penn, Nelson and Peckinpah are akin to 'descriptive theory'.[13] Althusser argues that such recognition that bourgeois democracy is covertly supported by state brutality should not be seen as a revelation in itself, but merely as the starting point for analysis.

Taken as an organic whole, the contemporaneous radicalism arising from within the Italian Western affirms this argument: while the 'RSA' narrative seeks to lay bare latent fascism, the 'insurgency' narrative proposes resistance against it. There is in these films little sense of authorial surprise or shock that an outwardly democratic government might be corrupt and coercive. Certainly, the identification of state-sanctioned cruelty was hardly revelatory in a country with a living memory of totalitarianism and a rich tradition of militant insubordination. Accordingly, compared to the momentous depictions of violent death being explored in contemporary Hollywood, the stylistics of the Italian Western as a whole reflect a considerably more blasé outlook towards brutality. In this respect, the militant offshoot of this *filone* did not fall far from the tree. This countercultural community was speaking in a different language from that of its American equivalent cinematically and politically, as well as verbally.

This is not to say that the innovations of this *filone* did not leave their mark on US cinema. The stylistic impact of the Italian Western on Hollywood is an indisputably significant, and well documented, phenomenon which commenced from the very moment the films were released. The consensus holds that the style, mood and levels of violence in the Western were changed forever more, heralding a self-consciously nihilistic West of casual, frequent and darkly comic killing. In a detailed appendix, Frayling sets out a variety of stylistic and industrial influences, including the increasing preponderance of desolate 'Leone towns', the elaborate use of zooms practiced by Ralph Nelson and the opportunities opened for increased levels of viciousness in Hollywood by Leone's success.[14] We have already seen that Peckinpah was encouraged by the brutality on show in films emanating from Rome when conceiving *The Wild Bunch*: an important point which has nevertheless been made by so many critics that it has become a cliché.

The popularity and profitability of the *filone* in foreign markets is most conspicuous on a topographical level. American film crews descended on the deserts of Andalucía in the late 1960s and early 1970s to replicate the look of Cinecittà Westerns in such films as *100 Rifles* (1969), *El Condor* (1970), *Doc* (1971), *Hannie Caulder* (1971), *Chato's Land* (1972) and *The Spikes Gang* (1974). Equally, Hollywood Westerns began to display signs of influence in their cinematographic style, as in the rapidly cross-cut deep-focus shots and close-ups which punctuate the climax of Edwin Sherin's *Valdez is Coming* (1971).

There is also evidence to suggest that, beyond the obvious influence of Leone, certain of Damiani's and Sollima's tics were carried over into Hollywood film-making. Both Buzz Kulik's *Villa Rides* (1968) and Tom Gries's *100 Rifles* (1969), for example, display clear parallels with the narrative framework common to the 'insurgency' plot, each centring on an uneasy partnership between a Mexican, and a North American who becomes reluctantly embroiled in the Revolution. Gries's plot device of a US sheriff pursuing a wanted Mexican vagabond over the border also apes *La resa dei conti*, while the pair's quest to smuggle rifles to a revolutionary general parallels *Quien sabe?* (itself released in the USA just one month after *100 Rifles*). Additionally, *Valdez is Coming* (1971) and Michael Winner's *Chato's Land* (1972) both display the influence of *La resa dei conti* in depicting a native pursued through the wilderness by avaricious, corrupt Westerners and their henchmen. Both films repeat Sollima's framing devices by bestowing a privileged vantage point, shared with the camera, on the guileful hero hiding in rocky outcrops. *Chato's Land*, indeed, displays a host of Italian Western quotations while overtly referencing Vietnam through a Third Worldist chic (the cat-and-mouse pursuit giving way to native retribution recalling not only Sollima's film but also Corbucci's *Un dollaro a testa* (1966)). Unlike in the pacifist *Soldier Blue* (1970), this murderous band of white Americans is massacred in righteous vengeance. While such influences are certainly testament to an irreverent and countercultural drive within the Hollywood Western, however, for the most part these films merely rehearse their Italian antecedents' plot devices, characterisations and rebellious tenor without expressing a programmatic ideological discourse.

We can therefore see that the increasingly bleak and amoral universe in which Western characters were operating certainly owed much to the nihilism evident in much of the Italian *filone*. Equally, numerous methodologies emerging from Cinecittà were imported into the mainstream Hollywood Western. It is therefore significant that those methodologies relating specifically to the stylistic portrayal of violence were by no means a compulsory component of a bulk shipment. It is in this key aspect of cinematic style, which above all others in contemporary Hollywood was carrying increasingly explicit radical inscriptions, that the *filone*'s influence is abruptly curtailed. Far from a linear progression from the violence depicted in Italian Westerns to that appearing in US cinema by the late 1960s, there were divergent and simultaneous modes of stylistic representation at work. The depictions of brutality ubiquitous to the Spaghettis in fact owed more to an older, less earnest tradition of representation than to the blood-soaked ultra-violence which was putting such an indelible stamp upon the American Western (and New Hollywood generally).

Don Medford's *The Hunting Party* (1971) illustrates this point through a curious fusion of the various stylistic directions in which the Western was being steered by the early 1970s. Co-authored by British writer Gilbert Alexander and pioneering producer of *The Magnificent Seven* Lou Morheim, and shot with British money in Almería, Medford's film displays a hybrid 'American' imaginary born from a European-oriented sensibility (in Morheim's case, a production record attuned to European cinematic tastes). Unsurprisingly, given this background, the 'West' presented here owes much to the Italian version. Far from a hero, the outlaw Frank Calder (Oliver Reed) abducts and rapes the wife of cattle baron Brandt Ruger (Gene Hackman). Calder is only afforded the audience's identification because the world in which he lives is so irredeemably brutal that simply by resisting corporate power he approaches the role of a romantic bandit. This approaches, and emulates, the milieu of ubiquitous corruption evident throughout Leone's 'Dollars' trilogy where, in Raymond Durgnat's words, 'in so black a world […] every faintly good deed […] has all the more power'.[15] The evacuation of violence's noble purpose, the sadistic relish with which Ruger kills the outlaw's band and the nihilism of the conclusion, in which he shoots both his wife and Calder before himself perishing in the desert, belong firmly to the desolate West of Leone and Corbucci. Additionally, the corrupt magnate obsessively hunting down an outlaw superficially recalls *La resa dei conti*.

These lines of influence notwithstanding, *The Hunting Party* is most remarkable for the manner in which its frequent acts of violence are filmed. In one scene, Calder and one of his men stand peering up at a rocky outcrop, where Ruger and his henchmen are perched with their long-range rifles, picking off the outlaws one-by-one. A point-of-view shot showing the rocks at which Calder and his companion are looking is spliced between side-on close-ups showing the two men looking up and out of frame to the right with Calder, closest to the camera, occupying the extreme left hand side of the frame. The angle of the shot places an empty gap, centre-frame, between him and his companion who stands in deeper focus. 'There ain't no son of a bitch can shoot from that far', mutters Calder's ill-fated buddy, a split second before the back of his head explodes courtesy of a blood-squib hidden in the actor's hair. The camera angle then cuts immediately to a frontal shot showing the body falling to the ground, where the centre of the frame is again occupied by a gap between the two men, filled with brain-matter gushing from the victim's head.

Both shot compositions focus attention on the gruesome details of this sequence, both gaps between the two men occupying centre-frame, to become filled with the ample contents of the blood-bag in the course of the shot. Furthermore, the palpably lethal damage done to the man's head demands a visual association with the graphic images of the JFK assassination so indelibly etched in the collective memory. This elaborate use of squibs, repeated throughout with similarly graphic results, underlines the stylistic debt owed to Sam Peckinpah by Medford's film. In a later scene, when the outlaws are massacred at a watering hole, this indebtedness becomes undisguised imitation. The absence of *The Wild Bunch*'s rapid montage and visceral sound effects attests to an inferior deployment of the technique; yet the slow-motion inserts of exploding squibs and bodies falling through the air intercut with real-time footage directly reference Peckinpah's infamous massacres of San Rafael and Agua Verde.

Such an aesthetic, which focuses on the graphic details of bullet impact wounds, derives not only from Peckinpah, but from Arthur Penn's ground-breaking depictions of violence in *Bonnie and Clyde*. Stephen Prince illustrates the extent to which the multi-camera, multi-speed montage which concludes this film (and is also central to *The Wild Bunch*'s stylistics) is a development from Akira Kurosawa's cinematography in *Seven Samurai* (1954).[16] Furthermore Penn's collaborator in this project, Warren Beatty, cited Wilson's shooting of Stonewall in *Shane* (1953) as the inspiration for this new breed of visceral brutality:[17] a scene which, as we have seen in Chapter Two, contrasts markedly with the predominant staging of violence emanating from Italy. The squibbed convulsions of the eponymous couple's bodies as they are riddled with machine gun fire at the climax of *Bonnie and Clyde* was designed with the express intention of shocking the audience, and of reminding them of the JFK shooting four years previously.[18]

Penn rejected the outcry provoked by his method by drawing contemporary parallels: 'Every night on the news we saw kids in Vietnam being lifted out in body bags, with blood all over the place. Why, suddenly, the cinema had to be immaculate, I'll never know.'[19] The graphic violence of *The Hunting Party*, too, pertains to allegory. The clinical ruthlessness of corporate power shooting outlaws from long range operates as a symbol for the bombing campaigns in Vietnam (and this very conceit would be repeated in Penn's *The Missouri Breaks* (1976)). That *The Hunting Party*, ostensibly a film grasping at the coat-tails of the Italian Western, should emulate this nascent countercultural tradition is significant, since the ample violence depicted in the Italian Western tends toward an altogether divergent aesthetic. While David Lusted is broadly correct in saying that 'by [...] the mid-1970s, Italian Westerns set the tone and style of American Westerns and the action film more generally',[20] the stylistic legacy of Cinecittà should not be overstated.

The opening sequence of Leone's *Per qualche dollaro in più* (1965) presents an identical spatial scenario to the scene from *The Hunting Party* discussed above, with a sniper in an elevated position shooting a man dead from long range. The *mise en scène*, however, differs markedly. A static camera shows the mountainous landscape in an extended long shot, and the only person in the frame is the victim, approaching on horseback in the distance. A nonchalant whistle and the sound of a gun being loaded are the only clues that this is a point-of-view shot, until a gunshot is heard, smoke rises from the near foreground, and the rider falls from his horse. At no point does the camera descend to show either the details of the killing or the victim, whose identity is never established. Instead, as the credits float into position, it becomes evident that this sequence's sole purpose is to set the moral tone of the film to come, as the subsequent epigraph makes abundantly clear: 'Where life had no value, death, sometimes, had its price.' In Leone's 'Dollars' trilogy, violence is indeed a casual and frequent affair, with few implications for the perpetrator other than financial gain. While the narrative function of this opening is to establish the unforgiving environment to come, it equally emblematises the stylistics of Leone's depictions of death by gunfire, which are often detached, casual and light-hearted. When Blondie (Clint Eastwood) enters the narrative of *Il buono, il brutto, il cattivo*, for example, it is to shoot three men with a superhuman gun-slinging panache. There are no squibs, no blood-bags, and no slow-motion inserts or close-ups emphasising the damage done to the men's bodies. Instead, all three immediately fall dead in comically elaborate pirouettes in the background of a deep-focus shot, as Blondie's pistol fires in the foreground. The attention here is placed firmly on the character's gun-slinging skills, not on the damage done to his victims. This is in stark contrast to the aforementioned victim of Ruger's long-range rifle in *The Hunting Party*, whose wounding is caught in centre-frame detail and who lies moaning and slowly bleeding to death.

As we have seen, Leone's pans, tilts and extreme close-ups became highly influential in global popular culture. He has, however, been erroneously[21] credited with innovations in the framing of gun fights, when this aspect of his technique in fact displays influences from an earlier, sanitised aesthetic. Indeed, Leone's method of depicting gunshot fatalities throughout the 'Dollars' trilogy bears a close, if exaggeratedly parodic, resemblance to the Hollywood practice prior to the 1960s, which Prince terms the 'clutch and fall' technique.[22] This bloodless staging of death, involving 'falling asleep' with no signs of pain, was precisely the convention against which Peckinpah was reacting in his efforts to shake audiences out of passive acceptance of violence. Both Frayling and Wagstaff underline the industrial resemblance between the *filone* production line and that of 1930s Hollywood 'B' Westerns, with their rapid turnaround, low budgets and frequently light-hearted treatment of established paradigms.[23] Nowhere is this notion illustrated more clearly than in the stylistics of gun violence which proliferated in the films of Leone, and through much of the Italian Western. Wagstaff, indeed, identifies the Italians' depictions with a comic-book seriality, aimed at holding the attention of an otherwise easily distracted audience: 'To attribute too much meaning to the violence would be to fail to see how much these films resembled, in that respect, American cartoons like *Road Runner* for example.'[24]

This is by no means to say that graphic brutality of other kinds is absent from this *filone*. Sergio Corbucci for one displayed a penchant for gruesome depictions of torture in the ear-cutting sequence of *Django* (1966); the horror influences on Lucio Fulci's *Quattro dell'apocalisse* (1975) are palpable in the skinning alive of a bandit in extreme close-up; and Giulio Questi's camera dwells upon hangings, a scalping, and a detailed depiction of lethal surgery in *Se sei vivo, spara!* (1967). Such indulgences do not, however, extend to gunshot wounds and are in any case the extremes of a *filone* largely characterised by its exuberantly parodic framings. As the Hollywood Western's depictions were already becoming more brutal, in such films as *One-Eyed Jacks* (1961) and *The Professionals* (1966), Peckinpah and Penn were preparing stylistically to heighten the graphic detail of violent death. The vast majority of Italy's Westerns, meanwhile, adopted a distinctly comic-book style, inheriting and elaborating the antiquated conventions of the Production Code era. Warshow's 'serious orientation to the problem of violence' is hard to discern in the films of Leone, Tessari, Carnimeo and Parolini (as we have seen in Chapter Two in the case of Tessari's *Una pistola per Ringo* (1965)). Their self-conscious, often sardonic deployment of these techniques was a far cry from the altogether more earnest framings of *Bonnie and Clyde* and *The Wild Bunch*. For example, as is alluded to by both Frayling and Prince, not once in all of Leone's Westerns does blood spurt from a bullet wound.[25]

With this in mind, it is initially curious to read, in *Time* magazine's 1968 review of *Il buono, il brutto, il cattivo*, that by the end of the film, 'liters of fake blood have oozed, dripped, spilled and spouted over the landscape'.[26] Such a hyperbolic description is clearly intended in jest, but it betrays a conflation of Leone's technique with the contemporaneous vogue for a considerably more graphic violence: the very trend, in such films as *Bonnie and Clyde*, *Point Blank*, *The Dirty Dozen* (all 1967) and *Bullitt* (1968), from which *The Wild Bunch* would emerge. As we have seen, a preoccupation with the issue of violence both in society and on the cinema screen grew steadily through the late 1960s, at precisely the time when many Italian Westerns were finding their way into American movie theatres.[27] The critical reception these films received upon their release in the US market accordingly focussed overwhelmingly on the very bone of contention dominating contemporary filmic discourse: namely, their abundantly violent content. Bosley Crowther, whose fiercely disparaging *New York Times* review of *Bonnie and Clyde* – 'as pointless as it is lacking in taste'[28] – famously divided critical opinion, did not pull his punches when dealing with this influx. Identifying 'an excitement of morbid lust' in the casual attitude towards death evident throughout *Per qualche dollaro in più*, he stated:

> The fact that this film is constructed to endorse the exercise of murderers, to emphasize killer bravado and generate glee in frantic manifestations of death is, to my mind, a sharp indictment of it as so-called entertainment in this day.[29]

Crowther's attitude towards Leone, indeed, is characteristic of the reception afforded Italian Westerns generally in US critical circles. Even the relatively innocuous *Una pistola per Ringo* (1965) incurred such condemnation, with Tony Galluzzo of the *Motion Picture Herald* announcing that 'one seriously questions whether a continuous barrage of senseless slaughter doth an action film make'.[30]

Appendix D tabulates my corpus of reviews, taken from US and UK publications, of a representative sample of 50 Italian Westerns released into those nations' markets between 1965 and 1977. The words 'violence' or 'violent' appear at least once in reviews of 32 of these films; the words 'bloodthirsty', 'bloody', 'bloodlust', 'bloodbath', 'bloodshed' or 'blood' appear in reviews of 22; and the words 'sadism' or 'sadistic' in 17. 'Torture', 'brutality', 'gore', 'carnage' and 'slaughter' are all applied to more than one film in this list, while only nine of the 50 films are exempted altogether from such a lexicon. Even some films which are recognised to have a relatively low body count (such as Corbucci's *Johnny Oro* (1966): 'Much less sadistic than its recent continental rivals'[31]) are discussed from within this frame of reference. Kevin Thomas epitomises the critical consensus in his *Los Angeles Times* review of *Indio Black, sai che ti dico? Sei un gran figlio di ...* (1970), released internationally as *Adios Sabata*:

> Since *Adios Sabata* is so relentlessly typical of its bloody genre – and therefore literally a bloody bore – it seemed worthwhile to concentrate primarily on counting corpses to find out just how many bodies do bite the dust in the course of one of these cretinous "entertainments".[32]

As is alluded to here, the deluge of Italian Westerns released in the USA led many critics to the conclusion that this *filone* constituted not only a sadistic, but a homogeneous, mass of low-budget trash. Carlo Lizzani's *Un fiume di dollari* (1966), for example, was described in *Variety* as 'another of what is apparently an endless supply of European-made blood-and-guts oaters'.[33] Most notable in Kevin Thomas's review, however, is his decision to count the number of corpses in the film, and he was not alone. On reviewing Leone's *Giù la testa* (1971) in *The Evening Standard*, Valerie Jenkins wrote that she was once asked to count shootings and knifings in an Italian Western (significantly, she does not specify which one, suggesting that they have all merged for this critic) for a survey on violence in the cinema: 'I fell fast asleep after getting up to 138.'[34] As well as illustrating the extent to which Italian Westerns were often thought of as a unified body of sadistic ephemera, these body-counting exercises go some way towards explaining the frequent conflation of the *filone* with contemporaneous trends towards graphic brutality in US cinema. The light-hearted stylistics of Italian Western violence were less the issue than was the narrative frequency of violent death *per se*.

If critics were up in arms at the frequent brutality on show, however, distributors swiftly came to see the lucrative appeal commanded by the Spaghetti Western. The violent content therein, far from being played down, was often the primary selling point (as in the case of Corbucci's *Un dollaro a testa*, whose 1967 US release was punctuated with the poster slogans 'Relentless in his vengeance! Deadly in his violence!' and 'Navajo revenge slashes ... burns ... ravages the screen!'). 'Reception' is an elusive concept, and gauging that of mainstream critical establishments is by no means a reliable method by which to understand how audiences themselves were viewing these films (many of which were considerable financial successes). Changes towards the end of the 1960s, however, are to some extent reflected by a more 'hip' tendency in a minority of reviews, more attuned to pop and youth sensibilities. The displacement of Bosley Crowther at the *New York Times* by Vincent Canby (whose sardonic riposte to outrage at the violence in *The Wild Bunch* we have already observed) was emblematic of these shifting mores. James Price in *The Times*, for example, saw *Il buono, il brutto, il cattivo*'s characters as 'conceived on purely cut-out, comic-strip lines' while, writing of the numerous killings in Gianfranco Parolini's *Ehi amico ... c'è Sabata, hai chiuso!* (1969), Eric Braun observed that 'they have the effect of a cartoon where creatures are often run-over, mangled, elongated, scalped, flattened, blown out [*sic*] and so on'.[35]

Rather than focussing purely on the very presence of violent death, these reviews recognised, however disparagingly, that many Italian Westerns reflected an altogether different aesthetic from the graphic brutality emanating from such directors as Penn and Peckinpah. The pop culture stylistics of this *filone*, invisible to many such as Crowther, were centre-frame in such countercultural publications as *Time Out*. One of the earliest champions of the Spaghetti Western, Mike Wallington, wrote in its pages in 1970 that these films should be read in the context of 'the time-opera and peplum [...] by way of the spy-movie [...] all self conscious genres susceptible to parody and spoof'.[36] This, as we shall see, was the very cultural milieu from which the *filone*'s subsequent cult status would emerge, giving rise to its eventual apotheosis in the annals of 'cool' cinema and the postmodern tributes of Rodriguez and Tarantino.

Given this environment, into which the films of Damiani and Sollima were released in 1968 and 1969, it is little wonder that their intended political expositions were almost entirely overlooked. Caught between a critical preoccupation with gratuitous screen brutality (and the attendant habit of viewing all Italian Westerns as one and the same) and a hip appreciation of wildly irreverent comic-book panache, their attempts at serious discourses on political violence would face a considerable battle just to be noticed. Reviewing *Quien sabe?* in May 1969, *The New York Times*'s AH Weiler expressed distaste for 'the latest in the series of bargain-priced, gory Italian Westerns [...] the standard, unending explosive carnage that is guaranteed to keep the customer awake, but not informed'.[37] While Damiani's Mexican Revolution setting at least garnered a modicum of political recognition (its full length showing at the Moscow Film Festival credited with 'a certain attempt at reasoning out its social-political implications'[38] in *Variety*), Sollima's contributions were damned with the faintest of praise. *La resa dei conti* was seen as 'all pretty old hat and of a calibre long forgotten by Hollywood'[39] (*Variety*) and 'not a bad little Western, as these dubbed, Italian-Spanish efforts go. [...] There are gunfights, knife-fights, a whipping and a couple of punch-ups to be going on with'[40] (*Kine Weekly*). *Faccia a faccia*'s studied eschewal of spectacle was seen as 'somewhat lacking in violent action. [...] This is really just another Western'[41] (*Kine Weekly*). In critical circles at least, these films were not differentiated from the mass of Italian Westerns to any notable extent, and the issue of violence remained purely on the level of cinematic context. Crucially, Franco Solinas's involvement in *Quien sabe?* and *La resa dei conti* was never discussed.

Moreover, these films' bracketing under an 'action' category led to them being cut severely to fit into grindhouse double bills and, more often than not, it was expositional (and 'political') dialogue which was shorn. *La resa dei conti* was edited down from 106 minutes to 85, *Quien sabe?* from 115 minutes to 77, and *Faccia a faccia*'s 107 minutes were cut to 92.[42] When *Quien sabe?* was released in the USA and the UK in 1969, its titular focus on the inarticulate peasant striking a violent blow against the West[43] was replaced by 'A Bullet for the General'. This title not only describes Tate's mission; it also promises action aplenty. The film's US distributor, Avco Embassy, was quick to exploit this with irrelevant tag lines such as 'Like the Bandit ... Like the Gringo ... A bullet doesn't care who it kills' and 'Nothing can stop the Bandit except the Gringo ... Nothing can stop the Gringo except the General ... Nothing can stop the General except a bullet!'. Ultimately, the film's close resemblance to the Western genre offered far more lucrative returns than did its political content: a pattern repeated in the case of *La resa dei conti*, which was marketed as a Sergio Leone spin-off. For the film's American release in August 1968, under the action-adventure title 'The Big Gundown', its publicity poster announced: 'Mr Ugly Comes to Town Today!' (though, this pedant must protest, Van Cleef had in fact played 'The Bad' in Leone's most recent film).

Quite clearly, the generic dominance of Leone, along with the cinematic and cultural contexts of the late 1960s, acted as barriers to serious political comprehension of these films in the US and UK markets. While distributors were brutal in their cutting, however, violent scenes were not their target. Indeed, pivotal sequences of on-screen violence by which, it was intended, serious political messages might be communicated remained intact: the killings of Tate in *Quien sabe?*, Shep in *La resa dei conti* and Wallace in *Faccia a faccia*. The question must therefore be raised as to what extent the films themselves can be seen to invite such oversights on their own terms, through either adherence to, or eschewal of, the Italian Western's stylistic norms. Do they in fact attempt to differentiate their depictions from the wider *filone*'s exuberance to offer an audience cinematic violence of a style which invites political discourse, as do Penn and Peckinpah?

The low-angle, deep-focus framings and the rapid cross-cutting which punctuate Cuchillo's drawn-out showdown with Shep in *La resa dei conti* adhere closely to the cinematographic norms, established largely by Leone, of the Italian Western. In particular, the deep-focus shot pointing between the hero's legs splayed in the foreground at his adversary waiting for combat in the background demands an association with similar low-angle framings throughout the 'Dollars' trilogy. If Sollima's professed intentions are to be taken at face value, however, the climactic moment of violence itself is supposed to symbolise the revenge of the Third World on the capitalist West as the primitive blade defeats the Western six-shooter. A shot of Shep's hand reaching for his gun is briefly spliced with Cuchillo, throwing his knife in centre-frame close-up, before the film cuts to another deep-focus shot with Shep in the foreground, his back to the camera as his gun fires. As he slowly turns around, it is evident that the knife has embedded itself in his head, the handle protruding from his brow. Returning to Stephen Prince's invaluable study of cinematic violence in Hollywood's Production Code era, he emphasises that one of the Code's most rigidly-enforced regulations was that prohibiting the graphic depiction of knife wounds, and specifically those shown on bare flesh.[44] While *La resa dei conti*'s 1968 release coincided with the final collapse of the Code, however, this brief and bloodless depiction was not in fact blazing a gory trail, even within the Italian Western *filone* itself. Sergio Corbucci, for one, had got there first with a considerably more gruesome framing of the death of Duncan in *Un dollaro a testa* (released in the USA in December 1967), which depicts the hero's axe embedded in the villain's skull in lurid close-up. *Variety*'s comment that Sollima's film was 'all pretty old hat' is a telling sign that violations of the defunct Code were no longer anything out of the ordinary.

It is indeed the case that the most politically-charged sequences of violence in both Damiani's and Sollima's films present nothing new in the cinematographic context of the Italian Western. In fact, as the above example of Corbucci's penchant for gruesomeness attests, those of *Quién sabe?* and *Faccia a faccia* are among the more innocuous examples to be found within the already parodic *filone*. They adhere remarkably closely to tried-and-tested (and by this time often violated) stylistic methodologies from the era of the Production Code. It is true that the glee with which Chuncho kills Tate, emptying his gun into the limp body at point-blank range, would have violated the Code's taboos on sadistic enjoyment of violence. So too, Brad Fletcher's cold-blooded, remorseless execution of Wallace would surely have drawn censure. Prince argues, however, that the Code's efforts to placate censors, far from imposing repressive regulations, compelled film-makers to innovate stylistic techniques to suggest violence instead of depicting its graphic details. In this respect, the specific techniques employed by Damiani and Sollima to frame the moment of violence itself are straight out of the 1940s. Tate loses consciousness immediately he is struck by the first bullet and slumps to the floor in an exemplary deployment of the 'clutch and fall' technique, while Sollima's camera cuts away from the close-up of Wallace a split second before the trigger is pulled. The reverse shot depicting his hand going limp adheres to what Prince terms 'indexical pointing': an action subsequent to, and caused by, the act of violence inserted to stand in for the act itself.[45]

In Chapter Two I posited the theory that for film-makers such as Damiani, Sollima and Petroni who sought to expound radical polemics in this era, the Spaghetti Western was seen to be a singularly suitable medium. As we examine the patterns of reception here summarised, however, one thing becomes increasingly clear: that the enduring legacy of their films would be shaped more by the political and cultural outlooks of international audiences than it would by their narrative content. Such factors may at first appear to have been beyond the control of the film-makers, yet we have seen on numerous levels that their decision to work within the stylistic conventions of the Italian Western placed obstacles in the way of political communication.

Firstly, the *filone*'s humorously detached violent aesthetic was not a framework within which radicalism was easily discernible at the very time when Penn and Peckinpah were redefining the visual stylistics of outrage and anger for a new generation. Outside countercultural communities, meanwhile, the very presence of abundant violence was obscuring political messages. The final collapse of the Production Code ushered in a new era of cinematic ultra-violence just as the films of Damiani and Sollima were being released in the USA. Both the moral outrage of critics and the 'hip' admiration of fans overlooked their attempts to provoke ideological debate. By heralding a fundamental shift in production (as profitable formulae from abroad were assimilated) and distribution (as the 'mass' market gave way to the niche market), the collapse of the Code ensured that their films were destined to be consumed as nothing more nor less than violent 'grindhouse' fare alongside Kung Fu, horror and blaxploitation movies, and other Spaghetti Westerns.

That the stylistic choices made by these film-makers jeopardised their chances of successful translation, however, is not necessarily to say that the ideologies carried by their films went entirely unnoticed in US cinema. The American counterculture was a diverse set of communities, and there were affinities between many of these and the Italian protest movements. It is therefore to patterns of political influence within the film industry itself that I now turn, to examine the extent to which Italian militancy bled into America's own cinematic radicalism. Here, we shall firstly observe that there were indeed ideological agreements between the radical Westerns of Italy and those of Hollywood. These certainly reflect pre-existing points of contact between the transatlantic countercultures, but the extent to which direct influences from Damiani and Sollima can be extrapolated therein is doubtful. More significantly, we shall see that the militancy expounded in some of the Italian films found an apt bedfellow in the very milieu of grindhouse cinema mentioned above. In the 'blaxploitation' genre, violent action similarly rubbed shoulders with belligerent ideological discourse in independent films aimed at audiences marginalised from mainstream culture.

### Points of Contact in Transatlantic Radicalism

Chuncho's gleeful instruction to Tate's limp body to 'go back to the United States, Niño' puts a stamp on the final awakening of the native, as he sends a bullet-riddled message to interfering gringos that they are no longer to be tolerated. Insofar as the didactic exposition of *Quien sabe?* is directed as much at the audience in the movie theatre as it is at the characters on the screen, this exclamation equally symbolises the motivation behind Damiani's and Solinas's collaboration. By inverting the Western genre's ideological assumptions they too seek to send a clear message back across a cultural divide, delivering an acerbic critique of US foreign policy. When this film was itself sent 'back to the United States' in April 1969 it arrived in the midst of protests in this target nation, as countercultural movements rallied in increasing numbers against the war in Vietnam. In the early 1970s, however, as the Western itself became a key ideological battleground, the more overtly militant Italian appropriations of this genre failed to gain a political foothold in mainstream US cinema. Instead of adopting the bravura tone of such polemics, the North American counterculture frequently expressed itself through films marked by despair, revulsion and anger. The programmatic endorsement of violent reprisals arising from such Roman diatribes as *Quien sabe?* was largely absent.

As I have shown, however, this aggressive militancy is a dominant feature in some, not all, of the key films examined in this book. The ideological heterogeneity of political trends emanating from Rome has been illustrated by the contrast between those films discussed in Chapter Three, and those in Chapter Four. Peckinpah's simultaneous revulsion for, and deliberate aesthetic elevation of, violent acts in *The Wild Bunch* reflected both ambiguity and incoherence in his political stance. The Italian 'RSA' plot arose from a similarly ambiguous ideological slant on violence – at once condemning a brutal machine while expounding the very rationale by which the Red Brigades would later justify their own violence – equally reflecting an incoherent political cause. This chapter has so far demonstrated public and critical neglect of these films' political content. In the RSA narrative, however, there are notable points of similarity with trends which arose in the Hollywood Western after 1969.

Michael Cimino's *Heaven's Gate* (1980) is at first sight an odd point of comparison with the Spaghetti Western. Its budgetary excesses, its interminable shooting schedule and its elaborately magisterial aesthetic could hardly be more distant from the playfully low-budget, rapidly-produced burlesque prevalent throughout this *filone*. When analysed alongside, for example, Michael Winner's *Lawman* (1971) and *Chato's Land* (1972), or Clint Eastwood's *High Plains Drifter* (1973), Cimino's earnest film is poles apart from the baroque cruelty frequently imported into 1970s Hollywood from Roman studios. It was, nevertheless, the culmination of a significant countercultural trend within the Hollywood Western of that decade, which reflected ideological parallels with aspects of the Italian protest movements. It is therefore a useful place-marker for the purposes of this chapter. From 1969 until the release of *Heaven's Gate*, the Hollywood Western frequently framed mechanisms of government and corporate power as murderous, corrupt cabals.

Power, in the Western, had always come from the barrel of a gun. The fetishism with which the people of Dodge City stare at 'the gun that won the West' on Independence Day in the opening sequence of *Winchester 73* (1950) inextricably ties the eponymous weapon to US nationhood. In *My Darling Clementine* (1946), the Earps can purge Tombstone of lawlessness only through bearing arms, and Ransom Stoddard is respected and influential because the collective imagination holds that he was the man who shot Liberty Valance. As the 1970s dawned, however, the violence with which the genre's powerful men were asserting their socio-political status was becoming ever more pernicious, coercive and sadistic. Peckinpah's railroad magnate Mr. Harrigan proved to be the prototype for a distinctly unsavoury breed of conspicuously wealthy thugs and brutal corporate employees, in such films as *McCabe and Mrs Miller* (1971), *The Hunting Party* (1971), *Valdez is Coming* (1971), *Pat Garrett and Billy the Kid* (1973) and *The Missouri Breaks* (1976). As Michael Coyne puts it, 'at the end of *Stagecoach* the corrupt banker, Gatewood, had been exposed and arrested. Yet now, in the age of Nixon and Watergate, Gatewood had triumphed. […] Finally, America was *his*'.[46] In Dick Richards's *The Culpepper Cattle Company* (1972), Frank Culpepper questions the right of avaricious land baron Thornton Pierce to evict people from his land. 'Seems to me you got an awful lot of land', observes the eponymous cowboy. 'You got a deed to it?' Nodding towards his gun-toting henchmen, Pierce wryly replies: 'These are all the deeds I need.' The anti-establishment, countercultural sentiments of *Little Big Man* (1970), *Soldier Blue* (1970), *Bad Company* (1972) and *Buck and the Preacher* (1972) propose that US militarism and white expansionism arise from a coercive, even genocidal, appetite. In a similar sentiment, the depictions of rapacious businessmen listed above suggest that corporate power is driven by that same violent urge.

The scene from *The Culpepper Cattle Company* cited above highlights the unease emanating from Hollywood Westerns in this period, which displays some equivalence with the Italian 'RSA' plot variant. The relationship between material wealth and subjective power is assumed to be a basic condition of society by Thornton Pierce, and his barely veiled threat of violence arises in response to a questioning of this very assumption. When the pastor, Nathaniel, further casts doubt on Pierce's material right to dictate access rights by asserting the field to be 'God's land', the landowner's rage unveils the violent base supporting his ideology: '*My* land! […] Squatter! Round here we shoot squatters. When we come back there ain't nobody better be here, because we're coming in to blast whatever trespassers is left.'

Such officially-sanctioned coercion is characteristic of power relations in some of this period's most significant Westerns. In the Harrison and Shaughnessy mining company, Robert Altman's *McCabe and Mrs Miller* (1971) offers a vivid representation of brutal realities beneath the surface of the corporate elite. The polite tones of Messrs Hollander and Sears, as they attempt to buy McCabe out of his property, barely conceal the threatening nature of the company they represent: 'Listen Mr McCabe, if we can't talk this over reasonably … We were led to believe that you were … a man of good common sense, if you know what I mean.' The lawyer Clement Samuels's subsequent posturing to McCabe that 'the law is here to protect the little guy' would sit comfortably in the pantheon of Hollywood films sticking up for individual enterprise, were it not for Altman's sardonic authorial voice, which fundamentally rejects the sentiment of Capra and Ford. 'Now do you think [the mining company] want their stockholders and the public thinking that their management isn't imbued with all the principles of fair play and justice, the very values that make this country what it is today?', Samuels asks. The appearance of Butler and his fellow hired assassins renders this faith in the institutions of justice and business hollow, but the lawyer inadvertently identifies the reality behind the company's actions. As long as the public face of corporate power presents a reasonable and rational façade, the coercive and murderous base can continue about its business.

Arising from a concept spawned in the early 1970s, but not released until 1980, *Heaven's Gate* is both the political and the chronological culmination of these countercultural trends. The film's ideological framework equally arises from radical outlooks of the late 1960s and the early 1970s concerning the oppressive 'system'. By insisting on the presence of brutal class struggle on the Western frontier, however, it expresses these in their most uncompromising tones. Frederick Jackson Turner's 'Frontier Thesis' of 1893 is most commonly applied to the Western genre for its elegiac affirmation of American exceptionalism: the 'safety valve' averting European class conflict by offering immigrants and workers the chance to forge their own destinies. Cimino's film demands instead that attention is turned towards Turner's lesser-dramatised disquiet at the officially-declared closing of the frontier in 1890, along with the socio-political implications of this onset of modernity. Articulated throughout is a dual notion: that the cattle barons comprise an elite cabal psychotically determined to slaughter immigrants; and that the US military and institutions of government are constituent parts of this murderous machine, endorsing the genocidal impulses of landed capital.

In seeking to uncover the repressed history of class struggle in the Wild West, Cimino recreates the precise 'brief epoch' which Owen Wister summoned in *The Virginian* – the 1892 Johnson County War – in a radically oppositional tenor. This oft-mythologised and richly-coded episode had been appropriated as a lens through which to assess contemporary oppositions on more than one occasion since Wister's elitist agenda first identified its resonance. The steadily more hostile depictions of the violent campaign waged against smallholders by the wealthy Wyoming Stock Growers Association (WSGA) themselves reflect the increasing ambivalence to corporate power within the Western genre. While Wister champions the cattle barons' right to lynch 'rustlers', for example, *Shane* (1953) locates the homesteaders as the pioneers of the nation. George

Stevens's film thus offers an emphatic riposte to *The Virginian*'s advocacy of such vigilantism while simultaneously bidding a fond farewell to the cattle drives and the 'Old West'. This ambiguity emblematises that which lies at the heart of the Western – the elegiac lament mixed with progressive zeal – partially explaining the film's frequently asserted 'classic' status. *Heaven's Gate* is therefore a self-conscious intervention in this pre-existing discourse. Cimino's counter-historical occupation of Wister's hallowed epoch directly implicates the upper classes of the East – of whom Wister was one – in both the oppression of the working classes and the obfuscation of this brutal history.

By so openly presenting history and myth as ideological constructs, and seeking to expose their repressed undercurrents, Cimino insists upon the epoch's continuing relevance to contemporary American society. This posits a continuum of exploitation and coercion in an agenda closely resembling that of *Faccia a faccia*, and *Heaven's Gate*'s philosophical parallels with the 'RSA' plot do not end with Sollima's film. Cimino's symbolic deployment of *mise en scène* towards his film's beginning, indeed, bears a marked similarity to Sergio Corbucci's at the end of *Il grande Silenzio*. Both make use of flat surfaces upon which two-dimensional projections of oppressive forces temporarily cover up the social realities hidden beneath. As illustrated in Chapter Three, Corbucci makes effective use of Tigrero's reflection in the saloon window to symbolise the murderousness barely concealed beneath the surface of legality throughout the film. Cimino's shot composition similarly projects a representative of legalised brutality onto a 'screen' when WSGA enforcer Nate Champion (Christopher Walken) menacingly approaches the hut of a rustler. In this instance, the white sheets draped all around the homestead are an attempt to conceal the theft, to which the family of immigrants has been driven, from the outside world. The starving underclass of the frontier whose plight, Cimino suggests, is traditionally concealed by the Western myth, remains hidden until the shadow of Nate, projected on the sheets, approaches. He remains only a vague apparition to both rustler and audience until his rifle shot pierces the sheet to reveal his face peering through the newly-created bullet hole at the now dead immigrant. The cognitive barrier between the violent mechanisms of landed capital and the victims of that violence is literally torn down at this early juncture, and from this point onwards each is clearly visible to the other, and to the audience.

On a narrative level, too, there are notable parallels between *Heaven's Gate* and *Il grande Silenzio*.[47] When the diabolical Frank Canton describes the poverty-stricken immigrants as 'thieves, anarchists and outlaws', this inverted moral compass recalls Tigrero's almost identical condemnation of the starving outlaws in the hills above Snow Hill ('They're enemies of God, of humanity, of morality, of order. It's a patriotic duty to exterminate them'). Later, Canton declares 'we are the law' before executing a bound immigrant in cold blood, exactly repeating Tigero's final act in the saloon. The legalised hunt for innocents and the desolation of the final massacre, as the malicious forces of law and order triumph, arise from an equivalently bleak ideological outlook on Western society to Corbucci's. The hand of Western Marxism weighs equally heavily upon the works of Penn, Peckinpah, Altman and Cimino as it does upon those of Sollima and Corbucci in their intended deconstructions of American history, culture and adventurism. Both Althusser's writings on Ideological State Apparatuses and Benjamin's historical theses inform a study of the apocalyptic agenda at work throughout this group of films. Furthermore, Marcuse's notions of 'repressive desublimation' and 'democratic unfreedom'[48] pertain to the pretence of propriety constructed to conceal the 'system's' coercive base, most visible in *McCabe and Mrs Miller*. Such parallels suggest a potentially receptive audience amongst certain US film-makers for radical Italian appropriations of the Western genre.

This is not, however, to say that the countercultural trend of which *Heaven's Gate* is the culmination was directly influenced by its Italian precursor. The limitations of drawing such influences become clear when we observe again the divergence in both stylistic and ideological tenor between the radical Westerns of the USA and those of Italy. Firstly, the burlesque tone infused throughout the Italian *filone* is almost entirely absent from New Hollywood's countercultural appropriations of the genre. Arthur Penn's *The Missouri Breaks* (1976), it is true, signals an alternative aesthetic, more closely resembling the playful irreverence for the genre's traditions to be found throughout the Italian Western. This film, however, is a notable exception in a trend otherwise characterised by earnest despair and solemn treatment of the Western's central role in defining US nationhood (a reverence for the genre's traditions particularly palpable throughout the work of Peckinpah). Secondly, while individual points of contact between the ideological outlooks discussed above attest to some crossovers between transatlantic countercultures, the strain of political commitment peculiar to the Italian Western – the confrontational militancy of *Quien sabe?* and *La resa dei conti* – was not taken up by mainstream Hollywood directors to any meaningful extent.

Above all, to attribute the outlooks of Peckinpah, Penn and Cimino to direct influences from the Italian Western would be to overlook the extent to which said outlooks arose from issues specifically preoccupying US society.

As the above quotation from Michael Coyne stresses, the first half of the 1970s was the era of the invasion of Cambodia, of My Lai becoming public knowledge, of the killings at Kent and Jackson States, and of Watergate. The messages at the heart of these Hollywood films depicting corrupt corporations, sadistic military institutions and deceitful governments are inextricably tied to the parochial concerns of the Nixon era.

There is also to be considered once more the fact that Italian Westerns *per se* were by no means received in mainstream circles – countercultural or otherwise – as films with a capacity for radicalism at all. The amoral nihilism of Leone (and of the majority of Spaghettis) most certainly resonated with the zeitgeist at a time when Vietnam was dismantling what Engelhardt dubs 'victory culture' and a perceived social breakdown was bedevilling conceptions of the American Dream. Such a representation of a broken society, however, was by no means one with appeal exclusively to the radical Left. Possibly the single most visible influence from the *filone* in mainstream Hollywood cinema of the early 1970s, indeed, while engaging openly with these contemporary concerns, advocated not a countercultural, but a reactionary response. Don Siegel's *Dirty Harry* (1971) directly exploits the most significant contribution made by Sergio Leone to Hollywood: the introduction of Clint Eastwood to American audiences.

The popularity of Eastwood's cynical persona driven by self-preservation in an unforgiving universe, described by Pauline Kael as 'the hero of a totally nihilistic dream world',[49] in part reflects this crisis in US national identity. This persona, repeated in all three 'Dollars' films and marketed in America as 'the Man with no Name', introduced a new breed of laconic, impassive and supremely deadly superhero to the English-speaking world. Ted Post's *Hang 'Em High* (1968), Siegel's *Two Mules for Sister Sara* (1969) and Eastwood's own *High Plains Drifter* (1973) perpetuated and entrenched the persona in popular culture within the generic boundaries of the Western. It was ironically with Siegel's transpositions of this lucrative archetype to the modern city, however, that the character took on its most ideologically 'Western' resonance. After *Coogan's Bluff* (1968) depicted the clash between a bureaucratic legal system and Eastwood's individualistic Westerner, *Dirty Harry* placed this 'tough cop' persona in the midst of Nixon-era neuroses over urban violence and social breakdown.

An amalgam of Western motifs, *Dirty Harry* asserts the individual gunman's duty to defy the whims of institutional law in the face of a ruthless threat to a weak and cowardly society. Such a discourse over vigilantism stretches all the way back to Owen Wister, and informs the Western's tense oppositions concerning violence and its relationship to society throughout the genre's development. By directly quoting *High Noon* in the final sequence, however, as Harry Callaghan discards his tin star in disgust at the society he has defended, Siegel performs an act of cinematic sleight of hand. *Dirty Harry*, unlike Zinnemann's film, is no radical polemic. On the contrary, the film engages contemporary countercultural ideologies from an explicitly antagonistic perspective.

On 6 October 1969, 'Weathermen' Bill Ayers and Terry Robbins blew up a statue commemorating police deaths in Chicago's 1886 riots. The incident was part of a concerted, but ultimately abortive, attempt amongst factions of the American New Left to instigate the 'Days of Rage'. This armed campaign aimed simultaneously to 'bring the war home' and to provoke high-profile police brutality in riots through Chicago which lasted until 10 October. The episode entrenched establishment and media views of the Weathermen as the 'New Barbarians', and divided the revolutionary Left yet further over the issue of violent insurrection.[50] Two years later, *Dirty Harry* opens with a close-up of a memorial to San Francisco police officers who gave their lives in the line of duty. From this point onwards Siegel's anti-'Miranda rights' invective is aimed squarely, not only at a liberal judicial system, but at America's radicalised youth culture. Harry is dismissive of his partner's sociology degree ('Just what I need: a college boy'), and the psychotic killer Scorpio sports shoulder-length hair. Also, the 'crosshair' symbol of the real-life Zodiac killer (upon whom Scorpio is based) is transformed into a CND badge on the killer's belt buckle, clearly signifying the fading hippie movement a year after the Charles Manson trial had soured the countercultural dream. In depicting Scorpio hiring somebody to beat him up then telling the press that Harry did it, the film openly dismisses the frequent accusations of police brutality made by contemporary radicals. Indeed, in asserting Harry's essential righteousness in using torture and lethal force where society dare not, *Dirty Harry* is a purposefully reactionary response to the contemporary fears over violent crime on the streets of America.

That Harry Callaghan is the progeny of Leone's 'Man with no Name' does not mean that the ideologies behind such an application of the persona can in any way be traced back to the 'Dollars' trilogy itself. What this does display, however, is that the influential and lucrative archetypes spawned by Leone were fluidly assimilated into mainstream, big-budget Hollywood cinema alongside such instantly recognisable cultural reference points as *High Noon*. Leone's widely-distributed contributions symbolised the Italian Western as a whole for mainstream critics and audiences alike. From whichever side of the political spectrum one looked, this sense of a nihilistic, amoral world of desolation was the prevailing perception of the *filone* and its relationship to society.

In stark contrast, *Quien sabe?*, *La resa dei conti*, *Corri, uomo, corri*, *Tepepa*, *Il mercenario* and *Compañeros*, far from expressing despair or nihilism, end on triumphalist, bravura expressions of ascendant Third World militancy. The closest Hollywood came to such an endorsement of subaltern violence was in *Chato's Land* (1972). Here, however, the native is a mysterious angel of death, wreaking symbolic revenge for the sins of Vietnam (itself an archetype displaying the vogue for deadly superheroes in part fostered by Leone). The tragedy here (as in Aldrich's *Ulzana's Raid* (1972)) is that of white America's loss of innocence, as the heterogeneous posse are picked off one-by-one by a taciturn native avenger. This film is also more notable for its foreshadowing of Michael Winner's and Charles Bronson's later, modern-day, *Death Wish* franchise (in which Bronson again plays a ruthless avenger whose wife has been brutally attacked). While we have seen that certain of Winner's cinematic framing devices attest to some degree of influence, this characterisation contrasts with Tomas Milian's charming native rogue. Cuchillo represents an alternative political stance and himself flees from a ruthless corporate posse before striking a blow against the system.

The lesser-known examples of the Italian Western *filone*, however, were not playing in these mainstream film circuits revolving around the Hollywood product, instead emerging amongst an eclectic mix of low-budget independent and foreign movies in grindhouse cinemas. While this milieu of niche distribution certainly obscured their political visibility, it is nevertheless here that we find the most linear ideological influence brought to bear in US cinema by the confrontational tones of Italy's militant Left. In the Black Panthers, and their own low-budget practices of cultural dissemination, there was an altogether more receptive audience for such belligerent postcolonial polemics. This bravura insubordination was precisely the tradition of 'ethnic' radicalism into which Melvin Van Peebles plugged when he closed *Sweet Sweetback's Baadasssss Song* (1971), to the backdrop of a south-western desert locale, with the caption: 'Watch out. A baad asssss nigger is coming back to collect some dues.'

Released in the very same year as *Dirty Harry*, this micro-budget film arose from within the Black Power movement, and is diametrically opposed to the ideologies expounded by Siegel. 'In the early 70s, when white [...] mainstream cinema was about defeat', claims Elvis Mitchell, 'black movies had heroes who won, people that could effect change [...] laying claim to the screen for the first time'.[51] *Sweet Sweetback's Baadasssss Song* is indeed a radical and confrontational assertion of ethnic pride in the face of police brutality. Moreover, its plot, cinematography and ideological intentions bear a remarkably close resemblance to *La resa dei conti*.

Firstly, the eponymous hero is, like Cuchillo, on the run from a corrupt white man's law. For most of the film, the guileful Sweetback is fleeing police sirens, hiding under bridges and running through the streets of downtown Los Angeles. The cinematography, too, echoes the framing of Cuchillo's flight. His progression through this desolate urban desert is punctuated by rapidly cross-cut montages, as the camera repeatedly 'discovers' him with pans and long shots giving the audience alone fleeting glimpses of his hiding places beneath underpasses and atop moving vehicles. As with Jonathan Corbett's shooting of Paco Molinas, the pursuant police kill one black man and savagely beat another in cases of mistaken identity. When, armed only with a knife, Sweetback flees into the desert, heading for the Mexican border while being pursued through cane fields by police dogs, the film's climax openly echoes that of Sollima's earlier work.

While Van Peebles has not publicly cited *La resa dei conti* as an influence, such direct and clear parallels should come as no surprise. Spaghetti Westerns were in this era a key ingredient in filling double bills at grindhouse cinemas along New York's 42nd Street and Los Angeles's Broadway and Hollywood Boulevard. They played alongside not only Kung Fu films, horror films and soft-core pornography, but also the genre, in part spawned by Van Peebles's pioneering independent film, which came to be known as 'blaxploitation'. This milieu of low-budget, frequently violent cinema attracted precisely the 'hip' young audience who defied the critical establishment by bestowing cult status on the much-reviled Italian Western *filone* in the 1970s. That militant factions amongst the practitioners of such popular genres might both identify with each other's intended ideological messages and draw direct inspiration from one another's films is an entirely plausible notion.

The political motivations driving *Sweet Sweetback's Baadasssss Song* are indeed similar to those of Sollima, Damiani and, especially, Solinas. Just as militant Italian Westerns were broadly addressed to subaltern groups marginalised by US-led modernity, so Van Peebles's polemic affirms Fanonist doctrine early on in its narrative, when the initially easy-going Sweetback uses handcuffs to beat two policemen unconscious. In turning the oppressive tools of 'the Man' against him this symbolic sequence of violence (repeated when the hero strangles another policeman, again with handcuffs), narrates an awakening of political consciousness akin to those of Chuncho in *Quien sabe?* and Jose in *Queimada!*. An exemplary portrayal of 'internal colonisation' and the right to armed self-defence against a racist state proclaimed by the Black Panther Party, the film opens with the dedication: 'To all the Brothers and Sisters who had enough of the Man.'

The frequent miscegenation of grindhouse genres hinted at by Van Peebles's film was unmasked on numerous occasions in the cycle of 'blaxploitation Westerns' which appeared in the early 1970s. Such films as *The Red, White, and Black* (1970), *The Legend of Nigger Charlie* (1972) and *Boss Nigger* (1975) further colonised white America's hallowed mythic turf with belligerent assertions of a black urban sensibility. Sidney Poitier's *Buck and the Preacher* (1972) simultaneously contributes to the countercultural 'RSA' trend in Hollywood cinema and elaborates upon the ethnic reversals of *Soldier Blue* by depicting black pioneers being murdered by barbaric whites in the employ of wealthy racists. Furthermore, both this film and Gordon Parks Jr.'s *Thomasine and Bushrod* (1974) depict black outlaws fleeing from 'the Man' while finding haven from the oppression of white America amongst other people of colour (most notably, Native Americans). In depicting their black heroes' flight from representatives of bourgeois capital both films directly overlay racial politics onto such recently-filmed legends of white rebellion as Jesse James, Butch Cassidy and the Sundance Kid, and Bonnie and Clyde. The Western was becoming increasingly decoupled, not only from its national roots, but from its traditional obfuscation of the ethnic history of the West.

It is therefore significant that, when Melvin Van Peebles's son, Mario, sought to re-inscribe the Western's ideologies with a counter-historical narrative of black pioneers in *Posse* (1993), it was the Italian Western which formed his primary generic source material. In his elaborate use, during one duel, of low-angle tilts and ground-level deep-focus shots, the director displays an undisguised cinematographic debt to Sergio Leone. The flashback sequences and the hero's revenge-driven revelations echo *Per qualche dollaro in più* and *C'era una volta il West* (a shot from which is played behind the end credits), as well as Petroni's *Da uomo a uomo* (1967) and Antonio Margheriti's *Joko, invoca Dio … e muori!* (1968). *Posse*'s purposeful resemblance to parts of the Italian Western *filone*, however, equally extends to its political agenda. Alexandra Keller identifies in the casting of blaxploitation legends (Pam Grier, Melvin Van Peebles and Isaac Hayes) and rap stars (Big Daddy Kane and Tone Loc), alongside the visual echoes of the Rodney King beating of 1991, an agenda 'drawing the connection between nineteenth and twentieth century racism [using] the suppressed history of blacks in the West to point up the suppressed present of blacks in mainstream American filmmaking'.[52] The film's postscript claims that the history of blacks on the frontier has been 'ignored by Hollywood'. While not strictly accurate (*Buck and the*

*Preacher* addressed the very same themes), this statement is a clear indication that the counter-historical 'West' through which Jesse and his posse travel owes little to that of Californian studios.

The purposeful selection instead of the Italian Western as an amenable space within which to 'brush history against the grain' and subvert the heavily coded signifiers of US culture with a contemporary racial imperative associates this *filone* with an innate countercultural trajectory. This is by no means the exclusive preserve of Leone. The film's political agenda, and the narrative through which that agenda is expounded, indeed, are the progeny of both the 'RSA' and the 'insurgency' plots. The lynch-happy townsfolk of Cutterstown, with their shallow affectations towards 'justice', could be straight out of Questi's *Se sei vivo, spara!*, while the psychopathic white lawmen corrupt the tin star by donning Ku Klux Klan robes (itself recalling the hoods of the racist Major Jackson and his men from *Django*). It is stressed on more than one occasion that the white man put the black man into slavery and stole the red man's land, and the hero insists that the black town of Freemanville must rise up and fight their white oppressors: a call answered when Melvin Van Peebles himself proclaims the rallying cry of the 1992 LA riots: 'No justice, no peace!'

If, as such a contemporary intervention suggests, *Posse* can be interpreted as a 'Black Panthers out West' parable, it is only the latest in a continuum of confrontational radical appropriations of a genre whose affirmative ideologies began to run out of steam in the late 1960s. Though originating as an imitative response to an increasingly Americanised popular culture, the innovations of the Italian Western in the 1960s would in turn contribute to the transformation of the Hollywood genre, foreshadowing shifts in American cinema of the 1970s. What is true of the wider *filone* can also be seen to apply to films emanating from its militant wing. These re-worked the Western's signifiers into radical critiques of bourgeois society and American adventurism before equivalent movements in America itself stripped the genre's ideologies of their erstwhile authority. It is worth noting that Alejandro Jodorowsky's countercultural exercise in hippie consciousness, *El Topo* (1970), not only borrows *Django*'s surrealism and Leone's cinematographic iconoclasm, but Giulio Questi's vicious town of hypocritical sadists. So too, by fusing 'blaxploitation' ideology with that of the political strain of the Italian Western, *Posse* uncovers the innate countercultural appeal commanded by the *filone* amongst marginalised groups.

That the subaltern militancy to be found within the Italian Western survives in its most uncontaminated form in this milieu, however, ironically goes a long way towards explaining why these very inscriptions have remained largely invisible. *Posse* is extraordinary for its purposeful engagement with the ideological imperatives attached to both genres. In his conscious application of 1960s political oppositions to contemporary America through a counter-history of the nation's most ideologically-charged mythology, Van Peebles Jr enacts a conceit akin to that of *Heaven's Gate*. Yet *Posse* is the exception to the rule, for behind the very portmanteau frequently attached both to this film and to *Sweet Sweetback's Baadasssss Song* lie processes of marketing and distribution which invite an altogether apolitical interpretation. 'Blaxploitation', it is true, arose in part as a response to the success of Van Peebles Sr's groundbreaking film. The genre's most characteristic features, however, as well as its enduring legacy, follow an altogether divergent trajectory, instead replicating the 'hip' tenor of Gordon Parks's *Shaft* (1971).

That Parks's black hero is a tough maverick cop provides the most obvious clue that any attempts to 'stick it to the Man' in this film are entirely engulfed by its all-action narrative, which ironically owes more to *Dirty Harry* than to *Sweet Sweetback*. The attendant evacuation of ideology from the black solidarity to which *Shaft* merely pays lip-service is manifest in the appearance of the Black Panthers as a rag-tag bunch of rogues who, remarkably, assist the eponymous policeman in his endeavours. In seeking to highlight innate countercultural thrusts behind both the Spaghetti Western and blaxploitation, the fusion of ideologies in *Posse* therefore performs a counter-historical gesture in cinematic as well as social terms. The tide was overwhelmingly flowing in the opposite direction. Each genre, as we have seen, contained militant elements pertaining to specific issues surrounding political violence in their country of origin. Each, however, has become assimilated into global popular culture as 'cool' shorthand for violent action and stylistic panache. Their indelible association with cult grindhouse cinema has proved the single most decisive factor in this process, and has been fostered by films with a considerably higher cachet than *Posse*. This notion is nowhere so evident as in the work of Sam Raimi, Robert Rodriguez and Quentin Tarantino.

## Spaghetti Westerns in the Postmodern Era

There is in *Posse*'s counter-historical agenda more than a hint of the postmodernist outlook termed by Jean-François Lyotard 'incredulity towards metanarratives'.[53] Certainly, the 'grand narrative' of the Hollywood Western, with its ideological claims towards universality, has been largely rejected in favour of suppressed 'little narratives' of which *Posse* is one. If

Van Peebles Jr succeeds in inscribing heterogeneous political and ethnic elements into a genre so long the preserve of white America, this owes much to the decoupling of the form from its attendant ideologies performed in part by the Italian Western.

Yet Van Peebles's 'little narrative' is a drop in the ocean of this *filone*'s inheritance in global popular culture. Of all the audience constituencies considered in this chapter, none have taken possession of the Italian Western's legacy as much as the 'hip' fans of grindhouse violence and 'cool' pop culture. In such an environment, political content has been evacuated. For example, this *filone*'s iconic status in post-1960s popular culture is at its most tangible in films from two of America's most acclaimed 'cult' directors: Sam Raimi's *The Quick and the Dead* (1995) and Robert Rodriguez's *Once Upon a Time in Mexico* (2003). Both film-makers' careers were launched with successful independently-funded films reprising a 'schlock' milieu of violent low-budget genre cinema (*The Evil Dead* (1981) and *El Mariachi* (1992) respectively). Both men accordingly bring to their meticulous imitations of the Italian Western a self-consciously postmodern sensibility. This engenders a keen sense that the *filone* they ape is synonymous with other modishly violent low-budget genres which filled American grindhouse cinemas in the late 1960s and early 1970s. Neither film, indeed, relies solely on the Italian Western, each instead fusing its instantly recognisable stylistic and narrative motifs with traces of horror, martial arts or Hong Kong action cinemas.

These processes, through which Raimi and Rodriguez filter the Italian Western, in fact emblematise what residual traces there are still to be found in US cinema of this *filone*'s more politically-engaged trends. The iconographic dominance of Sergio Leone is affirmed by their studied emulation of the camera angles, aural accompaniments and baroque confrontations indelibly associated with his work in the popular imagination. Nonetheless, aspects of the *filone* which are not common to his work, but are instead features of the political strands, are integrated into this broad pattern of genre pastiche.[54] These very processes of integration, however, serve to evacuate those motifs of the ideological functions with which they had originally been inscribed. An analysis of the two films will demonstrate this point.

From the moment an extreme close-up of an outlaw's grizzled visage abruptly intrudes upon a long shot of desert landscape (exactly repeating the opening if *Il buono, il brutto, il cattivo*), *The Quick and the Dead* presents a bravura array of undisguised references to Sergio Leone. The coffin maker who can measure the stranger in town for a wooden box with one glance, the heroine's 'resurrection' and the dynamite 'hellfire' she visits upon the town are lifted straight out of *Per un pugno di dollari*. The 'game' of shooting the legs of a stool from beneath a victim in a noose and the heroine's shooting of the rope repeat the elaborate playfulness of Blondie and Tuco. The gradual revelation, through childhood flashback, of the heroine's revenge motive as her father is tormented by the villain and ultimately killed by the child's unwilling agency rehearses *C'era una volta il West* almost by rote. The rapid zooms to extreme close-up and the deep-focus compositions with which Raimi draws out preludes to gunfire merely re-enforce the impression that this is a film 'about' the stylistics of Italian Westerns.

Amongst these obvious quotations, however, appear features common to the *filone* which are nevertheless absent from the cinema of the (by 1995) revered *auteur* Leone. The villain John Herod (Gene Hackman), for example, inhabits a grand mansion, appears in a smoking jacket and bow-tie, and sits atop a throne as he leeches the inhabitants of Redemption dry. This distinctly gothic characterisation of a vice-ridden grandee displays the imprint of *Il grande Silenzio* (1968) and *Ehi amico ... c'è Sabata, hai chiuso!* (1969), both of which incorporate features of Italian horror into their diabolical villains. The credulous, bloodthirsty townsfolk, meanwhile, equally situate this narrative among other such 'RSA' Westerns as *Se sei vivo, spara!* (1967), *Da uomo a uomo* (1967) and *Il prezzo del potere* (1969). This tale is delivered with a similarly comic-book panache to that with which such directors as Carnimeo, Parolini and Corbucci elaborated upon Leone's early work. Divorced from the specific context of 1960s Italy, though, the quotations remain purely on the level of the cinematic. This film is a patchwork quilt of the Italian Western's style, narrative and characterisation; not of its politics.

The final chapter of Rodriguez's modern-day 'El Mariachi' series, *Once Upon a Time in Mexico*, operates on a similar level to Raimi's film. The conspicuous influences from the Spaghetti Western throughout this overtly intertextual trilogy are legion: El Mariachi's guitar case loaded with guns is a nod to Django's similarly deadly coffin; the repeated uses of this object variously as a flamethrower, a bomb and a bazooka directly echo the character of Banjo from *Ehi amico ... c'è Sabata, hai chiuso!*, whose minstrel persona conceals his instrument's hidden firearm attachment; and the blind gunslinger miraculously finding his targets at the end of *Once Upon a Time in Mexico* repeats an identical characterisation in Ferdinando Baldi's *Il pistolero cieco* (1971). Additionally, as the title of this third instalment displays quite openly, the work of Sergio Leone provides the all-encompassing inspiration for the entire trilogy.[55] Equally evident in *Once Upon a Time in Mexico*, however, is a direct narrative parallel with *Quien sabe?*, as CIA agent Sheldon Sands (Johnny Depp) ventures south of the border both to engineer an indigenous revolution and to kill an insurgent general. Like Bill Tate, Sands exploits the film's native hero to further his scheme. 'Sometimes a revolution is exactly what is needed to clean up the system', declares this Western interloper. 'One giant enema which just so happens to be my area of expertise.' Even down to the small Mexican boy who is at first dismissed by the American only to reappear in the midst of the insurrectionary turmoil, Rodriguez's 'insurgency' film displays the legacy of Damiani's militant trailblazer.

As Edward Buscombe observes, however, 'despite its revolutionary subject matter, *Once upon a Time in Mexico* is more interested in the stylistics of the spaghetti Western than in its ideology'.[56] These clear lines of narrative influence, indeed, function not as political tracts but as self-conscious re-enactments informing Rodriguez's postmodern project of evoking a Spaghetti Western aura. Accordingly, recurrent features whose appearances in the work of Franco Solinas denote specific ideological hypotheses are in this film humorously elaborated and subsumed into a stylistic homage constructed from a multitude of *filone* echoes. The conspicuousness of the Western interloper in a Mexican locale could hardly be more comically pronounced than with the spectacle of Sands, in the crowd of a bull-fight, sporting a tee-shirt with the large letters 'CIA' emblazoned across the chest. His subsequent comeuppance heralds not his death but his apotheosis as a leather-clad blind pistolero: a baroque incarnation recalling Henry Silva's similarly attired villain Mendez from *Un fiume di dollari* (1966) as well as the aforementioned *Il pistolero cieco*. The righteous violence enacted by the Mexican hero El Mariachi, meanwhile, carries none of the postcolonial subaltern inscription with which Chuncho, Cuchillo and Tepepa strike their oppressors. As a ruthless avenger performing ever more spectacular acts of carnage, this characterisation instead adheres to the archetypes of Django, Colonel Mortimer and Harmonica. He functions alongside Rodriguez's other stylistic nods to the larger *filone* such as elaborate zoom shots, ritualised showdowns, and frequent 'Ennio Morricone' pastiche soundtracks.

Rodriguez's modern-day setting also highlights the extent to which the Italian Western has become indelibly tied to processes of generic miscegenation. Narrative and stylistic features of the *filone* have frequently been removed from the specific chronology of the Western and fused with the stylistic tics of Japanese *anime*, Hong Kong action cinema and blaxploitation. Of all the enthralled 'Spaghetti' pastiches, Quentin Tarantino's two volumes of *Kill Bill* (2003/2004) are the prime examples of this porosity. These films present a bewildering array of pop culture references, each playfully inviting an audience to identify musical refrains, excerpts of dialogue, cinematographic techniques and visual quotations. Each is culled from disparate national cinemas united only by their grindhouse distribution or related 'cult' status in the USA. The full list would take up another chapter on its own, but a merely cursory summary displays the diversity of Tarantino's project: the vigilante heroine borrows Bruce Lee's yellow tracksuit from *Game of Death* (1978) and pursues her brutal vengeance in a plot based directly on Jack Hill's blaxploitation classic *Coffy* (1973), Toshiya Fujita's Japanese revenge saga *Lady Snowblood* (1973) and Bo Arne Vibenius's Swedish exploitation film *Thriller – en grym film* (1974).[57] The life-story of one of her enemies is narrated through the stark brush-strokes of *anime*, and punctuating the action throughout are the theme tunes of *Per un pugno di dollari*, *Un dollaro a testa*, *Il buono, il brutto, il cattivo*, *Il mercenario* and *I giorni dell'ira*.

These quotations are all stylistic or narrative and, operating purely at this 'textual' level, each evacuates its source material of national or chronological specificity. Steve Rose notes this very tendency:

> One problem with *Kill Bill*'s quotation of all these 'cool' movies [...] is that when the films are divorced from their original contexts, they are drained of all meaning. Beyond their aesthetic attributes [they] are remarkable for their political purpose: *Lady Snowblood* addresses Japan's postwar purification and reintegration. One of the victims in *Female Convict Scorpion* boasts of raping Chinese women during the second world war, while *Thriller*, for all its sex and violence, is a scathing attack on patriarchal 1970s society. What does *Kill Bill* represent? Is it about anything other than being cool?[58]

It barely requires the addendum that in the Italian Western, too, is to be found a genre emptied of its local significance in this postmodern assimilation. It is worth noting that, after Sergio Leone, the chief 'Spaghetti' reference point for Tarantino's pastiches is Sergio Corbucci. The contemplative tenor of *Il grande Silenzio* is an exception in a directorial career otherwise characterised by outrageously comic flamboyance. As we have seen, Corbucci professed sincere political significances to lie behind such narratives as *Django*, *Un dollaro a testa* and *Il mercenario*. The quotations of each of these films which appear in the work of Tarantino, however, replicate solely their stylistics, or the gruesomeness for which the director is most commonly remembered (most notably in the ear-cutting sequence of *Reservoir Dogs* (1992), lifted directly from *Django*).

As *Kill Bill: Vol. 2* enters its denouement, Bill (David Carradine) delivers a lecture to the Bride/Beatrix Kiddo (Uma Thurman), relating the significance of comic-book superheroes and their alter-egos to her own bipolar persona: 'Superman didn't become Superman. Superman was born Superman. When Superman wakes up in the morning, he's Superman. His alter-ego is Clark Kent. [...] The glasses, the business suit [...] that's the costume Superman wears to blend in with us.' In this unique feature of the character of Superman Bill identifies a parallel with the heroine's true nature, and the futility of her denial of it. 'Are you calling me a superhero?', she asks. 'I'm calling you a killer. [...] You always have been, and you always will be', he replies.

This lecture which, as Philip French notes, is lifted almost verbatim from Jules Feiffer's *The Great Comic Book Heroes* (1965),[59] is on the one hand a narrative delivery of home truths as the heroine prepares to face her nemesis. On the other, however, the speech is an overt unmasking of Tarantino's film itself, which Bill self-consciously refers to as 'this tale of bloody revenge'. As Bill correctly implies, the character of the Bride is lifted from an amalgam of pop culture reference points. She is a mythical comic-book avenger in the tradition of Django, Harmonica, Chato, Coffy, and El Mariachi. It is in this continuum that the Italian Western and its attendant archetypes find a cultural home. Violence is indeed the legacy of this *filone*; not the violence of the exploited subaltern, but that of cinematic 'exploitation'. As the Bride tells the audience, looking straight into the camera: 'I went on what the movie advertisements refer to as "A Roaring Rampage of Revenge".'

It is once again in the key issue of on-screen violence and its stylistic framing that we can most clearly see the processes at work in the negotiation of the Spaghetti Western's enduring meanings. Violence, indeed, is the key to the identities of the films discussed above, uniting the otherwise disparate cinematic influences which formulate their networks of citations. Raimi's depictions of gunshot injuries, for example, while comically elaborate, place gaping bullet wounds centre-frame true to the director's horror film credentials. When *Kill Bill*'s Bride lops off the limbs of the 'Crazy 88' gang, the litres of blood that gush gleefully across the screen flow directly from 'splatter' films and *anime*. As we have seen, rarely in the Italian Western is such abundant gore in evidence. In a similar vein, while Rodriguez is indeed meticulous in his evocation of a Spaghetti Western locale, when bullets hit flesh (as they do with considerable frequency throughout the 'El Mariachi' trilogy) the stylistic debt shifts fundamentally to an altogether divergent aesthetic. The bodies that fall through the air in carefully choreographed slow-motion as blood-squibs explode in the actors' clothes bear no relation to the Italian Western, instead being lifted directly from Hong Kong action cinema.[60]

This is a characteristic feature of films whose postmodern credentials ostensibly rest on the Spaghetti Western. Gene Quintano's Spanish-American co-production *Dollar for the Dead* (1998), for example, is an explicit attempt to resurrect this long-defunct *filone*. Shot in Almería and aping *Il buono, il brutto, il cattivo* with a plot concerning hidden gold whose secret is divided amongst uneasy partnerships, the film was even released with the tag-line 'An Action-Packed Tribute to Sergio Leone'. Given these clearly-stated intentions, that the Italian Western has become merely one amongst many generic by-words for cinematic violence is manifest in the jarring stylistic framing of the film. Quintano's acrobatic slow-motion gunfights quite openly show that the action in this 'action-packed tribute' is indebted not to Leone but to John Woo.

There are in fact numerous processes of political evacuation converging in these films. Italy's militant Westerns were by no means alone in having their violent content stripped of its ideological imperative by contact with the industrial milieu of post-1960s US cinema. We have already seen that the violence of *The Wild Bunch*, for all its stylistic divergence, was frequently conflated with the same debates which surrounded the Italian Western. Indeed, the very presence of Hong Kong action stylistics alongside those of the *filone* in these apolitical pastiches attests to the ambiguous legacy of Peckinpah's own cinematic innovations. John Woo is nothing if not the heir to 'Bloody Sam's' slow-motion choreography and spurting blood-squibs. To a considerably greater extent than is the case with the films of Damiani or Sollima, Peckinpah's enduring influence has been one of stylised violence and visceral brutality revolutionising action cinema, while the political inscriptions attached to his techniques have been largely ignored. Since the sea-change in cinematic practice heralded by the Production Code's disappearance, on-screen violence has become an ever more ubiquitous, and constantly contentious, feature of mainstream Hollywood film-making. These stylistically opposed depictions of politicised violence have therefore together been assimilated into revolutions occurring not on the streets of America and Italy, nor in the huts and villages across the globe, but in the production and distribution sectors of US cinema.

On observing these melting-pots of stylistic quotations evacuating historically specific imperatives, one cannot help but recall Fredric Jameson's condemnations of postmodernism for its repudiation of universal representation in favour of nostalgic pastiche: 'An alarming and pathological symptom of a society that has become incapable of dealing with time and history.'[61] Certainly, the agendas of Tarantino and Rodriguez, seeking to resurrect defunct genres in such ambitious projects as their aptly-titled collaboration *Grindhouse* (2007), set out solely to replicate those genres' stylish tics and 'hip' milieus. This process has removed these very tics from their original socio-political contexts, and sealed them within the hermetic world of movie quotations inhabited most conspicuously by Tarantino. That such doyens of cult cinema as these directors (as well as their progenitor in the purposeful resurrection of budget genre cinema, Sam Raimi) have become the foremost guardians of the Italian Western's legacy in contemporary cinema goes some way towards illustrating why political messages have fallen by the wayside. In an environment so obsessed with violence of a purely cinematic nature, discourses pertaining to specific disputes within the 1960s Italian New Left become somewhat obscured.

In truth, the failure of these polemics to be translated adequately cannot be ascribed to these directors' appropriations some 35 years after the films' international releases. The generic fusions of pop violence discussed above are in fact most revealing for the ways in which they merely replicate the dominant patterns of reception afforded this *filone* from the late 1960s onwards. As we have seen, from the moment the films of Damiani and Sollima came into contact with the US market, their political imperatives were being stripped away by a collection of audience sectors. Rodriguez, Tarantino and Raimi are merely the heirs of one such constituency: that of the film buff and the 'movie geek'. *Kill Bill* is most certainly an example of what Jean Baudrillard termed 'hyperreal simulacra': empty signs without 'original' referents in reality.[62] Tarantino's participation in this ongoing discourse surrounding the 'meanings' attached to the Italian Western, however, above all serves to highlight the fact that the *filone* is itself a prime example of a 'hyperreal simulacrum'. It, too, is a 'signifier' without a 'signified', a copy without an 'original', in its postmodern evacuation of ideology from the 'grand narrative' of the Hollywood Western. The ethnic re-inscription of *Posse*'s 'little narrative' may be one available corollary of this process, but *Kill Bill* is its logical conclusion.

The political Italian Western's authorial capacity to dictate meaning is therefore inherently precarious. The very framework from within which Damiani and Sollima attempt to build didactic narratives is always already engaged in processes of ideological evacuation. If Jameson's thesis concerning 'the emergence of a new kind of flatness or depthlessness, a new kind of superficiality'[63] indeed applies to *Kill Bill*, it is merely describing the latest stage in a process which begins with the Italian Western itself. By liberating the Western form, rejecting Hollywood's grand narrative and, as an oppositional 'audience', seeking to create its own meanings, the *filone*'s militant wing participates in this continuum. That it has in turn been appropriated, removed from its native milieu and drained of ideological significance by disparate audiences is a by-product of such a postmodern project.

# 6

# Along the Radical Spectrum

Fight the bourgeois concept of representation. Wrest the control of cinema, photography and television from the hands of the controlling ideology. […] To make cinema a revolutionary weapon you must think through and with the revolutionary struggle. Think and work out the methods. Class struggle! Armed struggle!

*Vent d'Est* (Groupe Dziga Vertov, 1970).

Throughout this book I have argued that the radicalism of such films as *Quien sabe?*, *La resa dei conti* and *Faccia a faccia* is defined by a purposeful negotiation with the codes of the Hollywood Western. Far from rejecting this model, Damiani and Sollima work within its central oppositions and with its established signifiers, reflecting the cultural shifts of post-war Italy and embracing the 'belching stomach' of the Roman studio system. By no means, however, was this approach to genre cinema the only one available for militant ends. Indeed, the very act of utilising such an established model as a conduit for revolutionary polemics was a highly contentious one in the context of late 1960s radicalism. Though they seek to undermine the Western genre's ideological inflections, these films paradoxically affirm the dominance of Hollywood in the semiotic marketplace: a contradiction only too apparent to many on the Far Left. To conclude I shall therefore situate the key films of this book within this fractious milieu, and question some of the assumptions inherent to such disputes.

In *Vent d'Est* we find a European 'Western' which seeks to espouse a philosophy of militant dissemination in polar opposition to that simultaneously being practiced within the walls of Cinecittà and Elios studios.[1] In fact, 'Western' is a somewhat inappropriate moniker for Jean-Luc Godard's and Jean-Pierre Gorin's project, since archetypes common

Figures 7–8    'Fight the bourgeois concept of representation.' *Vent d'Est* (1970), a film by Jean-Luc Godard © 1969 GAUMONT (France)/POLIFILM (Italy)/C.C.C. FILMKUNST (Germany)

to this genre – a cavalryman, an Indian and a well-to-do eastern lady – are paraded purely as cognitive concepts in a dialectic concerning militant art and the depiction of repression. Invasive inter-titles and didactic voice-overs insist throughout that revolutionary cinema must reject bourgeois modes of representation. This agenda is articulated by the exhortation cited as this chapter's epigraph, and is symbolised by the audio-visual sequence which precedes it: an effect achieved through the juxtaposition of two shots, separated by 25 seconds of the film's running time. In the first shot, the upper-class lady in her eastern finery surveys her surroundings through a film camera (Figure 7); in the second, the Indian – less a character, more a Brechtian study of the subaltern archetype 'Indian' – stops inspecting a pistol and exchanges the weapon for a camera. The epigraph is uttered as he proceeds to take photographs of a rifle protruding from the mud in front of him (Figure 8). As befits a film which harangues its audience throughout, the symbolism is transparent: the Indian analyses the tools of resistance through the lens, or 'concept of representation', hitherto controlled by the bourgeoisie. When the inter-title 'Armed Struggle' then intrudes, followed by images depicting the manufacture of home-made bombs, it is clear that the insurgent now commands the medium.

Manifest in this sequence are the purposeful concordances between Godard's and Gorin's film-making collective – the Groupe Dziga Vertov – and Louis Althusser's contemporaneous conceptions of ideology as 'a representation of the imaginary relationship of individuals to their real conditions of existence'.[2] Of all the various Ideological State Apparatuses (in Althusser's terminology) which, Godard holds, perpetuate bourgeois hegemony, it is the Western which comes under the most trenchant scrutiny in this film. Accordingly, the concept of these apparatuses under the control of the ruling class is ably symbolised by the film camera in the hands of a bourgeois archetype lifted from this very genre. By proceeding to transfer control of the means of representation to the subaltern, *Vent d'Est* seeks to construct a revolutionary cinema in polar opposition to those dominant codes which Damiani and Sollima on the contrary opt to utilise.

It is, however, my contention in this concluding chapter that what is represented here is not a rupture within the European New Left. Instead, when considered alongside the key films analysed in this book, this reflects a nuanced spectrum of opinion within radical circles concerning methods of political dissemination. The act of physically placing a camera in the hands of the Indian is simply a more far-reaching example of the subversion of generic conventions enacted on behalf of Chuncho, Cuchillo and Tepepa (all of whom wrest control of their narratives, and the point-of-view of the movie camera, from bourgeois Westerners). In particular, the reverse shot commanded by Chuncho's gaze in the closing moments of *Quien sabe?* enacts a corresponding appropriation of the medium on behalf of the subaltern. Godard's unravelling of received models of representation is more pronounced, not diametrically opposed.

By the late 1960s, profound suspicion of US popular culture within Europe's political Left came by no means exclusively from such institutions as the PCI. As Herbert Marcuse's notions of a 'one dimensional' society augured, and Althusser's demarcation of Ideological State Apparatuses reflected, many in the New Left held the mass media and attendant forms of mass communication in contempt. From 1966 onwards, Godard's increasingly Maoist agenda incrementally rejected the generic frameworks with which his earlier work had engaged: in *Week-end* (1967), *Le Gai Savoir* (1968) and to an even greater extent in his collaborations with Gorin as the Groupe Dziga Vertov after the ferments of the student movement. Situating a perceived aesthetic imperialism alongside more visible systems of oppression preoccupying the contemporary Left, he announced this fundamental rejection of bourgeois (American) cinema in the press book for *La Chinoise* (1967): 'American cinema dominates world cinema. [...] We must also create two or three Vietnams at the heart of the immense empire, Hollywood-Cinecittà-Mosfilms-Pinewood [...] to create national cinemas.'[3] In other words, at precisely the time Godard was reacting to international events by reformulating his aesthetic and departing from studio-driven forms to express militant political standpoints, *Quien sabe?* emerged, seeking to expound equivalent ideologies from within those very generic frameworks.

This considered, it is little surprise that the appropriation of genre cinema for revolutionary politics undertaken by Damiani, Sollima, Petroni and (especially) Corbucci came under attack in the pages of *Cahiers du cinéma* (the cradle of Godard's own career). In 1971 Pierre Baudry identified in *Compañeros*, not only a failure to communicate a radical message, but an active disarming of revolutionary discourse. Thus these supposedly militant Westerns conceal a reactionary process of subsuming subversion within dominant semantic structures. 'It is […] no longer a question of ignoring revolutionary discourse', writes Baudry, 'or even of overtly criticising it, but of producing a double, a *faux-semblant* which, by "miming" it, destroys it'.[4] Using *Vent d'Est* as his primary exhibit, Christopher Frayling outlines in some detail the debates provoked by these attempts at radical exposition from within the referential framework of Hollywood genre cinema. Derided as 'the emotional revenge of the repressed' by James Roy MacBean, for example, the popular aesthetic of Franco Solinas's political treatises led Godard to conclude that '[Hollywood studios] don't even need to make movies themselves anymore, they have found slaves everywhere to make the movies they want'.[5] Cited on the other side of this argument is Bernardo Bertolucci, whose own political film-making career moved in a reverse arc to that of Godard in the late 1960s, as he increasingly embraced the mass audience with such films as *La strategia del ragno* (1970), *Ultimo tango a Parigi* (1973) and *1900* (1976). He accuses the extreme Brechtianism of films like *Vent d'Est* of precluding any meaningful contact with an audience: 'This was a non-communication model […] a cinema for the elite.'[6]

The debate thus summarised by Frayling is informative more for what it tells us about contemporary attitudes towards popular culture within the European New Left than it is for any socio-political deconstruction of revolutionary genre cinema. Clearly, radicals were divided in their outlook, and the events of 1968 in particular brought issues of political communication into sharp focus. On one side of the debate, outright hostility to the mechanisms of the mass media manifested itself in uncompromising dismissals of genre cinema as an agent of bourgeois indoctrination. On the other, such purposefully obscure diatribes as are found in the late 1960s cinema of Godard were seen to be merely preaching to the converted. In reality, such voices were at the edges of a spectrum of opinion within the innately fractious New Left, and in any case it would be a mistake to take such dichotomous critiques at face value. In Chapter One, we saw that the ideological battle lines drawn around neorealism and Hollywood genre cinema by the DC and the PCI in the late 1940s were largely erroneous. Processes of cultural blending, more than linear subordination, describe the evolution of popular Italian cinema both in this period and in the late 1960s. Diametrically to oppose politically-committed cinema to a capitulation under the hegemony of Hollywood signifiers would be to misread the heterogeneous nature of the New Left's attitudes to cultural dissemination.

The political Italian Westerns are situated within a divergent, not opposite, late 1960s radical trajectory from that of Godard and Gorin. This cycle's constituent films make no pretence towards depicting inviolable narrative forms, instead frequently arresting the viewer with intertextual quotations, extra-diegetic asides and didactic manipulations of the medium. Very rarely in these films is an audience permitted passive acceptance of naturalistic representation. Clearly, their unashamed engagement with the norms of Hollywood genre convention places them at odds with the later cinema of Godard. This is, however, less a diametrical opposition than an alternative inheritance, for both trends display clear, though differing, parallels with the highly influential French Nouvelle Vague of the early 1960s. In a number of ways – stylistic and cultural – the political Westerns emerging from Roman studios between 1966 and 1970 share preoccupations and techniques with this earlier, more internationally celebrated trend, and in particular with the transformations effected in European cinema by Godard himself.

While I am not suggesting that *Quien sabe?* or *Faccia a faccia* should be considered the peers of such pioneering works of the early 1960s as *À bout de souffle* (1960), *Une femme est une femme* (1961) or *Bande à part* (1964), this frame of reference is not as fanciful as it may at first appear. The deliberate and undisguised adoption of a generic milieu lifted directly from Hollywood fantasy, the didactic manipulation of the cinematic medium and the attendant re-inscription of recognisable signifiers which characterise the films of Cinecittà's radical wing were by 1966 well-established traits of this illustrious *auteur*.

Certainly, the tension between a European fascination for US cinema on the one hand, and unease towards its attendant ideologies on the other – palpable throughout the frequently confused political expositions of Damiani, Sollima, Petroni and Corbucci – was nothing new. As we have seen in the case of *Un americano a Roma*, the aspirant fantasies fuelled by American cinema in post-war Europe were apt to be inflected with ambivalence at a perceived confusion of identity. So too in France, films of the Nouvelle Vague such as *À bout de souffle* and François Truffaut's *Tirez sur le pianiste* (1960) register European infatuation with Hollywood noir, while re-inscribing the transatlantic format with a localised 'modern' idiom. In the early works of

Godard in particular, this postmodern tendency is enacted in a Brechtian tenor, with a frequently exuberant unmasking of the medium. When, in *À bout de souffle*, Michel (Jean-Paul Belmondo) stops outside a cinema at which *The Harder They Fall* (1956) is showing, he mutters 'Bogey!' as his eye is drawn to the photographed visage of Humphrey Bogart. A close-up of Michel's admiring gaze is spliced with a reverse shot of Bogart, looking back from the film poster. As the camera returns to Michel, and again to Bogart, the plasticity of this conventional shot construction narrating an exchange between two people is exposed. That the Hollywood star appears only as a two dimensional image, yet is afforded close-ups normally reserved for people physically present draws attention to the fact that such icons of American popular culture are never in fact 'present', but are forever projected onto a screen or printed on posters and in magazines for re-formulation by aspirant Europeans.

Insofar as Michel's 'exchange' is not with 'America', so much as with a phantasm of the European imagination, this scene offers a finely constructed symbol for the synthetic American imaginary inherited by the Italian Western. This is the 'America' of the cigarette card, the news stand and the movie screen emulated by Nando Moriconi and evoked by the Tex Willer *fumetti*. It is also the cognitive milieu with which the political Italian Western self-consciously engages, to the point of postmodern pastiche. By re-enacting scenes from *Viva Zapata!* almost by rote, for example, *Tepepa* effects another kind of 'conversation' with an American movie star, this time Marlon Brando. Its ambivalent interrogation of Hollywood's hegemony simultaneously functions as both an aesthetic tribute and a political riposte to Elia Kazan's iconic film.

It is above all in the playfulness and wit of Godard's early films, which the director himself would later eschew, that these Westerns display their resemblance to such techniques. This can be seen in the aural displacement common to Godard's cinema of the early 1960s. Geoffrey Nowell-Smith highlights the unmasking of the medium effected by the opening sequence of *Une femme est une femme*.[7] As Angela (Anna Karina) enters a café, we hear Charles Aznavour singing of 'la petite fille', clearly directing the audience into an acceptance of the song as an extra-diegetic backing track. Her visit to the café's juke box, however, reveals that the characters, too, are party to the music. Throughout this film, musical leitmotifs intrude upon the narrative at unexpected points, frequently drowning out dialogue and constantly emphasising the non-naturalism of the Hollywood musical format (and indeed of cinema itself). Such alienation from inviolable narrative forms, which came increasingly to characterise Godard's approach to cinema as the decade wore on, is elaborated upon in *Bande à part* (1964). This is most evident in both the emptying of all background noise announced by the characters themselves in the 'one minute silence' and in their impromptu dance routine, abruptly alternating between an extra-diegetic score and the hush of their ostensible surroundings.

These celebrated examples of aural displacement offer conspicuous precedents to the similar panache with which Cuchillo enters the narrative of *Corri, uomo, corri*, whistling the apparently non-diegetic theme tune. It is, indeed, with the exuberant clowning of Tomas Milian's Cuchillo persona that the most visible signs of influence from Godard's early cinema are to be found in either the 'insurgency' or the 'RSA' narratives. Milian's most overt moment of breaking the 'fourth wall' comes when, in the same film, he 'joins' the audience to watch the show and confide with an (un-)imaginary spectator. This, too, is presaged by *Une femme est une femme*, with characters frequently looking straight into the camera to acknowledge the presence of the audience. Jean-Paul Belmondo's continual winks and grins, along with the self-conscious bow performed by Anna Karina and Jean-Claude Brialy provide iconic blueprints for Cuchillo's comically audacious act.

That such stylistic parallels exist is not to say that Sergio Sollima was consciously emulating Godard's earlier work. Nor do they so shake up one's perception of these Westerns that they must be considered alongside Godard's later films, such as *La Chinoise* and *Week-end*, in the annals of Brechtian New Left cinema. Italy's political Westerns are, however, testament to the fact that the tendencies towards playful manipulation of the medium which arose in European cinema in the 1960s (in large part fostered by Godard) were infused in popular forms by mid-decade, alongside more celebrated examples in what are frequently referred to as 'art' films. These ostensibly dichotomous radical cinematic trends emerged simultaneously around 1966 and, by 1968, each was expounding equivalent revolutionary doctrine according to its own aesthetic. Their methodologies are not as antithetical as is at first apparent. Godard simply steered to an erudite extreme the audacity with which Sollima sought to communicate his own polemics. Considered together, they reflect the heterogeneity of attitudes within the radical European Left towards political dissemination in and around the years of the student movement.

A key feature of the activism within the 'New Left' of the late 1960s was a heightened awareness of the role of culture and ideology, both in assisting the state's apparatuses of control and in fostering a critique of those very mechanisms. Reinterpretations of Marx, Lenin and Gramsci, along with enthusiastic readings of Marcuse, Benjamin, Fanon and

Althusser, informed an outlook disparate in its ideological reference points, yet broadly characterised by a media-savvy consciousness. In Italy, the rapid growth of the mass media during and after the years of the 'Economic Miracle' provoked an ambivalent response amongst such radical groups. On the one hand the national press and television were seen to be outlets for governmental lies, since the PCI were certainly not alone in their disdain for the burgeoning mass media. During the student movement of 1967–68, for example, the term *controinformazione* (counter-information) was coined, to describe the widespread form of activism which sought to expose the ideological mechanisms at the heart of bourgeois means of communication. On the other hand, however, these very same media were acting as conduits for the spread of radicalism by bringing the atrocities of the Cold War into people's living rooms. By 1968 the vogue for Third Worldism was being fuelled by television transmitting not only the ferment of Vietnam – the first 'television war' – but also that of the wider student and protest movements themselves to the Italian public. Ginsborg records:

> The Vietnam War changed the way a whole generation of Italians thought about America. The American dream of the 1950s was shattered by the newsreels of the napalming of Vietnamese villages in the 1960s and by the example of peasant resistance to the American war machine.[8]

What Engelhardt terms the end of 'victory culture', as the USA's narrative of righteous triumph became soured in South-East Asia, was exacerbated by this globalised dissemination driven by precisely the media looked upon with suspicion by many on the Left.

This fundamental ambivalence towards the role of the mass media in society was reflected by the spectrum of cultural activities practiced within the Italian New Left during and after the era of protest. Attempts to disseminate *controinformazione* took on multifarious formats and displayed a range of responses to the expansion of mass communications. Parallel to Godard's stylistic shift in the second half of the 1960s, a desire to reject the cognitive frameworks of the bourgeoisie characterised significant parts of this tendency. The increasingly Maoist cultural association, the ARCI, for example, offered its support to such enterprises as Dario Fo's and Franca Rame's dramatic collective *Nuova scena*. Deserting the theatre and its middle-class audiences to take their message directly to the workers, they performed contemporary militant drama in factories and *Case del popolo*. Endorsed by leading militant actor Gian Maria Volonté,[9] the ARCI set up alternative film circuits and coordinated demonstrations against the governmental bias of the mass media. Recording a less organised level of activism, meanwhile, Robert Lumley highlights a considerably more anarchic form of counter-information in the form of anti-establishment graffiti which proliferated during this period. Seeking simultaneously to expose the ideological agendas of the press and to bypass conventionally regulated modes of political interaction, many such slogans expounded notions pertaining directly to Marcuse's theories of 'repressive tolerance' from *One Dimensional Man*. As one put it, 'eliminiamo il poliziotto che è nel nostro cervello' ('we eliminate the policeman in our head').[10]

It is therefore evident that many forms of *controinformazione* sought to reject every possible manifestation of what Fo described as 'bourgeois baubles'.[11] Conventional modes of communication, however, remained the primary source of dissemination amongst New Left activists. From November 1969, the weekly journal *Lotta Continua* (from which the extra-parliamentary group of the same name emerged) offered an outlet for countercultural perspectives. A radical periodical, *Lotta Continua* was nevertheless designed to attract a broad readership, with sensational stories and investigative journalism (within a month of its initial publication, for example, it would play a central role in refuting mainstream analysis of the Piazza Fontana bombing). By 1969, indeed, this method – 'smuggling' revolutionary ideas amongst material with a wider appeal – was a well established strategy in radical circles, thanks largely to the efforts of entrepreneur Giangiacomo Feltrinelli. His publishing house was founded with the explicit aim of widening the appeal of global communism through distributing a broad range of profitable material alongside more highbrow political treatises. That the works of radical icons such as Mao, Marcuse, Debray and Guevara gained a political currency in Europe owed much to the fact that they were widely distributed in Italy by Feltrinelli himself. Such dissident leftist intellectuals identified opportunities offered by the burgeoning mass media for the wide dissemination of militant ideas, and dreamt of imitating Third World guerrilla methods in Italy. His brand of populist radicalism became most famous for the mass distribution of agitprop such as Alberto Korda's world-famous photograph of Che Guevara, yet Feltrinelli's engagement with nascent revolutionary groupings was genuinely influential. Ginsborg records that the two volumes he published on the Uruguayan Tupamaros became do-it-yourself insurrectionary manuals for the early members of the Red Brigades.[12]

In the midst of such a wide spectrum of cultural responses from within the New Left to burgeoning forms of mass dissemination, the political Italian

Westerns here analysed partook in this ongoing discourse. Collectively, their engagements with key preoccupations of the protest movements, while frequently overlooked, often incoherent and occasionally banal, extended to this very issue: the recognition that mass communications media (in this case genre cinema), though outwardly in thrall to the ideological mechanisms of advanced capitalism, offered immediate and widespread formats for radical dissemination. While I have demonstrated in Chapter Five that their adherence to popular paradigms frequently jeopardised their political efficacy, their releases alongside 'mainstream' Italian Westerns must equally be seen in the context of Feltrinelli's 'entryist' cultural strategy. The rapid turnaround of the Western *filone*'s industrial milieu meant that, while political messages were apt to become confused, this was occasionally counterbalanced by an extraordinary prescience. *Faccia a faccia*'s simultaneous depiction of a corrupted academia and anticipation of a resurgent fascist threat, for example, was released just a month after the Trento campus occupation had begun.

There is, finally, one more important protest community which must be considered; one which situates the ideological methodologies of these Westerns within incipient extremities of radical thought. That the international New Left's extremist wings frequently sought to utilise the media to broadcast their messages was both a tactical continuation and a heightening of sophistication amongst those striving to spread *controinformazione*. Prior to the 'Days of Rage' in October 1969, for example, Weatherwoman Susan Stern gleefully anticipated the police brutality that would await the protesters for the propaganda victory it would offer them: she predicted 'human blood spilling and splattering all over the streets of Chicago for NBC and CBS to pick up in gory, gory Technicolor'.[13] Focussing on the Italian situation, David Moss sets out the central strategic role of explaining the need for violence carried out by various insurgent groups in the 1970s. Insurrectionary violence, it was perceived, could only attain its full political significance through processes of 'translation'. By this was meant a widely disseminated attribution of recognisable political imperatives to violent acts, carried out through a set of resources such as leaflets, banners and video cassettes. Such processes frequently lifted violent scenarios from the past – most commonly the Risorgimento, the rise of Fascism and the Resistance – and overlaid them directly onto contemporary conflicts. Moss continues:

> Examples of clandestine violence from the past could easily be adduced to render plausible the attribution of the assault after 1969 to widely

different points on the political spectrum. [...] The past provided ready reference points in the translation manuals of the present.[14]

Régis Debray warned against intellectual tendencies 'to grasp the present through preconceived ideological constructs'.[15] Chapters Three and Four, however, make clear that such a pell-mell adherence to historical models was practiced amongst many sections of the New Left to inform their contemporary outlooks. The use made in the 'RSA' and 'insurgency' variants of the Fascist era and the Mexican Revolution respectively presaged similar exercises in historical legitimation carried out by the practitioners of violence themselves in the early 1970s. The persistence of such cognitive practices amongst insurgent groups like the Red Brigades, who openly emulated the fighters of the Resistance, was the peak of a trajectory which manifested itself early on in overt and confrontational tones in many of the films discussed in this book.

If such an explanation of radicalism was indeed the purpose of these films, it is worthy of note that their ideological content was occasionally identified and discussed in Italy's film press. Each of *Quien sabe?*, *La resa dei conti* and *Tepepa*, for example, is situated as a constituent part of Franco Solinas's radical oeuvre.[16] More notably, on reviewing *Faccia a faccia* in the esteemed pages of *Rivista del cinematografo*, Enzo Natta describes the bandit leader Beauregard Bennett as 'the romantic, anarchic, libertarian, popular, I would say almost Guevarian soul of the peasant revolution of the Third World'.[17] Writing in January 1968, at the height of both the Vietnam War and the Italian student movement, this reviewer identifies Brad Fletcher as the embodiment of both Maoism and Stalinism, while the innocent victims of the vigilantes are seen as 'those same women and children who die in the "dirty war" of Vietnam'. Such reception is remarkable purely for the contrast it provides with the international critical patterns already analysed, which overlooked any political significance whatsoever. Natta's review is largely unfocused and tendentious, evoking a vast array of political reference points without identifying the film's clear references to Italian Fascism. It does not, I suggest, provide evidence that these films were in any way effective as propaganda tools. Instead, I would argue that the contrast between readings in Italy's mainstream film press and those further afield are testament to two things: the deleteriousness of the editorial cuts visited upon the English language versions, and the parochialism of these films' political expositions.

This parochialism goes some way towards explaining the failure of these films' political messages to be translated beyond the discourses of the European New Left. We saw in Chapter Five, for example, that the confrontational radicalism expounded by Sollima and Damiani was of a peculiarly Italian temperament, and broadly failed to translate into mainstream US cinema even while the counterculture increasingly took possession of it. Yet this tells only a part of the story. My focus throughout this book has been on the related choices made by these directors to work within the industrial milieu of Cinecittà and Elios studios, and within the generic one of the Western. Their stylistic options were largely determined by the conventions of the Italian *filone*, and their radicalism arose in direct response to the codes of the Hollywood Western: that grandest of genre cinema's 'grand narratives'. Though I repudiate the dichotomous outlook of Godard and Baudry it is true that Godard himself, as an esteemed *auteur*, enjoyed an artistic and industrial freedom of expression which was denied to films arising from within the *filone* system.[18] The failure of the latter to be received as they were intended therefore rests on the very choice to make Italian Westerns.

The implications of this choice for radical dissemination are illustrated in quite jarring terms by contrasting two fictional student debates. Both address the audience directly, both seek explicitly to articulate contemporary militant oppositions by assessing the value of violent resistance and both culminate in the bearing of arms by the students involved. The first – from Godard's *La Chinoise* (1967) – takes up almost the entirety of the film's 96 minute running time. The director enjoys free reign to indulge his fascination with the Chinese Cultural Revolution and nascent youth countercultures. The various acts, or 'dialogues', of this extended debate cover Mao, Brecht, the politics of representation and political violence. Ideological schisms and counter-arguments are depicted and interrogated at length before the act of terrorism is at last committed. That this is a stylistic forerunner to the Brechtian extremes explored by the Groupe Dziga Vertov becomes clear when Jean-Pierre Léaud looks into the camera (which is then shown to the viewer in reverse shot) and states: 'I'm an actor.' The audience is simply not permitted to overlook the didactic purpose of this film.

The second debate, which I have already analysed in some detail, is from Sergio Corbucci's *Compañeros* (1970) and takes up less than two minutes of the running time. Professor Xantos's equivalent extra-diegetic address to the audience lasts only 20 seconds. After the legitimacy of violence has been perfunctorily affirmed the result is an action-packed spectacle of machine gun fire, explosions and countless cackling *bandidos* meeting their maker while adhering to an elaborate, comic-book aesthetic. The debate's primary narrative function is as a framing device for this final sequence, which locates the film firmly in the formulaic milieu of *filone* cinema. From such a 'political economy' perspective, political Italian Westerns were inherently restricted by such stylistic imperatives, which arose directly from their industrial context.

The political limitations of working within the codes of such a 'grand narrative' as the Western, however, go beyond the stylistic concerns of Cinecittà and the *filone* system. The very engagement with the Western genre which we have seen operating throughout the key films of this book, indeed, is founded on an innately contradictory premise. I have identified in Chapter Two, and analysed at length in Chapters Three and Four, a dual function which these films set out to fulfil: to both unmask the hegemonic codes of the Hollywood Western and replenish the form with oppositional meaning. In the first instance they therefore claim the Western and its signifiers as arenas of contested semantic terrain, amenable to reinterpretation, negotiation and creative participation. On the other hand, however, they seek themselves to disseminate didactic theses, steering the audience down the path of militant insubordination. Even while they dismantle the authoritative structures of Hollywood's grand narrative, they simultaneously assume the power to impose a particular reading on their own audiences – from within that same paradigm. That their own attempts at didacticism have in turn been appropriated for purposes entirely divergent from their authorial intentions can hardly come as a surprise.

The year 1968 has been a pivotal one – historically, politically and cinematically – throughout my arguments. It is therefore apt that in this same year – at the cultural 'moment' these films were finding an international audience and passing into global circulation – Roland Barthes proclaimed 'the Death of the Author'. Insofar as readers themselves shape a text's meaning, we can see that attempts to work within the structures of genre cinema are fraught with peril for the militant artist. The films I have analysed in these pages inadvertently lean towards that textual ideal which Barthes termed 'writerly' or *scriptible*: a permanently open signifier which turns the reader into the primary producer of meaning.[19] In this chapter I have shown that, despite the objections of Godard and Baudry, these films warrant consideration within the cultural spectrum of late 1960s European radicalism. Yet this argument itself relies upon a 'textual' reading, analysing the processes by which an author (or more pertinently in this filmic context, *auteur*) purposefully bestows meaning to an audience. Throughout the book, we have seen time and again that readers and audiences themselves create 'meanings' through the artefacts of popular culture once they enter the public domain. The 'political Italian Western' originates from the creative participation of one such audience, and is inescapably caught up in these ongoing processes of negotiation, appropriation and reformulation.

# APPENDICES

# APPENDIX A

# Highest Grossing Italian Westerns, 1962–1980 (Domestic *Prima Visione* Box-office Returns)[1]

|    | Film title (key films in bold) | Release date | Gross income (lire) |
|----|-------------------------------|--------------|---------------------|
| 1  | … continuavano a chiamarlo Trinità | 19/10/1971 | 5,268,718,000 |
| 2  | Per qualche dollaro in più | 17/12/1965 | 3,492,268,000 |
| 3  | Il mio nome è Nessuno | 01/12/1973 | 3,385,835,000 |
| 4  | Il buono, il brutto, il cattivo | 20/12/1966 | 3,210,701,000 |
| 5  | Per un pugno di dollari | 01/09/1964 | 3,182,833,000 |
| 6  | Lo chiamavano Trinità | 15/12/1970 | 3,104,061,000 |
| 7  | … E poi lo chiamarono il magnifico | 07/09/1972 | 2,971,735,000 |
| 8  | Un genio, due compari, un pollo | 19/12/1975 | 2,684,413,000 |
| 9  | C'era una volta il West | 20/12/1968 | 2,503,669,000 |
| 10 | Zanna Bianca | 19/12/1973 | 2,471,222,000 |
| 11 | Sole Rosso | 19/10/1971 | 2,327,987,000 |
| 12 | I quattro dell'ave Maria | 29/10/1968 | 2,225,784,000 |
| 13 | Dio perdona … io no | 24/10/1967 | 2,067,440,000 |
| 14 | I giorni dell'ira | 05/12/1967 | 1,997,410,000 |
| 15 | Il bianco, il giallo, il nero | 19/12/1974 | 1,897,807,000 |
| 16 | Giù la testa | 23/10/1971 | 1,829,402,000 |
| 17 | La collina degli stivali | 18/12/1969 | 1,741,827,000 |

| | Film title (key films in bold) | Release date | Gross income (lire) |
|---|---|---|---|
| 18 | Un dollaro bucato | 04/08/1965 | 1,590,886,000 |
| 19 | Adiós Gringo | 08/12/1965 | 1,577,007,000 |
| 20 | Keoma | 01/01/1976 | 1,571,995,000 |
| 21 | **Vamos a matar, compañeros** | 18/12/1970 | 1,451,782,000 |
| 22 | **La resa dei conti** | 03/03/1967 | 1,440,849,000 |
| 23 | Si può fare … amigo! | 29/03/1972 | 1,410,463,000 |
| 24 | La vita, a volte, è molto dura, vero Provvidenza? | 24/10/1972 | 1,360,391,000 |
| 25 | Una pistola per Ringo | 11/05/1965 | 1,351,605,000 |
| 26 | Il ritorno di Ringo | 07/12/1965 | 1,317,664,000 |
| 27 | Per pochi dollari ancora | 01/10/1966 | 1,309,699,000 |
| 28 | **Il prezzo del potere** | 10/12/1969 | 1,273,858,000 |
| 29 | Una ragione per vivere e una per morire | 26/10/1972 | 1,264,826,000 |
| 30 | **Da uomo a uomo** | 24/08/1967 | 1,261,929,000 |
| 31 | Arizona Colt | 12/08/1966 | 1,249,041,000 |
| 32 | Centomilla dollari per Ringo | 14/11/1965 | 1,236,276,000 |
| 33 | Vivi o preferibilmente morti | 06/09/1969 | 1,202,368,000 |
| 34 | Cipolla Colt | 01/01/1975 | 1,190,585,000 |
| 35 | …e per tetto un cielo di stelle | 22/06/1968 | 1,145,950,000 |
| 36 | Che c'entriamo noi con la rivoluzione? | 29/11/1972 | 1,141,887,000 |
| 37 | Wanted | 18/03/1967 | 1,132,590,000 |
| 38 | Due mafiosi nel Far West | 27/06/1964 | 1,119,247,000 |
| 39 | Ehi amico … c'è Sabata, hai chiuso! | 10/09/1969 | 1,117,152,000 |
| 40 | **Faccia a faccia** | 21/11/1967 | 1,116,721,000 |
| 41 | **Il mercenario** | 17/12/1968 | 1,101,445,000 |
| 42 | Amico stammi lontano almena en palmo | 22/01/1972 | 1,091,133,000 |
| 43 | Valdez il mezzosangue | 29/08/1973 | 1,077,383,000 |
| 44 | I lunghi giorni della vendetta | 21/02/1967 | 1,072,359,000 |
| 45 | Ci risiamo, vero Provvidenza? | 08/11/1973 | 1,068,676,000 |
| 46 | Django | 01/04/1966 | 1,026,084,000 |
| 47 | Viva la muerte … tua! | 18/12/1971 | 1,019,096,000 |
| 48 | **Corri, uomo, corri** | 27/08/1968 | 1,000,146,000 |

| | Film title (key films in bold) | Release date | Gross income (lire) |
|---|---|---|---|
| 49 | Sette pistole per i MacGregor | 22/01/1966 | 976,430,000 |
| 50 | Vado ... l'amazzo e torno | 19/09/1967 | 951,521,000 |
| 51 | Oggi a me ... domani a te! | 26/03/1968 | 940,997,000 |
| 52 | Indio Black, sai che ti dico: Sei un gran figlio di ... | 24/09/1970 | 929,925,000 |
| 53 | Texas addio | 26/08/1966 | 902,690,000 |
| 54 | Al di là della legge | 09/04/1968 | 896,584,000 |
| 55 | La spina dorsale del diavolo | 15/10/1970 | 886,218,000 |
| 56 | **Tepepa** | 30/01/1969 | 858,936,000 |
| 57 | Tempo di massacro | 04/08/1966 | 848,814,000 |
| 58 | 5000 dollari sull'asso | 30/12/1964 | 847,563,000 |
| 59 | Ciccio perdona ... io no! | 25/09/1968 | 841,612,000 |
| 60 | Sette dollari sul rosso | 12/03/1966 | 839,548,000 |
| 61 | Il bello, il brutto, il cretino | 05/08/1967 | 830,852,000 |
| 62 | Per un pugno nell'occhio | 12/04/1965 | 826,143,000 |
| 63 | Se incontri Sartana prega per la tua morte | 13/08/1968 | 822,515,000 |
| 64 | I due sergenti del generale Custer | 11/08/1965 | 817,370,000 |
| 65 | I due figli di Ringo | 01/12/1966 | 798,306,000 |
| 66 | Testa t'ammazzo, croce ... sei morto ... | 03/04/1971 | 787,555,000 |
| 67 | I magnifici tre | 25/10/1961 | 745,171,000 |
| 68 | È tornato Sabata ... hai chiuso un'altra volta | 02/09/1971 | 730,592,000 |
| 69 | Odio per odio | 10/08/1967 | 711,100,000 |
| 70 | Un esercito di 5 uomini | 09/10/1969 | 705,030,000 |
| 71 | I tre spietati | 13/12/1963 | 699,604,000 |
| 72 | Il West ti va stretto, amico... è arrivato Alleluja | 08/08/1972 | 692,621,000 |
| 73 | **¿El Chuncho, quién sabe?** | 02/12/1966 | 687,118,000 |
| 74 | Sono Sartana il vostro becchino | 20/11/1969 | 684,154,000 |
| 75 | Preparati la bara! | 25/01/1968 | 683,271,000 |
| 76 | Lo chiamavano Tresette ... giocava sempre col morto | 09/03/1973 | 679,834,000 |
| 77 | La più grande rapina del west | 26/10/1967 | 663,969,000 |

| | Film title (key films in bold) | Release date | Gross income (lire) |
|---|---|---|---|
| 78 | Storia di karatè, pugni e fagioli | 14/06/1973 | 656,868,000 |
| 79 | Te deum | 21/11/1972 | 653,835,000 |
| 80 | El precio de un hombre | 27/10/1966 | 648,762,000 |
| 81 | Sette donne per i MacGregor | 01/03/1967 | 646,133,000 |
| 82 | Ammazzali tutti e torna solo | 11/12/1968 | 644,494,000 |
| 83 | C'e Sartana … vendi la pistola e comprati la bara! | 21/07/1970 | 642,321,000 |
| 84 | Pochi dollari per Django | 24/08/1966 | 642,139,000 |
| 85 | Così Sia | 11/08/1972 | 624,795,000 |
| 86 | Due contro tutti | 26/11/1962 | 613,435,000 |
| 87 | Mille dollari sul nero | 16/12/1966 | 607,849,000 |
| 88 | E continuavano a fregarsi il milione di dollari | 18/12/1971 | 605,516,000 |
| 89 | I due figli di Trinità | 11/07/1972 | 603,318,000 |
| 90 | Ringo, il volto della vendetta | 26/08/1966 | 600,682,000 |
| 91 | Il pistolero dell'Ave Maria | 14/10/1969 | 599,350,000 |
| 92 | I quattro inesorabile | 13/08/1965 | 596,223,000 |
| 93 | Django spara per primo | 21/10/1966 | 588,813,000 |
| 94 | L'uomo, l'orgoglio, la vendetta | 21/12/1967 | 586,203,000 |
| 95 | Gli eroi del West | 27/11/1963 | 585,899,000 |
| 96 | I tre implacabili | 14/05/1963 | 585,539,000 |
| 97 | Minnesota Clay | 09/10/1964 | 581,802,000 |
| 98 | Sugar Colt | 01/10/1966 | 571,183,000 |
| 99 | I sette del Texas | 09/09/1964 | 567,551,000 |
| 100 | … E divenne il più spietato bandito del sud | 04/03/1967 | 565,299,000 |

# APPENDIX B

## Italian Western[1] Releases in Italy,[2] 1962–1980

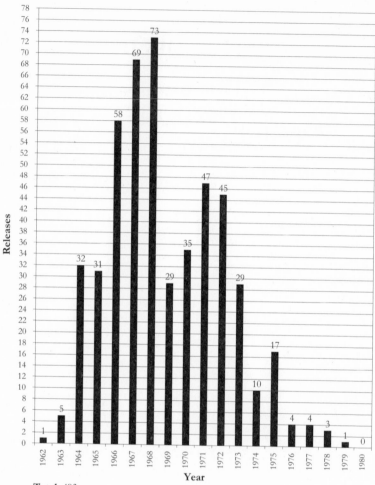

Total: 493

# APPENDIX C

## Italian Western Releases in the USA,[1] 1962–1980

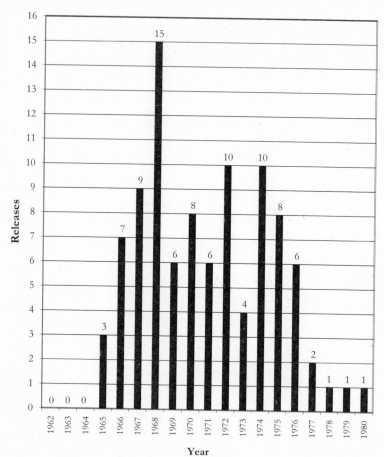

**Total: 95**

# APPENDIX D

## Corpus of US and UK Reviews of Fifty Italian Westerns, 1965–1977[1]

| Film title (by Italian release date) | 'Sadism', 'Sadistic' | 'Violence', 'Violent' | 'Bloodthirsty', 'Bloody', 'Bloodlust', 'Bloodbath', 'Bloodshed', 'Blood' | Other |
|---|---|---|---|---|
| Per un pugno di dollari | French (1967), Hawk (1964), Hibbin (1967), Pacey (1967), Walker (1967) | Barker (1967), Crowther (1967), Hawk (1964), Hirscholm, (1967), Pacey (1967), Wilson, C. (1967) | Alpert (1967), Coleman (1967), Hibbin (1967), Landry (1967), Wilson, C. (1967) | 'Brutal' (Clarke, 1967); 'Brutality' (Christie, 1967; Hibbin, 1967; Hirscholm, 1967); 'Gory' (Hinxman, 1967); 'Torture' (Hinxman, 1967; Robinson, R., 1967); 'Vicious' (Wilson, C., 1967) |
| Minnesota Clay | – | | – | 'Brutality' (Hinxman, 1967) |
| Una pistola per Ringo | – | – | – | 'Senseless slaughter' (Galluzzo, 1966) |
| Un dollaro bucato | – | Anon (1967) | – | 'Gore', 'Lashings of shooting' (Hinxman, 1967) |
| Per qualche dollaro in piu | Anon (1967), Bilbow (1967), Hawk (1966), Herbstman (1967) | Clarke (1967), Hawk (1966) | Bilbow (1967), Crowther (1967), Taylor, J.R. (1967) | 'Brutal' (Bilbow, 1967; Mahoney, 1967); 'Killing', 'Morbid lust' (Crowther, 1967); 'Torture' (Anon, 1967; Bilbow, 1967); 'Vicious' (Bilbow, 1967) |
| Il ritorno di Ringo | – | Clarke (1970) | – | 'Sudden death' (Clarke, 1970) |
| Sfida a Rio Bravo | – | – | – | – |
| Sette pistole per i MacGregor | | – | Anon (1967), Hinxman (1967) | – |
| Johnny Oro | Anon (1968), Bilbow (1967) | – | – | 'Brutality' (Bilbow, 1967; Clarke, 1967) |

| Film title (by Italian release date) | 'Sadism', 'Sadistic' | 'Violence', 'Violent' | 'Bloodthirsty', 'Bloody', 'Bloodlust', 'Bloodbath', 'Bloodshed', 'Blood' | Other |
|---|---|---|---|---|
| Arizona Colt | Anon (1970) | Anon (1970) | – | 'Killings' (Clarke, 1970) |
| Un fiume di dollari | – | T.H. (1967) | Dool (1967) | 'Savagery' (T.H., 1967) |
| Pochi dollari per Django | – | – | Anon (1967) | 'Corpses' (Clarke, 1967; Hinxman, 1967); 'Grotesque' (Anon, 1967) |
| Un dollaro a testa | Bilbow (1968) | Anon (1970), Clarke (1968) | Bilbow (1968), Clarke (1968), Orloff (1967), Weiler (1967) | 'Brutality' (Bilbow, 1968) |
| Il buono, il brutto, il cattivo | Adler (1968), Beau (1967), Hall (1968), Knight (1968), Walker (1968) | Beau (1967), Bilbow (1968), Day–Lewis (1968), Ottaway (1968), Pacey (1968), Powell (1968), Richards (1968), Wilson, D. (1968) | Anon (1968), Clarke (1968), Galluzzo (1968), Hall (1968), Myers (1968), Taylor, W. (1968), Wilson, C. (1968) | 'Brutality' (Mahoney, 1967; Milne, 1968); 'Gore' (Hinxman, 1968); 'Necrophilia' (Walker, 1968); 'Vicious' (Pacey, 1968); 'Flagellation' (Myers, 1968) |
| ¿El Chuncho, quién sabe? | – | – | Bilbow (1969) | 'Carnage', 'Gory' (Weiler, 1969) |
| Per pochi dollari ancora | – | – | – | 'Torture' (Anon, 1968); 'Corpses' (Bilbow, 1968); 'Brutal' (Clarke, 1968) |
| Texas Addio | – | – | – | – |
| Se sei vivo, spara! | Anon (1970) | Clarke (1969) | Bilbow (1969) | – |

| Film title (by Italian release date) | 'Sadism', 'Sadistic' | 'Violence', 'Violent' | 'Bloodthirsty', 'Bloody', 'Bloodlust', 'Bloodbath', 'Bloodshed', 'Blood' | Other |
|---|---|---|---|---|
| I crudeli | – | Anon (1969), Byro (1967), Clarke (1969) | Clarke (1969) | – |
| La resa dei conti | – | Whit (1968) | Clarke (1969) | – |
| Sette donne per i MacGregor | – | Byro (1968), Pelegrine (1967) | Byro (1968) | 'Gore' (Byro, 1968) |
| Da uomo a uomo | – | Anon (1969), Landry (1969) | – | 'Brutality' (Clarke, 1969); 'Vicious' (Bilbow, 1969) |
| Wanted | – | Anon (1970) | – | 'Brutal', 'Corpses' (Bilbow, 1969); 'Killings' (Clarke, 1969) |
| Dio perdona ... io no | Wilson, D. (1972) | Whit (1969) | – | – |
| Faccia a faccia | – | Bilbow (1969), Clarke (1969) | – | – |
| Vado ... l'amazzo e torno | – | – | – | 'Slaughter' (Thompson, 1968c) |
| I giorni dell'ira | Landry (1969) | Mahoney (1969) | Landry (1969) | 'Carnage' (Clarke, 1970); 'Mass shootings' (Bilbow, 1970) |
| Sette Winchester per un massacre | Loynd (1968) | Anon (1968), Loynd (1968) | – | – |
| Quella sporca storia nel West | – | Landry (1972) | – | 'Gore' (Landry, 1972) |

| Film title (by Italian release date) | 'Sadism', 'Sadistic' | 'Violence', 'Violent' | 'Bloodthirsty', 'Bloody', 'Bloodlust', 'Bloodbath', 'Bloodshed', 'Blood' | Other |
|---|---|---|---|---|
| I quattro dell'ave Maria | – | Anon (1969), Clarke (1969) | – | 'Brutality' (Lipton, 1969) |
| C'era una volta il West | Taylor, J.R. (1969) | Bilbow (1969), Gillett (1969) | Bilbow (1969) | 'Sudden death' (Clarke, 1969); 'Vicious' (Gillett, 1969) |
| Il mercenario | Taylor, J.R. (1969) | Clarke (1969), Landry (1970) | Taylor, J.R. (1969) | 'Corpses' (Bilbow, 1969); 'Slaughter', 'Sudden death' (Clarke, 1969) |
| Joko, invoca Dio … e muori! | – | – | – | – |
| Un minuto per pregare, un istante per morire | Davis (1969), Thompson (1968) | Bilbow (1968), Davis (1969), Gertner (1968) | – | 'Brutality' (Murf, 1968); 'Corpses' (Bilbow, 1968; Clarke, 1968); 'Cruel' (Clarke, 1968) |
| Ehi amico …c'è Sabata, hai chiuso! | – | Cohen (1970) | Greenspun (1970), Taylor, J.R. (1971) | – |
| Il prezzo del potere | – | Bilbow (1971) | – | – |
| Django il bastardo | – | – | – | – |
| Gli specialisti | – | – | – | – |
| Indio Black, sai che ti dico: Sei un gran figlio di … | – | Bilbow (1973), Thomas (1971) | Anon (1971), Mosk (1971) | 'Corpses', 'Slaughter' (Thomas, 1971); 'Gore' (Mosk, 1971); 'Killings' (Mahern, 1972) |
| Vamos a matar, compañeros | Taylor, J.R. (1972) | Braun (1972) | Bilbow (1972), Braun (1972) | 'Brutish' (Anon, 1972) |

| Film title (by Italian release date) | 'Sadism', 'Sadistic' | 'Violence', 'Violent' | 'Bloodthirsty', 'Bloody', 'Bloodlust', 'Bloodbath', 'Bloodshed', 'Blood' | Other |
|---|---|---|---|---|
| Lo chiamavano Trinità | Bilbow (1972) | Pennington (1971), Thomas (1971) | Bilbow (1972), Pennington (1971), Thomas (1971), Thompson (1972) | 'Brutal' (Thomas, 1971); 'Gore' (Thompson, 1972) |
| Una nuvola di polvere un grido di morte ...arriva Sartana | — | Bilbow (1975) | — | — |
| ...continuavano a chiamarlo Trinità | — | Bilbow (1974) | Bilbow (1974) | — |
| Giù la testa | Wilson, C. (1972) | Canby (1972), Ebert (1972) | Christie (1972), Melly (1972) | 'Corpses' (Melly, 1972); 'Killing' (Thirkell, 1972); 'Shootings' (Jenkins, 1972); 'Vicious' (Wilson, C, 1972) |
| È tornato Sabata ... hai chiuso un'altra volta | — | — | — | — |
| Il pistolero cieco | Bilbow (1974), Braun (1974), Mayerson (1972), Thompson (1972) | Mayerson (1972) | Parker (1972), Thompson (1972) | 'Crunching bones' (Thompson, 1972); 'Killings' (Mayerson, 1972); 'Torture' (Vine, 1972) |
| Viva la muerte ...tua! | — | — | — | — |

| Film title (by Italian release date) | 'Sadism', 'Sadistic' | 'Violence', 'Violent' | 'Bloodthirsty', 'Bloody', 'Bloodlust', 'Bloodbath', 'Bloodshed', 'Blood' | Other |
|---|---|---|---|---|
| Testa t'ammazzo, croce … sei morto … | — | — | — | 'Littered with dead bodies' (Bilbow, 1972) |
| Il mio nome è Nessuno | — | — | — | — |
| Keoma | — | — | — | — |

# Notes

URLs were correct at the time of writing.

### Introduction

1 See Appendix B for a more detailed breakdown of this figure.

2 Italian for 'tradition' or 'vein', the *filone* (singular form) reflected a rather different set of production practices to that signified by the more conventional appellation 'genre'. This distinction will be explored further in Chapter One.

3 See Eleftheriotis, Dimitris, *Popular Cinemas of Europe: Studies of Texts, Contexts and Frameworks* (London: Continuum, 2001) and Eleftheriotis, Dimitris, 'Spaghetti Western, genre criticism and national cinema: re-defining the frame of reference', in Yvonne Tasker (ed.), *Action Cinema Reader* (London: Routledge, 2004).

4 See Wagstaff, Christopher, 'A forkful of Westerns: industry, audiences and the Italian Western', in Richard Dyer and Ginette Vincendeau (eds), *Popular European Cinema* (London: Routledge, 1992); Wagstaff, Christopher, 'Italy in the post-war international cinema market', in Christopher Duggan and Christopher Wagstaff (eds), *Italy in the Cold War: Politics, Culture and Society 1948–1958* (Oxford: Berg, 1995); and Wagstaff, Christopher, 'Italian genre films in the world market', in Geoffrey Nowell-Smith and Stephen Ricci (eds), *Hollywood and Europe: Economics, Culture, National Identity 1945–95* (London: British Film Institute, 1998).

5 See Frayling, Christopher, *Spaghetti Westerns: Cowboys and Europeans from Karl May to Sergio Leone* (London: I.B.Tauris, [1981] 1998); Frayling, Christopher, *Sergio Leone: Something to Do with Death* (London: Faber and Faber, 2000); and Frayling, Christopher, *Sergio Leone: Once Upon a Time in Italy* (London: Thames and Hudson, 2005).

6 To date, indeed, one chapter by Frayling (*Spaghetti Westerns*, pp.217–244) remains the only scholarly discussion of the political content in the films addressed by this book.

7 Clifford, James, *The Predicament of Culture* (Cambridge, MA: Harvard University Press, 1988), p.147.

8    Frayling highlights the fact that spaghetti originated in the East and was a poor man's food before it spread beyond the borders of Italy to become a symbol of sophisticated cuisine, just as Sergio Leone's *Per un pugno di dollari* borrowed Akira Kurosawa's eastern-ness to spawn a 'poor man's cinema' which spread world-wide (*Spaghetti Westerns*, p.x).

# 1
# Imagining America: US Influence and American Mythology in Post-War Italy

1    Ellwood, David, '*Un americano a Roma*', *History Today* 46/5 (May 1996), pp.45–49 (p.49).

2    Stein, Gertrude, *Lectures in America* (New York: Random House, 1935), p.490.

3    This critique of consumerism is subordinate to the more conventional reading of *Nineteen Eighty-Four* as a comment on Stalinist totalitarianism.

4    Hoggart, Richard, *The Uses of Literacy* (London: Pelican, [1957] 1958), p.206.

5    Hoggart: *The Uses of Literacy*, pp.247–248.

6    By the time PCI leader Palmiro Togliatti died in 1964, the party was the largest Communist organisation in the Western world, and around one million people attended his funeral in Rome. His leadership led the party to over 25 per cent of the national vote in the 1963 elections, and the party daily, *L'Unità*, commanded the second highest sales after the *Corriere della sera* (Ginsborg, Paul, *A History of Contemporary Italy: Society and Politics, 1943–1980* (London: Penguin, 1990), p.291).

7    Gundle, Stephen, *Between Hollywood and Moscow: the Italian Communists and the Challenge of Mass Culture, 1943–1991* (London: Duke University Press, 2000), p.49.

8    Kroes, Rob, 'Americanisation: what are we talking about?', in Rob Kroes, RW Rydell and DFJ Bosscher (eds), *Cultural Transmissions and Receptions: American Mass Culture in Europe* (Amsterdam: VU University Press, 1993), p.303.

9    Forgacs, David, 'Americanisation: the Italian case 1938–1954', *Borderlines: Studies in American Culture* 1/2 (1993), pp.157–169 (p.158).

10    Barzini, Luigi, *The Europeans* (London: Penguin, 1983), pp.171–172.

11    De Mauro, Tullio, 'L'italiano dei non lettori', *Problemi dell'informazione* 3, pp.419–431 (p.420).

12    As Robert Lumley records, in 1952 Italians bought 107 daily newspapers per 1000 inhabitants, compared to 353 in the USA and 615 in the UK. This relative unpopularity was due both to the regional nature of even apparently 'national' papers such as the *Corriere della sera*, and to their use of an esoteric, literary idiom: 'Many Italians did not feel at home with the national language even if they could speak it [...] newspapers made no attempt to make themselves more accessible' (Lumley, Robert, 'Peculiarities of the Italian newspaper', in David Forgacs and Robert Lumley (eds), *Italian Cultural Studies: an Introduction* (Oxford: Oxford University Press, 1996), pp.203–204).

13    In this way, Italy's delayed experience was unique amongst Europe's post-war free-market democracies. While the Northern economy enjoyed rapid growth,

the South's remained comparable with those of surrounding Mediterranean dictatorships. Standards of living, meanwhile, were commensurate with those of Eastern Europe and the developing world (see Ginsborg: *A History of Contemporary Italy*, pp.210–217).

14   Gundle, Stephen, 'L'americanizzazione del quotidiano: televisione e consumismo nell'Italia degli anni cinquanta', *Quaderni Storici* 21/22 (1986), pp.561–594 (p.591).

15   Wagstaff, Christopher, 'Italian genre films in the world market', in Geoffrey Nowell-Smith and Stephen Ricci (eds), *Hollywood and Europe: Economics, Culture, National Identity 1945–95* (London: British Film Institute, 1998), p.75.

16   This propaganda tool was also exploited in other European countries where the communist threat was seen to be strong. In France, for example, a similar process led to *The Grapes of Wrath* (1940) being held back due to its unfavourable portrayal of American life, so as not to offer ammunition to the French Communist Party (Judt, Tony, *Postwar* (London: William Heinemann, 2005), p.231).

17   Scrivano, Paolo, 'Signs of Americanization in Italian domestic life: Italy's postwar conversion to consumerism', *Journal of Contemporary History* 40 (2005), pp.317–340 (p.327).

18   In 1956, this figure was 366,151. By 1961, it had risen to 2,761,738 (Forgacs, David, 'Cultural consumption, 1940s to 1990s', in David Forgacs and Robert Lumley (eds), *Italian Cultural Studies: an Introduction* (Oxford: Oxford University Press, 1996), p.283).

19   In 1960, 20 per cent of Italian families owned a television set (Ginsborg: *A History of Contemporary Italy*, p.432). In Britain in the same year, this figure was approximately 60 per cent (Judt: *Postwar*, p.345).

20   Average life expectancy in Italy rose by 14 years between 1946 and 1971 (Clark, Martin, *Modern Italy, 1871–1982* (London: Longman, 1984), p.363).

21   Scrivano: 'Signs of Americanization', p.317.

22   Scrivano: 'Signs of Americanization', p.338.

23   Ginsborg: *A History of Contemporary Italy*, pp.221–222.

24   Between 1951 and 1961, around 1.75 million people – nearly 10 per cent of the region's 1951 population – emigrated from the South (Clark: *Modern Italy*, p.360). Moreover, between 1958 and 1963 over 900 thousand southerners moved to other parts of Italy, where overcrowded trains jettisoned many passengers into exploitative building sites, child labour and, in some cases, petty crime and prostitution (Ginsborg: *A History of Contemporary Italy*, pp.220–225).

25   Clark: *Modern Italy*, p.362.

26   Sorlin, Pierre, *Italian National Cinema, 1896–1996* (London: Routledge, 1996), p.116.

27   Gundle: *Between Hollywood and Moscow*, p.55.

28   Torriglia, Anna Maria, *Broken Time, Fragmented Space: A Cultural Map for Postwar Italy* (London: University of Toronto Press, 2002), p.86.

29   Ginsborg: *A History of Contemporary Italy*, p.115.

30  Williams, Raymond, *Communications* (London: Chatto and Windus, 1966), p.109.

31  De Certeau, Michel, *The Practice of Everyday Life* (Berkeley: University of California Press, [1984] 1988), pp.xiii–xiv.

32  Clifford, James, *The Predicament of Culture* (Cambridge, MA: Harvard University Press, 1988), p.147.

33  To demonstrate the extent to which this issue split the party in the post-war years, I have made extensive use of the source material collated by Stephen Gundle in *Between Hollywood and Moscow*.

34  Gundle: *Between Hollywood and Moscow*, pp.38–39.

35  Forgacs, David, 'The Italian Communist Party and culture', in Zygmunt G. Baranski and Robert Lumley (eds), *Culture and Conflict in Postwar Italy: Essays on Mass and Popular Culture* (London: Macmillan, 1990), p.106.

36  It is therefore ironic to recall that, far from being considered a conservative influence, Gramsci's legacy in Britain has been that of a major New Left figure. He was, for example, appropriated by cultural studies to inform critiques of contemporary popular culture in what Tony Bennett terms 'the turn to Gramsci' at the Centre for Contemporary Cultural Studies at Birmingham University (Bennett, Tony, 'Introduction: "the turn to Gramsci"', in Tony Bennett, Colin Mercer and Janet Woollacott (eds), *Popular Culture and Social Relations* (Milton Keynes: Open University Press, 1986)).

37  Gundle: *Between Hollywood and Moscow*, pp.61–62.

38  Gundle: *Between Hollywood and Moscow*, p.69.

39  Forgacs: 'The Italian Communist Party and culture', p.102.

40  Hoggart: *The Uses of Literacy*, p.193.

41  Torriglia: *Broken Time, Fragmented Space*, p.82.

42  Gundle: *Between Hollywood and Moscow*, pp.67, 97.

43  Gundle: *Between Hollywood and Moscow*, p.66.

44  Hebdige, Dick, *Hiding in the Light: On Images and Things* (London: Routledge, 1988), p.74.

45  Such an outlook had a rich history, dating back to pulp novels and early cinema. It is also notable that it expanded with the onset of European modernism in (for example) Bertolt Brecht's mythical visions of Chicago, which emerged amidst another insecure national identity: that of 1920s Weimar Germany.

46  Torriglia: *Broken Time, Fragmented Space*, p.79.

47  Baudrillard, Jean, *America*, trans. Chris Turner (London: Verso, [1986] 1988), p.72.

48  Bazin, André, *What is Cinema?*, Vol. 2 (London: University of California Press, 2005), p.140.

49  This particular Western possesses a singular symbolic currency as a romanticised depiction of both American society and cinema, replicated in a nostalgic tenor by Peter Bogdanovich in *The Last Picture Show* (1971), which is also set in the early 1950s.

50  Brauer, David, Jim Edwards, Christopher Finch and Walter Hopps, *Pop Art: US/UK Connections, 1956–66* (Houston: Menil Collection, 2001), p.55.

51  Wilson, Alexandra, '*Fanciulla*'s transatlantic trials', in *La fanciulla del West* (opera programme) (London: Royal Opera House, 2005), p.42.

52  Wilson: '*Fanciulla*'s transatlantic trials', p.46.

53  Wilson: '*Fanciulla*'s transatlantic trials', p.46.

54  Forgacs: 'Americanisation: the Italian case', p.158.

55  'Fumetti' literally translates as 'little puffs of smoke', in reference to speech balloons.

56  Hall, Stuart, 'New cultures for old', in Doreen Massey and Pat Jess (eds), *A Place in the World?* (Oxford: Oxford University Press, 1995), p.181.

57  Judt: *Postwar*, p.352.

58  Everson, William K., 'Europe produces Westerns too. In the essentials of this universal genre they resemble our own', *Films in Review* (February 1953), pp.74–79 (p.74).

59  Frayling, Christopher, *Sergio Leone: Something to Do with Death* (London: Faber and Faber, 2000), pp.28–30, 121.

60  Frayling, Christopher, *Spaghetti Westerns: Cowboys and Europeans from Karl May to Sergio Leone* (London: I.B.Tauris, [1981] 1998), p.33.

61  See Appendix B.

62  Gundle: *Between Hollywood and Moscow*, p.49.

63  Wagstaff, Christopher, 'Italy in the post-war international cinema market', in Christopher Duggan and Christopher Wagstaff (eds), *Italy in the Cold War: Politics, Culture and Society 1948–1958* (Oxford: Berg, 1995), p.93.

64  Gundle, Stephen, 'From neo-realism to *luci rosse*: cinema, politics, society, 1945–85', in Zygmunt G. Baranski and Robert Lumley (eds), *Culture and Conflict in Postwar Italy: Essays on Mass and Popular Culture* (London: Macmillan, 1990), p.209.

65  Wood, Mary P., *Italian Cinema* (Oxford: Berg, 2005), p.14.

66  Gunning, Tom, *DW Griffith and the Origins of American Narrative Film* (Chicago, University of Illinois Press, 1994), p.258.

67  Pierre Leprohon writes that 220 Italian films were produced in 1920, 100 in 1921, 50 in 1922, dwindling to 'less than a dozen' in 1927–28 (Leprohon, Pierre, *The Italian Cinema*, trans. Roger Greaves and Oliver Stallybrass (London: Secker and Warburg, 1972), p.51). Pierre Sorlin (*Italian National Cinema*, pp.52–53) depicts an even sharper slump, from 371 films in 1920, to 114 in 1923 and eight in 1930.

68  Nowell-Smith, Geoffrey, James Hay and Gianni Volpi, *The Companion to Italian Cinema* (London: Cassell, 1996), p.1.

69  Literally, 'cinema city'.

70  The Bolshevik leader had actually said in 1922 that, for his purposes, film was 'the most important of all the arts'. It was Leon Trotsky who claimed that film was 'the most important weapon [...] this weapon which cries out to be used, is the best instrument for propaganda [...] a propaganda which is accessible to everyone' (Gillespie, David, *Early Soviet Cinema: Innovation, Ideology and Propaganda* (London: Wallfower, 2000), p.19).

71   Ginsborg: *A History of Contemporary Italy*, p.441.

72   It is here worth recording that Lenin, too, acknowledged the importance of US formats. Frayling records his realisation that, to keep urban cinemas open, double bills would have to mix 'entertainment pictures especially for advertising and revenue [...] [and] pictures with a specifically propagandist content' (*Spaghetti Westerns*, p.6). Indeed, Americana commanded a singular fascination in the early years of Bolshevik power: Fordism was to be exported wholesale to build Russian industry, and the Bolsheviks assimilated American popular culture into their own agenda. This is displayed in the imitations of US comedies in such founding texts of montage cinema as Lev Kuleshov's *The Extraordinary Adventures of Mr. West in the Land of the Bolsheviks* (1924) and Vsevolod Pudovkin's *Chess Fever* (1925). It is an interesting aside, therefore, that the PCI's post-war hostility towards American culture, while adhering to the official Soviet line in the Cold War, was in fact a break with the founding philosophies of Bolshevism.

73   Dalle Vacche, Angela, *The Body in the Mirror: Shapes of History in Italian Cinema* (Princeton, NJ: Princeton University Press, 1992), pp.27–29.

74   Landy, Marcia, *Italian Film* (Cambridge: Cambridge University Press, 2000), pp.76–77.

75   Gundle: 'From neo-realism to *luci rosse*', p.210.

76   Sorlin: *Italian National Cinema*, p.77.

77   Leprohon: *The Italian Cinema*, p.86.

78   Sorlin: *Italian National Cinema*, p.97.

79   Wagstaff, Christopher, 'Cinema', in David Forgacs and Robert Lumley (eds), *Italian Cultural Studies: an Introduction* (Oxford: Oxford University Press, 1996), p.227; Bondanella, Peter, 'Italian cinema', in Zygmunt G. Baranski and Rebecca J. West (eds), *The Cambridge Companion to Modern Italian Culture* (Cambridge: Cambridge University Press, 2001), p.223; Wood: *Italian Cinema*, pp.101–109.

80   Torriglia: *Broken Time, Fragmented Space*, p.96.

81   By this I intend both meanings of the word: well-attended and appealing to a working-class audience.

82   Bondanella: 'Italian cinema', p.224.

83   Landy: *Italian Film*, p.111.

84   Ellwood: '*Un americano a Roma*', p.45.

85   Wood: *Italian Cinema*, p.88.

86   Wagstaff: 'Italy in the post-war international cinema market', p.103.

87   Wagstaff: 'Italian genre films in the world market', p.84.

88   In 1946, 411 million cinema tickets were sold in Italy. In 1955, this number was 819 million (Wagstaff: 'Italy in the post-war international cinema market', p.95). Commercially operating cinemas in Italy numbered 6,551 in 1948, and 10,570 in 1955 (Gundle: 'From neo-realism to *luci rosse*', p.199).

89   Italy's cinematic output outnumbered Hollywood's by 242 films to 174 in 1962, 241 to 155 in 1963, 270 to 181 in 1964, 245 to 168 in 1966 and 258 to 215 in 1967 (Eleftheriotis, Dimitris, *Popular Cinemas of Europe: Studies of Texts, Contexts and Frameworks* (London: Continuum, 2001), p.105). Moreover, from a situation in

1947 whereby American films took 75 per cent of Italian box-office receipts to Italians' 10 per cent, by 1960 home-grown products had overtaken US imports by 50 per cent to 35 per cent (Wagstaff: 'Italy in the post-war international cinema market', p.108).

90  Wagstaff: 'Italy in the post-war international cinema market', pp.90, 114.

91  Faldini, Franca and Goffredo Fofi, *L'avventurosa storia del cinema italiano raccontata dai suoi protagonisti 1960–1969* (Milan: Mondadori, 1981), p.154.

92  Baudrillard, Jean, *America*, trans. Chris Turner (London: Verso, [1986] 1988), p.76.

93  Carrano, P., 'Divismo', in Marino Livolsi (ed.), *Schermi e ombre: gli Italiani e il cinema nel dopoguerra* (Scandicci: La Nuova Italia, 1988), p.231.

94  Gundle, Stephen, 'Fame, fashion, and style: the Italian star system', in David Forgacs and Robert Lumley (eds), *Italian Cultural Studies: an Introduction* (Oxford: Oxford University Press, 1996), pp.316–317.

95  Dalle Vacche: *The Body in the Mirror*, p.55.

96  Wagstaff, Christopher, 'A forkful of Westerns: industry, audiences and the Italian Western', in Richard Dyer and Ginette Vincendeau (eds), *Popular European Cinema* (London: Routledge, 1992), p.250.

97  The word 'peplum' refers to a short classical tunic often worn by extras in these budget revivals of the 'sword and sandal' movie.

98  Between 1950 and 1965, 1149 co-productions involving Italian investment were made. 764 of these were with France, 190 with Spain, 46 with Germany and 141 with two other countries. By 1965, 75 per cent of Italian production was shared in such a way (Wagstaff: 'Italy in the post-war international cinema market', pp.100–101).

99  Frayling: *Spaghetti Westerns*, p.68.

100 Frayling: *Spaghetti Westerns*, p.68.

101 Stanfield, Peter, *Hollywood Westerns and the 1930s: The Lost Trail* (Exeter: University of Exeter Press, 2001).

102 Wagstaff: 'A forkful of Westerns', p.253.

103 Wagstaff: 'Italian genre films in the world market', p.81.

104 Del Buono, Oreste and Lietta Tornabuoni (eds), *Era Cinecittà* (Milan: Bompiani, 1979), p.23.

105 Wagstaff: 'Italy in the post-war international cinema market', p.106.

106 The US distribution rights to *Le fatiche di Ercole* were bought by Joseph E. Levine in 1958 for $35 thousand, making a $4 million profit (Frayling: *Spaghetti Westerns*, p.73).

107 Frayling: *Something to Do with Death*, pp.115–116.

108 Eleftheriotis: *Popular Cinemas of Europe*, p.104.

109 In 1955, commercially operating cinemas peaked at 10,570. By 1965, this figure was still 10,517 (Gundle: 'From neo-realism to *luci rosse*', p.199).

110 As noted previously, in 1956, 366,151 television licenses were sold. In 1961, this figure was up to 2,761,738, and by 1966 it was 6,855,298 (Forgacs: 'Cultural consumption', p.283).

111 Westerns fell from making up 34 per cent of Hollywood's output in 1950 to 9 per cent in 1963 (Frayling: *Something to Do with Death*, p.121). John Sturges's *The Magnificent Seven* (1960), however, quadrupled its takings when released outside the USA (Parkinson, Michael and Clyde Jeavons, *A Pictorial History of Westerns* (London: Hamlyn, 1983), p.195).

112 Faldini and Fofi: *L'avventurosa storia del cinema italiano*, p.304.

113 Marsili, Mario, 'The other Sergio' (online), available: http://www.strangeher.net/bennetts_raiders/othersergio.htm (accessed 20 September 2004).

114 Sandler, Dorothy L., 'Damiano Damiani', *Daily American Weekly* (December 1963).

## 2
## A Marxist's Gotta Do What a Marxist's Gotta Do: National Identity and Political Violence on the Italian Frontier

1   Tuska, John, *The American West in Film: Critical Approaches to the Western* (London: Greenwood Press, 1985), p.141.

2   The James brothers' mother, Zerelda Samuel, was wounded, not killed, by an explosion caused by agents of the Pinkerton detective agency on the night of 26 January 1875.

3   Settle, William A., *Jesse James Was His Name* (London: University of Nebraska Press, [1966] 1977), p.46.

4   The Western being such an elusive genre, exceptions to this rule of course exist. *The Ox-Bow Incident* (1943), *High Noon* (1952) and *Johnny Guitar* (1954) openly question the genre's received ideologies. The significance of such films in relation to the Italian Western is discussed in Chapter Three.

5   In this chapter, I use the words 'South' and '*Mezzogiorno*' interchangeably. These terms are traditionally used to denote a large and diverse section of Italy comprising Campania, Molise, Puglia, Basilicata, Calabria, Sicily and Sardinia. It is to this conceptual entity, rather than to any genuine social or economic unit, that I refer. Where appropriate, I instead refer to the sovereign state of the Kingdom of Naples, which was made up of most of these regions prior to Italian unification in 1860.

6   Frayling, Christopher, *Spaghetti Westerns: Cowboys and Europeans from Karl May to Sergio Leone* (London: I.B.Tauris, [1981] 1998), p.58.

7   Landy, Marcia, *Italian Film* (Cambridge: Cambridge University Press, 2000), pp.183–184.

8   Frayling: *Spaghetti Westerns*, p.61.

9   Gribaudi, Gabriella, 'Images of the South', in David Forgacs and Robert Lumley (eds), *Italian Cultural Studies: an Introduction* (Oxford: Oxford University Press, 1996), pp.72–73.

10  In examining this topic, I have utilised the abundant source material collated by both John Dickie (*Darkest Italy: the Nation and Stereotypes of the Mezzogiorno, 1860–1900* (London: Macmillan, 1999)) and Nelson Moe (*The View from Vesuvius:*

*Italian Culture and the Southern Question* (London: University of California Press, 2002)).

11  Moe: *The View from Vesuvius*, pp.75–76.

12  Wister, Owen, *The Virginian* (London: Macmillan, [1902] 1949), p.7.

13  Dickie: *Darkest Italy*, pp.93–111; Moe: *The View from Vesuvius*, pp.124–153.

14  Dickie: *Darkest Italy*, p.19.

15  Moe: *The View from Vesuvius*, p.137.

16  Wister: *The Virginian*, p.12.

17  Such intellectuals as Pasquale Villari, Giustino Fortunato, Leopoldo Franchetti and Sidney Sonnino were collectively known as the *meridionalisti*. Villari and Fortunato were in fact southerners, eager to alert the government to their region's plight. This does not, however, preclude their presence in this argument concerning northern stereotypes of the South, since notions propagated by this school of thought did much to influence perceptions of these stereotypes in national discourse.

18  Dickie: *Darkest Italy*, p.54.

19  An alternative reading of the Western's relationship to these representational models will be explored in Chapter Four. The modern nation's fascinated gaze at a backward, subaltern neighbour will be seen to parallel the Hollywood Western's depictions of Mexico, which are directly appropriated and reversed by the militant Italian Westerns under consideration in that chapter.

20  Moe: *The View from Vesuvius*, p.50.

21  Wister: *The Virginian*, p.viii.

22  Dickie: *Darkest Italy*, p.104.

23  Moravia, Alberto, *Contempt*, trans. Angus Davidson (London: Prion, [1954] 1999), p.144.

24  Moe: *The View from Vesuvius*, p.295.

25  Levi, Carlo, *Christ Stopped at Eboli* (London: Cassell Levi, 1948), p.75.

26  Ginsborg, Paul, *A History of Contemporary Italy: Society and Politics, 1943–1980* (London: Penguin, 1990), p.33.

27  Moe: *The View from Vesuvius*, p.167.

28  Ginsborg (*A History of Contemporary Italy*, p.30) records that *latifondi* made up 80 per cent of all cultivated land in Sicily in 1930.

29  Chubb, Judith, *Patronage, Power and Poverty in Southern Italy* (Cambridge: Cambridge University Press, 1982), p.162.

30  Judt, Tony, *Postwar* (London: William Heinemann, 2005), p.257.

31  Only 0.4 per cent of redistributed land in Sicily under this scheme was described as 'well-irrigated' (Ginsborg: *A History of Contemporary Italy*, pp.131–132).

32  Clark, Martin, *Modern Italy, 1871–1982* (London: Longman, 1984), p.360.

33  Barzini, Luigi, *The Europeans* (London: Penguin, 1983), pp.171–172.

34  Hudson, Anne, '*Rocco e i suoi fratelli*', in Giorgio Bertellini (ed.), *The Cinema of Italy* (London: Wallflower Press, 2004), p.96.

35  Moss, David, *The Politics of Left-Wing Violence in Italy, 1969–85* (London: MacMillan, 1989), p.44.

36    Wagstaff does however stress that exact figures for *terza visione* cinemas are unavailable, due to the nature of such theatres as 'a huge stew-pot of small independent cinemas, open-air summer cinemas and parish cinemas' (Wagstaff, Christopher, 'Italy in the post-war international cinema market', in Christopher Duggan and Christopher Wagstaff (eds), *Italy in the Cold War: Politics, Culture and Society 1948–1958* (Oxford: Berg, 1995), p.113).

37    Wagstaff, Christopher, 'A forkful of Westerns: industry, audiences and the Italian Western', in Richard Dyer and Ginette Vincendeau (eds), *Popular European Cinema* (London: Routledge, 1992), p.253.

38    Frayling: *Spaghetti Westerns*, pp.189, 60.

39    Gundle, Stephen, 'Fame, fashion, and style: the Italian star system', in David Forgacs and Robert Lumley (eds), *Italian Cultural Studies: an Introduction* (Oxford: Oxford University Press, 1996), pp.316–317.

40    It should be pointed out here that some of the key films under consideration in this book – most notably *Quien sabe?* and *La resa dei conti* – were not in fact *terza visione*, but large-scale and internationally-released, productions. This argument nevertheless describes the generic milieu, and the traditions of representation, with which such films consciously engage.

41    Wister: *The Virginian*, pp.435–436.

42    Wright, Will, *Sixguns and Society: A Structural Study of the Western* (London: University of California Press, [1975] 1977).

43    John Tuska states that 'the actual plots of the films [Wright] selected to illustrate these basic plot types do not fit into his categories without all manner of exceptions and unconventional interpretations' (*The American West in Film*, p.14). Barry Langford questions the reliability of using such major works as the sole referent for understanding the genre, considering the thousands of series 'B' films which constitute the vast majority of all Westerns ever made (Langford, Barry, *Film Genre: Hollywood and Beyond* (Edinburgh: Edinburgh University Press, 2005), p.58).

44    Wagstaff: 'Italy in the post-war international cinema market', p.106.

45    Wright: *Sixguns and Society*, p.34.

46    Cawelti, John G., *The Six-Gun Mystique Sequel* (Bowling Green: Bowling Green State University Press, 1999), p.68.

47    McGee, Patrick, *From Shane to Kill Bill: Rethinking the Western* (Oxford: Blackwell, 2007), p.25.

48    Frayling: *Spaghetti Westerns*, p.60.

49    Frayling: *Spaghetti Westerns*, p.59.

50    Clark: *Modern Italy*, p.361.

51    Dickie: *Darkest Italy*, p.25.

52    Dickie: *Darkest Italy*, p.37.

53    Dickie: *Darkest Italy*, p.33.

54    Hobsbawm, Eric, *Bandits* (London: Orion, [1969] 2000), p.152.

55    Hobsbawm: *Bandits*, pp.142–143.

56 Restivo, Angelo, 'The economic miracle and its discontents: bandit films in Spain and Italy', *Film Quarterly* 49/2 (Winter 1995–96), pp.30–40 (pp.31, 33).

57 Frayling: *Spaghetti Westerns*, p.58.

58 French, Philip, *Westerns* (Manchester: Carcanet, 2005), p.69.

59 Warshow, Robert, *The Immediate Experience: Movies, Comics, Theatre and Other Aspects of Popular Culture* (London: Harvard University Press, 2001), p.121.

60 Warshow: *The Immediate Experience*, p.123.

61 Tompkins, Jane, *West of Everything: The Inner Life of Westerns* (Oxford: Oxford University Press, 1992), p.41.

62 Mitchell, Lee Clark, *Westerns: Making the Man in Fiction and Film* (London: University of Chicago Press, 1996).

63 Schaefer, Jack, *Shane* (London: Heinemann, [1953] 1967), p.61.

64 Calder, Jenni, *There Must Be a Lone Ranger* (Gateshead: Northumberland Press, 1974), p.114.

65 Kitses, Jim, *Horizons West: Directing the Western from John Ford to Clint Eastwood* (London: BFI, 2004), p.17.

66 Prince, Stephen, *Classical Film Violence: Designing and Regulating Brutality in Hollywood Cinema, 1930–1968* (London: Rutgers University Press, 2003), p.19.

67 Tompkins: *West of Everything*, p.228.

68 Beale, Lewis, 'The American way west', *Films and Filming* (18 April 1972), pp.24–30 (p.27).

69 Kael, Pauline, 'Killing time', in Karl French (ed.), *Screen Violence* (London: Bloomsbury, 1974), p.172.

70 I shall examine this issue further in Chapter Five, when my argument will consider the countercultural uses to which the Western genre was being put in America itself by the end of the 1960s. As I shall demonstrate, the framing of violence in fact signifies Hollywood's most notable departure from the Italian model.

71 Mitchell: *Westerns*, p.226.

72 Mitchell: *Westerns*, p.252.

73 Frayling, Christopher, *Sergio Leone: Once Upon a Time in Italy* (London: Thames and Hudson, 2005), p.82.

74 Leone stated that *Il buono, il brutto, il cattivo*'s pacifistic stance was influenced by Chaplin's *Monsieur Verdoux* (1947) (Frayling: *Once Upon a Time in Italy*, p.82), and that *C'era una volta il West* depicted 'the relentless force of capitalism, at whatever the cost' (Frayling: *Once Upon a Time in Italy*, p.78).

75 Frayling, Christopher, 'The wretched of the Earth', *Sight and Sound* 3/6 (June 1993), pp.26–29 (p.29).

76 De Fornari, Oreste, *Sergio Leone: The Great Italian Dream of Legendary America*, trans. Charles Nopar (Rome: Gremese, 1997), p.23.

77 Especially revealing in this context is Leone's posturing that: 'I'm a *moderate* anarchist who doesn't go around throwing bombs' (Frayling, Christopher, *Sergio Leone: Something to Do with Death* (London: Faber and Faber, 2000), p.306). Perhaps it is this comment that occupied Mitchell's train of thought.

78   This is not to say that the resulting turn to violence was the same in both
     countries. Such clandestine American groups as the Weathermen operated on
     a much smaller scale than those of the Italian Red Brigades and, unlike their
     Italian counterparts, did not carry their confrontational rhetoric over into
     murder. I shall return to the implications of this divergence in Chapters Four
     and Five.

79   Judt: *Postwar*, p.415.

80   Della Porta, Donatella, *Social Movements, Political Violence, and the State: A
     Comparative Analysis of Italy and Germany* (Cambridge: Cambridge University
     Press, 1995), p.23.

81   La Palombara, Joseph, *Democracy, Italian Style* (London: Yale University Press,
     1987).

82   Tarrow, Sidney, 'Violence and institutionalisation after the Italian protest cycle',
     in Raimondo Catanzaro (ed.), *The Red Brigades and Left-Wing Terrorism in Italy*
     (London: Pinter Publishers, 1991), pp.52, 54.

83   The *Corriere della sera* recorded that only 19 per cent of student demonstrations
     involved any form of violence, compared to 23 per cent of protests as a whole
     (Tarrow: 'Violence and institutionalisation', p.50).

84   Tarrow: 'Violence and institutionalisation', pp.42–43.

85   Ginsborg: *A History of Contemporary Italy*, pp.318–319.

86   Mitchell: *Westerns*, p.224.

87   Frayling: 'The wretched of the Earth', p.27.

88   Prince: *Classical Film Violence*, p.153.

89   Kael: 'Killing time', p.172.

### 3
### Go West, Comrade! Defining the Absolute Enemy

1   Faldini, Franca and Goffredo Fofi, *L'avventurosa storia del cinema italiano raccontata
    dai suoi protagonisti 1960–1969* (Milan: Mondadori, 1981), p.303.

2   Sollima elucidates further: 'The origin of the story is that my girlfriend
    denounced me to the Germans, because her father was a Fascist' (Faldini and
    Fofi: *L'avventurosa storia del cinema italiano*, p.303). In 2004 he added that the
    characters in the film 'are children of my own personal experience during World
    War Two, when I saw people changing from cowards to heroes and heroes
    becoming cowards' (Marsili, Mario, 'The other Sergio' (online), available:
    http://www.strangeher.net/bennetts_raiders/othersergio.htm   (accessed   20
    September 2004)).

3   Moss, David, *The Politics of Left-Wing Violence in Italy, 1969–85* (London:
    MacMillan, 1989), p.11.

4   Curcio drew his own inspiration from his uncle, who died fighting the Nazis: 'I
    have picked up the rifle that only death, arriving through the murderous hand
    of nazi-fascists, had wrested from him' (Weinberg, Leonard, 'The violent life:
    left- and right-wing terrorism in Italy', in Peter H. Merkl (ed.), *Political Violence*

*and Terror: Motifs and Motivations* (London: University of California Press, 1986), p.148).

5   Manconi, Luigi, 'The political ideology of the Red Brigades', in Raimondo Catanzaro (ed.), *The Red Brigades and Left-Wing Terrorism in Italy* (London: Pinter Publishers, 1991), p.122.

6   Wright, Will, *Sixguns and Society: A Structural Study of the Western* (London: University of California Press, [1975] 1977), p.32.

7   Frayling, Christopher, *Spaghetti Westerns: Cowboys and Europeans from Karl May to Sergio Leone* (London: I.B.Tauris, [1981] 1998), p.51.

8   Fridlund, Bert, *The Spaghetti Western: A Thematic Analysis* (Jefferson: MacFarland, 2006).

9   Fridlund includes *Faccia a faccia* in his 'infiltrator' plot (*The Spaghetti Western*, pp.27–28) – which accords closely with Frayling's 'foundation' scenario – due to the Pinkerton agent's infiltration of Brad and Beau's gang. While this narrative motif's appearance in the film displays signs of influence from the common variant, it is a secondary sub-plot and does not suffice in an analysis of this film's complexities.

10   Althusser, Louis, *Lenin and Philosophy and Other Essays*, trans. Ben Brewster (New York: Monthly Review Press, [1971] 2001), pp.92–94.

11   Weidhorn, Manfred, '*High Noon*: liberal classic? Conservative screed?', *Bright Lights* (February 2005).

12   Don Siegel further affirms this symbolic potency by quoting *High Noon* in the closing shot of *Dirty Harry* (1971). This film's significance in the context of cinematic violence and the legacy of the Italian Western will be addressed in more detail in Chapter Five.

13   Marcuse, Herbert, *One Dimensional Man* (London: Ark, [1964] 1986), pp.1, 56.

14   Marcuse, Herbert, 'Repressive Tolerance', in Robert Paul Wolff, Barrington Moore Jr. and Herbert Marcuse, *A Critique of Pure Tolerance* (London: Jonathan Cape, 1969), p.116.

15   Varon, Jeremy, *Bringing the War Home: The Weather Underground, the Red Army Faction, and Revolutionary Violence in the Sixties and Seventies* (London: University of California Press, 2004), p.44.

16   Wagstaff, Christopher, 'A forkful of Westerns: industry, audiences and the Italian Western', in Richard Dyer and Ginette Vincendeau (eds), *Popular European Cinema* (London: Routledge, 1992), p.250; Dalle Vacche, Angela, *The Body in the Mirror: Shapes of History in Italian Cinema* (Princeton, NJ: Princeton University Press, 1992), p.55.

17   Fridlund: *The Spaghetti Western*, p.42.

18   In many 'RSA' films – for example, *Se sei vivo, spara!*, *Ehi amico … c'è Sabata, hai chiuso!* and *Una nuvola di polvere … un grido di morte … arriva Sartana* – a hero is faced with factions of a hostile community whom he plays off against one another: the basis of the 'foundation' narrative.

19   Cox, Alex, *10,000 Ways to Die* (online), available: http://www.alexcox.com/freestuff/10000_WAYS_TO_DIE.pdf (accessed 4 January 2008).

20  Dalle Vacche: *The Body in the Mirror*, p.55.

21  Leone said that *Shane* was particularly important in the construction of the film, describing it as 'an abstraction, a walking piece of myth', but stating that he admired Jack Palance's villain more than Alan Ladd's hero (Frayling, Christopher, *Sergio Leone: Something to Do with Death* (London: Faber and Faber, 2000), p.127).

22  Frayling: *Something to Do with Death*, p.127.

23  Calder, Jenni, *There Must Be a Lone Ranger* (Gateshead: Northumberland Press, 1974), p.122.

24  Derderain, Stephane, '"I made one, and to tell the truth I only like one": an interview with Giulio Questi', trans. Alain Petit, *Spaghetti Cinema* 67 (July 1997), pp.18–26 (p.22).

25  In depicting a gang of outlaws riding into a town in which malevolent forces conspire beneath the surface, this sequence anticipates a similar framing in the opening of Sam Peckinpah's *The Wild Bunch* (1969). As we shall see in Chapter Five, the professed ideologies behind Peckinpah's film also have certain points of contact with Questi's outlook on bourgeois society.

26  The most striking aspect of this allegory is the rape of a young man by black-shirted muchachos. I shall return to the theme of fascist sexuality at the end of this chapter.

27  8 September 1943 saw the declaration of the armistice between Italy and the Allies, leaving Italy invaded from both north and south, and engulfed in civil war. King Victor Emanuel III and his Prime Minister, Marshal Badoglio, fled Rome, leaving the city to its fate, and an estimated 600 Italians were killed resisting the German seizure of the capital (Ginsborg, Paul, *A History of Contemporary Italy: Society and Politics, 1943–1980* (London: Penguin, 1990), p.14).

28  Faldini and Fofi: *L'avventurosa storia del cinema italiano*, p.302.

29  Faldini and Fofi: *L'avventurosa storia del cinema italiano*, p.302.

30  The story on which *La resa dei conti* was based was also written by a former Resistance fighter: Franco Solinas.

31  Ramonet, Ignacio, 'Italian Westerns as political parables', *Cineaste* 15/1 (1986), pp.30–35 (p.35).

32  *La resa dei conti* was the third highest-grossing Italian Western in *prima visione* receipts in 1967, bringing in 1,440,849,000 lire; *Da uomo a uomo* was fourth (1,261,929,000) and *Faccia a faccia* sixth (1,116,721,000). *Un fiume di dollari* made 524,568,000, with *Se sei vivo, spara!* making 374,256,000 (see Appendix A).

33  Macherey, Pierre, *A Theory of Literary Production* (New York: Routledge, [1978] 2006), p.95.

34  I refer throughout to the full 107 minute release.

35  In the English language dub the theatrical symbolism of the scene is further emphasised, with Williams's line being translated as 'ah, I believe the performance is about to begin'. Since this chapter's primary focus is on Italian reception, however, I have opted for a more faithful translation of the Italian soundtrack's 'ecco, mi pare proprio ci siamo'.

36  Van Cleef had recently finished work on *Il buono, il brutto, il cattivo* when he appeared in *La resa dei conti*. The former film was released in December 1966; the latter in March 1967.

37  I refer throughout to the full 106 minute release.

38  Hughes, Howard, *Once Upon a Time in the Italian West* (London: I.B.Tauris, 2004), p.148.

39  Hall, Keith, 'The hunt's over', *Spaghetti Cinema* 11 (1986), pp.10–13 (p.12).

40  Cox: *10,000 Ways to Die*, p.31.

41  Hughes: *Once Upon a Time in the Italian West*, p.147.

42  Sollima claimed in a 2004 interview that after the first screening of *La resa dei conti*, Leone approached him and admitted 'it is better than mine' (Marsili: 'The other Sergio'). Leone himself in fact publicly expressed distaste for the film: 'Solinas's screenplay was wonderful. The film was not' (Faldini and Fofi: *L'avventurosa storia del cinema italiano*, p.303).

43  Catanzaro, Raimondo, 'Subjective experience and objective reality: an account of violence in the words of its protagonists', in Raimondo Catanzaro (ed.), *The Red Brigades and Left-Wing Terrorism in Italy* (London: Pinter Publishers, 1991), p.175.

44  Varon: *Bringing the War Home*, p.39.

45  Wood, Robin, *Hollywood from Vietnam to Reagan... and Beyond* (Chichester: Columbia University Press, [1986] 2003), p.42.

46  Frayling: *Spaghetti Westerns*, p.236.

47  Smith, Douglas, 'Introduction', in Friedrich Nietzsche, *On the Genealogy of Morals*, trans. Douglas Smith (Oxford: Oxford University Press, [1887] 1996), p.xxviii.

48  Benjamin, Walter, *Illuminations*, trans. Harry Zorn (London: Pimlico, 1999), p.248.

49  Wister, Owen, *The Virginian* (London: MacMillan, [1902] 1949), p.viii.

50  Nachbar, Jack, 'Introduction: a century on the trail', *Journal of Popular Film and Television* 30/4 (2003), pp.178–180 (p.179).

51  Benjamin: *Illuminations*, p.247.

52  Benjamin: *Illuminations*, p.253.

53  Langford, Barry, *Film Genre: Hollywood and Beyond* (Edinburgh: Edinburgh University Press, 2005), p.68.

54  Benjamin: *Illuminations*, p.248.

55  Benjamin: *Illuminations*, p.251.

56  Wagstaff: 'A forkful of Westerns', p.253.

57  Günsberg, Maggie, *Italian Cinema: Gender and Genre* (London: Palgrave, 2005), p.186.

58  Günsberg: *Italian Cinema*, p.186.

59  Calder: *There Must Be a Lone Ranger*, p.114.

60  Theweleit, Klaus, *Male Fantasies*, Vols. 1 and 2 (Cambridge: Polity, [1977] 1987).

61  This is, of course, a generalisation, but not one without foundation. Wagstaff records that Italian audience surveys of the era showed that adventure formulae

were preferred more by men than by women ('A forkful of Westerns', pp.253, 260).

62   Varon: *Bringing the War Home*, p.43.

63   Catanzaro: 'Subjective experience and objective reality', p.184.

4

## Violent Mexico: 'Crossing the Border' into Armed Insurgency

1   *Quien sabe?*, *Tepepa*, *Il mercenario* and *Compañeros* are all set in the period most often referred to as 'the Mexican Revolution', of 1910–20. *Corri, uomo, corri* inhabits a more abstract timeline, but is set in the late nineteenth century, at an early but unspecified stage during the reign of Porfirio Díaz (1877–80, 1884–1911).

2   Slotkin, Richard, *Gunfighter Nation: The Myth of the Frontier in Twentieth-Century America* (New York: Atheneum, 1992), pp.405–440.

3   Wistrich, Robert, *Trotsky: Fate of a Revolutionary* (London: Robson Books, 1979), p.207.

4   Ginsborg, Paul, *A History of Contemporary Italy: Society and Politics, 1943–1980* (London: Penguin, 1990), p.303.

5   Weinberg, Leonard, 'The violent life: left- and right-wing terrorism in Italy', in Peter H. Merkl (ed.), *Political Violence and Terror: Motifs and Motivations* (London: University of California Press, 1986), p.162.

6   Engelhardt, Tom, *The End of Victory Culture: Cold War America and the Disillusioning of a Generation* (New York: BasicBooks, 1995), p.201.

7   The killing of 502 Vietnamese villagers in the My Lai sub-hamlet at the hands of First Lieutenant William Calley's platoon actually took place on 16 March 1968, but the story did not break in *Time*, *Life* and *Newsweek* until December 1969 (Engelhardt: *The End of Victory Culture*, pp.216–220).

8   Wise, David and Thomas B. Ross, *The Invisible Government* (New York: Random House, 1964).

9   Marcuse, Herbert, 'Repressive tolerance', in Robert Paul Wolff, Barrington Moore Jr. and Herbert Marcuse, *A Critique of Pure Tolerance* (London: Jonathan Cape, 1965), p.116.

10  The militant manifesto 'You Don't Need a Weatherman to Know Which Way the Wind Blows', written principally by 'JJ' (John Jacobs), was published in 1969. It signalled the final rejection by the Revolutionary Youth Movement of the proletarian focus of the Progressive Labor Party, asserting a more internationalist support for the Black Panthers and the Vietnamese NLF (Varon, Jeremy, *Bringing the War Home: The Weather Underground, the Red Army Faction, and Revolutionary Violence in the Sixties and Seventies* (London: University of California Press, 2004), p.50).

11  Varon: *Bringing the War Home*, p.39.

12  Ginsborg: *A History of Contemporary Italy*, p.302.

13  Faldini, Franca and Goffredo Fofi, *L'avventurosa storia del cinema italiano raccontata dai suoi protagonisti 1960–1969* (Milan: Mondadori, 1981), p.300.

14  Coyne, Michael, *The Crowded Prairie: American National Identity in the Hollywood Western* (London: I.B.Tauris, 1997), p.70.

15  Kitses, Jim, *Horizons West: Anthony Mann, Budd Boetticher, Sam Peckinpah: Studies of Authorship Within the Western* (London: Thames and Hudson, 1969).

16  Hall, Linda B. and Don M. Coerver, *Revolution on the Border: The United States and Mexico 1910–1920* (Albuquerque: University of New Mexico Press, 1988), p.89.

17  De Orellana, Margherita, *Filming Pancho Villa: How Hollywood Shaped the Mexican Revolution* (New York: Verso Books, 2004).

18  Burns and Charlip record: 'One version of his life story contends that he fled the hacienda after shooting and wounding the haçendado, who had raped his sister' (Burns, E. Bradford and Julie A. Charlip, *Latin America: A Concise Interpretative History* (New Jersey: Prentice Hall, 2002), p.203). In Jack Conway's *Viva Villa!* (1934), the death of Villa's father similarly gives just cause for his banditry, efficiently enabling audience sympathy without the need for overtly 'political' examinations of his motives.

19  O'Malley, Ilene, *The Myth of the Revolution: Hero Cults and the Institutionalisation of the Mexican State 1920–1940* (London: Greenwood Press, 1986), p.88.

20  Moe, Nelson, *The View from Vesuvius: Italian Culture and the Southern Question* (London: University of California Press, 2002), p.101.

21  Slotkin: *Gunfighter Nation*, p.415.

22  Slotkin: *Gunfighter Nation*, p.440; Corkin, Stanley, *Cowboys as Cold Warriors: The Western and US History* (Philadelphia: Temple University Press, 2004).

23  Slotkin: *Gunfighter Nation*, pp.408–409.

24  Slotkin: *Gunfighter Nation*, p.436.

25  Corkin: *Cowboys as Cold Warriors*, p.180.

26  Corkin: *Cowboys as Cold Warriors*, p.10.

27  Engelhardt: *The End of Victory Culture*, pp.190, 193.

28  Engelhardt: *The End of Victory Culture*, p.10.

29  It is significant that Lancaster's role here closely echoes that of Joe Erin from *Vera Cruz*. In *The Professionals*, unlike in Aldrich's film, this cynical, mercenary character survives and remains a hero, suggesting that Ben Trane's chivalric wholesomeness was no longer expected to triumph in 1966.

30  Fanon, Frantz, *The Wretched of the Earth* (London: Penguin, [1961] 2001), p.74.

31  Michalczyk, John, 'Franco Solinas: the dialectic of screenwriting', *Cineaste* 13/2 (1984), pp.30–33 (p.30).

32  De Fornari, Oreste, *Sergio Leone: The Great Italian Dream of Legendary America*, trans. Charles Nopar (Rome: Gremese, 1997), p.86.

33  *La battaglia di Algeri* presents a considerably more even-handed representation of the colonial situation during the Algerian war of independence (the precise historical 'moment' to which Fanon chiefly referred in his writings). The carnage inflicted by insurgent atrocities, for example, is depicted in the same harrowing detail as those caused by the French army, and Colonel Mathieu, far from a jack-booted oppressor, is a veteran of the French Resistance who empathises with the guerrillas' cause and understands their tactics. In this film, as in *Quien sabe?*

and *Queimada!*, however, the dichotomous incompatibility of the clashing forces is clear.

34  Fanon: *The Wretched of the Earth*, p.73.

35  Solinas later insisted that he played no part in the actual writing of *Tepepa*, and only gave assistance to Della Mea, who was the film's sole author (Faldini and Fofi: *L'avventurosa storia del cinema italiano*, p.300). The influence, if not necessarily the hand, of the writer of *Quien sabe?* and *Queimada!* is however evident in the most cursory plot summary: an English doctor enters Mexico with the intention of killing a native revolutionary leader, with whom he eventually forms an uneasy partnership. The final scene depicts a violent rejection of his intervention in Mexican affairs.

36  *La resa dei conti* is the exception, since it narrates instead the political awakening of a 'gringo': Jonathan Corbett. It does, however, provide its sequel, *Corri, uomo, corri*, with a peasant figure – Cuchillo – who becomes a revolutionary in this later film.

37  As Appendix A displays, *Quien sabe?*, while not rivaling such phenomena as *Il buono, il brutto, il cattivo* and *Django*, was nevertheless the tenth most successful Italian Western at the *prima visione* box-office in 1966, making 687,118,000 lire: this in a year in which 58 such productions emerged (see Appendix B).

38  Frayling, Christopher, *Spaghetti Westerns: Cowboys and Europeans from Karl May to Sergio Leone* (London: I.B.Tauris, [1981] 1998), p.52.

39  Fridlund, Bert, *The Spaghetti Western: A Thematic Analysis* (Jefferson: MacFarland, 2006), p.173.

40  Ginsborg: *A History of Contemporary Italy*, pp.221–222.

41  I refer throughout to the original 115 minute long cut, released in Italian cinemas in December 1966.

42  Faldini and Fofi: *L'avventurosa storia del cinema italiano*, p.303.

43  Frayling, Christopher, *Sergio Leone: Something to Do with Death* (London: Faber and Faber, 2000), p.307.

44  Crowdus, Gary and Dan Georgakas, 'Acting and the collective filmmaking experience: an interview with Gian Maria Volonté', *Cineaste* 15/1 (1986), pp.9–11 (p.10).

45  Anon, 'Italian actors outwit police', *The Times* (16 February 1965), p.12.

46  Braucourt, Guy, 'Gian Maria Volonté talks about cinema and politics', trans. Renée Delforge, *Cineaste* 7/1 (1975), pp.10–13 (p.11).

47  The very final moment of this portrayal jeopardises this pattern with its overt exuberance. I shall return to this flaw at the end of the chapter.

48  Mead, Taylor, 'Inter/View with Tomas Milian', *Inter/View* 2/3, pp.12–3 (p.13).

49  Engelhardt: *The End of Victory Culture*, p.40.

50  Engelhardt: *The End of Victory Culture*, p.41.

51  Günsberg, Maggie, *Italian Cinema: Gender and Genre* (London: Palgrave, 2005), pp.213–214.

52  Clifford, James, *The Predicament of Culture* (Cambridge, MA: Harvard University Press, 1988), p.147.

53 Eleftheriotis, Dimitris, *Popular Cinemas of Europe: Studies of Texts, Contexts and Frameworks* (London: Continuum, 2001), pp.97–98.

54 Günsberg: *Italian Cinema*, p.214.

55 Eleftheriotis: *Popular Cinemas of Europe*, p.128.

56 Slotkin: *Gunfighter Nation*, pp.417–418.

57 De Certeau, Michel, *The Practice of Everyday Life* (Berkeley: University of California Press, [1984] 1988), pp.xiii-xiv.

58 Fanon: *The Wretched of the Earth*, p.200.

59 So too Cuchillo in *Corri, uomo, corri* is dressed up in the garb of a Westerner when he crosses into Texas, only to reject these clothes and resume his peon dress as the climax approaches.

60 Fanon: *The Wretched of the Earth*, p.178.

61 Varon: *Bringing the War Home*, p.8.

62 Chaliand, Gérard, *Revolution in the Third World*, trans. Diana Johnstone and Tony Berrett (Harmondsworth: Penguin, 1989), p.217.

63 Faldini and Fofi: *L'avventurosa storia del cinema italiano*, p.302.

64 Frayling: *Spaghetti Westerns*, p.76.

65 Della Porta, Donatella, *Social Movements, Political Violence, and the State: A Comparative Analysis of Italy and Germany* (Cambridge: Cambridge University Press, 1995), p.121.

66 Judt, Tony, *Postwar* (London: William Heinemann, 2005), p.415.

67 Della Porta: *Social Movements*, p.87.

68 Tarrow, Sidney, 'Violence and institutionalisation after the Italian protest cycle', in Raimondo Catanzaro (ed.), *The Red Brigades and Left-Wing Terrorism in Italy* (London: Pinter Publishers, 1991), p.43.

69 *Compañeros*, too, is narrated through the flashback of Franco Nero's European outsider. As we have seen, this film's extra-diegetic engagement with the New Left is conspicuous, but the identification with the native similarly compromised by this framing.

70 Fanon: *The Wretched of the Earth*, p.73.

71 Ginsborg: *A History of Contemporary Italy*, p.313.

72 Woddis, Jack, *New Theories of Revolution: A Commentary on the Views of Frantz Fanon, Régis Debray and Herbert Marcuse* (London: Lawrence and Wishart, 1972), p.27.

# 5
## Revolutionising Violence: Radical Translation and Postmodern Residues in US Cinema

1 Hall, William, '*The Wild Bunch*', *The Evening News* (20 June 1969).

2 Kitses, Jim, *Horizons West: Directing the Western from John Ford to Clint Eastwood* (London: BFI, 2004), p.202.

3 Prince, Stephen, *Savage Cinema: Sam Peckinpah and the Rise of Ultraviolent Movies* (London: Athlone, 1998), p.24.

4   Peckinpah responded to criticisms of his films' violent content thus: 'We watch wars and see men die, really die, every day on television, but it doesn't seem real [...] We've been anaesthetized by the media [...] When people complain about the way I handle violence, what they're really saying is, "Please don't show me; I don't want to know; and get me another beer out of the icebox"' (Prince: *Savage Cinema*, p.49).

5   Prince: *Savage Cinema*, p.70.

6   Goff, John, '*The Wild Bunch*', *The Hollywood Reporter* 206/25 (1969), p.3.

7   Hall: '*The Wild Bunch*'.

8   Canby, Vincent, '*The Wild Bunch*', *The New York Times* (26 June), p.45.

9   Sragow, Michael, '*The Wild Bunch*', *Film Society Review* 5/3 (1969), pp.31–37 (p.35).

10   Hibbin, Nina, '*The Wild Bunch*', *The Morning Star* (23 August 1969).

11   Sharrett, Christopher, 'Peckinpah the radical: the politics of *The Wild Bunch*', in Stephen Prince (ed.), *Sam Peckinpah's* The Wild Bunch (Cambridge: Cambridge University Press, 1999), p.98.

12   These two films will therefore be the chief, though not exclusive, frames of reference in this chapter when discussing the political trends examined in the book as a whole. *Faccia a faccia* was released in the UK in May 1969, and *Se sei vivo, spara!* followed in January 1970. These films are also therefore incorporated to inform my analysis of international critical reception. Each of *Tepepa, Corri, uomo, corri* and *Il grande Silenzio* failed to find distributors in either the USA or the UK, whose markets are this chapter's primary focus.

13   Althusser, Louis, *Lenin and Philosophy and Other Essays*, trans. Ben Brewster (New York: Monthly Review Press, [1971] 2001), pp.92–94.

14   Frayling, Christopher, *Spaghetti Westerns: Cowboys and Europeans from Karl May to Sergio Leone* (London: I.B.Tauris, [1981] 1998), pp.280–286.

15   Durgnat, Raymond, '*The Good, the Bad and the Ugly*', *Films and Filming* 15/2 (1968), pp.48–49 (p.48).

16   Prince: *Savage Cinema*, pp.50–62.

17   French, Philip, 'How violent taboos were blown away', *The Guardian Review* (26 August 2007), pp.6–7 (p.7).

18   Biskind, Peter, *Easy Riders, Raging Bulls* (London: Bloomsbury, 1998), p.35.

19   Prince: *Savage Cinema*, p.26.

20   Lusted, David, *The Western* (London: Pearson, 2003), p.192.

21   Wheeler Winston Dixon repeats Clint Eastwood's claim that in framing shooter and victim in the same shot, Leone broke 'rigidly enforced Hollywood taboos' (Dixon, Wheeler Winston, 'Re-visioning the Western: code, myth, and genre in Peckinpah's *The Wild Bunch*', in Stephen Prince (ed.), *Sam Peckinpah's* The Wild Bunch (Cambridge: Cambridge University Press, 1999), p.169). Stephen Prince refutes this, highlighting the fact that this shot construction appears as early as *Scarface* (1932), *G-Men* (1935), *This Gun for Hire* (1943) and *The Big Sleep* (1946) (Prince, Stephen, *Classical Film Violence: Designing and Regulating Brutality in Hollywood Cinema, 1930–1968* (London: Rutgers University Press, 2003), p.106).

22   Prince: *Classical Film Violence*, p.153.

23 Frayling: *Spaghetti Westerns*, p.68; Wagstaff, Christopher, 'A forkful of Westerns: industry, audiences and the Italian Western', in Richard Dyer and Ginette Vincendeau (eds), *Popular European Cinema* (London: Routledge, 1992), p.257.

24 Wagstaff: 'A forkful of Westerns', p.257.

25 Frayling: *Spaghetti Westerns*, p.280; Prince: *Savage Cinema*, p.18.

26 Anon, '*The Good, the Bad and the Ugly*', *Time* (9 December 1968).

27 See Appendix C.

28 Crowther, Bosley, '*Bonnie and Clyde*', *The New York Times* (14 April 1967).

29 Crowther, Bosley, '*For a Few Dollars More*', *The New York Times* (4 July 1967), p.23.

30 Galluzzo, Tony, '*A Pistol for Ringo*', *Motion Picture Herald* (9 November 1966), p.627.

31 Anon, '*Ringo and his Golden Pistol*', *Monthly Film Bulletin* 35/408 (1968), pp.9–10 (p.10).

32 Thomas, Kevin, '*Adios Sabata*', *The Los Angeles Times* (9 September 1971).

33 Dool, '*The Hills Run Red*', *Variety* (11 October 1967), p.6.

34 Jenkins, Valerie, '*A Fistful of Dynamite*', *The Evening Standard* (14 September 1972).

35 Price, James, '*The Good, the Bad and the Ugly*', *The Times* (30 August 1968); Braun, Eric, '*Sabata*', *Films and Filming* 17/9 (1971), pp.76–78 (p.77).

36 Wallington, Mike, 'Spaghettis', *Time Out* (2–16 May 1970), p.25.

37 Weiler, AH, '*A Bullet for the General*', *The New York Times* (1 May 1969), p.52.

38 Hawk, '*A Bullet for the General*', *Variety* (19 July 1967).

39 Whit, '*The Big Gundown*', *Variety* (14 August 1968).

40 Clarke, Graham, '*The Big Gundown*', *Kinematograph Weekly* 3200 (1969), p.10.

41 Clarke, Graham, '*Face to Face*', *Kinematograph Weekly* 3211 (1960), p.10.

42 The patterns of critical reception summarised here are, of course, responding to these cut versions. This factor doubtless played a part in framing the Italian Western as superficial and apolitical in the USA.

43 Spanish for 'who knows?', 'Quien sabe?' is Chuncho's final utterance to Tate before he shoots him dead, in response to the question 'but why must you kill me?'.

44 Prince: *Classical Film Violence*, p.153.

45 Prince: *Classical Film Violence*, p.238.

46 Coyne, Michael, *The Crowded Prairie: American National Identity in the Hollywood Western* (London: I.B.Tauris, 1997), p.164.

47 While neither *Il grande Silenzio* nor *Django* secured full releases in the USA, both were highly successful in Europe, and Corbucci's work was most certainly known amongst American cineastes. Hughes records, for example, that Jack Nicholson attempted to acquire the rights to *Django* in 1967 (Hughes, Howard, *Once Upon a Time in the Italian West* (London: I.B.Tauris, 2004), p.65).

48 Marcuse, Herbert, *One Dimensional Man* (London: Ark, [1964] 1986), pp.1, 56.

49 Kael, Pauline, 'Killing time', in Karl French (ed.), *Screen Violence* (London: Bloomsbury, 1974), p.174.

50  Varon, Jeremy, *Bringing the War Home: The Weather Underground, the Red Army Faction, and Revolutionary Violence in the Sixties and Seventies* (London: University of California Press, 2004), p.83.

51  Julien, Isaac, *BaadAsssss Cinema: A Bold Look at 70's Blaxploitation Films* (DVD) (Direct Video, 2002).

52  Keller, Alexandra, 'Generic subversion as counterhistory: Mario Van Peebles's *Posse*', in Janet Walker (ed.), *Westerns: Films Through History* (London: Routledge, 2001), p.40.

53  Lyotard, Jean-François, *The Postmodern Condition: A Report on Knowledge*, trans. Geoffrey Bennington and Brian Massumi (Manchester: Manchester University Press, 1979).

54  The 'insurgency' formulation does admittedly appear in *Giù la testa* (1971). As we have seen in Chapter Four, however, this operates as a conscious riposte to the 'political' trends and should not be identified as a characteristic feature of Leone himself.

55  The director's DVD commentary for *Once Upon a Time in Mexico* cites Leone at every turn and reports that, on the set of *Desperado* (1995), Quentin Tarantino told Rodriguez: 'This is your Dollars trilogy.'

56  Buscombe, Edward, 'Border control' (online), available: http://www.bfi.org. uk/sightandsound/feature/10/ (accessed 5 September 2006).

57  This flashback-driven revenge plot, as we have seen in the case of *Posse*, equally owes a debt to the Italian Western.

58  Rose, Steve, 'Found: where Tarantino gets his ideas', *The Guardian* (6 April 2004).

59  French, Philip, 'Mother of all battles', *The Observer* (25 April 2004).

60  In his commentary for the *Desperado* DVD, Rodriguez emphasises that the action sequences in this film were meticulously choreographed precisely because such films as John Woo's *The Killer* (1989) and *Hard Boiled* (1992) had raised the bar of stylised cinematic violence.

61  Jameson, Fredric, 'Postmodernism and consumer society', in Hal Foster (ed.), *The Anti-Aesthetic: Essays on Postmodern* Culture (Port Townsend, Wash.: Bay Press, 1983), p.117.

62  Baudrillard, Jean, *Simulacra and Simulations*, trans. Paul Foss, Paul Patton and Philip Beitchmann (New York: Semiotext, [1981] 1983).

63  Jameson, Fredric, *Postmodernism, or the Cultural Logic of Late Capitalism* (Durham, NC: Duke University Press, 1991), p.9.

# 6
## Along the Radical Spectrum

1  Since *Vent d'Est* was in fact partly shot at Elios, my meaning here is figurative, referring to the industrial milieu of Italian *filone* cinema, which Godard seeks fundamentally to reject.

2  Althusser, Louis, *Lenin and Philosophy and Other Essays*, trans. Ben Brewster (New York: Monthly Review Press, [1971] 2001), p.109.

3  MacCabe, Colin, *Godard: A Portrait of the Artist at 70* (London: Bloomsbury, 2003), p.182.

4  Baudry, Pierre, 'L'idéologie du western italien', *Cahiers du cinéma* 233 (1971), pp.55–56 (p.55).

5  Frayling, Christopher, *Spaghetti Westerns: Cowboys and Europeans from Karl May to Sergio Leone* (London: I.B.Tauris, [1981] 1998), p.230.

6  Frayling: *Spaghetti Westerns*, p.230.

7  Nowell-Smith, Geoffrey, *Making Waves: New Cinemas of the 1960s* (London: Continuum, 2008), pp.191–192.

8  Ginsborg, Paul, *A History of Contemporary Italy: Society and Politics, 1943–1980* (London: Penguin, 1990), pp.301–302.

9  Volonté's appearances in *Quien sabe?*, *Faccia a faccia* and *Vent d'Est* therefore display a personal journey along the spectrum of New Left opinion here summarised.

10  Lumley, Robert, *States of Emergency: Cultures of Revolt in Italy from 1968–1978* (London: Verso, 1990), p.122.

11  Lumley: *States of Emergency*, p.126.

12  Ginsborg: *A History of Contemporary Italy*, p.362.

13  Varon, Jeremy, *Bringing the War Home: The Weather Underground, the Red Army Faction, and Revolutionary Violence in the Sixties and Seventies* (London: University of California Press, 2004), p.76.

14  Moss, David, *The Politics of Left-Wing Violence in Italy, 1969–85* (London: MacMillan, 1989), p.12.

15  Debray, Régis, *Revolution in the Revolution?: Armed Struggle and Political Struggle in Latin America*, trans. Bobbye Ortiz (Harmondsworth: Penguin, 1968), p.21.

16  Bernardini, Aldo, '*Quien sabe?*', *Cineforum* 62 (1967), pp.172–173 (p.173); Natta, Enzo, '*La resa dei conti*', *Rivista del Cinematografo* 6 (1967), pp.364–365 (p.364); Saitta, Luigi, '*Tepepa*', *Rivista del Cinematografo* 2 (1969), pp.93–94 (p.93).

17  Natta, Enzo, '*Faccia a faccia*', *Rivista del Cinematografo* 1 (1968), pp.43–44 (p.43).

18  It is largely for this reason that analyses of my key films in relation to contemporaneous works of such political *auteurs* as Rosi and Pontecorvo have been only secondary in this book. Such an approach could well uncover notable parallels between, for example, the concerns of the political Italian Western and those of Pier Paolo Pasolini. Any one of agrarianism, the alienation of the *Mezzogiorno* in the Economic Miracle, Third Worldism or the psychopathology of fascism would offer ample material for comparative research (Pasolini even appeared in a Mexican Revolution-set Italian Western in 1967: Carlo Lizzani's *Requiescant*). My specific focus on the institutional milieu of the *filone* system and on the codes of the Western genre, however, would make such a tangent extraneous in this study.

19  Barthes, Roland, *S/Z*, trans. Richard Miller (Oxford: Blackwell, 1970).

## Appendix A

1   Sources: Associazione Generale Italiana dello Spettacolo, *Catalogo generale dei film italiani dal 1956 al 1975* (Rome: AGIS, 1975), The Internet Movie Database (www.imdb.com), The Spaghetti Western Database (www.spaghetti-western.net), various reviews in the pages of *Bianco e nero*.

## Appendix B

1   I include in the category 'Italian Westerns' films produced or co-produced by Italian studios, whose narratives are located in the USA, Mexico or Canada and set between the start of the Gold Rush (1848) and the Mexican Revolution of 1910–1920.

2   Sources: Associazione Generale Italiana dello Spettacolo, *Catalogo generale dei film italiani dal 1956 al 1975* (Rome: AGIS, 1975), Giusti, Marco, *Dizionario del Western all'italiana* (Milan: Oscar Mondadori, 2007), The Internet Movie Database (www.imdb.com), The Spaghetti Western Database (www.spaghetti-western.net), various reviews in the pages of *Bianco e nero*.

## Appendix C

1   These statistics are based largely on the collation of reviews in *Variety* and the *New York Times*, and thus give a good indication of release patterns. They are not necessarily exhaustive, however, due to the inherently independent, 'grindhouse' nature of these films' international distribution.

## Appendix D

1   Each film review listed here can be located in the bibliography. This corpus is discussed in the text on pp.175–178.

# Bibliography

Adams, Les and Buck Rainey, *Shoot-Em-Ups: The Complete Reference Guide to Westerns of the Sound Era* (New Rochelle, NY: Arlington House, 1978).

Adler, Renata, '*The Good, the Bad and the Ugly*', *The New York Times* (25 January 1968), p.33.

Alexander, Robert J., *Trotskyism in Latin America* (Stanford, CA: Hoover Institution Press, 1973).

Allum, PA, *Politics and Society in Postwar Naples* (Cambridge: Cambridge University Press, 1973).

Alpert, Hollis, '*A Fistful of Dollars*', *Saturday Review* (18 February 1967).

——, '*The Wild Bunch*', *Saturday Review* (27 September 1969).

Althusser, Louis, *Lenin and Philosophy and Other Essays*, trans. Ben Brewster (New York: Monthly Review Press, [1971] 2001).

Altman, Rick, *Film / Genre* (London: BFI, 1999).

Amyot, Grant, *The Italian Communist Party: the Crisis of the Popular Front Strategy* (London: Croom Helm, 1981).

Anderson, Jon Lee, *Che Guevara: A Revolutionary Life* (London: Bantam, 1997).

Anderson, Perry, *Considerations on Western Marxism* (London: Verso, 1976).

Andreychuk, Ed, *The Golden Corral: a Roundup of Magnificent Western Films* (London: McFarland, 1997).

Anon., 'Italian actors outwit police', *The Times* (16 February 1965), p.12.

Anon., '*Una pistola per Ringo*', *Intermezzo* 20/11 (1965), p.7.

Anon., '*Duel at Rio Bravo*', *Monthly Film Bulletin* 32/381 (1965), p.150.

Anon., '*Per qualche dollaro in più*', *Intermezzo* 21/1–2 (1966), p.6.

Anon., '*Sette pistole per i MacGregor*', *Intermezzo* 21/7–8 (1966), p.6.

Anon., '*Django*', *Intermezzo* 21/9–10 (1966), p.5.

Anon., '*A Pistol for Ringo*', *Monthly Film Bulletin* 33/394 (1966), p.171.

Anon., '*A Fistful of Dollars*', *Time* (10 January 1967).

Anon., '*Il buono, il brutto, il cattivo*', *Intermezzo* 22/1 (1967), p.7.

Anon., '*Quien sabe?*', *Intermezzo* 22/2–3 (1967), p.5.

Anon., '*Se sei vivo spara*', *Intermezzo* 22/2–3 (1967), p.10.

Anon., '*Minnesota Clay*', *Monthly Film Bulletin* 34/398 (1967), p.45.

Anon., '*La resa dei conti*', *Intermezzo* 22/6–7 (1967), p.11.

Anon., '*Sette donne per i MacGregor*', *Intermezzo* 22/6–7 (1967), p.11.

Anon., '*I crudeli*', *Intermezzo* 22/6–7 (1967), p.12.

Anon., '*A Fistful of Dollars*', *Monthly Film Bulletin* 34/401 (1967), p.96.

Anon., '*A Few Dollars for Django*', *Monthly Film Bulletin* 34/401 (1967), p.96.

Anon., '*Pochi dollari per Django*', *Intermezzo* 22/11–12 (1967), p.13.

Anon., '*One Silver Dollar*', *Monthly Film Bulletin* 34/402 (1967), p.106.

Anon., '*The Hills Run Red*', *Monthly Film Bulletin* 34/403 (1967), p.124.

Anon., '*Seven Guns for the MacGregors*', *Monthly Film Bulletin* 34/405 (1967), p.158.

Anon., '*Vado … l'ammazzo e torno*', *Cinema d'oggi* (23 October 1967), p.10.

Anon., '*For a Few Dollars More*', *Monthly Film Bulletin*, 34/406 (1967), p.176.

Anon., '*Dio perdona … io no!*', *Cinema d'oggi* (27 November 1967), p.10.

Anon., '*Faccia a faccia*', *Cinema d'oggi* (27 November 1967), p.10.

Anon., '*Vado … l'ammazzo e torno*', *Intermezzo* 22/21–22, p.11.

Anon., '*Dio perdona … io no!*', *Intermezzo* 22/23–24, p.6.

Anon., '*Faccia a faccia*', *Intermezzo* 22/23–24 (1967), p.6.

Anon., '*I giorni dell'ira*', *Cinema d'oggi* (8 January 1968), p.10.

Anon., '*Ringo and his Golden Pistol*', *Monthly Film Bulletin* 35/408 (1968), pp.9–10.

Anon., '*I giorni dell'ira*', *Intermezzo* 23/1–2 (1968), pp.6, 11.

Anon., '*Preparati la bara!*', *Intermezzo* 23/5–6 (1968), p.6.

Anon., '*Quella sporca storia nel West*', *Cinema d'oggi* (16 April 1968), p.10.

Anon., '*Quella sporca storia nel West*', *Intermezzo* 23/11–12 (1968), p.7.

Anon., '*Corri, uomo, corri*', *Cinema d'oggi* (28 August 1968), p.10.

Anon., '*Se incontri Sartana prega per la tua morte*', *Cinema d'oggi* (9 September 1968), p.10.

Anon., ' *… e per tetto un cielo di stelle*', *Cinema d'oggi* (23 September 1968), p.12.

Anon., ' *… e per tetto un cielo di stelle*', *Intermezzo* 23/17–18 (1968), p.11.

Anon., '*The Good, the Bad and the Ugly*', *Monthly Film Bulletin* 35/417 (1968), p.154.

Anon., '*Fort Yuma Gold*', *Monthly Film Bulletin* 35/417 (1968), p.159

Anon., '*I quattro dell'Ave Maria*', *Cinema d'oggi* (18 November 1968), p.8.

Anon., '*I quattro dell'Ave Maria*', *Intermezzo* 23/21–22 (1968), p.12.

Anon., '*The Good, the Bad and the Ugly*', *Time* (9 December 1968).

Anon., '*Payment in Blood*', *Variety* (11 December 1968), p.33.

Anon., '*Il grande Silenzio*', *Intermezzo* 23/24 (1968), p.7.

Anon., '*C'era una volta il West*', *Cinema d'oggi* (21 December 1968), p.12.

Anon., '*Dead or Alive*', *Monthly Film Bulletin* 36/420 (1969), p.9.

Anon., '*Il mercenario*', *Cinema d'oggi* (7 January 1969), p.10.

Anon., '*C'era una volta il West*', *Intermezzo* 24/1–2 (1969), p.5.

Anon., '*Il mercenario*', *Intermezzo* 24/1–2 (1969), p.8.

Anon., '*C'era una volta il West*', *Cinema Nuovo* 22/197 (1969), p.60.

Anon., '*Tepepa*', *Cinema d'oggi* (3 March 1969), p.10.

Anon., '*Death Rides a Horse*', *Monthly Film Bulletin* 36/422 (1969), p.57.

Anon., '*The Big Gundown*', *Monthly Film Bulletin* 36/422 (1969), pp.59–60.

Anon., '*Tepepa*', *Intermezzo* 24/5–6 (1969), p.10.

Anon., '*The Hellbenders*', *Monthly Film Bulletin* 36/424 (1969), pp.99–100.

Anon., '*Face to Face*', *Monthly Film Bulletin* 36/425 (1969), p.124.

Anon., '*A Bullet for the General*', *Monthly Film Bulletin* 36/425 (1969), p.128.

Anon., '*Once Upon a Time in the West*', *Films and Filming* 16/1 (1969), p.42.

Anon., '*Vivi o preferibilmente morti*', *Cinema d'oggi* (10 November 1969), p.10.

Anon., '*Sono Sartana il vostro Becchino*', *Cinema d'oggi* (24 November 1969), p.4.

Anon., '*A Professional Gun*', *Monthly Film Bulletin* 36/431 (1969), pp.269–270.

Anon., '*Ace High*', *Monthly Film Bulletin* 36/431 (1969), p.270.

Anon., '*Vivi o preferibilmente morti*', *Intermezzo* 24/23–24 (1969), p.7.

Anon., '*Gli specialisti*', *Cinema d'oggi* (19 January 1970), p.11.

Anon., '*La collina degli stivali*', *Cinema d'oggi* (26 January 1970), p.4.

Anon., '*La notte dei serpenti*', *Intermezzo* 25/1–2 (1970), p.12.

Anon., '*Il prezzo del potere*', *Intermezzo* 25/1–2 (1970), p.12.

Anon., '*Django Kill! (If You Live, Shoot!)*', *Monthly Film Bulletin* 37/433 (1970), pp.35–36.

Anon., '*La collina degli stivali*', *Intermezzo* 25/3–4 (1970), p.7.

Anon., '*Gli specialisti*', *Intermezzo* 25/3–4 (1970), p.11.

Anon., '*Wanted*', *Monthly Film Bulletin* 37/433 (1970), p.38.

Anon., '*Day of Anger*', *Monthly Film Bulletin* 37/437 (1970), p.128.

Anon., '*Arizona Colt*', *Monthly Film Bulletin* 37/438 (1970), p.145.

Anon., '*Navajo Joe*', *Monthly Film Bulletin* 37/438 (1970), p.148.

Anon., '*Indio Black, sai che ti dico: sei un gran figlio di …*', *Intermezzo* 25/20–21 (1970), p.13.

Anon., '*Texas Adios*', *Monthly Film Bulletin* 37/442 (1970), p.233.

Anon., '*The Return of Ringo*', *Monthly Film Bulletin* 37/443 (1970), p.252.

Anon., '*Buon funerale amigos … paga Sartana*', *Intermezzo* 25/23–24 (1970), p.11.

Anon., '*Vamos a matar compañeros*', *Cinema d'oggi* (11 January 1971), p.5.

Anon., '*Vamos a matar compañeros*', *Intermezzo* 26/1–2 (1971), p.11.

Anon., '*Lo chiamavano Trinità*', *Cinema d'oggi* (8 February 1971), p.4.

Anon., '*Una nuvola di polvere, un grido di morte ... Arriva Sartana!*', *Cinema d'oggi* (8 February 1971), p.4.

Anon., '*Lo chiamavano Trinità*', *Intermezzo* 26/3–4 (1971), p.4.

Anon., '*Una nuvola di polvere, un grido di morte ... Arriva Sartana!*', *Intermezzo* 26/3–4 (1971), p.5.

Anon., '*Adios Sabata*', *Filmfacts* 14/23 (1971), p.630.

Anon., '*Adios Sabata*', *The Hollywood Reporter* 217/38 (1971), p.4.

Anon., '*È tornato Sabata ... hai chiuso un'altra volta*', *Intermezzo* 26/19–20 (1971), p.8.

Anon., '*Giù la testa*', *Intermezzo* 26/21–24 (1971), p.11.

Anon., '*Compañeros*', *Monthly Film Bulletin* 39/457 (1972), pp.38–39.

Anon., '*They Call Me Trinity*', *Filmfacts* 15/10 (1972), pp.222–223.

Anon., '*Blindman*', *Filmfacts* 15/12 (1972), pp.274–276.

Anon., '*Duck, You Sucker!*', *Filmfacts* 15/15 (1972), pp.337–340.

Anon., '*Johnny Hamlet*', *Filmfacts* 15/17 (1972), pp.413–414.

Anon., '*Return of Sabata*', *Filmfacts* 15/17 (1972), pp.415–416.

Anon., '*Il mio nome è Nessuno*', *Cinematografo ITA* 40/9/10 (1973), pp.45–46.

Anon., 'Damiano Damiani', *Film Dope* (9 April 1976), pp.26–27.

Anon., 'Obituary: Sergio Corbucci', *Variety* (December 1990), pp.101–102.

Anon., *Che Guevara: Revolutionary and Icon* (Exhibition Guide) (London: Victoria and Albert Museum, 2006).

Associazione Generale Italiana dello Spettacolo, *Catalogo generale dei film italiani dal 1956 al 1975* (Rome: AGIS, 1975).

Aubrey, Crispin, '*A Fistful of Dynamite*', *The Morning Star* (15 September 1972).

Austen, David, '*Fort Yuma Gold*', *Films and Filming* 16/1 (1969), pp.55–56.

Bach, Stephen, *Final Cut: Dreams and Disaster in the Making of* Heaven's Gate (New York: Morrow, 1985).

Bailey, Kenneth, '*A Fistful of Dynamite*', *The Sunday People* (17 September 1972).

Banfield, Edward C., *The Moral Basis of a Backward Society* (Glencoe, IL: University of Chicago Press, 1958).

Barker, Felix, '*A Fistful of Dollars*', *The Evening News* (8 June 1967).

Barzini, Luigi, *The Europeans* (London: Penguin, 1983).

Basso, Matthew, Laura McCall and Dee Garceau (eds), *Across the Great Divide: Cultures of Manhood in the American West* (New York: Routledge, 2001).

Bates, Hal, '*Duck, You Sucker!*', *The Hollywood Reporter* 221/38 (1972), p.3.

Barthes, Roland, *S/Z*, trans. Richard Miller (Oxford: Blackwell, 1970).

Barthes, Roland, *Image, Music, Text*, trans. Stephen Heath (New York: Noonday, 1978).

Baudrillard, Jean, *Simulacra and Simulations*, trans. Paul Foss, Paul Patton and Philip Beitchmann (New York: Semiotext, [1981] 1983).

——, *America*, trans. Chris Turner (London: Verso, [1986] 1988).

Baudry, Pierre, 'L'idéologie du western italien', *Cahiers du cinéma* 233 (1971), pp.55–56.

Baxter, Monique James, '*Giant* helps America recognize the cost of discrimination', in Peter C. Rollins and John E. O'Connor (eds), *Hollywood's West: The American Frontier in Film, Television, and History* (Lexington: The University of Kentucky Press, 2005).

Bazin, André, *What is Cinema?*, vol. 2 (London: University of California Press, 2005).

Beale, Lewis, 'The American way west', *Films and Filming* (18 April 1972), pp.24–30.

Beatrice, Luca, *Al cuore, Ramon, al cuore – La leggenda del western all'italiana*, (Florence: Tarab, 1996).

Beau, '*The Good, the Bad and the Ugly*', *Variety* (27 December 1967), p.6.

Belton, Neil, 'Giangiacomo Feltrinelli' (online), available: http://www.granta.com/features/2001/11/belton (accessed 8 September 2006).

Benjamin, Walter, *Illuminations*, trans. Harry Zorn (London: Pimlico, 1999).

Bennett, Tony, 'Introduction: "the turn to Gramsci"', in Tony Bennett, Colin Mercer and Janet Woollacott (eds), *Popular Culture and Social Relations* (Milton Keynes: Open University Press, 1986).

Bergan, Ronald, 'Obituary: Sergio Corbucci: beefcake and spaghetti', *The Guardian* (December 1990), p.39.

Bernardini, Aldo, '*Quien sabe?*', *Cineforum* 62 (1967), pp.172–173.

Betts, Ernest, '*The Good, the Bad and the Ugly*', *The People* (7 September 1968).

——, '*The Wild Bunch*', *The People* (24 August 1969).

Bianchi, Franco, Massimo Torrigiani and Rinella Cere 'Cultural policy', in David Forgacs and Robert Lumley (eds), *Italian Cultural Studies: an Introduction* (Oxford: Oxford University Press, 1996).

Bilbow, Marjorie, '*For a Few Dollars More*', *The Daily Cinema* 9428 (1967), p.3.

——, '*Ringo and his Golden Pistol*', *The Daily Cinema* 9457 (1967), p.5.

——, '*Navajo Joe*', *The Daily Cinema* 9496 (1968), p.12.

——, '*The Good, the Bad and the Ugly*', *The Daily Cinema* 9565 (1968), p.6.

——, '*Fort Yuma Gold*', *The Daily Cinema* 9567 (1968), p.6.

——, '*Dead or Alive*', *The Daily Cinema* 9597 (1968), p.11.

——, '*The Big Gundown*', *Today's Cinema* 9636 (1969), p.8.

——, '*Death Rides a Horse*', *Today's Cinema* 9645 (1969), p.8.

——, '*100 Rifles*', *Today's Cinema* 9654 (1969), p.12.

——, '*The Hellbenders*', *Today's Cinema* 9654 (1969), p.13.

——, '*A Bullet for the General*', *Today's Cinema* 9664 (1969), p.8.

——, '*Face to Face*', *Today's Cinema* 9664 (1969), p.9.

——, '*Once Upon a Time in the West*', *Today's Cinema* 9705 (1969).

——, '*The Wild Bunch*', *Today's Cinema* 9714 (1969), p.6.

——, '*Revenge in El Paso*', *Today's Cinema* 9746 (1969), p.6.

——, '*A Professional Gun*', *Today's Cinema* 9749 (1969), pp.6–7.

——, '*Django Kill! (If You Live, Shoot!)*', *Today's Cinema* 9764 (1969), p.5.

——, '*Wanted*', *Today's Cinema* 9764 (1969), p.5.

——, '*Arizona Colt*', *Today's Cinema* 9810 (1970), p.8.

——, '*Day of Anger*', *Today's Cinema* 9810 (1970), p.8.

——, '*The Return of Ringo*', *Today's Cinema* 9854 (1970), p.8.

——, '*For a Few Dollars More*', *Today's Cinema* 9868 (1971), p.14.

——, '*Sabata*', *Today's Cinema* 9897 (1971), p.7.

——, '*The Price of Power*', *Today's Cinema* 9954 (1971), p.13.

——, '*Compañeros*', *Cinema TV Today* 9963 (1972), p.29.

——, '*God Forgives … I Don't!*', *Cinema TV Today* 9989 (1972), p.19.

——, '*They Call Me Trinity*', *Cinema TV Today* 9994 (1972), p.24.

——, '*A Fistful of Dynamite*', *Cinema TV Today* 9998 (1972), p.17.

——, '*Head I Kill You – Tails You Die*', *Cinema TV Today* 10008 (1972), p.20.

——, '*The Bounty Hunters*', *Cinema TV Today* 10019 (1973), p.16.

——, '*Drop Them or I'll Shoot*', *Cinema TV Today* 10049 (1973), p.12.

——, '*Vengeance*', *Cinema TV Today* 10058 (1973), pp.24–25.

——, '*Blindman*', *Cinema TV Today* 10065 (1974), p.14.

——, '*Trinity is Still My Name*', *Cinema TV Today* 10071 (1974), p.14.

——, '*Gunman in Town*', *Screen International* 8 (1975), p.14.

——, '*My Name is Nobody*', *Screen International* 67 (1976), p.16.

——, '*Keoma*', *Screen International* 108 (1977), p.30.

Biskind, Peter, *Easy Riders, Raging Bulls* (London: Bloomsbury, 1998).

Bondanella, Peter, *Italian Cinema: From Neorealism to the Present* (New York: Continuum, 2001).

——, 'Italian cinema', in Zygmunt G. Baranski and Rebecca J. West (eds), *The Cambridge Companion to Modern Italian Culture* (Cambridge: Cambridge University Press, 2001).

Braucourt, Guy, 'Gian Maria Volonté talks about cinema and politics', trans. Renée Delforge, *Cineaste* 7/1 (1975), pp.10–13.

Brauer, David, Jim Edwards, Christopher Finch and Walter Hopps, *Pop Art: US/UK Connections, 1956–66* (Houston: Menil Collection, 2001).

Braun, Eric, '*Sabata*', *Films and Filming* 17/9 (1971), pp.76–78.

——, '*Compañeros*', *Films and Filming* 18/7 (1972), p.56.

——, '*Blindman*', *Films and Filming* 20/5 (1974), pp.39–40.

Bronner, Stephen, 'Reclaiming the fragments: on the Messianic materialism of Walter Benjamin' (online), available: http://www.ominiverdi.com/walterbenjamin/cf/pdf/Stephen_Bronner.pdf (accessed 20 December 2006).

Brownlow, Kevin, *The War, the West and the Wilderness* (London: Secker and Warburg, 1979).

Bruschini, Antonio and Antonio Tentori, *Western all'italiana: The Specialists* (Florence: Glittering Images, 1998).

Buchanan, Loren G., '*A Fistful of Dollars*', *Motion Picture Herald* 237/1 (1967), p.646.

——, '*For a Few Dollars More*', *Motion Picture Herald* 237/20 (1967), p.685.

Burns, E. Bradford and Julie A. Charlip, *Latin America: A Concise Interpretative History* (New Jersey: Prentice Hall, 2002).

Buscombe, Edward (ed.), *The BFI Companion to the Western* (London: BFI, 1993).

——, 'Border control' (online), available: http://www.bfi.org.uk/sightandsound/feature/10/ (accessed 5 September 2006).

Buss, Robin, *Italian Films* (London: B.T. Batsford Ltd, 1989).

Byro, '*The Hellbenders*', *Variety* (6 September 1967), p.6.

——, '*Seven Women for the MacGregors*', *Variety* (24 April 1968), p.6.

Calder, Jenni, *There Must Be a Lone Ranger* (Gateshead: Northumberland Press, 1974).

Caldiron, Orio, *Sergio Corbucci* (Rimini: Ramberti, 1993).

Calvert, Peter, *Mexico* (London: Ernest Benn Limited, 1973).

Cameron, Ian and Douglas Pye (eds), *The Movie Book of the Western* (London: Studio Vista, 1996).

Campbell, Neil, Jude Davies, and George McKay 'Introduction: issues in Americanisation and culture', in Neil Campbell, Jude Davies and George McKay (eds), *Issues in Americanisation and Culture* (Edinburgh: Edinburgh University Press, 2004).

Campbell, Neil, 'Landscapes of Americanisation in Britain: learning from the 1950s', in Neil Campbell, Jude Davies and George McKay (eds), *Issues in Americanisation and Culture* (Edinburgh: Edinburgh University Press, 2004).

Canby, Vincent, '*Once Upon a Time in the West*', *The New York Times* (29 May 1969), p.43.

——, '*The Wild Bunch*', *The New York Times* (26 June 1969), p.45.

——, '*Ace High*', *The New York Times* (9 October 1969), p.55.

——, '*Duck, You Sucker!*', *The New York Times* (1 July 1972), p.11.

——, '*My Name is Nobody*', *The New York Times* (18 July 1974), p.30.

——, 'Boss Nigger', The New York Times (27 February 1975), p.30.

Cano, 'One Silver Dollar', Variety (18 June 1975), p.19.

Carrano, P., 'Divismo', in Marino Livolsi (ed.), Schermi e ombre: gli Italiani e il cinema nel dopoguerra (Scandicci: La Nuova Italia, 1988).

Carroll, Noël, 'The professional Western: south of the border', in Edward Buscombe and Roberta E. Pearson (eds), Back in the Saddle Again: New Essays on the Western (London: BFI, 1998).

Castellani, Leandro, 'Per un pugno di dollari', Cineforum 41 (1965), pp.61–63.

Catanzaro, Raimondo, 'Subjective experience and objective reality: an account of violence in the words of its protagonists', in Raimondo Catanzaro (ed.), The Red Brigades and Left-Wing Terrorism in Italy (London: Pinter Publishers, 1991).

Cawelti, John G., The Six-Gun Mystique (Bowling Green: Bowling Green State University Press, 1971).

——, 'Reflections on the new Western films', in Jack Nachbar (ed.), Focus on the Western (New Jersey: Englewood Cliffs, 1974).

——, The Six-Gun Mystique Sequel (Bowling Green: Bowling Green State University Press, 1999).

Cèbe, Gilles, Sergio Leone ou le triomphe d'Arlequin (Paris: H. Veyrier, 1984).

Celli, Carlo and Marga Cottino-Jones, A New Guide to Italian Cinema (New York: Palgrave Macmillan, 2007).

Cento Bull, Anna, 'Social and political cultures in Italy from 1860 to the present day', in Zygmunt G. Baranski and Rebecca J. West (eds), The Cambridge Companion to Modern Italian Culture (Cambridge: Cambridge University Press, 2001).

Chaliand, Gérard, Revolution in the Third World, trans. Diana Johnstone and Tony Berrett (Harmondsworth: Penguin, 1989).

Christie, Ian, 'A Fistful of Dollars', The Daily Express (18 April 1967).

——, 'A Fistful of Dollars', The Daily Express (9 June 1967).

——, 'The Wild Bunch', The Daily Express (20 August 1969).

——, 'A Fistful of Dynamite', The Daily Express (15 September 1972).

Chubb, Judith, Patronage, Power and Poverty in Southern Italy (Cambridge: Cambridge University Press, 1982).

Ciaccio, Giacinto, 'Per un pugno di dollari', Rivista del Cinematografo 12 (1964), pp.584–585.

——, 'Una pistola per Ringo', Rivista del Cinematografo 7 (1965), p.387.

——, 'Sette pistole per i MacGregor', Rivista del Cinematografo 4 (1966), pp.297–298.

——, 'Il buono, il brutto, il cattivo', Rivista del Cinematografo, 2 (1967), p.126.

——, 'Quien sabe?', Rivista del Cinematografo 2 (1967), pp.136–137.

Clapham, Walter C., *Western Movies* (London: Octopus, 1974).

Clark, Martin, *Modern Italy, 1871–1982* (London: Longman, 1984).

Clarke, Graham, '*Duel at Rio Bravo*', *Kinematograph Weekly* 3020 (1965), p.11.

——, '*A Pistol for Ringo*', *Kinematograph Weekly* 3077 (1966), p.17.

——, '*Minnesota Clay*', *Kinematograph Weekly* 3095 (1967), p.18.

——, '*A Fistful of Dollars*', *Kinematograph Weekly* 3108 (1967), p.7.

——, '*A Few Dollars for Django*', *Kinematograph Weekly* 3108 (1967), pp.7–8.

——, '*One Silver Dollar*', *Kinematograph Weekly* 3109 (1967), p.17.

——, '*The Hills Run Red*', *Kinematograph Weekly* 3112 (1967), pp.10–11.

——, '*Seven Guns for the MacGregors*', *Kinematograph Weekly* 3123 (1967), p.14.

——, '*For a Few Dollars More*', *Kinematograph Weekly* 3128 (1967), p.11.

——, '*Ringo and his Golden Pistol*', *Kinematograph Weekly* 3139 (1967), p.8.

——, '*Navajo Joe*', *Kinematograph Weekly* 3151 (1968), p.12.

——, '*The Good, the Bad and the Ugly*', *Kinematograph Weekly* 3176 (1968), p.20.

——, '*Fort Yuma Gold*', *Kinematograph Weekly* 3176 (1968), p.21.

——, '*Dead or Alive*', *Kinematograph Weekly* 3188 (1968), p.20.

——, '*The Big Gundown*', *Kinematograph Weekly* 3200 (1969), p.10.

——, '*Death Rides a Horse*', *Kinematograph Weekly* 3200 (1969), p.16.

——, '*100 Rifles*', *Kinematograph Weekly* 3207 (1969), p.11.

——, '*The Hellbenders*', *Kinematograph Weekly* 3208 (1969), p.17.

——, '*A Bullet for the General*', *Kinematograph Weekly* 3211 (1969), p.10, 16.

——, '*Face to Face*', *Kinematograph Weekly* 3211 (1969), p.10.

——, '*Once Upon a Time in the West*', *Kinematograph Weekly* 3227 (1969), p.10.

——, '*The Wild Bunch*', *Kinematograph Weekly* 3228 (1969), p.13.

——, '*A Professional Gun*', *Kinematograph Weekly* 3239 (1969), p.17.

——, '*Ace High*', *Kinematograph Weekly* 3240 (1969), p.15.

——, '*Django Kill! (If You Live, Shoot!)*', *Kinematograph Weekly* 3246 (1969), p.12.

——, '*Wanted*', *Kinematograph Weekly* 3246 (1969), p.12.

——, '*Day of Anger*', *Kinematograph Weekly* 3265 (1970), p.18.

——, '*Arizona Colt*', *Kinematograph Weekly* 3269 (1970), p.91.

——, '*The Return of Ringo*', *Kinematograph Weekly* 3291 (1970), p.12.

——, '*For a Few Bullets More*', *Kinematograph Weekly* 3298 (1970), p.8.

——, '*Sabata*', *Kinematograph Weekly* 3315 (1971), p.12.

Clifford, James, *The Predicament of Culture* (Cambridge, MA: Harvard University Press, 1988).

Cocks, Jay, '*Duck, You Sucker!*', *Time* (31 July 1972).

Cohen, Larry, '*Sabata*', *The Hollywood Reporter* 212/34 (1970).

Coleman, John, '*A Fistful of Dollars*', *The New Statesman* (9 June 1967).

Combs, Richard, '*Sabata*', *Monthly Film Bulletin* 38/448 (1971), p.95.

Comuzio, Ermanno, '*Requiescant*', *Cineforum* 68 (1967), pp.667–668.

Connolly, William, 'Franco Solinas and the commie cowboys', *Spaghetti Cinema* 1/3 (December 1984), pp. 35–49.

Corkin, Stanley, *Cowboys as Cold Warriors: The Western and US History* (Philadelphia: Temple University Press, 2004).

Corneau, Ernest N., *The Hall of Fame of Western Film Stars* (North Quincy, Mass.: Christopher Publishing House, 1969).

Costello, Matthew J., 'Rewriting *High Noon*: transformation in American popular political culture during the Cold War, 1952–1968', in Peter C. Rollins and John E. O'Connor (eds), *Hollywood's West: The American Frontier in Film, Television, and History* (Lexington, KY: The University of Kentucky Press, 2005).

Cox, Alex, *10,000 Ways to Die* (online), available: http://www.alexcox.com/ freestuff/10000_WAYS_TO_DIE.pdf (accessed 4 January 2008).

——, *10,000 Ways to Die: A Director's Take on the Spaghetti Western* (Harpenden: Kamera Books, 2009).

Coyne, Michael, *The Crowded Prairie: American National Identity in the Hollywood Western* (London: I.B.Tauris, 1997).

Crowdus, Gary, '*Spaghetti Westerns: Cowboys and Europeans from Karl May to Sergio Leone* by Christopher Frayling', *Cinéaste* 11/3 (1981), pp.44–46.

—— and Dan Georgakas, 'Acting and the collective filmmaking experience: an interview with Gian Maria Volonté', *Cineaste* 15/1 (1986), pp.9–11.

Crowther, Bosley, '*A Fistful of Dollars*', *The New York Times* (2 February 1967), p.29.

——, '*Bonnie and Clyde*', *The New York Times* (14 April 1967).

——, '*For a Few Dollars More*', *The New York Times* (4 July 1967), p.23.

Cumbow, Robert C., '*Spaghetti Westerns: Cowboys and Europeans from Karl May to Sergio Leone* by Christopher Frayling', *Film Quarterly* 34/4 (1981), pp. 37–38.

——, *Once Upon a Time: The Films of Sergio Leone* (London: The Scarecrow Press, 1987).

Curtis, Thomas Quinn, '*The Good, the Bad and the Ugly*', *International Herald Tribune* (23 March 1968).

Dalle Vacche, Angela, *The Body in the Mirror: Shapes of History in Italian Cinema* (Princeton, NJ: Princeton University Press, 1992).

Damiani, Bruno, '… *continuavano a chiamarlo Trinità*', *Cineforum* 108 (1971), pp.86–88.

Davis, Richard, '*Dead or Alive*', *Films and Filming* 15/6 (1969), p.50.

Davis, Robert Murray, *Playing Cowboys: Low Culture and High Art in the Western* (Norman: University of Oklahoma Press, 1992).

Dawson, Jan, '*The Wild Bunch*', *The Listener* (4 September 1969).

Day-Lewis, Sean, 'The Good, the Bad and the Ugly', The Daily Telegraph (23 August 1968).

——, 'The Wild Bunch', The Daily Telegraph (22 August 1969).

De Certeau, Michel, The Practice of Everyday Life (Berkeley: University of California Press, [1984] 1988).

De Fornari, Oreste, Sergio Leone: The Great Italian Dream of Legendary America, trans. Charles Nopar (Rome: Gremese, 1997).

De Martino, Paola, 'Fifty years of Tex Willer: memories from the Western renaissance in Italy' (online), available: http://www.ubcfumetti.com/tx/50year1_en.htm (accessed 4 September 2006).

De Mauro, Tullio, 'L'italiano dei non lettori', Problemi dell'informazione 3 (1979), pp.419–431.

De Orellana, Margherita, Filming Pancho Villa: How Hollywood Shaped the Mexican Revolution (New York: Verso Books, 2004).

Debray, Régis, Revolution in the Revolution?: Armed Struggle and Political Struggle in Latin America, trans. Bobbye Ortiz (Harmondsworth: Penguin, 1968).

Del Buono, Oreste and Lietta Tornabuoni (eds), Era Cinecittà (Milan: Bompiani, 1979).

Della Porta, Donatella, Social Movements, Political Violence, and the State: A Comparative Analysis of Italy and Germany (Cambridge: Cambridge University Press, 1995).

Derderain, Stephane, '"I made one, and to tell the truth I only like one": an interview with Giulio Questi', trans. Alain Petit, Spaghetti Cinema 67 (July1997), pp.18–26.

Deutschmann, David (ed.), Che Guevara: A New Society (Melbourne: Ocean Press, 1991).

Di Claudio, Gianni, Directed by Sergio Leone (Rome: Libreria Universitaria, 1990).

Dickie, John, Darkest Italy: the Nation and Stereotypes of the Mezzogiorno, 1860–1900 (London: Macmillan, 1999).

——, 'The notion of Italy', in Zygmunt G. Baranski and Rebecca J. West (eds), The Cambridge Companion to Modern Italian Culture (Cambridge: Cambridge University Press, 2001).

Dixon, Wheeler Winston, The Films of Jean-Luc Godard (Albany: State University of New York Press, 1997).

——, 'Re-visioning the Western: code, myth, and genre in Peckinpah's The Wild Bunch', in Stephen Prince (ed.), Sam Peckinpah's The Wild Bunch (Cambridge: Cambridge University Press, 1999).

Dombroski, Robert S., 'Socialism, Communism and other "isms"', in Zygmunt G. Baranski and Rebecca J. West (eds), *The Cambridge Companion to Modern Italian Culture* (Cambridge: Cambridge University Press, 2001).

Dool, '*The Hills Run Red*', *Variety* (11 October 1967), p.6.

Dorfman, Ariel, 'The *Time* 100: Che Guevara' (online), available: http://www.time.com/time/time100/heroes/profile/guevara01.html (accessed 24 June 2006).

Doyle, Michael V., *American West on Film* (Dubuque: Kendall/Hunt, 1996).

Durgnat, Raymond, '*The Good, the Bad and the Ugly*', *Films and Filming* 15/2 (1968), pp.48–49.

Ebert, Roger, '*Duck, You Sucker!*', *Chicago Sun-Times* (19 October 1972).

Eleftheriotis, Dimitris, *Popular Cinemas of Europe: Studies of Texts, Contexts and Frameworks* (London: Continuum, 2001).

——, 'Spaghetti Western, genre criticism and national cinema: re-defining the frame of reference', in Yvonne Tasker (ed.), *Action Cinema Reader* (London: Routledge, 2004).

Ellwood, David, 'Il cinema e la proiezione del modello americano', in Gian Piero Brunetta and David W. Ellwood, *Hollywood in Europa* (Florence: Usher, 1991).

——, '*Un americano a Roma*', *History Today* 46/5 (May 1996), pp.45–49.

Engelhardt, Tom, *The End of Victory Culture: Cold War America and the Disillusioning of a Generation* (New York: BasicBooks, 1995).

Everson, William K., 'Europe produces Westerns too. In the essentials of this universal genre they resemble our own', *Films in Review* (February 1953), pp.74–79.

——, *A Pictorial History of the Western Film* (New York: Citadel Press, 1969).

Eyles, Allen, *The Western: an Illustrated Guide* (London: A. Zwemmer, [1967] 1975).

Fagen, Herb, *The Encyclopaedia of Westerns* (London: Eurospan, 2003).

Faldini, Franca and Goffredo Fofi, *L'avventurosa storia del cinema italiano raccontata dai suoi protagonisti 1960–1969* (Milan: Mondadori, 1981).

Fanon, Frantz, *Black Skin, White Masks* (London: Pluto, [1952] 1986).

——, *The Wretched of the Earth* (London: Penguin, [1961] 2001).

Farber, Stephen, '*The Wild Bunch*', *Film Quarterly* 23/1 (1969), pp.2–11.

Feiffer, Jules, *The Great Comic Book Heroes* (London: Allen Lane the Penguin Press, [1965] 1967).

Feltrinelli, Carlo, *Senior Service*, trans. Alastair McEwen (London: Granta Books, 2001).

Fenin, George, *The Western: From Silents to the Seventies* (New York: Grossman, 1973).

Ferguson, Ken and Sylvia Ferguson, *Western Stars of Television and Film* (London: Purnell & Sons, 1967).

Fisher, Austin, 'A Marxist's gotta do what a Marxist's gotta do: political violence on the Italian frontier', *Scope: an Online Journal of Film and Television Studies* 15 (2009).

——, 'Out West down south: gazing at America in reverse shot through Damiano Damiani's *Quien sabe?*', *The Italianist* 30 (2010), pp.182–200.

Fofi, Goffredo, *L'immigrazione meridionale a Torino* (Milan: Feltrinelli, 1964).

Forgacs, David, 'The Italian Communist Party and culture', in Zygmunt G. Baranski and Robert Lumley (eds), *Culture and Conflict in Postwar Italy: Essays on Mass and Popular Culture* (London: Macmillan, 1990).

——, 'Americanisation: the Italian case 1938–1954', *Borderlines: Studies in American Culture* 1/2 (1993), pp.157–169.

——, 'Cultural consumption, 1940s to 1990s', in David Forgacs and Robert Lumley (eds), *Italian Cultural Studies: an Introduction* (Oxford: Oxford University Press, 1996).

Forshaw, Barry, *Italian Cinema: Arthouse to Exploitation* (Harpenden: Pocket Essentials, 2006).

Fotia, Maria, '*Che c'entriamo noi con la rivoluzione?*', *Rivista del Cinematografo* 3/4 (1973), pp.157–158.

Fox, Julian, '*They Call Me Trinity*', *Films and Filming* 19/3 (1972), p.52.

Frame, Colin, '*A Fistful of Dynamite*', *The Evening News* (15 September 1972).

Frayling, Christopher, '*Django*', *Monthly Film Bulletin* 53/625 (1986), pp.55–56.

——, 'Obituary: Sergio Corbucci', *The Independent* (December 1990), p.46.

——, 'The wretched of the Earth', *Sight and Sound* 3/6 (June 1993), pp. 26–29.

——, 'Mexico', in Edward Buscombe (ed.), *The BFI Companion to the Western* (London: BFI, 1993).

——, *Spaghetti Westerns: Cowboys and Europeans from Karl May to Sergio Leone* (London: I.B.Tauris, [1981] 1998).

——, *Sergio Leone: Something to Do with Death* (London: Faber and Faber, 2000).

——, '*Per un pugno di dollari / A Fistful of Dollars*', in Giorgio Bertellini (ed.), *The Cinema of Italy* (London: Wallflower Press, 2004).

——, *Sergio Leone: Once Upon a Time in Italy* (London: Thames and Hudson, 2005).

French, Philip, '*A Fistful of Dollars*', *The Observer* (11 June 1967).

——, *Westerns: Aspects of a Movie Genre* (London: Secker and Warburg, [1973] 1977).

——, 'Mother of all battles', *The Observer* (25 April 2004).

——, *Westerns* (Manchester: Carcanet, 2005).

——, 'How violent taboos were blown away', *The Guardian Review* (26 August 2007), pp.6–7.

Fridlund, Bert, *The Spaghetti Western: A Thematic Analysis* (Jefferson: MacFarland, 2006).

——, '"A first class pallbearer!": the Sartana/Sabata cycle in Spaghetti Westerns', *Film International* 33 (2008), pp.44–55.

Galluzzo, Tony, '*A Pistol for Ringo*', *Motion Picture Herald* (9 November 1966), p.627.

——, '*The Good, the Bad and the Ugly*', *Motion Picture Herald* 238/3 (1968), p.760.

Garfield, Brian, *Western Films: a Complete Guide* (New York: Rawson Associates, 1982).

Garofalo, Marcello, *Tutto il cinema di Sergio Leone* (Milano: Baldini & Castoldi, 1999).

Gertner, Richard, '*A Minute to Pray, A Second to Die*', *Motion Picture Herald* 238/18 (1968), pp.805–806.

——, '*The Wild Bunch*', *Motion Picture Herald* 239/27 (1969), p.219.

Gibbs, Patrick, '*A Fistful of Dynamite*', *The Daily Telegraph* (15 September 1972).

Gili, Jean A., *Italian Filmmakers: Self Portraits: A Selection of Interviews*, trans. Sandra E. Tokunaga (Rome: Gremese, 1998).

Gillespie, David, *Early Soviet Cinema: Innovation, Ideology and Propaganda* (London: Wallfower, 2000).

Gillett, John, '*Once Upon a Time in the West*', *Monthly Film Bulletin* 36/428 (1969), pp.187–188.

Ginsborg, Paul, *A History of Contemporary Italy: Society and Politics, 1943–1980* (London: Penguin, 1990).

Giusti, Marco, *Dizionario del Western all'italiana* (Milan: Oscar Mondadori, 2007).

Glaessner, Verina, '*Gunman in Town*', *Monthly Film Bulletin* 42/503 (1975), p.266.

——, '*My Name is Nobody*', *Time Out* 351 (1976).

Glasser, Barry, '*Death Rides a Horse*', *Motion Picture Herald* 239/29 (1969), p.234.

Godard, Jean-Luc, Weekend *and* Wind from the East: *Two Films by Jean-Luc Godard* (London: Lorrimer Publishing, 1972).

Goff, John, '*The Wild Bunch*', *The Hollywood Reporter* 206/25 (1969), p.3.

Gordon, Lewis R., T. Denean Sharpley-Whiting and Renée T. White, 'Five stages of Fanon studies', in Lewis R. Gordon, T. Denean Sharpley-

Whiting and Renée T. White (eds), *Fanon: A Critical Reader* (Oxford: Blackwell, 1996).

Gow, Gordon, '*A Fistful of Dynamite*', *Films and Filming* 19/2 (1972), p.46.

Gramsci, Antonio, 'The Italian situation and the tasks of the PCI "The Lyons theses"', trans. Quintin Hoare (online), available: http://www.marxists.org/archive/gramsci/1926/01/lyon_congress/lyon_thesis.htm (accessed 2 October 2006).

——, *An Antonio Gramsci Reader: Selected Writings 1916–1935* (New York: Schocken Books, 1988).

Greenspun, Roger, '*Sabata*', *The New York Times* (3 September 1970), p.38.

——, '*Day of Anger*', *The New York Times* (5 December 1970), p.40.

——, '*Return of Sabata*', *The New York Times* (10 August 1972), p.27.

Gressard, Gilles, *Sergio Leone* (Paris: J'ai lu, 1989).

Gribaudi, Gabriella, 'Images of the South', in David Forgacs and Robert Lumley (eds), *Italian Cultural Studies: an Introduction* (Oxford: Oxford University Press, 1996).

Gundle, Stephen, 'L'americanizzazione del quotidiano: televisione e consumismo nell'Italia degli anni cinquanta', *Quaderni Storici* 21/22 (1986), pp.561–594.

——, 'From neo-realism to *Luci Rosse*: cinema, politics, society, 1945–85', in Zygmunt G. Baranski and Robert Lumley (eds), *Culture and Conflict in Postwar Italy: Essays on Mass and Popular Culture* (London: Macmillan, 1990).

——, 'Fame, fashion, and style: the Italian star system', in David Forgacs and Robert Lumley (eds), *Italian Cultural Studies: an Introduction* (Oxford: Oxford University Press, 1996).

——, *Between Hollywood and Moscow: the Italian Communists and the Challenge of Mass Culture, 1943–1991* (London: Duke University Press, 2000).

Gunning, Tom, *DW Griffith and the Origins of American Narrative Film* (Chicago: University of Illinois Press, 1994).

Günsberg, Maggie, *Italian Cinema: Gender and Genre* (London: Palgrave, 2005).

Guttmacher, Peter, *Legendary Westerns* (New York: MetroBooks, 1995).

Hall, Keith, 'The hunt's over', *Spaghetti Cinema* 11 (1986), pp.10–13.

Hall, Linda B. and Don M. Coerver, *Revolution on the Border: The United States and Mexico 1910–1920* (Albuquerque: University of New Mexico Press, 1988).

Hall, Stuart, 'New cultures for old', in Doreen Massey and Pat Jess (eds), *A Place in the World?* (Oxford: Oxford University Press, 1995).

Hall, William, '*The Good, the Bad and the Ugly*', *The Evening News* (23 August 1968).

——, 'The Wild Bunch', The Evening News (20 June 1969).

Hardy, Phil, The Western (London: Aurum, 1991).

Harris, David, From Class Struggle to the Politics of Pleasure (London: Routledge, 1992).

Harris, Paul, 'Franco Nero: an interview', Cinema Papers 73 (May 1989), pp.12–16.

Hart, Henry, 'A Fistful of Dollars', Films in Review 18/3 (1967), pp.174–175.

Hawk, 'A Fistful of Dollars', Variety (18 November 1964), p.22.

——, 'Minnesota Clay', Variety (10 February 1965), p.6.

——, 'A Pistol for Ringo', Variety (23 June 1965).

——, 'The Return of Ringo', Variety (2 February 1966).

——, 'For a Few Dollars More', Variety (16 February 1966), p.6.

——, 'A Bullet for the General', Variety (19 July 1967).

Heard, Colin, 'Death Rides a Horse', Films and Filming 9 (1969), p.54.

Hebdige, D., Hiding in the Light: On Images and Things (London: Routledge, 1988).

Herbstman, Mandel, 'A Pistol for Ringo', The Film Daily 129/52 (1966), p.7.

——, 'A Fistful of Dollars', The Film Daily 129/85 (1966), p.4.

——, 'For a Few Dollars More', The Film Daily 130/86 (1967), p.5.

——, 'Navajo Joe', The Film Daily 131/88 (1967), p.6.

——, 'A Minute to Pray, A Second to Die', Film and Television Daily 132/91 (1968), p.3.

——, 'Payment in Blood', The Film Daily (1968), p.7.

Hibbin, Nina, 'A Fistful of Dollars', The Morning Star (10 June 1967).

——, 'The Wild Bunch', The Morning Star (23 August 1969).

Hinxman, Margaret, 'Minnesota Clay', The Daily Cinema 9325 (1967), p.4.

——, 'A Few Dollars for Django', The Daily Cinema 9361 (1967), p.6.

——, 'One Silver Dollar', The Daily Cinema 9365 (1967), p.4.

——, 'A Fistful of Dollars', The Daily Cinema 9365 (1967), p.4.

——, 'Seven Guns for the MacGregors', The Daily Cinema 9411 (1967), p.5.

——, 'The Good, the Bad and the Ugly', The Sunday Telegraph (25 August 1968).

——, 'The Wild Bunch', The Sunday Telegraph (24 August 1969).

——, 'A Fistful of Dynamite', The Sunday Telegraph (17 September 1972).

Hirscholm, Clive, 'A Fistful of Dollars', The Sunday Express (11 June 1967).

——, 'The Wild Bunch', The Sunday Express (24 August 1969).

Hitt, Jim, The American West from Fiction (1823–1976) into Film (1909–1986) (London: McFarland, 1990).

Hoberman, J., 'How the Western was lost', in Jim Kitses and Gregg Rickman (eds), The Western Reader (New York: Limelight Editions, 1998).

Hobsbawm, Eric, *Primitive Rebels* (Manchester: Manchester University Press, [1959] 1978).

——, *Bandits* (London: Orion, [1969] 2000).

Hoggart, Richard, *The Uses of Literacy* (London: Pelican, [1957] 1958).

Hoskins, WG, *The Making of the English Landscape* (London: Penguin, [1955] 1985).

Hough, Penelope, '*A Fistful of Dollars*', *The Spectator* (16 June 1967).

Houston, Penelope, '*The Wild Bunch*', *The Spectator* (30 August 1969).

Howard, Alan R., '*My Name is Nobody*', *The Hollywood Reporter* (11 June 1974), pp.4, 9.

Hudson, Anne, '*Rocco e i suoi fratelli*', in Giorgio Bertellini (ed.), *The Cinema of Italy* (London: Wallflower Press, 2004).

Hughes, Howard, *Spaghetti Westerns* (Harpenden: Pocket Essentials, 2001).

——, *Once Upon a Time in the Italian West* (London: I.B.Tauris, 2004).

Hutchison, David, '*100 Rifles*', *Films and Filming* 15/9 (1969), p.54.

Jameson, Fredric, 'Postmodernism and consumer society', in Hal Foster (ed.), *The Anti-Aesthetic: Essays on Postmodern Culture* (Port Townsend, WA: Bay Press, 1983).

——, *Postmodernism, or the Cultural Logic of Late Capitalism* (Durham, NC: Duke University Press, 1991).

Japa, '*Seven Guns for the MacGregors*', *Variety* (4 December 1968), p.6.

Jay, Martin, 'Anamnestic totalization: reflections on Marcuse's theory of remembrance', *Theory and Society* 11/1 (January 1982), pp.1–15.

Jenkins, Valerie, '*A Fistful of Dynamite*', *The Evening Standard* (14 September 1972).

Judt, Tony, *Postwar* (London: William Heinemann, 2005).

Julien, Isaac, *BaadAsssss Cinema: A Bold Look at 70s Blaxploitation Films* (DVD) (Direct Video, 2002).

Kaase, Max, 'Political participation, political values and political violence', in Raimondo Catanzaro (ed.), *The Red Brigades and Left-Wing Terrorism in Italy* (London: Pinter Publishers, 1991).

Kael, Pauline, *Kiss Kiss Bang Bang* (Boston: Little, Brown and Company, 1968).

——, 'Killing time', in Karl French (ed.), *Screen Violence* (London: Bloomsbury, 1996).

Kaminsky, Stuart M., *American Film Genres* (Chicago: Nelson-Hall, 1985).

Katz, Ephraim, *The Film Encyclopedia* (New York: Perigee Books, 1979).

Keller, Alexandra, 'Generic subversion as counterhistory: Mario Van Peebles's *Posse*', in Janet Walker (ed.), *Westerns: Films Through History* (London: Routledge, 2001).

Kellner, Douglas M. and Meenakshi Gigi Durham, 'Adventures in media and cultural studies: introducing the KeyWorks', in Meenakshi Gigi Durham and Douglas M. Kellner (eds), *Media and Cultural Studies: KeyWorks* (Oxford: Blackwell, 2006).

Kezich, Tullio, '*Per un pugno di dollari*', *Bianco e Nero* 25/11–12 (1964), pp.113–115.

Kitses, Jim, *Horizons West: Anthony Mann, Budd Boetticher, Sam Peckinpah: Studies of Authorship Within the Western* (London: Thames and Hudson, 1969).

——, 'Introduction: post-modernism and the Western', in Jim Kitses and Gregg Rickman (eds), *The Western Reader* (New York: Limelight Editions, 1998).

——, *Horizons West: Directing the Western from John Ford to Clint Eastwood* (London: BFI, 2004).

Knight, Arthur, '*The Good, the Bad and the Ugly*', *Saturday Review* (13 January 1968).

——, '*Blindman*', *The Hollywood Reporter* 220/42 (1972), p.3.

Kroes, Rob, 'Americanisation: what are we talking about?', in Rob Kroes, RW Rydell and DFJ Bosscher (eds), *Cultural Transmissions and Receptions: American Mass Culture in Europe* (Amsterdam: VU University Press, 1993).

La Palombara, Joseph, *Democracy, Italian Style* (London: Yale University Press, 1987).

Landry, Robert J., '*A Fistful of Dollars*', *Variety* (8 February 1967).

——, '*Any Gun Can Play*', *Variety* (18 September 1968), p.26.

——, '*Death Rides a Horse*', *Variety* (16 July 1969).

——, '*Day of Anger*', *Variety* (5 November 1969).

——, '*A Professional Gun*', *Variety* (4 March 1970).

——, '*Johnny Hamlet*', *Variety* (10 May 1972), p.20.

Landy, Marcia, 'He went thataway: the form and style of Leone's Italian Westerns', in Jim Kitses and Gregg Rickman (eds), *The Western Reader* (New York: Limelight, 1998).

——, *Italian Film* (Cambridge: Cambridge University Press, 2000).

Langford, Barry, *Film Genre: Hollywood and Beyond* (Edinburgh: Edinburgh University Press, 2005).

Lasagna, Roberto, *Sergio Leone* (Roma: Ripostes, 1996).

Lenihan, John H., *Showdown: Confronting Modern America in the Western Film* (Urbana: University of Illinois Press, 1985).

Lenin, VI, *Collected Works* (Moscow: Progress, 1973).

Leprohon, Pierre, *The Italian Cinema*, trans. Roger Greaves and Oliver Stallybrass (London: Secker and Warburg, 1972).

Levi, Carlo, *Christ Stopped at Eboli* (London: Cassell, 1948).

Liehm, Mira, *Passion and Defiance: Film in Italy from 1942 to the Present* (London: University of California Press, 1984).

Lipton, Edward, '*Ace High*', *The Film Daily* (14 October 1969), p.12.

Lowy, Michael, *The Marxism of Che Guevara*, trans. Brian Pearce (London: Monthly Review Press, 1973).

Loy, R. Philip, *Westerns in a Changing America, 1955–2000* (London: McFarland, 2004).

Loynd, Ray, '*Payment in Blood*', *The Hollywood Reporter* 203/41 (1968), p.4.

Lumley, Robert, *States of Emergency: Cultures of Revolt in Italy from 1968–1978* (London: Verso, 1990).

——, 'Challenging traditions: social movements, cultural change and the ecology question', in Zygmunt G. Baranski and Robert Lumley (eds), *Culture and Conflict in Postwar Italy: Essays on Mass and Popular Culture* (London: Macmillan, 1990).

——, 'Peculiarities of the Italian newspaper', in David Forgacs and Robert Lumley (eds), *Italian Cultural Studies: an Introduction* (Oxford: Oxford University Press, 1996).

Lusted, David, *The Western* (London: Pearson, 2003).

Lyotard, Jean-François, *The Postmodern Condition: A Report on Knowledge*, trans. Geoffrey Bennington and Brian Massumi (Manchester: Manchester University Press, 1979).

MacCabe, Colin, *Godard: A Portrait of the Artist at 70* (London: Bloomsbury, 2003).

Macherey, Pierre, *A Theory of Literary Production* (New York: Routledge, [1978] 2006).

Mack Smith, Denis, *Mussolini* (London: Weidenfeld & Nicolson, 1981).

Mahern, Michael, '*Adios Sabata*', *Focus!* (Spring 1972), pp.21–23.

Mahoney, John, '*A Pistol for Ringo*', *The Hollywood Reporter* 193/3 (1966), p.3.

——, '*For a Few Dollars More*', *The Hollywood Reporter* 195/36 (1967), p.3.

——, '*The Hills Run Red*', *The Hollywood Reporter* 197/38 (1967), p.3.

——, '*The Good, the Bad and the Ugly*', *The Hollywood Reporter* 198/46 (1967), p.3.

——, '*Once Upon a Time in the West*', *The Hollywood Reporter* 207/5 (1969), p.4.

——, '*Ace High*', *The Hollywood Reporter* 208/7 (1969), p.3.

——, '*Day of Anger*', *The Hollywood Reporter* 208/48 (1969), p.15.

Malcolm, Derek, '*A Fistful of Dynamite*', *The Guardian* (14 September 1972).

Malley, Robert, *The Call from Algeria: Third Worldism, Revolution, and the Turn to Islam* (London: University of California Press, 1996).

Manchel, Frank, *Cameras West* (New Jersey: Englewood Cliffs, 1971).

Manconi, Luigi, 'The political ideology of the Red Brigades', in Raimondo Catanzaro (ed.), *The Red Brigades and Left-Wing Terrorism in Italy* (London: Pinter Publishers, 1991).

Marcuse, Herbert, *One Dimensional Man* (London: Ark, [1964] 1986).

——, 'Repressive tolerance', in Robert Paul Wolff, Barrington Moore Jr. and Herbert Marcuse, *A Critique of Pure Tolerance* (London: Jonathan Cape, 1969).

——, *The New Left and the 1960s* (London: Routledge, 2005).

Marinetti, Filippo Tommaso, 'Manifesto of Futurism' (online), available: http://users.dickinson.edu/~rhyne/232/Eight/Marinetti.html (accessed 15 May 2008).

Marsili, Mario, 'The other Sergio' (online), available: http://www.strangeher.net/bennetts_raiders/othersergio.htm (accessed 20 September 2004).

Mayerson, Donald J., '*Blindman*', *Cue* (4 August 1972).

Maynard, Richard A., *The American West on Film: Myth and Reality* (Rochelle Park, New Jersey: Hayden Book Company, 1974).

McCarty, John Alan, '*The Wild Bunch*', *Film Heritage* 5/2 (1969), pp.1–10.

McGee, Patrick, *From* Shane *to* Kill Bill*: Rethinking the Western* (Oxford: Blackwell, 2007).

Mead, Taylor, 'Inter/View with Tomas Milian', *Inter/View* 2/3 (1970), pp.12–13.

Melly, George, '*A Fistful of Dynamite*', *The Observer* (17 September 1972).

Menello, Richard, 'Sergio Sollima plays cowboys and politics', *European Trash Cinema* 2/11 (1995), pp.28–34.

——, 'Sergio Sollima plays cowboys and politics', *European Trash Cinema* 2/12 (1995), pp.31–34.

Meyer, William R., *The Making of the Great Westerns* (New Rochelle, NY: Arlington House, 1979).

Michalczyk, John, 'Franco Solinas: the dialectic of screenwriting', *Cineaste* 13/2 (1984), pp.30–33.

——, *The Italian Political Filmmakers* (London: Associated University Press, 1986).

Milne, Tom, '*The Good, the Bad and the Ugly*', *The Observer* (1 September 1968).

——, '*The Wild Bunch*', *The Observer* (24 August 1969).

——, '*The Wild Bunch*', *Sight and Sound* 38/4 (1969), pp.208–209.

——, '*They Call Me Trinity*', *Monthly Film Bulletin* 39/464 (1972), p.191.

——, '*The Bounty Hunters*', *Monthly Film Bulletin* 40/470 (1973), p.52.

——, '*Blindman*', *Monthly Film Bulletin* 41/480 (1974), p.4.

——, '*Trinity is Still My Name*', *Monthly Film Bulletin* 41/482 (1974), p.44.

Mininni, Francesco (1995). *Sergio Leone*. Florence: Il Castoro.

Mitchell, Lee Clark , *Westerns: Making the Man in Fiction and Film* (London: University of Chicago Press, 1996).

Moe, Nelson, *The View from Vesuvius: Italian Culture and the Southern Question* (London: University of California Press, 2002).

Monterisi, Giancarlo, '*Per qualche dollaro in più*', *Rivista del Cinematografo* 2 (1966), pp.131–132.

Mora, Carl J., *Mexican Cinema: Reflections of a Society* (London: University of California Press, 1982).

Moravia, Alberto, *Contempt*, trans. Angus Davidson (London: Prion, [1954] 1999).

Mosk, '*Adios Sabata*', *Variety* (1 September 1971), p.26.

Moss, David, *The Politics of Left-Wing Violence in Italy, 1969–85* (London: MacMillan, 1989).

Murf, '*A Minute to Pray, A Second to Die*', *Variety* (1 May 1968), p.25.

——, '*They Call Me Trinity*', *Variety* (3 November 1971), p.16.

Myers, Nell, '*The Good, the Bad and the Ugly*', *The Morning Star* (31 August 1968).

Nachbar, Jack, 'Riding shotgun: the scattered formula in contemporary Western movies', in Nachbar, Jack, (ed.), *Focus on the Western* (New Jersey: Englewood Cliffs, 1974).

——, 'Introduction: a century on the trail', *Journal of Popular Film and Television* 30/4 (2003), pp.178–180.

Napoli, Gregorio, '*Il buono, il brutto, il cattivo*', *Civiltà dell'immagine* 1 (1967), pp.62–63.

Natta, Enzo, '*Per qualche dollaro in più*', *Cineforum* 51 (1966), pp.75–76.

——, '*Il buono, il brutto, il cattivo*', *Cineforum* 61 (1967), pp.74–76.

——, '*La resa dei conti*', *Rivista del Cinematografo* 6 (1967), pp.364–365.

——, '*Faccia a faccia*', *Rivista del Cinematografo* 1 (1968), pp.43–44.

——, '*C'era una volta il West*', *Rivista del Cinematografo* 1 (1969), pp.32–33.

Negarville, Massimo, '*Requiescant*', *Ombre Rosse* 2 (1967), p.102.

Newman, Kim, 'Thirty years in another town: the history of Italian exploitation', *Monthly Film Bulletin* 53/624 (January 1986), pp.20–24.

——, 'Thirty years in another town: the history of Italian exploitation II', *Monthly Film Bulletin* 53/625 (February 1986), pp.51–55.

——, 'Thirty years in another town: the history of Italian exploitation III', *Monthly Film Bulletin* 53/626 (March 1986), pp.88–91.

——, *Wild West Movies* (London: Bloomsbury, 1990).

Nicholls, David, 'Once upon a time in Italy', *Sight and Sound* (Winter 1980/81), pp.46–49.

Nietzsche, Friedrich, *On the Genealogy of Morals*, trans. Douglas Smith (Oxford: Oxford University Press, [1887] 1996).

Noble, Andrea, *Mexican National Cinema* (London: Routledge, 2005).

Nowell-Smith, Geoffrey, 'Italy: tradition, backwardness and modernity', in Zygmunt G. Baranski and Robert Lumley (eds), *Culture and Conflict in Postwar Italy: Essays on Mass and Popular Culture* (London: Macmillan, 1990).

——, James Hay and Gianni Volpi, *The Companion to Italian Cinema* (London: Cassell, 1996).

——, *Making Waves: New Cinemas of the 1960s* (London: Continuum, 2008).

Nuara, Ettore, '*Il grande silenzio*', *Cinema d'oggi* (2 December 1968), p.12.

O'Malley, Ilene, *The Myth of the Revolution: Hero Cults and the Institutionalisation of the Mexican State 1920–1940* (London: Greenwood Press, 1986).

Orloff, Kathy, '*Navajo Joe*', *The Hollywood Reporter* 198/13 (1967), p.3.

Ottaway, Robert, '*The Good, the Bad and the Ugly*', *The Daily Sketch* (22 August 1968).

——, '*The Wild Bunch*', *The Daily Sketch* (20 August 1969).

PJD, '*Duel at Rio Bravo*', *The Daily Cinema* 9105 (1965), p.6.

——, '*A Pistol for Ringo*', *The Daily Cinema* 9271 (1966), p.6.

Pacey, Ann, '*A Fistful of Dollars*', *The Sun* (6 June 1967).

——, '*The Good, the Bad and the Ugly*', *The Sun* (23 August 1968).

——, '*The Wild Bunch*', *The Sun* (20 August 1969).

Paganelli, Mauro and Sergio Valzania, *Conversazione con Gianluigi Bonelli* (Siena: Editori del Grifo, 1982).

Pahlow, Colin, '*Keoma*', *Monthly Film Bulletin* 44/526 (1977), p.235.

Parish, James R. and Michael R. Pitts, *The Great Western Pictures*, Vol. 1 (London: Scarecrow Press, 1976).

——, *The Great Western Pictures*, Vol. 2 (London: Scarecrow Press, 1976).

Parker, Jerry, '*Blindman*', *Newsday* (4 March 1972).

Parkinson, Michael and Clyde Jeavons, *A Pictorial History of Westerns* (London: Hamlyn, 1983).

Parks, Rita, *The Western Hero in Film and Television: Mass Media Mythology* (Ann Arbor: UMI Research Press, 1982).

Pasquino, Gianfranco and Donatella Della Porta, 'Interpretations of Italian left-wing terrorism', in Peter H. Merkl (ed.), *Political Violence and Terror: Motifs and Motivations* (London: University of California Press, 1986).

Pattison, Barry, 'Dollars in the bank?: Sergio Corbucci', *Montage* 24 (1973), pp.13–16.

——, 'Sergio Corbucci: obituary', *Cinema Papers* 82 (March 1991), pp.46–47.

Pelegrine, Louis, '*Seven women for the MacGregors*', *The Film Daily* 131/96 (1967), p.4.

Pennington, Ron, '*They Call Me Trinity*', *The Hollywood Reporter* 218/28 (1971), p.3.

Perona, Piero, '*Se sei vivo, spara*', *Civiltà dell'immagine* 2/3 (1967), p.69.

——, '*La resa dei conti*', *Civiltà dell'immagine* 2/3 (1967), p.70.

——, '*Sette donne per i MacGregor*', *Civiltà dell'immagine* 2/4 (1967), pp.80–81.

——, '*Wanted*', *Civiltà dell'immagine* 2/4 (1967), p.82.

Petley, Julian, 'Franco Solinas' (online), available: http://www.filmreference. com/Writers-and-Production-Artists-Sh-Sy/Solinas-Franco.html (accessed 8 September 2006).

Philo, Simon and Neil Campbell, 'Biff! Bang! Pow! The transatlantic pop aesthetic, 1956–66', in Neil Campbell, Jude Davies and George McKay (eds), *Issues in Americanisation and Culture* (Edinburgh: Edinburgh University Press, 2004).

Pilkington, William T. and Don Graham, *Western Movies* (Albuquerque: University of New Mexico Press, 1979).

Pirie, David, '*Vengeance*', *Monthly Film Bulletin* 40/479 (1973), pp.251–252.

Pithon, Rémy, '*Spaghetti Westerns: Cowboys and Europeans from Karl May to Sergio Leone* by Christopher Frayling', *Historical Journal of Film, Radio and Television* 1/2 (1981), pp.204–205.

Pitts, Michael R., *Western Movies: a TV and Video Guide to 4200 Genre Films* (London: McFarland, 1986).

Pontecorvo, Gillo, Interview, *La battaglia di Algeri* (DVD) (Argent Films, 2003).

Powell, Dilys, '*A Fistful of Dollars*', *The Sunday Times* (11 June 1967).

——, '*The Good, the Bad and the Ugly*', *The Sunday Times* (25 August 1968).

——, '*The Wild Bunch*', *The Sunday Times* (28 August 1969).

——, '*A Fistful of Dynamite*', *The Sunday Times* (17 September 1972).

Powers, James, '*A Fistful of Dollars*', *The Hollywood Reporter* 194/3 (1967), p.3.

Presley, Gail M., 'Fanon on the role of violence in liberation: a comparison with Gandhi and Mandela', in Lewis R. Gordon, T. Denean Sharpley-Whiting and Renée T. White (eds), *Fanon: A Critical Reader* (Oxford: Blackwell, 1996).

Price, James, '*The Good, the Bad and the Ugly*', *The Times* (30 August 1968).

Prince, Stephen, *Savage Cinema: Sam Peckinpah and the Rise of Ultraviolent Movies* (London: Athlone, 1998).

——, *Classical Film Violence: Designing and Regulating Brutality in Hollywood Cinema, 1930–1968* (London: Rutgers University Press, 2003).

Pye, Douglas, 'The Western (genre and movies)', in Barry Keith Grant (ed.), *Film Genre Reader III* (Austin: University of Texas Press, 2003).

Rainey, Buck, *The Reel Cowboy: Essays on the Myth in Movies and Literature* (Jefferson, NC: McFarland, 1995).

Ramonet, Ignacio, 'Italian Westerns as political parables', *Cineaste* 15/1 (1986), pp.30–35.

Rayns, Tony, '*The Price of Power*', *Monthly Film Bulletin* 38/455 (1971), p.245.

——, '*A Fistful of Dynamite*', *Monthly Film Bulletin* 39/464 (1972), pp.189–190.

——, '*The Specialists*', *Monthly Film Bulletin* 40/477 (1973), p.214.

——, '*My Name is Nobody*', *Monthly Film Bulletin* 44/517 (1977), p.26.

Restivo, Angelo, 'The Economic Miracle and its discontents: bandit films in Spain and Italy', *Film Quarterly* 49/2 (Winter 1995–96), pp.30–40.

Rhodes, John David, '*Divorzio all'italiana*', in Giorgio Bertellini (ed.), *The Cinema of Italy* (London: Wallflower Press, 2004).

Richards, Dick, '*The Good, the Bad and the Ugly*', *The Daily Mirror* (23 August 1968).

Richardson, Brian, 'Questions of language', in Zygmunt G. Baranski and Rebecca J. West (eds), *The Cambridge Companion to Modern Italian Culture* (Cambridge: Cambridge University Press, 2001).

Rick, '*Aces High*', *Variety* (1 October 1969), p.28.

——, '*Sabata*', *Variety* (2 September 1970), p.32.

Rider, David, '*The Big Gundown*', *Films and Filming* 15/7 (1969), pp.42–43.

Robey, David, 'Umberto Eco: theory and practice in the analysis of the media', in Zygmunt G. Baranski and Robert Lumley (eds), *Culture and Conflict in Postwar Italy: Essays on Mass and Popular Culture* (London: Macmillan, 1990).

Robinson, David, '*A Fistful of Dollars*', *The Financial Times* (9 June 1967).

——, '*The Wild Bunch*', *The Financial Times* (22 August 1969).

——, '*A Fistful of Dynamite*', *The Financial Times* (15 September 1972).

Robinson, Robert, '*A Fistful of Dollars*', *The Sunday Telegraph* (11 June 1967).

Robson, Mark, *Italy: Liberalism and Fascism 1870–1945* (London: Hodder & Stoughton, 1992).

Rose, Steve, 'Found: where Tarantino gets his ideas', *The Guardian* (6 April 2004).

Roth, Lane, *Film Semiotics: Metz and Leone's Trilogy* (London: Garland, 1983).

Ryweck, Charles, 'Don't turn the other cheek', *The Hollywood Reporter* 233/28 (1974), p.3.

Saitta, Luigi, '*Tepepa*', *Rivista del Cinematografo* 2 (1969), pp.93–94.

——, '*Viva la muerte … tua!*', *Rivista del Cinematografo* 1 (1972), p.50.

Salvadori, Maria Luisa, 'Apologizing to the ancient fable: Gianni Rodari and his influence on Italian children's literature', *The Lion and the Unicorn* 26/2 (2002), pp.169–202.

Sandler, Dorothy L., 'Damiano Damiani', *Daily American Weekly* (December 1963).

Sarris, Andrew, '*Duck, You Sucker!*', *The Village Voice* (6 July 1972).

Sassoon, Donald, *Contemporary Italy: Politics and Society since 1945* (London: Longman, 1986).

Saunders, John, *The Western Genre: From Lordsburg to Big Whiskey* (London: Wallflower, 2001).

Savioli, Aggeo, '*Tepepa*', *L'Unità* (16 February 1969).

Schaefer, Jack, *Shane* (London: Heinemann, [1953] 1967).

Schmitt, Richard, 'Racism and objectification: reflections on themes from Fanon', in Lewis R. Gordon, T. Denean Sharpley-Whiting and Renée T. White (eds), *Fanon: a Critical Reader* (Oxford: Blackwell, 1996).

Schneider, Tassilo, 'Finding a new *Heimat* in the Wild West: Karl May and the German Westerns of the 1960s', in Edward Buscombe and Roberta E. Pearson (eds), *Back in the Saddle Again: New Essays on the Western* (London: British Film Institute, 1998).

Scrivano, Paolo, 'Signs of Americanization in Italian domestic life: Italy's postwar conversion to consumerism', *Journal of Contemporary History* 40 (2005), pp. 317–340.

Sege, '*Don't Turn the Other Cheek*', *Variety* (9 October 1974), p.19.

Settle, William A., *Jesse James Was His Name* (London: University of Nebraska Press, [1966] 1977).

Sharrett, Christopher, 'Peckinpah the radical: the politics of *The Wild Bunch*', in Stephen Prince (ed.), *Sam Peckinpah's* The Wild Bunch (Cambridge: Cambridge University Press, 1999).

Shore, Cris, *Italian Communism: the Escape from Leninism* (London: Pluto, 1990).

Shorter, Eric, '*A Fistful of Dollars*', *The Daily Telegraph* (9 June 1967).

Sim, Stuart, *Introducing Critical Theory* (Royston: Icon Books, 2001).

Simmon Scott, 'Return of the badmen: *Spaghetti Westerns: Cowboys and Europeans from Karl May to Sergio Leone* by Christopher Frayling and *Peckinpah: the Western Films* by Paul Seydor', *Journal of Popular Film and Television* 9/3 (1981), pp.149–151.

Sitney, P. Adams, *Vital Crises in Italian Cinema: Iconography, Stylistics, Politics* (Austin: University of Texas Press, 1995).

Slotkin, Richard, 'Prologue to a study of myth and genre in American movies', *Prospects* 9 (1984), pp.407–432.

Slotkin, Richard, *Gunfighter Nation: The Myth of the Frontier in Twentieth-Century America* (New York: Atheneum, 1992).

Smith, Douglas, 'Introduction', in Friedrich Nietzsche, *On the Genealogy of Morals*, trans. Douglas Smith (Oxford: Oxford University Press, [1887] 1996).

Smith, Murray, 'Imagining from the inside', in Richard Allen and Murray Smith (eds), *Film Theory and Philosophy* (Oxford: Oxford University Press, 1997).

Sorlin, Pierre, *Italian National Cinema, 1896–1996* (London: Routledge, 1996).

Spini, Valdo, 'The New Left in Italy', *Journal of Contemporary History* 7/1–2 (April 1972), pp.512–571.

Sragow, Michael, '*The Wild Bunch*', *Film Society Review* 5/3 (1969), pp.31–37.

Staig, Laurence and Tony Williams, *Italian Western: The Opera of Violence* (London, Lorrimer, 1975).

Stanfield, Peter, *Hollywood Westerns and the 1930s: The Lost Trail* (Exeter: University of Exeter Press, 2001).

Steckmesser, Kent Ladd, *Western Outlaws: The 'Good Badman' in Fact, Film and Folklore* (Claremont: Regina Books, 1983).

Stein, Gertrude, *Lectures in America* (New York: Random House, 1935).

Strick, Philip, '*The Wild Bunch*', *Monthly Film Bulletin* 36/429 (1969), pp.211–212.

Strinati, Dominic, *An Introduction to Theories of Popular Culture* (London: Routledge, 1995).

TH, '*The Hills Run Red*', *The Daily Cinema* 9373 (1967), p.7.

Tarb, '*Once Upon a Time in the West*', *Variety* (28 May 1969), p.6.

Tarrow, Sidney, 'Violence and institutionalisation after the Italian protest cycle', in Raimondo Catanzaro (ed.), *The Red Brigades and Left-Wing Terrorism in Italy* (London: Pinter Publishers, 1991).

Taylor, John Russell, '*A Fistful of Dollars*', *The Times* (8 June 1967), p.8.

——, '*For a Few Dollars More*', *The Times* (5 October 1967), p.9.

——, '*Once Upon a Time in the West*', *The Times* (14 August 1969), p.11.

——, '*The Wild Bunch*', *The Times* (21 August 1969).

——, '*A Professional Gun*', *The Times* (27 November 1969), p.20.

——, '*Sabata*', *The Times* (16 April 1971), p.10.

——, '*Compañeros*', *The Times* (14 January 1972), p.8.

Taylor, Weston, '*The Good, the Bad and the Ugly*', *The News of the World* (25 August 1968).

Testa, Maurizio, '*Giù la testa*', *Rivista del Cinematografo* 12 (1971), pp.618–619.

Testa, Maurizio, ' … *continuavano a chiamarlo Trinità*', *Rivista del cinematografo* 12 (1971), pp.619–620.

Theweleit, Klaus, *Male Fantasies*, Vol. 1 (Cambridge: Polity, [1977] 1987).

——, *Male Fantasies*, Vol. 2 (Cambridge: Polity, [1977] 1987).

Thirkell, Arthur, '*A Fistful of Dynamite*', *The Daily Mirror* (15 September 1972).

Thomas, Kevin, '*Adios Sabata*', *The Los Angeles Times* (9 September 1971).

——, '*They Call Me Trinity*', *The Los Angeles Times* (28 October 1971).

Thomas, Tony, *The West That Never Was* (New York: Citadel Press, 1989).

Thompson, Howard, '*A Minute to Pray, A Second to Die*', *The New York Times* (23 May 1968), p.56.

——, '*The Big Gundown*', *The New York Times* (22 August 1968), p.47.

——, '*Any Gun Can Play*', *The New York Times* (14 September 1968), p.34.

——, '*100 Rifles*', *The New York Times* (27 March 1969), p.54.

——, '*A Professional Gun*', *The New York Times* (7 March 1970), p.36.

——, '*Blindman*', *The New York Times* (1 April 1972), p.30.

——, '*They Call Me Trinity*', *The New York Times* (11 May 1972), p.57.

Thur, '*Django the Bastard*', *Variety* (17 April 1974), p.20.

Tompkins, Jane, *West of Everything: The Inner Life of Westerns* (Oxford: Oxford University Press, 1992).

Torriglia, Anna Maria, *Broken Time, Fragmented Space: A Cultural Map for Postwar Italy* (London: University of Toronto Press, 2002).

Tuska, John, *The Filming of the West* (Garden City, NY: Doubleday, 1976).

——, *The American West in Film: Critical Approaches to the Western* (London: Greenwood Press, 1985).

Varon, Jeremy, *Bringing the War Home: The Weather Underground, the Red Army Faction, and Revolutionary Violence in the Sixties and Seventies* (London: University of California Press, 2004).

Verstraten, Peter, *Screening Cowboys: Reading Masculinities in Westerns* (Amsterdam: Bureau Grafisches Produkties, 1999).

Vine, '*Blindman*', *Variety* (12 April 1972), p.16.

Wagstaff, Christopher, 'A forkful of Westerns: industry, audiences and the Italian Western', in Richard Dyer and Ginette Vincendeau (eds), *Popular European Cinema* (London: Routledge, 1992).

——, 'Italy in the post-war international cinema market', in Christopher Duggan and Christopher Wagstaff (eds), *Italy in the Cold War: Politics, Culture and Society 1948–1958* (Oxford: Berg, 1995).

——, 'Cinema', in David Forgacs and Robert Lumley (eds), *Italian Cultural Studies: an Introduction* (Oxford: Oxford University Press, 1996).

——, 'Italian genre films in the world market', in Geoffrey Nowell-Smith and Stephen Ricci (eds), *Hollywood and Europe: Economics, Culture, National Identity 1945–95* (London: British Film Institute, 1998).

Walker, Alexander, '*A Fistful of Dollars*', *The Evening Standard* (8 June 1967).

——, '*The Good, the Bad and the Ugly*', *The Evening Standard* (29 August 1968).

——, '*The Wild Bunch*', *The Evening Standard* (21 August 1969). ·

Walker, Janet (ed.), *Westerns: Films through History* (London: Routledge, 2001).

Wallington, Mike, 'Spaghettis', *Time Out* (2–16 May 1970), p.25.

——, 'The Italian Western: a concordance', *Cinema* 6/7 (August 1970), pp.31–34.

——, '*For a Few Bullets More*', *Monthly Film Bulletin* 38/445 (1971), p.34.

Wallmann, Jeffrey, *The Western: Parables of the American Dream* (Lubbock: Texas Tech University Press, 1999).

Ward, David, 'Intellectuals, culture and power in modern Italy', in Zygmunt G. Baranski and Rebecca J. West (eds), *The Cambridge Companion to Modern Italian Culture* (Cambridge: Cambridge University Press, 2001).

Warshow, Robert, *The Immediate Experience: Movies, Comics, Theatre and Other Aspects of Popular Culture* (London: Harvard University Press, 2001).

Weidhorn, Manfred, '*High Noon*: liberal classic? Conservative screed?', *Bright Lights* (February 2005).

Weiler, AH, '*Navajo Joe*', *The New York Times* (7 December 1967), p.60.

——, '*A Bullet for the General*', *The New York Times* (1 May 1969), p.52.

——, '*Death Rides a Horse*', *The New York Times* (10 July 1969), p.28.

Weinberg, Leonard, 'The violent life: left- and right-wing terrorism in Italy', in Peter H. Merkl, (ed.), *Political Violence and Terror: Motifs and Motivations* (London: University of California Press, 1986).

Weisser, Thomas, *Spaghetti Westerns: the Good, the Bad and the Violent* (London: McFarland, 1992).

Werb, '*Trinity is Still My Name*', *Variety* (12 January 1972), p.26.

——, '*My Name is Nobody*', *Variety* (16 January 1974), p.18.

Whit, '*Navajo Joe*', *Variety* (1 November 1967), p.6.

——, '*The Big Gundown*', *Variety* (14 August 1968).

——, '*100 Rifles*', *Variety* (12 March 1969).

——, '*God Forgives … I Don't!*', *Variety* (21 May 1969), p.6.

——, '*The Wild Bunch*', *Variety* (18 June 1969), p.6.

——, '*Duck, You Sucker!*', *Variety* (21 June 1972), pp.18, 24.

Whyte, Alistair, '*Return of Sabata*', *Monthly Film Bulletin* 40/479 (1973), pp.247–248.

Williams, Raymond, *Communications* (London: Chatto and Windus, 1966).

Wilson, Alexandra, '*Fanciulla*'s transatlantic trials', in *La fanciulla del West* (opera programme) (London: Royal Opera House, 2005).

Wilson, Cecil, '*A Fistful of Dollars*', *The Daily Mail* (6 June 1967).

——, '*The Good, the Bad and the Ugly*', *The Daily Mail* (27 August 1968).

——, '*The Wild Bunch*', *The Daily Mail* (20 August 1969).

——, '*A Fistful of Dynamite*', *The Daily Mail* (14 September 1972).

Wilson, David, '*The Good, the Bad and the Ugly*', *The Guardian* (30 August 1968).

——, '*100 Rifles*', *Monthly Film Bulletin* 36/424 (1969), pp.94–95.

——, '*God Forgives … I Don't!*', *Monthly Film Bulletin* 39/463 (1972), pp.159–160.

Wise, David and Thomas B. Ross, *The Invisible Government* (New York: Random House, 1964).

Wister, Owen, *The Virginian* (London: Macmillan, [1902] 1949).

Wistrich, Robert, *Trotsky: Fate of a Revolutionary* (London: Robson Books, 1979).

Witcombe, RT, *The New Italian Cinema: Studies in Dance and Despair* (London: Secker and Warburg, 1982).

Woddis, Jack, *New Theories of Revolution: A Commentary on the Views of Frantz Fanon, Régis Debray and Herbert Marcuse* (London: Lawrence and Wishart, 1972).

Wolin, Richard, *Walter Benjamin: an Aesthetic of Redemption* (New York: Columbia University Press, 1982).

Wood, Mary P., *Italian Cinema* (Oxford: Berg, 2005).

Wood, Robin, *Hollywood from Vietnam to Reagan … and Beyond* (Chichester: Columbia University Press, [1986] 2003).

Worland, Rick and Edward Countryman, 'The new Western American historiography and the emergence of the new American Westerns', in Edward Buscombe and Roberta E. Pearson (eds), *Back in the Saddle Again: New Essays on the Western* (London: British Film Institute, 1998).

Wright, Will, *Sixguns and Society: A Structural Study of the Western* (London: University of California Press, [1975] 1977).

## Websites

URLs were correct at the time of writing.

Fondazione Franco Fossati (www.lfb.it)

The Internet Movie Database (www.imdb.com)

The Italophile (www.italo-phile.net)

Linea Rossa (Genova) (www.linearossage.it)

Novopress Italia (it.novopress.info)

The Spaghetti Western Database (www.spaghetti-western.net)
TEXBR (www.texbr.com)
uBC Fumetti (www.ubcfumetti.com)

# Index

λ